# The Early Church at Work and Worship

# The Early Church at Work and Worship

*Volume 2*
Catechesis, Baptism, Eschatology, and Martyrdom

EVERETT FERGUSON

CASCADE Books • Eugene, Oregon

THE EARLY CHURCH AT WORK AND WORSHIP
Volume 2: Catechesis, Baptism, Eschatology, and Martyrdom

Copyright © 2014 Everett Ferguson. All rights reserved. Except for brief quotations in critical publications or reviews, no part of this book may be reproduced in any manner without prior written permission from the publisher. Write: Permissions, Wipf and Stock Publishers, 199 W. 8th Ave., Suite 3, Eugene, OR 97401.

Cascade Books
An Imprint of Wipf and Stock Publishers
199 W. 8th Ave., Suite 3
Eugene, OR 97401

www.wipfandstock.com

ISBN 13: 978-1-60899-365-9

*Cataloging-in-Publication data:*

Ferguson, Everett, 1933–

The early church at work and worship / Everett Ferguson.

3 v.; xii + 358 p.; cm. Includes bibliographical references.

ISBN 13: 978-1-60899-365-9 (v. 2)
ISBN 13: 978–1–60899–307–9 (v. 1)

Contents: v. 1 Ministry, Ordination, Covenant, and Canon — v. 2. Catechesis, Baptism, Eschatology, and Martyrdom — v. 3. Worship, Eucharist, Music, and Gregory of Nyssa.

1. Christian literature. Early—History and criticism. 2. Fathers of the church. 3. Theology—History—Early church, ca. 30–600. 3. Baptism. 4. Millennialism. 5. Martyrdom—Christianity. I. Title.

BR67 F47 2014

Manufactured in the U.S.A.

To Thomas H. Olbricht,
my fellow Cappadocian,
Basil to my Gregory of Nyssa

# Contents

*Acknowledgments* | vii
*Abbreviations* | ix

1. Irenaeus' *Proof of the Apostolic Preaching* and Early Catechetical Instruction | 1
2. Catechesis and Initiation | 18
3. Christian and Jewish Baptism according to the *Epistle of Barnabas* | 52
4. Baptism according to Origen | 68
5. The Doctrine of Baptism in Gregory of Nyssa's *Oratio Catechetica* | 89
6. Exhortations to Baptism in the Cappadocians | 100
7. Basil's Protreptic to Baptism | 110
8. Preaching at Epiphany: Gregory of Nyssa and John Chrysostom on Baptism and the Church | 124
9. Spiritual Circumcision in Early Christianity | 144
10. Inscriptions and the Origin of Infant Baptism | 155
11. The Disgrace and the Glory: A Jewish Motif in Early Christianity | 166
12. The Kingdom of God in Early Patristic Literature | 176
13. Was Barnabas a Chiliast? An Example of Hellenistic Number Symbolism in *Barnabas* and Clement of Alexandria | 200
14. Millennial and Amillennial Expectations in Christian Eschatology: Ancient and Medieval Views | 213

15  Number Symbolism in the Ancient World | 244

16  Divine Pedagogy: Origen's Use of the Imagery of Education | 254

17  Early Christian Martyrdom and Civil Disobedience | 269

*Bibliography* | 281
*Ancient Sources Index* | 303
*Subject Index* | 337

# Acknowledgments

THE AUTHOR AND PUBLISHER are grateful to the original publications and publishers for permission to reprint articles in revised form. All are used by permission.

1. "Irenaeus' *Proof of the Apostolic Preaching* and Early Catechetical Instruction." *Studia Patristica* 18.3 (1989) 119–40.

2. "Catechesis and Initiation." In *The Origins of Christendom in the West*, edited by Alan Kreider, 229–68. Edinburgh: T. & T. Clark, 2001.

3. "Christian and Jewish Baptism according to the *Epistle of Barnabas*." In *Dimensions of Baptism: Biblical and Theological Studies*, edited by Stanley E. Porter, and Anthony R. Cross, 207–23. Journal for the Study of the New Testament Supplement 234. Sheffield: Sheffield Academic, 2002.

4. "Baptism according to Origen." *Evangelical Quarterly* 78 (2006) 117–35.

5. "The Doctrine of Baptism in Gregory of Nyssa's *Oratio Catechetica*." In *Dimensions of Baptism: Biblical and Theological Studies*, edited by Stanley E. Porter, and Anthony R. Cross, 224–34. Journal for the Study of the New Testament Supplement 234. Sheffield: Sheffield Academic, 2002.

6. "Exhortations to Baptism in the Cappadocians." *Studia Patristica* 32 (1997) 121–29.

7. "Basil's Protreptic to Baptism." In *Nova et Vetera: Patristic Studies in Honor of Thomas Patrick Halton*, edited by John Petruccione, 70–83. Washington, DC: Catholic University of America Press, 1998.

8. "Preaching at Epiphany: Gregory of Nyssa and John Chrysostom on Baptism and the Church." *Church History* 66 (1997) 1–17.

9. "Spiritual Circumcision in Early Christianity." *Scottish Journal of Theology* 41 (1988) 485–97.

*Acknowledgments*

10. "Inscriptions and the Origin of Infant Baptism." *Journal of Theological Studies* n.s. 30 (1979) 37–46.

11. "The Disgrace and the Glory: A Jewish Motif in Early Christianity." *Studia Patristica* 21 (1989) 86–94.

12. "The Kingdom of God in Early Patristic Literature." In *The Kingdom of God in 20th Century Interpretation*, edited by W. Willis, 191–208. Peabody, MA: Hendrickson, 1987.

13. "Was Barnabas a Chiliast? An Example of Hellenistic Number Symbolism in *Barnabas* and Clement of Alexandria." In *Greeks, Romans, and Christians: Essays in Honor of Abraham J. Malherbe*, edited by David Balch et al., 157–67. Minneapolis: Fortress, 1990.

14. "Millennial and Amillennial Expectations in Christian Eschatology: Ancient and Medieval Views." In *Apocalypticism and Millennialism: Shaping a Believers Church Eschatology for the 21st Century*, edited by L. Johns, 127–57. Kitchener: Pandora; Scottdale: Herald, 2000.

15. "Number Symbolism in the Ancient World." Previously unpublished paper delivered at the North American Patristics Society, May, 2008.

16. "Divine Pedagogy: Origen's Use of the Imagery of Education." In *Christian Teaching*, edited by Everett F. Ferguson, 343–62. Abilene: Abilene Christian University Bookstore, 1981.

17. "Early Christian Martyrdom and Civil Disobedience." *Journal of Early Christian Studies* 1 (1993) 73–83.

# Abbreviations

| | |
|---|---|
| ACW | Ancient Christian Writers |
| ANF | Ante-Nicene Fathers |
| *Aug* | *Augustiniana* |
| CH | *Church History* |
| DACL | *Dictionnaire d'archéologie chrétienne et de liturgie* |
| FC | Fathers of the Church |
| GNO | Gregorii Nysseni Opera |
| HTR | *Harvard Theological Review* |
| JBL | *Journal of Biblical Literature* |
| JECS | *Journal of Early Christian Studies* |
| JEH | *Journal of Ecclesiastical History* |
| JTS | *Journal of Theological Studies* |
| NHC | Nag Hammadi Codices |
| *NovT* | *Novum Testamentum* |
| NovTSup | Novum Testamentum Supplements |
| NPNF | Nicene and Post-Nicene Fathers |
| NTS | *New Testament Studies* |
| *PGM* | *Papyri graecae magicae: Die griechischen Zauberpapyri.* Edited by K. Preisendanz |
| PMS | Patristic Monograph Series |
| PG | Patrologia graeca. Edited by J. Migne |
| PL | Patrologia latina. Edited by J. Migne |

*Abbreviations*

| | |
|---|---|
| *RSPT* | *Revue sciences philosophiques et théologiques* |
| SC | Sources chrétiennes |
| SCA | Studies in Christian Antiquity |
| SEC | Studies in Early Christianity |
| *SecCent* | *The Second Century* |
| *SJT* | *Scottish Journal of Theology* |
| *StPatr* | *Studia Patristica* |
| TS | *Theological Studies* |
| TU | Texte und Untersuchungen zur Geschichte der altchristlichen Literatur |
| VC | *Vigiliae Christianae* |
| VCSup | Vigiliae Christianae Supplemens |
| WUNT | Wissenschaftliche Untersuchungen zum Neuen Testament |
| ZNW | *Zeitschrift für die neutestamentliche Wissenschaft und die Kunde der älteren Kirche* |

# 1

## Irenaeus' *Proof of the Apostolic Preaching* and Early Catechetical Instruction

GEORGE W. STROUP IN his book *The Promise of Narrative Theology* states the following:

> A community is a group of people who have come to share a common past, who understand particular events in the past to be of decisive importance for interpreting the present, who anticipate the future by means of a shared hope, and express their identity by means of a common narrative. What was true of the identity of persons is also true of that of communities—memory is a necessary if not sufficient category for the description of communal identity. What distinguishes a community from a crowd or a mob is a common memory which expresses itself in living traditions and institutions . . .
> 
> The community's common narrative is the glue that binds its members together. To be a true participant in a community is to share in that community's narratives, to recite the same stories as the other members of the community, and to allow one's identity to be shared by them . . . What is perhaps less clear is how a community's past and the narratives by which it preserves that past become a part of an individual's personal history and identity.[1]

---

1. Stroup, *The Promise of Narrative Theology*, 133, 134.

It is the thesis of this paper that catechetical instruction was the means by which the early church achieved this end of communal identity and that the common narrative transmitted in this instruction was the biblical history of salvation. Early Christian catechetical instruction, therefore, gives a confirmation of Stroup's affirmations and also provides a superb view of how the Christian self-identity was perceived.

The catechumenate as an organised, formal institution took shape toward the end of the second century, when the words "catechesis," "catechumen," and "catechise" acquired a technical sense.[2] The concern of this study will not be this formal catechumenate as such but the content of the instruction deemed important for new converts. For this purpose we follow Turck's definition of catechesis as elementary but comprehensive Christian teaching connected with baptism.[3] Whether that teaching was given before or after baptism is not significant for this study.

Twentieth-century study of early Christian instructional material for new converts received stimulation from the studies of Alfred Seeberg.[4] Working from New Testament material, Seeberg found two parts in the primitive catechism: a moral teaching drawn from Judaism and a specifically Christian "formula" of faith. To these were added explanations on baptism, the Holy Spirit, the Lord's prayer, and the words of the Lord at the Last Supper.[5]

The influential article on catechesis by H. Leclercq in *DACL* followed Seeberg's scheme into the extra-canonical literature. Leclercq saw the "Two Ways" as preserving the pattern of moral instruction and the "Apostles' Creed" as preserving a catechetical summary of the Christian faith.[6] DePuniet's companion article on the catechumenate—still a standard treatment, although not having assimilated the identification of the *Egyptian Church Order* as Hippolytus' *Apostolic Tradition*—carefully assembled the principal literary references bearing on admission to the catechumenate, the stages of instruction, and the content of instruction.[7]

---

2. Capelle, "L'introduction du catécheménat a Rome"; Turck, "Aux origines du catéchuménat." On the words see Turck, "Catéchein et Catéchèsis chez les premiers Pères."

3. Turck, *Évangélisation et catéchèse aux deux premiers siècles*, 10.

4. Seeberg, *Der Katechismus der Urchristenheit*.

5. See the summary of Seeberg and criticism of his reconstruction by Turck, *Évangélisation et catéchèse*, 15–22.

6. Leclercq, "Catéchèse. Catéchisme. Catéchumène."

7. DePuniet, "Catechumenate."

Most attention to catechetical instruction has continued to emphasise a two-fold content: moral and doctrinal.[8] That these elements were included seems obvious enough.[9] The *Didache* placed the "Two Ways" in the context of preliminary instruction for baptism. The creed is the basis of the *Catechetical Lectures* of Cyril of Jerusalem, and doctrinal[10] or sacramental/liturgical[11] material is the subject of the fourth and fifth-century catechetical lectures immediately before and after baptism.

Other authors, nonetheless, have offered other schemes. Under the influence of the three pairs in Heb 6:1–2, Turck and Maertens speak of moral conversion and doctrine (repentance = the two ways and faith = the symbol), liturgy (baptisms and laying on of hands), and eschatology (resurrection and judgment). They stress, however, that the catechesis was unified, having its center in Christ, and connected with baptism.[12] Daniélou, with the fourth century in mind, has a different three-fold classification: biblical, dogmatic, and sacramental.[13] In his course of instruction on catechesis in the early centuries, Daniélou organised the material as dogmatic, moral, and sacramental.[14] J. Lupi has seen the surviving evidence as indicating a catechesis in four sections: historical, moral, dogmatic, and liturgical.[15]

The biblical or historical type of catechesis mentioned as a separate category by some authors refers to the use of the history of salvation according to the scriptures as the basis of instruction. This approach in catechesis has been mainly known from Augustine's *De catechizandis rudibus*, where a narrative of biblical history serves as a preliminary instruction in

---

8. Robinson, "Historical Survey of the Church's Treatment of New Converts with Reference to Pre-and Post-Baptismal Instruction"; Folkemer, "A Study of the Catechumenate"; Bopp, "Katechese," 27–28; and Jungmann, "Katechumenat," 51

9. Origen, *Hom. in Num.* 27.1; *In Jer.* 5:13; Cyril, *Cat. lect.* IV.2; Ambrose, *De mys.* 1:1; Riggi, "La catéchèse adaptée aux temps chez Epiphane," studies the catechesis of Epiphanius in his *Ancoratus* according to its moral and doctrinal content.

10. Gregory of Nyssa, *Cat. or.*

11. Cyril, *Cat. mys.*; John Chrysostom, *Cat. ad illum.*; Theodore of Mopuestia, *Cat. Hom.*; Ambrose, *De mys.*; *De sacram.*

12. Turck, *Évangélisation et catéchèse*, 144–50; Maertens, *Histoire et pastorale du rituel du catéchumenat et du baptême*, 69–70.

13. Daniélou, "La Catéchèse dans la Tradition Patristique"; and "Introduction," in *L'initiation chrétienne*.

14. Daniélou, *La catéchèse aux premiers siècles*. Thus he seems to have moved away from the claim that "l'objet de la catéchèse est bien l'histoire du salut"—"L'histoire du salut dans la catechese," 19.

15. Lupi, "Catechetical Instruction in the Church of the First Two Centuries," 64.

essentials of the faith to inquirers before their formal enrollment in the catechumenate.[16] Augustine's work is especially valuable, because it gives two sample discourses, a longer and a shorter version, as recommendations for the actual practice in teaching potential converts.

There are other indications of this history of salvation approach to catechetical instruction. The compilation of church order material in the Apostolic Constitutions calls for a similar type of teaching.

> Let him, therefore, who is to be taught the truth in regard to piety be instructed before his baptism in the knowledge of the unbegotten God, in the understanding of his only begotten Son, in the assured acknowledgment of the Holy Spirit. Let him learn the order of the several parts of the creation, the series of providence, the different dispensations of thy laws. Let him be instructed why the world was made, and why man was appointed to be a citizen therein; let him know also his own nature, of what sort it is; let him be taught how God punished the wicked with water and fire, and did glorify the saints in every generation— I mean Seth, and Enosh, and Enoch, and Noah, and Abraham and his posterity, and Melchizedek, and Job, and Moses, and Joshua, and Caleb, and Phinehas the priest, and those that were holy in every generation; and how God still took care of and did not reject mankind, but called them from their error and vanity to the acknowledgment of the truth at various seasons, reducing them from bondage and impiety unto liberty and piety, from injustice to righteousness, from death eternal to everlasting life. Let him that offers himself to baptism learn these and the like things during the time that he is a catechumen; and let him who lays his hands upon him adore God, the Lord of the whole world, and thank him for his creation, for his sending Christ his only begotten Son, that he might save man by blotting out his transgressions...
>
> And after his thanksgiving, let him instruct him in the doctrines concerning our Lord's incarnation, and in those concerning his passion, and resurrection from the dead, and assumption.[17]

---

16. Among many studies of this work, note Folkemer, "A Study of the Catechumenate," 301–7; Touton, "La méthode catéchètique de St. Cyrille de Jérusalem comparée à celles de St. Augustin et de Théodore de Mopsueste"; Allard, "La nature du *De catechizandis rudibus* de S. Augustin"; Belche, "Die Bekehrung zum Christentum nach Augustins Buchlein De catechizandis rudibus" (4 parts); Kevane, *Catechesis in Augustine*.

17. *Apos. Const.* VII.39. Translation is taken from *Ante-Nicene Fathers*, vol. 7, 475–76.

## *Irenaeus'* Proof of the Apostolic Preaching *and Early Catechetical Instruction*

If the compiler is an Arian, then the agreement with Augustine becomes all the more significant as pointing to an earlier pattern of instruction. There is a further late fourth-century witness to biblical history as the content of teaching to new converts in the Journal of Egeria. She speaks about candidates for baptism undergoing special preparation during the Lenten season at Jerusalem. This seems to be the setting for the instructions in the *Apostolic Constitutions* also, in distinction from the pre-catechesis described by Augustine.

> All those who are to be baptized, both men and women, sit closely around the bishop, while the godmothers and godfathers stand there; and indeed all the people who wish to listen may enter and sit down, provided they are of the faithful. A catechumen, however, may not enter at the time when the bishop is teaching them the law. He does so in this way: beginning with Genesis he goes through the whole of Scripture during these forty days, expounding first its literal meaning and then explaining the spiritual meaning. In the course of these days everything is taught not only about the resurrection but concerning the body of faith. This is called catechetics.
>
> When five weeks of instruction have been completed, they then receive the Creed.[18]

Egeria explains that the teaching occupied three hours a day for seven weeks, but during the eighth week (the week before Easter Sunday) there were so many other activities that there was no more time for teaching. The baptismal ceremony itself was explained during the eight days after its reception on Easter Sunday. Egeria's diary thus testifies to a historical, doctrinal (the creed), and liturgical sequence in the instructions given to new converts. The *Catechetical Lectures* of Cyril of Jerusalem might not seem to agree with Egeria's summary. The passing of a generation and the presence of another bishop might have given another framework, yet there are similarities: the literal/spiritual approach to the Old Testament and the explanation of the sacraments during the week after the baptism (these *Mystagogical Catecheses* perhaps coming from a successor of Cyril). Although the outline of the *Catechetical Lectures* is provided by the creed, there are elements of a history of salvation exposition included.[19]

---

18. Egeria, *Journal* 46. Translation is by Gingras, *Egeria: Diary of a Pilgrimage*, 123–25. The description of the instruction corresponds to Irenaeus's approach also.

19. Note *Cat. Lect.* XII. Cyril's practice is to draw on Old Testament antecedents, prophecies, and types for each article of the creed. See Daniélou, *La catéchèse aux premiers siècles*, 103ff. Cyril has fully subordinated the history of salvation approach

Even apart from special lectures baptismal candidates could learn the scriptural story from the lections in the liturgy during this season.[20] In fact, these readings would have provided the point of departure for the bishop's specific instructions. It has been noted that there is a close correspondence between the scripture readings attested later at Rome during the period from Septuagisma to the second week after Easter and the pictures in the Roman catacombs. From this correspondence it has been argued that the catechetical instruction provided the program for the pictures depicted on the walls of the catacombs.[21] Other interpretations, of course, have been offered of the inspiration for the selection of pictures in the catacombs, but whatever element of truth there is in this hypothesis would further support the prominence of biblical history in the teaching of the church and encourage a look for ante-Nicene evidence for this framework of instruction.

In this context I propose another look at Irenaeus' *Proof of the Apostolic Preaching*. Harnack in his notes accompanying the *editio princeps* of the Armenian version described the *Proof* in a general sense as catechetical.[22] P. Drews argued that it was a catechetical work in the technical sense. He noted that the essential points in *Apostolic Constitutions* VII.39 (quoted above) occur in Irenaeus in the same order.[23] He further noted the parallels between Augustine, *De catechizandis rudibus*, and Irenaeus' *Proof*,[24] explaining that Augustine was not following Irenaeus but that the

---

to the credal framework and so completed the shift in framework begun by Irenaeus—see below at n. 44. Doval, "The Fourth Century Jerusalem Catechesis and the Development of the Creed," notes that catechesis was originally structured on salvation history (the thesis of this paper) and was later adapted to a Trinitarian style creed.

20. Surkau, "Katechetik," 1181.

21. Martimort, "L'inconographie des catacombs et la catéchèse antique." Martimort does not put this information in a specifically history of salvation setting, but that would complement the presentation.

22. Ter-Mekerttschian and Ter-Minassiantz, *Des Heiligen Irenäus Schrift zum Erweise der Apostolischen Verkündigung in Armenischer Version Entdeckt*, 55 ("sie zeigt uns den bedeutenden Bischof als Katecheten") and 65 ("unser Traktak ist katechetisch erbaulich").

23. Drews, "Der literarische Charakter der neuentdeckten Schrift des Irenaus 'Zum Erweise der apostolischen Verkündigung.'"

24. Ibid., 230–31, states that Augustine expanded the *Apostolic Constitutions* and Irenaeus by reference to the last judgment and ethical admonitions because the scheme of catechesis had been enlarged since Irenaeus; but moral instruction was early, and Irenaeus has an ethical section in chapters 95–96. Daniélou, "L'histoire du salut dans la catéchèse," 24–25, exaggerates the difference between Irenaeus and Augustine. Irenaeus uses types in his historical sketch, and when he comes to the prophecies, he is

verbal connections were due to the traditional scheme both were following. Of course, if both were following the biblical order, there would be parallels, but what is included and what is omitted would suggest a closer connection.

An alternative classification of the *Proof of the Apostolic Preaching* gives its purpose as apologetic. Influential patrologies have popularized this classification.[25] On the other hand, Turck and Maertens describe the *Proof* as the first catechetical manual, but neither develops the significance of the prominence of biblical history in its content for his reconstruction of early catechesis.[26] Daniélou has given his magisterial support to the *Proof* as the "first catechetical work we possess,"[27] and he does utilize the work fully in his treatment of early catechesis; hence to his studies we must return. Not everyone concurred: Michael Dujarier has written his history of the catechumenate without any reference to Irenaeus.[28] Others are content to describe the purpose of the *Proof* as both catechetical and apologetic.[29] Joseph P. Smith in the judicious introduction to his excellent English translation characterizes the *apparent* aim of the work as catechetical but the real aim as apologetic.[30] I would prefer to reverse the priorities. The question of the intention of the work is posed already by Irenaeus' own statement in chapter 1:

> What we are sending you is in the form of notes on the main points, so that you may find much matter in short space, comprehending in a few details all the members of the body of truth, and receiving in brief the proof of the things of God. In this way, not only will it bear fruit in your own salvation, but also you may confound all those who hold false views, and to all who wish to hear, you may with all confidence expound what we have to say in its integrity and purity.[31]

---

telling the history of Jesus.

25. Bardenhewer, *Geschichte der altkirchlichen Literatur*, 1:409–11; Quasten, *Patrology*, 1:292; Jungmann, "Katechumenat," 52.

26. Turck, *Évangélisation et catéchèse*, 72, 117, 128–32; cf. Grant, "Development of the Christian Catechumenate," 41; Peretto, ed., *Ireneo de Lione: Epideixis, Antico catechismo degli adulti*.

27. Daniélou, *La catéchèse aux premiers siècles*, 89; see his exposition on 89–102.

28. Dujarier, *A History of the Catechumenate*.

29. Hamman, "Introduction," in *La prédication des apôtres*, 12 and 17; Altaner, *Patrology*, 152.

30. J. P. Smith, *St. Irenaeus: Proof of the Apostolic Preaching*, 14, 19–20.

31. Ibid., 47.

Irenaeus thus saw a three-fold purpose for his writing: (1) the edification of the recipient, Marcianus, (2) the refutation of heresy, and (3) the instruction of those who wish to learn about Christianity. The question is, "Which of these purposes was primary?" The debate is between numbers (2) and (3).

A decision on the question requires consideration of the content of the *Proof of the Apostolic Preaching*. One approach is by way of rhetorical analysis, and Irenaeus was not as innocent of rhetorical training as he professes.[32] If rhetorical divisions are more obvious in the *Proof* than in *Against Heresies*, that may be due to the former being an educational work. The *Proof* may rather easily be outlined according to the following parts of a speech:

    I. Exordium, 1–2

    II. Divisio, 3–7

    III. Narratio, 8–42a

    IV. Confirmatio, 42b–97

    V. Conclusio, 98–100

This does not correspond to either of the two common divisions of a speech into four[33] or six[34] divisions, and Quintilian's five parts are different.[35] But Cicero refers to "four, five, six, or even seven subdivisions" into which different authorities distribute every speech.[36] The *Rhetorica ad Herennium* had recognized that "There is also another arrangement, which, when we must depart from the order imposed by the rules of the art, is accommodated to circumstance in accordance with the speaker's judgment."[37] Normally the *narratio*, or statement of the facts in the case

---

32. *Adv. haer.* I. pref. 3. See Grant, "Irenaeus and Hellenistic Culture"; Schoedel, "Philosophy and Rhetoric in the Adversus Haereses of Irenaeus"; and Perkins, "Irenaeus and the Gnostics."

33. Aristotle, *Rhet.* III.xiii.4 gives proem, statement, proof, and epilogue; Cicero, *De part. or.* 4 and 27 names them exordium, statement of the facts, proof, and peroration; cf. *Top.* 97–99 and *Or.* 122.

34. *Rhet. ad Heren.* I.iii.4 gives the six parts as introduction, statement of facts, division, proof, refutation, and conclusion; the same outline is in Cicero, *De inventione* 1.19.

35. *Inst. or.* III.ix.1–3 divides a forensic speech into exordium (*prooemium*), statement of facts (*narratio*), proof (*probatio*), refutation (*refutatio*), and peroration (*peroratio*).

36. *De or.* 11.79.

37. *Rhet. ad Heren.* III.ix.16–18; cf. Theon, *Progymnasmata* 12 (Spengel, 125).

preceded the *divisio*, or outline of the points, but Cicero cites an example in which a "narrative follows the plan laid down in the partition."[38] Or, alternatively, if one wanted to be a rhetorical purist, he could treat chapters 3–7 as the *narratio*, the statement of facts, and both the historical and prophetic parts of the treatise as part of the proof. I have preferred to treat the historical section as *narratio*, since Cicero presents *historia* as one kind of narrative and defines *historia* as "an account of actual occurrences remote from the recollection of our own age."[39] This arrangement brings the outline into harmony with the two main parts of Irenaeus' work, Old Testament history followed by proof from the prophecies. Nevertheless, Irenaeus' survey of history would seem to a student of ancient rhetoric a most unusual kind of *narratio*, but perhaps explainable by the special subject matter of his treatise.

Irenaeus himself had other interests which governed his presentation, and these might seem more obviously to determine the outline. These interests are doctrinal, and Irenaeus has imposed a modified Trinitarian framework on his presentation. The doctrinal content gives the following outline:

    I. Introduction, 1–2

    II. The Trinity, in Creation and Redemption, 3–7

    III. The Father, 8–29

    IV. The Son, 30–88

    V. The Holy Spirit and the Church, 89–97

    VI. Conclusion, 98–100

The Son of God clearly gets major attention. He was the fulfillment of words addressed to Adam, Abraham, and David (32–36), the subject of the theophanies to the patriarchs (44–46), and in his earthly life the object of the prophecies (53–85). The apparent lack of attention to the Holy Spirit is partially offset by the consideration that the prophecies of Christ are viewed as the work of the Holy Spirit (30; 42). But the work of the Holy Spirit is little developed apart from this prophetic function; and the last section treats more the calling of the Gentiles through the apostolic preaching than the work of the Holy Spirit as such,[40] although this ap-

---

38. *De inventione* 1.33.

39. Ibid., 1.27.

40. Justin Martyr too had included the mission of the apostles in his summary of the Christian faith—*Apology* I, 39; 45; *Dialogue* 109–10.

ostolic preaching is probably to be seen as inspired by the Holy Spirit, for it stands in parallel with the prophets' proclamation (86; cf. 41 and 98). The comparative neglect of the Holy Spirit can be explained from the anti-heretical perspective as arising from Irenaeus' concern with teachings which affected the Father and the Son but not the Holy Spirit.[41]

Although in general the content of the *Proof* corresponds to what is stated about Father, Son, and Holy Spirit in chapter 6, the material at the end of the work shows the difficulty of outlining the whole in terms of the Three Persons. Indeed, the chapters preceding the conclusion (86–97) still essentially present the sending of the apostles, the new covenant, the calling of the Gentiles, the pouring forth of the Holy Spirit, and the new life as part of the scheme of the fulfillment of prophecy which was employed about Christ (42–85). Moreover, the Trinitarian outline does not do justice to the major division at 42–43. Indeed as significant a treatment of the place of the Holy Spirit in the economy of salvation occurs in chapters 41–42 as in the latter part of the book.

The fact is, there was another scheme at work in Irenaeus' presentation, signalled already in Irenaeus' introduction: "the members of the body of truth" and "the proof of the things of God"(1).[42] Both the rhetorical and doctrinal outlines yield a somewhat artificial arrangement of what is essentially an account of biblical history centered on Christ with a baptismal/doctrinal introduction and a moral/anti-heretical conclusion. I would suggest an outline for the work in terms of the history of salvation. The body of the work consists of two major blocks of material. The first is largely a literal history of salvation as the mighty acts of God the Father, beginning with creation and continuing through the events of Genesis, the Mosaic covenant, taking the promised land, the sending of the prophets, the coming of Christ, the sending of the apostles, and the general resurrection (8–42a). The second block, also historically ordered, concerns the spiritual sense of scripture. Returning to Gen 1:1, Irenaeus treats Christ and his salvation and church from the standpoint of the fulfillment of the Old Testament. The quotations from the prophetic books are not taken

---

41. Grossi, "Regula veritatis e narratio battesimale in sant' Ireneo," 442–43.

42. See the outline in Barthoulot, trans., *La Prédication des Apôtres et ses Preuvres*: Prologue, 1–3. I. Exposition of the Preaching of the Apostles, 4–42. II. The Proof of the Preaching of the Apostles: Christ the Fulfillment of Scripture, 43–85. III. Christ and the New Law, 86–97. Conclusion, 98–100. Cf. Daniélou, *La catéchèse aux premiers siècles*, 90–91, for a similar structure. My debt to Daniélou is evident, but I want to advance additional arguments for the *Proof* as based on catechesis and carry the implications of its history of salvation approach further.

## *Irenaeus' Proof of the Apostolic Preaching and Early Catechetical Instruction*

in their biblical order but are arranged according to the story of Christ as testimonies to his preexistence, his nature, his virgin birth, his miracles, his passion, his resurrection, and his calling a new people through his apostles (42b–97).[43] The basic content of the work is provided by the biblical history of salvation from the preexistent Father and Son to the general resurrection, in general following the books of Law and then the books of the Prophets, all seen as culminating in the Christian age. The accommodation to the Trinitarian scheme has resulted in a certain repetition, since Irenaeus goes back to Genesis in chapter 32, when he turns from talking about the Father to talking about the Son, and again in chapter 43, when he begins the proof from prophecy. Nonetheless, history and prophecy still provide the two main bodies of material in the work, and the prophetic segment is arranged according to the history of Christ. This proposed outline keeps the advantages of the outline according to rhetorical divisions, i.e., a historical *narratio* and a *confirmatio* from prophecy. This history of salvation content has been brought into a Trinitarian framework by Irenaeus. The rough edges and lack of exact correspondence point to the arrangement according to biblical history being the earlier, traditional form of the material, and the "rule of faith" or the Trinitarian summary of Christian doctrine as being imposed by Irenaeus.[44]

If the historical rather than the doctrinal per se lies at the basis of the *Proof* then a catechetical purpose is primary. Several considerations support this conclusion. There are indeed anti-heretical comments scattered throughout the work, and the argument from prophecy as a demonstration of the continuity of the Old and New Testaments was of obvious value in refuting Gnostics and Marcionites.[45] Nevertheless, the content of the *Proof* as a whole does not show this as the primary thrust (much of the historical survey is irrelevant to an anti-heretical purpose) and seems to be dictated by other considerations. This may be readily demonstrated by a comparison of the Proof with an avowedly anti-heretical work by Irenaeus, the *Against Heresies*. The history of salvation perspective is the

---

43. Musurillo, "History and Symbol: A Study of Form in Early Christian Literature," *Theological Studies* 18 (1957) 357–86, notes the pattern in early Christian literature of literal history followed by its symbolic meaning (*theoria*) but does not discuss Irenaeus' *Proof* and Melito's *On the Pascha* (see below), two striking examples of this pattern. Cf. Egeria, *Journal* 46, quoted above.

44. Rules of faith first appear with this title about Irenaeus' time—Tertullian, *Praescr.* 13; *Vel. virg.* 1; *Adv. Prax.* 2. Cf. Clement of Alexandria, *Strom.* VI.xv.124–25. Irenaeus offers in *Adv. haer.* I.10.1 and III.4.2 similar summaries to that in *Proof* 6.

45. Cf. Tertullian, *C. Marc.*, esp. Book III.

standpoint from which the argument is constructed in that work too,[46] but the arrangement of the material is obviously for polemical purposes. The position opposed is stated, and then scriptural and historical arguments are introduced in refutation. The plan is quite different in the *Proof*. The history of salvation itself becomes the groundwork. Irenaeus could hardly write anything without a jab at his opponents where the subject matter suggested it, but that does not necessarily make anti-heretical arguments the dominant theme. The history of salvation scheme, which was being challenged by Gnostics and Marcionites, had its origin in the *Proof* elsewhere.

Irenaeus' warning against false teachers at the end of the work (99–100) specified three errors: positing a Father above the Creator, despising the incarnation, and rejecting the gifts of the Holy Spirit (i.e., prophecy). The first error was associated with Gnostic systems, the second was that of Docetism, and the third was part of the Marcionite rejection of the Old Testament. Actually all three positions against which Irenaeus warns apply to Marcion, but Gnostics too were especially in mind, and on the third point perhaps even Jews. Probably we should not try to think of specific heretics. The false teachings are singled out to correspond to the three articles of belief with which the work was introduced (6). The schematising of errors according to Father, Son, and Holy Spirit indicates that Irenaeus' main concern was not the various heresies themselves, but rather the contrast with the true faith. The presentation of the material had a positive goal.

When Irenaeus summarized what he had done, he affirmed: "This, beloved, is the preaching of the truth, and this is the manner of our salvation, and this is the way of life, announced by the prophets and ratified by Christ and handed over by the apostles and handed down by the Church in the whole world to her children. This must be kept in all security, with good will, and by being well-pleasing to God through good works and sound moral character" (98). The sequence of preaching, salvation, and way of life; the reference to what the church handed down to her children; and the insistence on maintaining a good moral life are all motifs

---

46. Lawson, *The Biblical Theology of Saint Irenaeus*; Benoît, *Saint Irénée*; P. and H. Lassiat, *Dieu veut-il des hommes libres?* Von Campenhausen, "Die Entstehung der Heilsgeschichte," concludes that Irenaeus, in express contrast to Justin and Melito, has the first developed statement of a Christian *Heilsgeschichte*. I would prefer to see this as an underlying pattern of instruction that finds its first full, systematic presentation in Irenaeus.

pertaining to the catechetical process.[47] May it be that "those who wish to hear" in chapter 1 are the "hearers," the term that became a technical designation of catechumens?[48]

In keeping with what is known of the concerns of catechetical instruction, Irenaeus integrates doctrine and morals into the historical framework of the *Proof*. Chapter 2 introduces the human person as a combination of body and soul and so requiring both holy deeds and true faith. Christians must keep "the rule of faith and carry out the commands of God" (3). Similarly, Irenaeus returns to faith in God and love for God and neighbor in chapters 41, 87, and 95. Moreover, Irenaeus begins with the theme of the two ways (1), and the teaching which he presents is that associated with baptism (3). I see the *Proof*, therefore, as a work based on and shaped by catechetical instruction but adapted here and there to include a refutation of Gnostic and/or Marcionite views.

Irenaeus refers in chapter 3 to the "rule of faith." It has been plausibly suggested that the *regula fidei* originated in the outlines of instruction for catechumens which bishops gave to their catechists.[49] These began as oral formulations of a common faith and pattern of instruction and so have come down to us in a variety of wordings. We may think of the *Proof* also as an elaboration in written form of such instructions for a teacher of new converts. Drews suggested that Marcianus may have been recently baptised and in need of elaboration of what was given him more briefly in catechesis.[50] But may not Marcianus have been himself a teacher and this work a manual for his use? If the fact that he was removed in distance from Irenaeus is thought to argue against this (1),[51] there is still the possibility that the kind of guidance Irenaeus gave to teachers in his own church has here been recorded for use elsewhere.

The prophecies cited by Irenaeus are used to narrate the gospel of Christ, not to construct a formal proof per se. As much as an argument

---

47. Cf. Turck, *Évangélisation et catéchèse*, passim. The *Apostolic Tradition* implies scriptural (17, 20, and 35), doctrinal (21); liturgical (22–23, 27, 33, 37–38, 41); and moral (42) instruction in the catechumenate.

48. Tertullian, *Paenit*. 6; *Cor*. 2; Origen, *C. Cels*. 111.51; *Apos. Const*. VIII.6.2.

49. Countryman, "Tertullian and the *Regula Fidei*," 221–26. For the catechist see Hippolytus, *Ap. Trad*. 16; 18; 19; Cyprian, *Ep*. 23 [29]. For references to the regula see n. 44. The connection of the regula in Irenaeus with baptism, specifically the baptismal interrogations, has been argued by Grossi, "Regula veritatis e narratio battesimale in sant' Ireneo." Smulders, "The *Sitz im Leben* of the Old Roman Creed," argued the creed was a *homologia*, not catechetical, polemic, nor a test of orthodoxy.

50. Drews, "Der literarische Charakter," 232.

51. But need the distance be any more than that between Lyons and Vienne?

from prophecy, the work is a telling of the story of Jesus out of the prophets. And there are other collections which indicate such an approach to Christian teaching.

Telling the Christian message in terms of Old Testament history has precedent already in the New Testament. Particularly to be noted are Stephen's speech in Acts 7 and the sermon attributed to Paul in Acts 13:16ff. The facts connected with the life of Jesus appear as the content of most Christian preaching in the New Testament, and the fulfillment of prophecy is prominent in that presentation.[52] These passages are in a kerygmatic context, but as Christianity moved from a Jewish to a Gentile setting the need must have been felt to acquaint those without a background in the synagogue with the Old Testament history, of which Christians claimed to be the heir. And in fact there is an impressive knowledge of the Old Testament scriptures shown in early Christianity and considerable influence from the Old Testament on the development of early Christianity. The case for the history of salvation providing the groundwork of early Christian catechesis is strengthened by looking at two other collections of Old Testament *testimonia* to Christ, one a near successor to Irenaeus' *Proof* and one an immediate predecessor.

The earliest surviving formal collection of *testimonia* is Cyprian's three books *Ad Quirinum*. Jean Daniélou has noted that Book II arranges the prophecies according to the order of the life of Christ and pointed to the formal parallel with the Old Roman Symbol and Irenaeus' approach in the *Proof of the Apostolic Preaching*.[53] Although Cyprian uses few of same proof texts from the Old Testament as Irenaeus, his ordering of the material covers the same points, beginning with the pre-existence (1–6; *Proof* 43; 50–51) and moving through the virgin birth (7–9; *Proof* 53–58), Christ's two natures (10; *Proof* 31; 37), his descent from David (11; *Proof* 59; 62; 64), birth in Bethlehem (12; *Proof* 63), the passion and crucifixion (13–23; *Proof* 68–77; 79–81), descent into Hades (24; *Proof* 78), resurrection and exaltation (25–27; *Proof* 83–84), and second coming for judgment (28–30; *Proof* 85). There are indications of a catechetical origin or motivation for Cyprian's collection. Book I is an anti-Jewish collection emphasising that

---

52. The classic statement is Dodd, *The Apostolic Preaching and its Developments*. Whatever criticisms of detail are sustained (as by Worley, *Preaching and Teaching in the Earliest Church*), Dodd has noted a consistent feature in the content of Christian preaching.

53. For this paragraph I draw on Daniélou, *The Origins of Latin Christianity*, 288–95. The Pseudo-Epiphanius Testimony Book similarly arranges the prophecies by the life of Christ: Hotchkiss, ed. and trans., *A Pseudo-Epiphanius Testimony Book*.

the church of the Gentiles has replaced the ancient people of God. This is a more elaborate development of the theme of the latter part of Irenaeus' treatise (87–96). Moreover, Cyprian's Book III of *Ad Quirinum* is a collection of Old and New Testament passages on Christian moral duties.[54] Cyprian here has made an original collection on a traditional theme of Christian teaching. We may, then categorise Cyprian's collection of *testimonia* as representing three themes of Christian catechesis: historical (the new Israel replacing the old—Book I), doctrinal (Christology—Book II), and moral (duties of the Christian life—Book III).

The argument from messianic proof texts in the Old Testament is pervasive in early Christianity, but we select here only Justin Martyr, who is clearly one of Irenaeus' important sources.[55] Justin's *Dialogue with Trypho* is much less systematic and organized than Irenaeus and Cyprian, but a broad outline may be observed: the replacement of the Jewish law, rites, and covenant (*Dialogue* 11–30; cf. Irenaeus, *Proof* 87–96; Cyprian, *Ad Quirinum* I.8–18); the two advents and deity of Christ (*Dialogue* 31–62; cf. *Proof* 43–51; *Ad Quirinum* II.1–7; 13); the incarnation (*Dialogue* 63–78; cf. *Proof* 51–64; *Ad Quirinum* II.7–12); the cross (*Dialogue* 86–105; cf. *Proof* 68–82; *Ad Quirinum* II.13–23); resurrection and ascension (*Dialogue* 106–8; cf. *Proof* 83–85; *Ad Quirinum* II.25–27); the calling of the Gentiles and the church (*Dialogue* 109 to end; cf. *Proof* 89–96; *Ad Quirinum* I.19–24). R. Way-Rider in a communication to the Seventh International Conference of Patristic Studies pointed out how Justin arranged his references to pagan parallels to Christianity according to the elements of the kerygma. The same sequence even more clearly provides an ordering principle for the Old Testament proof texts, and the history of salvation sequence closely approximates Irenaeus. Thus Justin's summary of the faith includes the calling of the Gentiles, a theme not normally found in the *regula*. The presence of this topic in both Justin and Irenaeus would fit a salvation history approach to catechetical instruction. Justin's purposes required putting the material on the rejection of the Jewish law early in his *Dialogue* separate from the discussion of the calling of the Gentiles, even as the needs of the anti-Jewish polemic have put all of this material in Book I of Cyprian's *testimonia*.

There is one other work to be considered, not a collection of *testimonia* but coming from a contemporary of Irenaeus, the *Homily on the Pascha* of Melito of Sardis. The paschal season, it will be remembered, was

---

54. Baker, "*Ad Quirinum* Book Three and Cyprian's Catechumenate."
55. Skarsaune, *The Proof from Prophecy*.

the time for the preparation for and administration of baptism.[56] I would not claim the *Peri Pascha* is a catechetical address, but once more the pattern of presenting the material has striking similarities to what appears to be a traditional method of approach.[57] Stuart Hall outlines the work in two major parts.[58] Part I is a historical account of the Old Testament Passover and its interpretation (1–45). Part II develops the Christian meaning of the Passover. Melito begins this section with the creation and fall of man (47–48). After discussing sin and its punishment in death (49–56), he presents types and prophecies from the Old Testament of the Lord's sufferings (57–65).[59] Then are described the Lord's coming, passion, and exaltation (66–71). The theme of the rejection of Israel (72–99), including a summary of her early history (83–89), is followed by the conclusion on the resurrection, salvation for all, and glory (100–105). The similarities to the development in Irenaeus' *Proof* are again obvious.

The examination of these few works indicates that the biblical history of salvation is more pervasive in early Christianity than perhaps even the biblical theology movement, now considered in some circles as *passé*, thought. That movement emphasised the saving acts of God as the structure of biblical faith. Jean Daniélou was one of the few who applied its insights to patristic studies. He has stimulated much of what is presented here, but he was still perhaps too much under the influence of traditional categories and did not push on to the full implications of his insights for the structure of catechetics. The Old Testament was more than an explication and proof of the New Testament message;[60] as the story of God's saving deeds it was the very framework of catechesis and provided the setting for presenting Christ, the very center of that catechesis.[61]

The *Proof of the Apostolic Preaching* is what it purports to be: a work for the teaching of inquirers about Christianity which also serves to refute false interpretations of the Christian message and so to confirm the faith of the reader. Therefore, a better rendering of the title than *Proof* would be *Demonstration* or *Presentation*, for the work is an exposition or a showing

---

56. Tertullian, *De bapt.* 19.
57. Winslow, "The Polemical Christology of Melito of Sardis."
58. Hall, *Melito of Sardis on Pascha and Fragments*, xxii–xxiii.
59. Perler, "Typologie der Leiden des Herrn in Melitons Peri Pascha." Justin and Irenaeus use types as well as prophecies—*Dial.* 40–42; 113; 132; 134; 138; *Proof* 12; 25; 26; 32; 33.
60. Daniélou, *La catéchèse aux premiers siècles*, 86–88.
61. Ibid., 231, 251–53 on Augustine have a wider validity.

forth.⁶² And if this work is indeed a guide for a catechist, or based on such a guide, then we not only know more about the framework of catechetical instruction than perhaps we thought we did, but we also know something very important about early Christian self-understanding. The importance of the theme of the history of salvation shows a sense of identity with old Israel and a sense of "roots" in a world where the modern was assumed to be erroneous. Biblical history provided for the early church the "common narrative" which shaped its identity.⁶³

---

62. The Greek ἐπίδειξις could go either way, but the primary meaning is exposition. The Latin *demonstratio* as used in rhetoric could be applied to the *narratio*; see the note in Fredouille, trans. and ed., *Tertullien: Contre les Valentiniens*.

63. Research for this paper has been supported in part by the Research Council of Abilene Christian University through the generosity of the Cullen Foundation.

# 2

# Catechesis and Initiation

Catechesis was central to the initiation of new Christians in the early centuries of Christianity. In the pre-Constantinian writers, evidence about the content of catechesis is sketchy. But Justin indicates that in mid-second-century Rome training in Christian lifestyle was as important as the teaching of doctrine. In Gaul a few years later, Irenaeus shows that an emphasis upon moral training in the Sermon on the Mount tradition was still strong, but evidently less prominent than doctrinal instruction. Cyprian's *Testimonia* demonstrate his concern in mid-third-century Carthage to establish a biblical basis for historical, doctrinal and moral instruction. In the large and rapidly growing church of the fourth and early fifth centuries, the evidence for catechesis becomes much fuller, and its focus appears to have altered somewhat. Cyril in Jerusalem concentrated on giving an exposition of the creed, with a post-baptismal emphasis upon mystagogy; moral instruction was present, but was incidental to instruction in orthodox doctrine. In Milan, Ambrose's catechesis similarly concentrated on doctrine and mystagogy; his homilies instructing catechumens in Christian lifestyle were based especially on Old Testament materials—the proverbs and the examples of the patriarchs. Augustine's many catechetical materials covered the entire span of the catechumenate and dealt with matters of doctrine, prayer and morals in eschatological perspective; the balance of materials was tilted towards doctrine, although Augustine was concerned that the new Christians in North Africa live lives of sexual chastity.

## Catechesis and Initiation

Lewis Rambo, in his book *Understanding Religious Conversion*,[1] identifies seven overlapping stages, or I might call them components or aspects, of conversion. These are context, crisis, quest (or search), encounter, interaction, commitment, and consequences. Of these stages, interaction describes the catechumenate of the ancient church. The goal of interaction between the potential convert and the group to which he or she is being converted is encapsulation.[2] The sphere of influence created by encapsulation involves four dimensions, according to Rambo: relationships, rituals, rhetoric, and roles.[3] The relationships that "create and consolidate emotional bonds to the group and establish the day-by-day reality of the new perspective"[4] remind us of the sponsors, who introduced to the teachers those who came "to hear the word" and who "bore witness" to their readiness to be instructed.[5] Rituals would have included such practices as the teacher's prayer and laying on of hands in blessing;[6] exorcism, which dramatized the process of a change of realms in which the convert lived;[7] and fasting.[8] By rhetoric, Rambo means "the language of transformation" that the new convert is taught; in the ancient church this was done by attendance at services of the word and instruction over a period of time,[9] and to this practice we shall return shortly. Roles, the enactment of the activities associated with the new life, included in the practice of the ancient church such items as prayer, renouncing Satan, and reciting the creed.[10] Rambo discusses Christian baptism as an example of commitment, and he includes in commitment adopting the story of a group as one's own,[11] but he does not discuss the early church's catechetical

---

1. Rambo, *Understanding Religious Conversion*.

2. Ibid., 103–8.

3. Ibid., 107–23.

4. Ibid., 197.

5. *Apostolic Tradition* 16 (Dix, *The Treatise on the Apostolic Tradition of St. Hippolytus of Rome*, 23). In spite of the doubts about the authorship of this treatise (see n. 16), it remains a valuable source for what was done by some in the early third century.

6. *Apostolic Tradition* 19.

7. *Apostolic Tradition* 20.3–4, 8; Finn, "Ritual Processes and the Survival of Early Christianity."

8. *Apostolic Tradition* 20.8.

9. *Apostolic Tradition* 17; 20.2.

10. *Apostolic Tradition* 18.1 (prayer by the catechumens), 21.9 (renunciation of Satan), 21:12–18 (profession of faith).

11. Rambo, *Understanding Religious Conversion*, 127–29, 138.

practices. This is the aspect of conversion, namely its rhetoric, that I want to consider.

What instruction did the early church, especially in the West, consider important to give to new converts? My purpose is to answer the question, What was taught to catechumens? Or, more broadly, how was the convert "formed" into a Christian? "Christian formation" certainly included ceremonies, actions, and practices as well as words, but the limitation to teachings is still quite ambitious.

Changes in emphasis may tell us something about both the changing circumstances of the church and changing understandings about Christianity itself. Conclusions must be drawn cautiously because we must allow for accidents of preservation. There is something capricious about what was preserved, but that is what we have to deal with. Moreover, preservation was not wholly capricious. Not only must we work with what we have, and for the fourth and fifth centuries that is rather considerable, but also we must assume that one factor in what was preserved was recognition by some persons that the contents of a document were important.

Therefore, I propose to take seriously what remains from the past. As historians we lament the fact of destroyed and lost source material. We speculate about what it would tell us. But also, there is a reason why we have many of the things we do. Contemporaries thought they were worth saving. That in itself tells us what they thought was important. Sometimes that favourable decision was made by later centuries and so may tell us more about the later century than an author's own time. Yet for the later century to transmit the material, it had to have been preserved to that day. So, with due allowance made for arbitrary and accidental features in the transmission, I conclude that what we have tells us something about what was important in a given period. That permits us in turn to make some tentative inferences concerning the thinking and concerns of people.

An observation on terminology is perhaps worth making at the outset.[12] The early church had a verb for giving instruction (κατηχέω), a noun for the instruction itself (κατήχησις), a noun for the teacher (κατηχετής), the participle as a technical term for the one being instructed (κατηχούμενος), and eventually a noun for the place where the instruction occurred (κατηχουμενιον or κατηχούμενον). There was no word, however, for catechism. Greek did not create a word for it from the κατηχ-root.[13] Ecclesiastical Latin borrowed the Greek terminology, and in

12. Turck, "*Catéchein* et *catéchèsis* chez les premiers Pères."
13. A search of the Thesaurus Linguae Graecae reveals no occurrences of

addition did create the word *catechismus*. Initially it had the same meaning as *catechesis*, the act of teaching, and not a formalized content. The first occurrences of *catechismus* are in Augustine.[14] Perhaps I am making too much of the late occurrence of the word and then only in Latin, but I find it corroborative of the fact that there was no fixed content to the instruction. Certainly there were common themes and subject matter, and the "Rule of Faith" and eventually the baptismal creeds provided an outline of doctrinal instruction for many catechists, but there was no fixed catechism such as emerged in the Medieval and Reformation churches. Hence, I have chosen the word "catechesis" for my title instead of "catechism."

Because of the limitation of my subject to the content of instruction to new converts, I omit the *Apostolic Tradition* from my survey, since it does not discuss the content of instruction during the three-year catechumenate it provides for.[15] There have been recently revived doubts about the title *Apostolic Tradition* and its attribution to Hippolytus of Rome as part of the observation that the work represents the genre of living institutional literature in the ancient church.[16] These doubts do not remove the importance of the work for the development of the catechumenate.[17] In this regard, we will refer to it once more in our conclusion.

---

κατήχισμος or κατήχεσμος. Nor is such a word to be found in the lexica of Liddell and Scott, *Greek-English Lexicon*, with Supplement; Lampe, *A Patristic Greek Lexicon*; Sophocles, *Greek Lexicon of the Roman and Byzantine Periods*; and Demetrakos, *Mega lexikon*.

14. The CETEDOC Library of Christian Latin Texts reveals none before Augustine, and lists four from him, all from *On Faith and Works*: 9.14 "those things to be said in catechizing"; 18.33 "rigorously disciplined by inculcation of precepts and catechizings"; and 19.35 "in the catechizings of candidates for baptism" are clearly the act of catechizing; 13.19 inclines more toward the content, referring to "all the teachings."

15. The *Apostolic Tradition* does stress the moral qualifications for admission to the catechumenate (chs. 16, 17, 20) and implies scriptural (chs. 20, 33), doctrinal (ch. 21; cf. 23.13—"you have already been instructed concerning the resurrection"), and liturgical (chs. 23, 32) teaching.

16. Metzger, "Nouvelies perspectives pour la prétendue Tradition apostolique"; Metzger, "Enquetes autour de la prétendue 'Tradition apostolique.'" Phillips, "Hippolytus and the So-Called 'Apostolic Tradition,'" reported support for a connection with Hippolytus based on the appearance of phrases in the *Apostolic Tradition* that occur also in other works attributed to Hippolytus but not elsewhere (or rarely) in the first four centuries.

17. For book-length surveys of the content of catechetical instruction, see Turck, *Évangelisation et catéchese aux deux premiers siecles*; and Daniélou with du Charlat, *La catéchèse aux premiers siècles*; older points of departure for study include Bareille, "Catéchèse"; and Leclercq, "Catéchèse, Catéchisme, Catéchumène." For the catechumenate itself, a brief overview is by Dujarier, *A History of the Catechumenate*; still

## JUSTIN MARTYR: TRAINING TO LIVE IN A DISTINCTIVE COMMUNITY

Justin Martyr, although coming from Palestine and converted in the East, is arguably our first witness to Christian initiatory practice in the West, since he spent his later years in Rome and did his writing there.[18] He, as the other apologists, was concerned to define the Christian community over against both the pagan world and Judaism. The *Acts of Justin* give some information of Justin's teaching activities in Rome: "Anyone who wished could come to my abode and I would impart to him the words of truth."[19] The prefect who examined Justin and his companions thought Justin converted them, but the answers by the students indicate that Justin was teaching those already Christians. Justin may have engaged in evangelistic and catechetical work as well as more advanced instruction, for catechesis and apologetics have much in common. He does give us information about conversion and how one became a Christian.

Justin explained to his intended imperial readership "how we dedicated ourselves to God and were made new through Christ." "As many as are persuaded and believe that the things taught and said by us are true and promise to be able to live accordingly" pray and fast in preparation for their baptism. He continues with another twofold statement about faith and life: the person baptized is "one who chooses to be regenerated and who repents of his sins."[20] Later he speaks of the one baptized as the one "who has been persuaded and agreed entirely with our teachings" (*1 Apol.* 65.1). The eucharist is for "the one who believes the things which have been taught by us to be true, and was washed with the washing for the remission of sins and for regeneration, and lives in the manner Christ taught" (*1 Apol.* 66.1). It is evident that for Justin faith, baptism, and conduct belong together. These statements may look back to the New Testament requirements of faith and repentance accompanying baptism[21]

---

standard is de Puniet, "Catéchuménat"; cf. Maertens, *Histoire et pastorale du rituel du catéchuménat et du Baptéme*, esp. ch. 3; still useful, covering both the stages and the instructions given, is Folkemer, "A Study of the Catechumenate"; bringing new material and perspectives is Grant, "Development of the Christian Catechumenate."

18. For introductions to Justin, see Barnard, *Justin Martyr*; Osborn, *Justin Martyr*.
19. *Acts of Justin*, A 3.3; Musurillo, *The Acts of the Christian Martyrs*, 45.
20. Justin Martyr, *1 Apol.*, 61.2, 10. Cf. the summary of Justin's evidence for practice in Rome before the introduction of a more formal catechumenate at the end of the second century by Capelle, "L'introduction du catechumenat á Rome," 131–33.
21. Acts 2:38; 18:8.

*Catechesis and Initiation*

or forward to catechetical instruction in faith (doctrine) and morals; or Justin may be seen as linking both.[22]

What Justin meant by the teachings about things to be believed and about how to live may be reflected earlier in his *First Apology*. Accepting an obligation to "furnish an account of [Christian] life and doctrine," Justin sets as his task to make possible for all to examine "our life and teachings" (*1 Apol.* 3.2, 4). As a summary of Christian doctrine, Justin refers to Christians offering the worship of "prayer and thanksgiving," "ceremonies and hymns" to the "Creator of the universe." "Our teacher ... is Jesus Christ, who was crucified under Pontius Pilate, the governor of Judea in the time of Tiberius Caesar. Having learned that he is the Son of the true God, we will show that with reason we honour him, holding him in the second place, and also the prophetic Spirit in the third rank" (*1 Apol.* 13 ).[23] Justin permits us to see the principal points in teaching to pagans: condemnation of idolatry; unity of God; existence of Father, Son, and Holy Spirit; creation; proof of the divinity of Christ—Son of God, incarnate, crucified, and raised; and eternal recompense.[24]

In addition to the brief summary of the *kerygma* about Christ inserted into the doctrinal statement in *First Apology* 13, Justin gives another brief reference in chapter 61 and a more extensive account in chapter 31.[25] Moreover, it has been pointed out that Justin arranges the heathen analogies to Christ according to the items of the *kerygma* in chapters 21 and 22.[26] Similarly the prophecies of Christ, with interruptions, are constructed according to the *kerygma* in chapters 32–35, 40, 41, 45, and 47–53.[27]

Justin gives more attention at the beginning of his apology to the teachings about Christian conduct, because he was concerned to rebut charges of Christian immorality. The summary of Christian doctrine in *First Apology* 13 is followed by a description of the changed life by converts in chapter 14 and a detailing of the moral teachings of Christ in chapters 15–17. These teachings cover chastity (σωφροσύνη), love for all, giving

---

22. Justin's characterization of the instruction prior to baptism as concerning faith and life is matched in the accounts found in the Apocryphal Acts—Turck, "Aux origines du catéchuménat," 24–26.

23. Other trinitarian statements of Christian belief occur in *1 Apol.* 6 and in connection with baptism in 61 (twice) and with prayer in 65 and 67.

24. Bareille, "Catéchèse," col. 1880.

25. Kerygmatic statements are also found in Justin's *Dialogue with Trypho* 30.3; 63.1; 132.1.

26. Way-Rider, "Justin Martyr's Use of Some Pagan and Jewish Material."

27. As is done by Irenaeus in his *Demonstration of the Apostolic Preaching*.

to the needy, patience, not swearing oaths, and paying taxes.[28] This use of moral teaching in the instruction of converts preparatory to baptism may be fleshed out further from the "Two Ways" in *Didache* 1–6, a document with which Justin otherwise seems to be familiar.[29] The moral teachings in Justin's account are followed by an eschatological sanction (chapters 18 and 19).

The Christian life served as an important part of the argument by second-century apologists, both to counter slanders against Christians and also to give a positive proof on the divine origin of Christian teaching.[30] Christ himself was the connection between doctrine and life, for he was both the object of worship as the Son of God and was the teacher of Christian conduct.[31]

The two subjects of doctrine and morals continued to be central to Christian catechetical instruction. This subject matter is related to a larger frame of reference in Irenaeus's *Demonstration of the Apostolic Preaching*.

## IRENAEUS: TRAINING TO LIVE IN A COMMUNITY IN THE HISTORY OF SALVATION

Beginning with Irenaeus, the authors of catechetical works in this survey are all bishops. Irenaeus was concerned to define orthodox Christianity over against various heresies, especially those of the Marcionites and Gnostics.[32] In order to do this he stresses the unity of God, the unity of the Lord Jesus Christ, and the unity of the plan of salvation. The new covenant in Christ is superior to God's earlier covenants with people, but is in continuity with them.[33] Irenaeus's favourite word for the plan of salvation is

28. The quotations from the teaching of Jesus are drawn primarily from the traditions found in the Sermon on the Mount/Plain in Matthew 5–7 and Luke 6. I have shown in "Love of Enemies and Non-Retaliation in the Second Century," the use of this material in the instruction of new converts (especially in the *Didache*).

29. M. A. Smith, "Did Justin Know the Didache?" discusses only the liturgical parallels, many of which were common Christian material. For the continued use of the *Didache* in catechesis, cf. Athanasius, *Festal Letters*, 39. For the use of the "Two Ways" in catechesis, see Turck, *Évangélisation et Catéchèse*, 23–48, who concludes that the theme of two ways was current in catechesis but that it was not specifically a baptismal catechesis, and Daniélou, *La catéchèse aux premiers siècles*, 127–30, who describes it as the preponderant but not the only element in ancient moral catechesis.

30. See Ferguson, *Early Christians Speak*, 189–202.

31. Justin Martyr, *1 Apol.* 13.3; 23.2.

32. For introductions to Irenaeus, see Benoit, *Saint Irénée*; and Minns, *Irenaeus*.

33. Ferguson, "The Covenant Idea in the Second Century," esp. 144–48 on Irenaeus.

## Catechesis and Initiation

"economy."[34] His *Demonstration of the Apostolic Preaching* sets forth this unified view of Christian teaching as based on one continuous history of God's saving acts.

I have argued that the *Demonstration of the Apostolic Preaching* was catechetical, not apologetic, in purpose and was perhaps indeed written as a guide for catechists.[35] Among the catechetical motifs are the possible technical reference to "hearers" ("those who wish to hear"—ch. 1), the use of the imagery of the two ways (ch. 1), and the association of the teaching with baptism (ch. 3). Hence, I would suggest that the title could be translated "Presentation of the Apostolic Preaching." In this work Irenaeus repeats the emphasis on doctrine and morals. He puts "truth in the soul" and "holiness in the body" together at the beginning of the treatise (ch. 2). Chapter 3 gives as twin emphases the keeping of "the rule of faith" and carrying out "the commands of God." "Our faith," he says, provides a "way of life" (ch. 6). "The preaching of the truth" and "good works and sound moral character" come together again at the end of the treatise (ch. 98). Faith in God and love for neighbour recur in combination (chs. 41, 87, 95).

The distinctive feature of the *Demonstration of the Apostolic Preaching* is that faith and morals are integrated into a historical framework. The introduction is a doctrinal/creedal summary (chs. 1–6). The Last section is a moral/practical application (chs. 87–98). The largest part of the work is the telling of the history of salvation from creation to judgment. This biblical/historical body of the work functions on two levels: a historical narrative followed by the meaning of the history. The latter is Christological. Prophecies in the Old Testament are arranged according to the story of Christ.[36] Some of the distinctive concerns of Irenaeus are shown in his assertion that the prophecies in Deuteronomy were "written about our Lord Jesus Christ and about the people and about the calling of the Gentiles and about the kingdom" (ch. 28). I rather think this biblical storyline was more central in early Christian teaching and preaching than is often

---

34. Barthoulot, trans., *La prédication des apôtres et ses preuvres ou La foi chrétienne*, 24.

35. Ferguson, "Irenaeus' Proof of the Apostolic Preaching and Early Catechetical Instruction," contra the conclusion of J. P. Smith, whose translation I use: *St. Irenaeus: Proof of the Apostolic Preaching*, 20. If Smith's translation, "those who look after the salvation of souls," in ch. 1 is correct (see his 132 n. 6), this could be a confirmation that the work is intended for catechists.

36. See also Justin, *Dialogue with Trypho*; Cyprian, *Testimonies* (below); and Pseudo-Epiphanius, *Testimony Book*.

realized,[37] appearing in other places than where it is as explicit as it is in Irenaeus.

The trinitarian ordering of the doctrinal statements appears to be a secondary imposition on the material, not consistently carried through. I gather from Irenaeus's references that the trinitarian structure of the instruction derives from the baptismal formula (chs. 3, 7, 100). The "rule of faith" (ch. 3; cf. ch. 6) is not a creed but the whole of the doctrinal content of Christian faith which the church teaches.[38] The christological centre is shown by the way in which the Spirit is treated as especially active in the prophets who foretold Christ (chs. 6, 30, 49).[39]

Salvation, according to Jrenaeus, is received not by the law but by faith and love, and love is defined by the two commandments to love God and the neighbour (ch. 87).[40] "Through faith in [the Son of God] we learn to love God with our whole heart, and our neighbour as ourselves" (ch. 95). The double commandment to love is followed by a treatment of the Decalogue (ch. 96).[41] Irenaeus continues the use of the "Sermon on the Mount" tradition in catechesis, taking up the commandments according to the interpretation in Matthew 5 but not in the Matthaean order. The moral teaching in Irenaeus's *Demonstration* is less prominent and less systematic than the doctrinal teaching. This work thus anticipates the ascendancy of doctrine and the decline of the moral element in catechesis in the fourth century. The biblical content continued to be important but not always as explicitly formulated in terms of God's saving history as it is in Irenaeus.

## CYPRIAN: TRAINING TO LIVE IN A COMMUNITY OF MARTYRS

Cyprian guided the church of Carthage and North Africa through its greatest crisis, the Decian persecution and the accompanying mass apostasy

---

37. Daniélou, "L'histoire du salut dans la catéchèse," made it central; in his "La catéchèse dans la tradition patristique," he classified catechesis as biblical, dogmatic, and sacramental (26); but then he omitted the biblical-historical from his classification of the types of catechesis (dogmatic, moral, and sacramental) in *La catéchèse aux premiers siècles*. Lupi, "Catechetical Instruction in the Church of the First Two Centuries," 64, combined the items into four: historical, moral, dogmatic, and liturgical.

38. Turck, *Évangelisation et catéchèse*, 72.

39. For Justin too, the Spirit is the "prophetic Spirit"—1 *Apol.* 6; 13; 31.

40. Cf. *Didache* 2.1; Justin, *Dialogue with Trypho*, 93.

41. Daniélou, *La catéchèse aux premiers siècles*, 133–34.

## Catechesis and Initiation

among its members.⁴² Although Quasten dates Cyprian's *Ad Quirinum* (*Testimoniorum libri III*) before 149, there is good reason to put book 3, which seems to be later than books 1 and 2, after the outbreak of the Decian persecution.⁴³ Even if this collection of biblical *excerpta*⁴⁴ does not directly reflect a martyr environment, it represents the teaching given on the eve of the Decian persecution. An early topos in book 3 is "On the benefits of martyrdom" (3.16), and the following four *topoi* ("That what we suffer in this world is of less account than is the reward which is promised"; "That nothing is to be preferred to the love of God and Christ"; "That we are not to obey our own will, but the will of God"; and "That the foundation and strength of hope and faith is fear") are related to this theme.⁴⁵ The ensuing persecution occasioned a separate collection of *testimonia*, the *Ad Fortunatum de exhortatione martyrii*. Cyprian in his correspondence showed an interest in catechumens. He knew that the "hearers" were in danger during persecution (*Epp.*, 18.2), and he declares that catechumens who were martyred received a baptism of blood (*Epp.*, 73.22).⁴⁶

It has been suggested that Quirinus was engaged in the instruction of catechumens and had need of a manual collecting passages of scripture on various points.⁴⁷ Danielou adds that there were two principal elements that gave structure to dogmatic catechesis: the formulas of faith or *symbola*, and collections of citations of the Old Testament or *testimonia*.⁴⁸ His suggestion that books 1 and 2 are dogmatic catechesis and book 3 is moral catechesis⁴⁹ I would like to revise and extend. Book 1 contains twenty-four topics on the theme of the church replacing the old Israel. This represents the historical framework of Christian teaching. Book 2 contains thirty topics on christology; this represents the central doctrinal affirmations of Christianity. Book 3 has a separate prologue and was apparently written later than the first two books; its 120 topics represent the moral duties of

---

42. On Cyprian, see Sage, *Cyprian*; C. Saumagne, *Saint Cyprian*; and Burns, *Cyprian the Bishop*.

43. Quasten, *Patrology*, 2:363. Turner, "Prolegomena to the *Testimonia* and *Ad Fortunatum* of St. Cyprian," 230–31, however, dates only books 1 and 2 to 249, book 3 to Cyprian's retirement during the early months of AD 250 after the outbreak of the Decian persecution, and the *Ad Fortunatum* to AD 253.

44. Quacquarelli, "Note retoriche sui *Testimonia* di Cipriano."

45. I use the translation of R. E. Wallis in the *Ante-Nicene Fathers* 5, 507–57.

46. So *Apostolic Tradition*, 19.2.

47. Quacquarelli, "Note retoriche sui *Testimonia* di Cipriano," 204.

48. Daniélou, *La catéchèse aux premiers siècles*, 71.

49. Ibid., 18; cf. his *The Origins of Latin Christianity*, 288–95.

the Christian life. The preface to the first two books employs language consistent with a catechetical use. Cyprian addresses Quirinus as "my beloved son," language used by teachers and by bishops to their clergy. Quirinus had requested "divine teachings," whereby he might be "led away from the darkness of error and enlightened by [the Lord's] pure and shining light"—definitely conversion language. Cyprian offers his treatise as advantageous "for forming the first lineaments of your faith." The thoroughly scriptural basis of the teaching is indicated by the encouragement to "read through the complete volumes" of the "Scriptures, old and new."

Most of the testimonia in books 1 and 2. are quite traditional, as may he seen from *Barnabas*, Justin, Irenaeus, and Tertullian.[50] The history of salvation has taken a decidedly anti-Judaic turn in Cyprian's book 1. Chapters 1–4 deal with the faithlessness of the Jews; chapters 5–18 with the loss of Israel's privileges; and chapters 19–24 with the church of the Gentiles. His passages are selective, tendentious, and out of context.

Book 2 arranges the prophecies according to the same scheme as Irenaeus's *Demonstration*, beginning with the pre-existence of the Wisdom of God, continuing with his virgin birth, his titles, and his death and resurrection, and concluding with his coming again as judge and king. The passages collected under each heading follow the order of the biblical books. The presence of quotations from the New Testament, more frequent in book 2 than in book 1, shows that the work was not directed to Jews (at least not immediately).

Book 2.30 seems to prepare for Book 3, although the latter was written later and separately. There was a conscious effort to link the two parts, for 3.1 begins with Isaiah 58:1–9 on fasting, a topic which elsewhere appears in an anti-Judaic context, and contains a quotation of Matthew 25:31–46, with which book 2 ended. The contents of book 3 are mostly negative—what the Christian is not to do. The topics seem to be in random order, and there is no discernible order in which the texts are cited on each topic. However, I would note that brotherly love appears early (3.3) and is followed shortly by some of the topics from the Sermon on the Mount—anger (8), trusting God for material needs (11), not swearing oaths and cursing (12–13), not judging (21), and forgiving wrongs (22).

The prologue to book 3 states, "You asked me to gather out for your instruction from the holy Scriptures some heads bearing upon the religious teaching of our school [*secta*]." Several items might reflect a specifically catechetical context: The necessity of baptism and warning against sin

---

50. Daniélou, *The Origins of Latin Christianity*, 288–45.

after baptism (3.25–27); "That we must hasten to faith and to attainment [*consecutionem*], a word used in Latin Christianity for attaining grace in baptism (97);[51] "That the catechumen ought now no longer to sin" (98); "That one ought to make confession while he is in the flesh" (114); "That God is more loved by him who has had many sins forgiven in baptism" (116); and the call to take up the yoke of the Lord (119).

Cyprian's collection of scriptural *testimonia* may have served other purposes than catechesis and at best would represent a resource, a skeleton as it were, for catechists to flesh out in their instruction. Nevertheless, it does remind us of the effort at a biblical basis for historical, doctrinal, and moral teachings in the early church.

## CYRIL OF JERUSALEM: TRAINING TO LIVE IN AN ORTHODOX CHURCH

With the fourth century we enter the full light of day in regard to the catechumenate, as with many other subjects. No longer is it necessary to draw inferences from documents written for other purposes, or argue for the catechetical intent of works not explicitly so designated, for we have texts for that express purpose and the words of actual catechetical instructions. The fourth century presented a different situation for the church: no longer a persecuted church of martyrs, it was the triumphant church of the emperor. The development and refinement of the catechumenate was a major response to the changed circumstances. This fact raises problems for using the fourth century as a model from which earlier practice can be inferred. There assuredly was some continuity in practice, but just as assuredly there was adaptation to new needs. The development of a more organized catechumenate around AD 200 may have had, in part, the purpose of making sure that candidates were ready to make a deep commitment to the church and were persons who could be trusted in a crisis. The number of apostasies in the Decian and Diocletian persecutions showed how real the problem was and how decades of relative peace had caused a slackening of seriousness. The development in the fourth century of a series of catechetical lectures during Lent leading up to baptism at Easter apparently was designed to handle more efficiently the larger number of

---

51. Cf. the inscriptions collected in Diehl, *Inscriptiones latinae christianae veteres*, 1523, "obtained the grace [*gratiam consecuta*] of the glorious font on Easter day and survived after holy baptism five months"; cf. the phrase in 1524 and 1527; the verb form is used alone with "[baptismal] grace" understood in 1525, 1528, 1539, 1540.

candidates for baptism and to make a serious effort at instructing them in the contents of the faith and at showing the special privileges of church membership for those who indeed took this step and did not delay their baptism, as many, following Constantine's example, did.

The surviving catechetical lectures of the fourth and fifth centuries are chiefly the instructions given during Lent and so are predominantly doctrinal. The fullest of these are from the Eastern realm, so I am going to stretch the meaning of "Western" and illustrate this development from one of the Greek bishops of the fourth century, Cyril of Jerusalem. There is some justification for doing so in the extensive use made of his *Catechetical Lectures* in Rufinus's *Commentary on the Apostles' Creed*.[52] Cyril was active during the time of the trinitarian controversies between the Councils of Nicaea (AD 325) and Constantinople (AD 381). Cyril's Catechetical Lectures were delivered in about AD 348 while he was a presbyter who prepared candidates for baptism.[53] They are our earliest extant example of the full course of actual instruction of those preparing for baptism. Cyril became bishop in 350 or early 351. I am leaving aside the *Mystagogical Lectures* attributed to Cyril that were delivered on the Monday to Friday in the week after the Easter baptism so will not enter into the controversy over whether they come from Cyril or his successor John.[54]

The *Procatechesis* was delivered on Sunday at a public service. It is an exhortation to come not "with soul bemired with sins" (4).[55] The candidates are given forty days in which to effect repentance for their sins. Fornication, uncleanness, and avarice are the specific sins mentioned; indeed, throughout the series sexual sin seems to be a special preoccupation, often taken as the representative sins.[56] Cyril warns about unworthy motives, but he welcomes all in the hope of making them alive (5), "but one should beware of receiving the title of "faithful" but having the will of the faithless" (6). The flavour of the exhortation is indicated by some representative appeals: "the water will receive, but the Spirit will not accept" the unrepentant (4); "Cease from this day from every evil deed" (8); "Prepare your heart for reception of doctrine, for fellowship in holy mysteries"

52. Kelly, trans. and ann., *Rufinus*, 9–11.

53. Paulin, *Saint Cyrille de Jerusalem*.

54. Cyril's authorship is rejected in Saxer and Maestri, *Cirillo e Giovanni di Gerusalemme*, but defended by Alexis Doval, *Cyril of Jerusalem, Mystagogue*. The mystagogical lectures are studied in Riley, *Christian Initiation*.

55. I use but update the wording of the translation of E. H. Gifford in *NPNF* ser. 2, 7.

56. *Cat. Lect.* 2.6, 9; 3.15; 4.2, 18, 21, 23, 24; 12.6, 26, 33–34; 18.1, 20.

(16). Thus a moral exhortation precedes the doctrinal instruction of the *Catechetical Lectures*, and even they begin with a discussion of repentance and confession of sin (*Cat.* 1 and 2).

This order seems to be the pattern that had earlier emerged, moral training followed by doctrinal teaching, but the latter seems to have gained prominence over the former in the fourth century; at least the surviving catechetical works, although containing considerable moral teaching, show few examples of works devoted explicitly to moral instruction. Gregory of Nyssa (who puts the moral teaching at the end after the doctrinal in his *Catechetical Oration*) and John Chrysostom (whose *Baptismal Instructions* are permeated with moral teaching) illustrate the concern with morals but also the absence of a curriculum for moral teaching comparable to the creed for teaching doctrine and the liturgy for teaching sacraments. The *Procatechesis* is an appeal to true conversion and then a moral catechesis as part of the data of faith. Thus, Daniélou takes Cyril as an example of the unity of moral and doctrinal catechesis.[57] He seems to me to be putting the best face on the minor role of morals in many fourth-century catecheses when he claims that the moral catechesis in the fourth century is only the moral aspect of the doctrinal catechesis. Morals were a part of the faith itself, its practical application in daily life.[58] One could wish for more evidence that more of those baptized got the point.

The eighteen *Catechetical Lectures* proper were distributed during the following forty days that began on Monday and ended on the night of Good Friday, except that *Catechesis* 18 was delivered a day later on the Saturday evening before Easter Sunday. *Catechesis* 1 is a general encouragement to the hearers to be faithful to their calling.[59] They are to "prepare for new birth" by confessing sins, devoting time to exorcisms, catechizings, ascetic exercises, forgiving others, attending church assemblies, and nourishing their souls with sacred readings. *Catechesis* 2 concentrates on repentance. Biblical history is employed in support of the topic by giving examples of sin and repentance in their biblical order. The conclusion summarizes the lecture: "Having therefore, brothers and sisters, many examples of those who have sinned and repented and been saved, do you also heartily make confession to the Lord, that you may both receive the forgiveness of your former sins and be counted worthy of the heavenly gift" (2.20).

---

57. Daniélou, *La catéchèse aux premiers siècles*, 161–62.
58. Ibid., 157–58.
59. Note the references to faith: 1 (twice), 2 (twice), 3 ("believer"), 5 (twice).

*Catechesis* 3 discusses the doctrinal meaning of baptism. Cyril repeatedly connects the effectiveness of baptism with faith and repentance (3.2, 15); his conception of faith, however, may be inadequate, since he often means by faith the creed. The confession of faith for him is the reciting of the creed (3.1.0). Baptism is necessary for salvation (except for the martyrs—3.10) and brings forgiveness of all sins (3.15). He emphasizes the necessity of bringing forth the fruits of good works (3.8, 16).

*Catechesis* 4 begins the doctrinal discussion proper with a summary of the principal points of Christian doctrine. Cyril defines godliness as consisting of two things, "pious doctrine and virtuous practice" (4.2), and he concludes the doctrinal survey with a statement of Christian living, especially avoiding pagan, Jewish, and heretical practices (4.37). The emphasis, however, lies on doctrine, and he develops the doctrinal points with more relish.

*Catechesis* 5 discusses faith, almost with the sense of "faithfulness." Cyril has in mind especially keeping the "dogmatic" faith, professing what is delivered by the church (5.12). He identifies two kinds of faith: the "dogmatic, involving an assent of the soul on some particular point," and the faith which is "a gift of grace," which "works things above human power" (5.10–11). Neither seems to be faith in the Pauline and Johannine sense of personal trust in the promises and work of God in Christ.

*Catecheses* 6–9 take up the phrases in the creed concerning the one God (especially directed against heretics—6), Father (7), Almighty (8), and Maker of heaven and earth (9). Cyril's method is on each article of the symbol to collect the "proof out of the Prophets" (13.13) for the teaching.[60] Throughout he uses passages and incidents from the Old and New Testaments, so the biblical content is quite extensive, although arranged topically and not historically or biblically. The principal concern of Cyril's lectures is, as a commentary on the creed, doctrinal, as expressed by the phrase, "the saving doctrines of the true faith" (7.1). He does add that it profits nothing to have the title of Christians unless the works also follow (7.14) and uses the title of God as Father as an occasion to teach the necessity of honouring parents (7.15–16).

Lectures 10–15 discuss the "one Lord Jesus Christ" (10), the "only begotten" (11), "incarnate" (12), "crucified and buried" (13), who "rose on the third day and ascended" (14), and who is coming again in judgment (15). There seems to be more of the sense of "trust" here in the call to believe in Christ and not to let him be blasphemed because of the hearers'

---

60. Daniélou, "La catéchèse dans la tradition patrisdque," 28.

*Catechesis and Initiation*

conduct (10.20). Faith is accepting what the prophecies say about Christ, but this gives a trust and commitment, for "You have taken your stand on the rock of the faith in the resurrection" (14.21). Nevertheless, there is the warning against falling away from Christ (14.30).

The discussion of the articles pertaining to Christ often contain anti-Judaic statements (10.2, 8, 16; 12.2, 13, 28; 13.7, 14.1, 15, 26). Cyril gives a survey of Old Testament history from Adam onward, including quotations from the prophets in order to demonstrate human sin and God's sending Christ as the remedy (12.5ff.). The use of the Old Testament throughout this section of the lectures is comparable to that of Irenaeus. Testimonies to the passion are collected (13.9ff.) and to the resurrection (14.3ff.). Those concerning the resurrection are particularly arbitrary and unconvincing to the modern reader, but the method is significant. The scriptures are read from the standpoint of the experience of Christ, and every word that has any reference to a "rising up" or the like is understood of the resurrection of Christ. There is a recurrent pattern involving the citing of Old Testament prophecies and then recording the witnesses or testimonies to the event.[61]

The concluding admonition of *Catechesis* 15, "Flee all heretical error" (15.33) sums up Cyril's principal concern in his dogmatic catechesis. The heretics are sometimes specifically the Gnostics (11.21); the Manichees, a special concern in *Catecheses* 4 and 6, appear in this section also (14.21). Sabellian and Arian teachings are opposed as contrasting errors, but not by name (e.g., 11.13–17; 15.9); for the most part Cyril deals with contemporary doctrinal issues through a positive exposition of his own understanding. The discussion of Christ's coming in judgment provides occasion to bring in the moral dimension by warning against immoral acts and, with reference to Matthew 25 (as in Cyprian), by giving the exhortation, "Let the light of your good works shine" coupled with the repetition of the admonition, "Let not Christ be blasphemed on your account" (15.23, 26).

Catecheses 16 and 17 instruct about the Holy Spirit. The same characteristics observed in the previous lectures obtain here too. The biblical content is pervasive. Passages about the "One and same Holy Spirit" who spoke in the Law and the Prophets and in the Gospels and Apostles (17.5; cf. 4.16 and 16.3–4) are collected: from the Old Testament in 16.25–31, and from the New Testament in 17—the Gospels (17.6–12), Acts (17.13–31), and Paul (17.32–38). The hearers were expected to continue in "the

---

61. On the resurrection, the prophecies are collected in 14.3–20 and the witnesses in 14.22–23; on the ascension, prophecies in 14.24, 27–28, testimonies in 14.29.

frequent reading of the sacred scriptures" (17.34). The thrust against the heretics remains strong; these include Sabellians, Gnostics, Marcionites, Montanists, and Manicheans (16.4, 6–10). The Spirit gives knowledge (16.17) and continues his work of enlightenment, a frequently mentioned feature of the Spirit's work,[62] and spiritual maturing in the present (16.22), but otherwise Cyril offers no discussion of the moral achievements by the Spirit.[63] Because baptism is the work of the Holy Spirit and not of the human administrator, one should not come to baptism in hypocrisy (17.35–36).

The last catechetical lecture in the series deals with the resurrection (18.2–21), the catholic church (18.22–27), and eternal life (18.27–31). Cyril affirms the hope of resurrection as the root of all good works (18.1). Fornication is once more the representative sin (18.1, 20). He declares again that the Jewish church "is cast off" and "the churches of Christ are increased over all the world" (18.25). The heavy content of scripture quotation continues, and as Cyril forecasts the coming mystagogical catecheses, he says the newly baptized will "receive proofs from the Old and New Testaments" about what they experienced on Easter Sunday.

During the fourth century a process that had begun with the Gnostic struggles of the second century reached a climax, namely to identify the true church more by correct doctrine than by manner of life.

The earliest of our surviving instructions on the sacraments of initiation are the *Mystagogical Catecheses* delivered on Monday to Friday after baptism on Easter Sunday and ascribed to Cyril of Jerusalem. However, to illustrate this aspect of catechetical instruction we will return to the West to Ambrose of Milan.

## AMBROSE: TRAINING TO LIVE IN A STATE CHURCH

Ambrose may be taken as representative of the situation in the church in the late fourth century when it was now the authorized state religion, receiving a multitude of new converts and struggling to incorporate them into its life and to accommodate itself to its new position. That often uneasy situation is well typified in the career of Ambrose. Coming directly

---

62. *Cat.* 16.3, 12, 16 (three times), 17, 18, 22 (twice).

63. For instance, the "fruits of the Holy Spirit" in Gal 5:22, 23 appears only in the closing doxology of *Cat.* 17.38. Cyril's treatment of the Holy Spirit bears many points of contact with the treatment in Novatian, *De Trinitate* 29, except that Novatian's briefer discussion offers proportionately more on the Spirit as effecting holiness through moral improvement.

from high government office to the bishopric of arguably the most important church in the West in his time, Ambrose found himself at the centre of the conflicts and tensions of his time, affirming the independence of the church and exerting its influence in the affairs of state.[64]

There are ascribed to Ambrose two sets of mystagogical catecheses, delivered during the week following baptism on Easter Sunday morning, the *De Mysteriis* and the *De Sacramentis*. There have been weighty objections to the common authorship of these works, but the argument in favour of Ambrose as the author of both works seems now to be in the ascendancy. I do not feel competent to address the stylistic arguments, but the content of the two works does not seem to me to be inconsistent with common authorship.[65] They may represent the mystagogical instruction given by Ambrose on two different occasions, essentially the same but varied from year to year. The six addresses of the *De Sacramentis* are certainly not so well organized as the *De Mysteriis*. They have the marks of oral delivery and may be notes on actual addresses only lightly retouched. The *De Mysteriis*, on the other hand, is more formal and exact; if not an epitome of the *De Sacramentis*,[66] it is a more polished literary presentation of the material.

The very terminology of "mysteries" says something about the accommodation to Graeco-Roman religious conceptions.[67] The comparison of Christian initiation to initiation in the pagan mysteries served both pedagogic and hortatory purposes. It was a way of teaching the solemnity and seriousness of the Christian rites and of making full initiation more appealing to those inclined to maintain only a minimal association with the church. Ambrose himself offers two reasons for postponing instruction about the mysteries until after baptism: "For if we had thought that such an account should be propounded before baptism to the uninitiated, we should be esteemed traitors rather than teachers; further, because it were better that the light of the mysteries should reveal itself unasked and unexpected than preceded by some discourse" (*Mys.* 1.2).[68] In other

64. For an introduction to Ambrose, see McLynn, *Ambrose of Milan*.

65. Botte, *Ambroise de Milan*, 12–24; further bibliography in Quasten and Di Berardino, *Patrology*, 4:171–72. Riley, *Christian Initiation*, uses both works for his comparative study.

66. Connolly, "The *Explanatio symboli ad initiandos*," 39.

67. Echle, "Sacramental Initiation as Christian Mystery"; and Daniélou, "Le Mystère du cube dans les sermons de Saint Grégoire de Nysse"; Hamilton, "The Church and the Language of Mystery."

68. I use for the English translation of these works by Thompson, *St. Ambrose*, "On

words, what had once been only an analogy to the mysteries (as I think is the case with Clement of Alexandria) had become by the fourth century a controlling imagery with the resultant conviction that only after initiation should full secrets be revealed. This is given the further pedagogical justification that one can understand better after experiencing the initiatory rites than only hearing about them.[69]

Contemporaries and successors of Ambrose preserved the *De Mysteriis* and *De Sacraments* in numerous manuscripts, because they found them useful and/or distinctive, at least containing what was not expressed so well elsewhere. This was an important part of his teaching and represents certain tendencies in him and his age, but the mystagogical catechesis was not all there was to Ambrose's preparation of new converts, so before discussing its contents, I want to say something about what preceded it in the ceremonies of initiation at Milan.[70]

Ambrose begins the *De Mysteriis* with this reminder: "On questions of right conduct we discoursed daily at the time when the lives of the patriarchs or the precepts of the Proverbs were being read, in order that, trained and instructed thereby, ... you might, after being renewed by baptism, continue to practice the life which befitted the regenerate" (1.1). The lives of the patriarchs provided appropriate models to imitate, and the Proverbs provided basic moral principles.[71] There survive several works by Ambrose on the lives of the patriarchs, the written texts of which appear to be revised, polished, and generalized versions of originally preached sermons. They may have been preached in the liturgical assemblies during Lent and so have been intended for the faithful as well as the *competentes*. The *De Abraham* contains express reference to the candidates for baptism during Lent.[72]

---

the Mysteries" and the Treatise "On the Sacraments" by an Unknown Author, 45; cf. the discussion on xiii. As the full title indicates, this work (the introduction and notes were prepared by J. H. Srawley) concludes separate authorship.

69. Daniélou, *La catéchèse aux premiers siècles*, 175.

70. Michiels, "L'initiation chrétienne selon saint Ambroise," 109–14, 164–69, gives a popular survey of the three components: catechumenate, sacraments of initiation, and the post-baptismal catechesis.

71. Harmless, *Augustine and the Catechumenate*, 94–95.

72. Ambrose, *De Abraham* 1.4.2.5 ("you who are proceeding to the grace of the Lord"); 1.7.59 ("you who are proceeding to the grace of baptism"); 1.9.89 ("you daughters who are proceeding to the grace of the Lord"). The first two statements are in passages teaching against adultery; cf. what is noted above about Cyril's concern with sexual sins.

Ambrose's biblical sermons at the beginning of Lent draw moral lessons from the stories of the patriarchs.[73] The introduction to *De Ioseph* provides a summary: "In him [Joseph] there shone forth above all the mark of chastity. In Abraham you have learned the undaunted devotion of faith, in Isaac the purity of a sincere heart, in Jacob the spirit's signal endurance of toils. For it is right that after the treatment of virtues in general you should give attention to moral principles in their specific kinds."[74] Joseph served as a type of Christ (*De Ioseph* 2.8 and *passim*) as well as a "mirror of purity" (ibid., 1.2).

Ambrose makes frequent use of Canticles (or Song of Solomon). He comments on Canticles 8:6,

> Christ is the seal on the forehead, the seal in the heart—on the forehead that we may always confess Him, in the heart that we may always love Him, and a seal on the arm, that we may always do His work. Therefore let His image shine forth in our profession of faith, let it shine forth in our love, let it shine forth in our works and deeds so that, if it is possible, all His beauty may be represented in us (*De Isaac* 8.74).[75]

As this quotation indicates, there is a fair amount in these sermons on confession.

*De Jacob et vita beata* develops the theme of 4 Maccabees that reason rules the passions. Biblical examples are given of various virtues, and Ambrose goes through Jacob's life in detail with spiritual lessons drawn. Thus the biblical framework serves as the basis for moral instruction. Ambrose lays out the history of salvation in three periods: there was the natural law, which was not kept, so the law of Moses was added to it, and now with Christ grace has come (*De Iacob* 1.6.20, 22).[76] "Happy indeed," he says, "is the young man who leads a good life, but happy also is the old man who has led a good life. What the young man hopes for, the old man has obtained" (*De Iacob* 1.8.35). Other biblical illustrations of the happy life are introduced (*De Iacob* 1.9.41ff.) before Ambrose returns to 4 Maccabees for his conclusion.

*De bono mortis* uses 2 Esdras extensively. It was probably intended as two sermons (1–29; 30–57), perhaps for catechumens awaiting baptism.[77]

---

73. Daniélou, "La catéchèse dans la tradition patristique," 30.
74. McHugh, trans., *Saint Ambrose*, 189.
75. Ibid., 59.
76. Cf. *De fuga saeculi*, 3.15 for a natural law in the heart and a written law.
77. McHugh, trans., *Saint Ambrose*, 69.

If so, there is a wide-ranging allegorical exegesis applied to death, as *De Isaac* does with the soul. *De fuga saeculi*, another sermon apparently delivered during Eastertide, was influenced by Philo and adduces numerous biblical examples.[78] "The flight consists in this: to keep away from sins, to take up the rule of the virtues unto the likeness and image of God, to enlarge our strength unto the imitation of God according to the limit of our potentiality. For the perfect man is the image and glory of God" (*De fuga* 4.17).[79] Ambrose particularly urges his hearers to flee immorality, avarice, and unbelief.

As Cyril drew moral instruction from the creed, Ambrose drew it from scripture. It could also be drawn from the sacraments, as in John Chrysostom's catechetical lectures.[80] I observe, and leave what its significance may be as a point to be pondered, that Ambrose draws his moral instruction from the Old Testament rather than from the teachings of Jesus, as earlier catechists had done.

Since we have given more extensive treatment of doctrinal catechesis in discussing Cyril of Jerusalem, we may treat it more briefly in Ambrose, by reference to his brief *Explanatio symboli ad initiandos*. This short address accompanied the delivery of the creed to the candidates for baptism following the scrutinies (exorcism) and was delivered on the Sunday before Easter.[81] Cyril expounded the baptismal creed of the Jerusalem church, which was similar to the creed that was the basis of the Nicene Creed. Ambrose delivered the "Apostles' Creed," as was common in the Western church.[82] He instructed his hearers not to write it down (ch. 12), for it was

---

78. Savon, *Saint Ambroise devant l'exégèse de Philon le Juif*, 1, 329–76.

79. McHugh, trans., *Saint Ambrose*, 195.

80. Daniélou, "La Catéchèse dans la tradition patristique," 30; Daniélou, *La catéchèse aux premiers siècles*, 162–70.

81. Connolly, "The *explanatio symboli ad initiandos*." Ambrose, *Epp.* 20.4: "[On Sunday] when the catechumens were dismissed, I was teaching the creed to certain candidates in the baptistery of the basilica." The same letter (20:14, 25) refers to the reading of the books of Job (cf. Ambrose's sermon *The Prayer of Job and David*, translated in McHugh, trans., *Saint Ambrose*, 327ff.) and Jonah at the season leading up to Easter.

82. Ambrose refers to the doctrinal instruction of baptismal candidates in his *Expositio Evangelii secundum Lucam*, 6:104–9: "When some from the Gentiles are called to the church, we must produce a series of precepts, so that at first we teach one God to be the maker of the world and all things ... When you are persuaded there is one God, then by his disclosure you add on the salvation given to us by Christ" (104); "Wherefore the catechumen who is proceeding to the sacraments of the faithful must receive initial instruction. It must be said that there is one God, from whom are all things, and one Jesus Christ, through whom are all things ..." (107).

part of the "secret" that belonged to the initiated alone. In his explanation of the name "symbol," Ambrose either confused *symbolum* ("token," "watchword") with *symbola* ("contribution") or made a play on the former by interpreting it in the latter sense. There are twelve pronouncements in the creed, as there are twelve Apostles (ch. 11). He justifies inclusion of the articles on the church, forgiveness of sins, and resurrection on the grounds that to believe in the Author is to believe in his works (ch. 9). He affirms, "This whole sacrament is concerned with your resurrection"; what is the "sacrament" here — baptism or the symbol?

The contents of the *De Mysteriis* and *De Sacramentis*, like the *Mystagogical Catecheses* of Cyril, are explanations after the event of what was experienced in the initiation on Easter. Ambrose in the former address calls on his hearers to "open their ears," for they were obligated to remember the answer of faith they had professed (1.3). When they descended into the font, they gave a pledge by their own voice, giving answer that they believed in the Father, in the Son, and in the Holy Spirit (5.28; cf. 4.21).[83] There is much use of scripture with the intention of showing the analogy of the acts of God in scripture and in the sacraments of the church.[84] Ambrose adduces Old Testament types of baptism—creation, Noah's ark, Israel's crossing of the Red Sea, the bitter waters of Marah made sweet by the rod of Moses, Naaman's cleansing of leprosy (3.9-18, all quite traditional and familiar from other sources);[85] and of the eucharist—Melchizedek, the manna from heaven, and water from the rock (8.43-49, likewise traditional).

The *De Mysteriis* concentrates on baptism and the eucharist. The newly baptized now have the "innocence of a dove" (*Mys.* 4.25). Regeneration by the Spirit in baptism is compared to and validated, by the Spirit's generation of Christ in the virgin Mary (*Mys.* 9.59). The eucharist is not bodily food, but spiritual (*Mys.* 9.58). In support of the bread and wine becoming the body and blood of Christ, Ambrose adduces biblical incidents where a blessing produced a miraculous transformation (several of which are baptismal types here used of the eucharist): the rod of Moses, the Red Sea becoming dry land, the turning back of the Jordan, water from the rock, the bitter waters of Marah, and Elisha's axehead that floated (*Mys.*

---

83. The creed was interrogatory, "Do you believe in . . . ?" to which the candidate answered, "I believe." The baptismal questions are more fully quoted in *Sacram.* 2.7.20.

84. Germain, "Baptême et éducation de la foi dans l'église ancienne," 17.

85. *Sacram.* 1.5.13—1.6.43 refers to the exodus, Naaman, and the flood, and adds from the New Testament the healing of the paralytic at the pool (2.2.3—2.3.9).

9.50–52).[86] Little is said about the unction, but it is affirmed that "we are all anointed with spiritual grace unto the kingdom of God and the priesthood" (6.30).

The *De Sacramentis* covers much the same ground but contains some significant additions to what is found in the shorter treatise. It begins with an explanation for delaying the interpretation of the initiatory rites that is couched in more "Christian" terms than in terms of the mysteries, "for in a Christian, faith must come first" (*Sacram.* 1.1.1). The explanation begins with the rite of *Ephpheta* ("opening") on Saturday night (1.1.2), only alluded to in *De Mysteriis* (1.3–4). The renunciation of "the devil and his works," and of "the world and its pleasures" is stated (1.2.5) and is interpreted as a binding promise before Christ (1.2.6, 8). The reason for Christ's baptism is stated to be that he might cleanse the flesh of our nature and set a pattern for us (*Sacram.* 1.5.16).[87]

Ambrose contrasts the "one baptism" of Christians with the baptisms of the Gentiles and Jews (*Sacram.* 2.1.2).[88] The efficacy of baptism is ascribed to the cross (*Sacram.* 2.2.6; 3.4.11–13),[89] to Christ (2.2.7; 2.7.23), to the name of the Trinity (2.3.9; 2.4.10–13; 2.5.14; 2.7.20–22), and to the Holy Spirit (1.5.15). The water of baptism is associated with the earth, so the font is, as it were, a burial" (2.6.19).[90] Baptism is a resurrection and a regeneration (*Sacram.* 3.1.2.); in it "all guilt is washed away" (3.1.7).

More is said in this treatise about the unction, but less than is said by Cyril's *Mystagogical Lectures*. The sealing' brings the seven gifts of the Spirit (3.2.8–10). Of greater concern is the justification of the ritual footwashing

---

86. Cf. *Sacram.* 4.4,17–20 for miracles of transformation. The argument is similar to that of Gregory of Nyssa in a baptismal context, *De baptisma Christi* (Gregorii Nysseni opera [henceforth GNO] 9:225, 10–227, 4). *De Sacram.* 1.3.9–10; 1.5.15 similarly asserts that the water of baptism is more than water.

87. For the treatment of the baptism of Jesus in patristic literature, see Wilken, "The Interpretation of the Baptism of Jesus in the Later Fathers"; Doignon, "La scène évangélique du Baptême de Jésus commentée par Lactance (*Diuinae institutiones*, 4.15) et Hilaire de Poitiers (*In Matthaeum*, 2, 5–6)"; McDonnell, "Jesus' Baptism in the Jordan."

88. Cf. Basil, *Exh. bapt.* 1–2 (PG, 31.425A–428B); Basil, *De Bapt.* 1.2. (PG, 31.1532C–1533C); John Chrysostom, *De Bapt. Chr. et Epiph.* 2–3 (PG, 49.366).

89. Cf. the wording of the baptismal interrogation, unique to these two treatises, "Do you believe in our Lord Jesus Christ and in his cross?" (*Sacram.* 2.7.20; *Mys.* 5.28).

90. Cf. the different yet similar comparison of burial in the earth of Jesus and in water of the convert by Gregory of Nyssa, *Bapt. Chr.* (GNO 9.228, 9–22); idem, *Catech. Or.* 35.

(*Sacram.* 3.1.4–7; cf. the stronger justification in *Mys.* 6.3 1–33), which Ambrose knew was not part of the Roman baptismal ceremony.

On the eucharist, Ambrose joins Cyril of Jerusalem and Gregory of Nyssa in making the earliest explicit arguments that the consecration effects a change in the elements themselves and not just in their use (*Sacram.* 4.4.14 of the bread; 4.4.19 of the wine and water).[91] Each communion is said to bring a remission of sins (*Sacram.* 5.3.17). There continues to he much use of scripture in Ambrose's instructions; quite striking in discourse 5 is the use of Canticles.

Another new feature of *De Sacramentis* is the instruction on prayer, beginning with an exposition of the Lord's prayer (5.4.18–30). The sixth discourse, after a brief review of earlier material, continues with instructions on how and where to pray (6.3.11—6.4.19) and on the order of contents of prayer (6.5.22–25).

Danielou identified three types of mystagogical catechesis: commentary on the rites, biblical theology of the sacraments (types from the Old Testament), and response to theological difficulties.[92] Ambrose (as also Cyril of Jerusalem) structures his instructions as a commentary on the rites, but includes within that commentary biblical typology and argumentation on theological points. The prominence of the liturgical catechesis following baptism shows the extent to which the process of salvation had become a drama, and the extent to which membership in the church was identified with a performance and an understanding of the ceremonies that were part of a state church. We must not forget what motivated much of this development. There was the worthy concern to make church membership meaningful and to incorporate the large numbers of new members into a new (for them) cohesive social community. Yet there was almost inevitably associated with these developments an emphasis on externals, in spite of the diligent efforts by church leaders to emphasize the spiritual. Their repeated affirmations along this line only confirm the need and the difficulty of achieving a truly spiritual formation.

---

91. Crockett, *Eucharist*, 61–62, 88–98; Dugmore, "Sacrament and Sacrifice in the Early Fathers"; Ferguson, "The Lord's Supper in Church History."

92. Danielou, *La catéchèse aux premiers siècles*, 61.

## AUGUSTINE: TRAINING TO LIVE IN THE HEAVENLY CITY

Augustine as Bishop of Hippo sits astride two ages, at the end of the ancient church and the beginning of the medieval church. He is usually remembered as a towering intellectual genius, the apex of Latin patristic theology and the seminal genius and authoritative church father of the Latin Middle Ages. Our concern here is with one aspect of Augustine's pastoral work,[93] his activity as a catechist. For this, we are fortunate to have an admirable recent synthesis by William Harmless, who looks at Augustine's material from an educator's point of view.[94] As the Roman world in which he had been educated and lived was coming to an end in the West under the force of the migration of Germanic peoples, Augustine directed attention to the "City of God," present as a spiritual reality in this world but having as its goal the future heavenly city. Although Augustine gave much attention, as we shall see, to life in the present world, his catechetical work is infused with a much more futuristic eschatology than is found in the Antiochians, John Chrysostom and Theodore of Mopsuestia, who present an almost realized eschatology in their baptismal catecheses.[95]

Augustine is the only church father from whom there survives a sampling of material from each of the four periods of initiation into the church: (1) pre-catechesis or evangelization (*On Catechizing Beginners* [or *Cat. rud.*]);[96] (2) the catechumenate proper (*Sermon* 132; *Exposition of the Psalms*, 81 [Lt. 80]; *Tractates on the Gospel of John*, 4, 10, and 11); (3)

---

93. For brief introductions to Augustitine, note Chadwick, *Augustine*; and Marrou, *St. Augustine and His Influence through the Ages*, text reprinted without the selections in Ferguson, ed., *Studies in Early Christianity* 1, 271–351. For his pastoral work, see Van der Meer, *Augustine the Bishop*, esp. 347–87 on Christian initiation according to Augustine.

94. Harmless, *Augustine and the Catechumenate*, to whose presentation my summary is greatly indebted. Busch, "De initiatione Christiana secundum sanctum Augustinum," covers this material but with primarily liturgical interests. The same applies to De Latte, "Saint Augustin et le bapteme: Etude liturgico-historique du rituel baptismal des adultes chez saint Augustin," 177–223, who organizes his study according to the two steps of first making one a catechumen and then making that person one of the faithful. For an overview of the North African catechumenate in the time of Augustine with an emphasis on the power of ritual, see Finn, "It Happened One Saturday Night."

95. Shippee, "Antioch's Separate Catechetical Classes and Curricula."

96. If we had the letter that Ambrose wrote to the queen of the Marcomanni in response to her request for information on what belief in Christ involved, we would have a sample of Ambrose's instruction at this stage (Paulinus, *Vita Ambrosii* 8.36).

*Catechesis and Initiation*

Lenten instructions to the *competentes* (*Sermons*, 56–59; 212–218); and (4) mystagogy (*Sermons*, 224–29; 260; 272).[97]

Augustine's *On Catechizing Beginners*, written perhaps in 399,[98] has been much studied, because, while revealing his "pedagogical acumen and psychological sensitivity,"[99] it also offers both a long and a short sample of instruction.[100] I find it particularly noteworthy that Augustine's recommendation of the content of the preliminary instruction (*Cat. rud.* 6.10) and both his long (16–25) and short (26.51—27.55) samples take the form of a survey of biblical and Christian history. This historical framework allows the catechist to adapt the presentation according to the needs of the hearers (*Cat. rud.* 15). Giving a salvation history overview was traditional, going back to Jewish roots,[101] and recognition of this common method of presentation may to some extent account for the way many fathers make abundant use of the scriptures, assuming their hearers will have a framework into which to put their frequent references. Augustine, moreover, extends the biblical history to include the church up to his time (*Cat. rud.* 6.10; 24.44–45).[102] He repeats some of his characteristic themes: the division of human history into seven ages (*Cat. rud.* 17.28; 22.39);[103] and the division of humanity into "two cities" (*Cat. rud.* 19.31), which is comparable to the "two ways" in earlier catechetical instruction and better known from his apologetic work, *The City of God.*[104] True Christians, he says, are "citizens of the heavenly Jerusalem" (*Cat. rud.* 7.11). Most characteristic is

---

97. Harmless, *Augustine and the Catechumenate*, 29.

98. Van der Lof, "The Date of the *De catechizandis rudibus*."

99. Harmless, *Augustine and the Catechumenate*, 108.

100. Note Touton, "La méthode catéchétique de St Cyrille de Jérusalem comparée à celles de St Augustin et de Théodore de Mopsuestia"; Allard, "La nature du *De catechizandis rudibus* de S. Augustin"; Belche, "Die Bekehrung zum Christentum nach Augustins Büchlein De carechizandis rudibus."

101. Harmless, *Augustine and the Catechumenate*, 127. For Christian practice, see Irenaeus, *Demonstration of the Apostolic Preaching* (see Ferguson, "Irenaeus' Proof of the Apostolic Preaching"); *Apostolic Constitutions*, 7.39; Egeria, *Travels*, 46 (the practice referred to by Egeria of the Bishop of Jerusalem going "through the whole of scripture" could explain why Cyril was able to draw so fully from Old Testament examples and prophecies in his creedal exposition). Christopher, *St. Augustine*, 7 (whose translation I use), concludes that the resemblances in these works indicate that all "derive from an original, well-defined catechetical model."

102. Both Justin, *1 Apol.* 39; 45; *Dial.* 109-10, and Irenaeus, *Dem.* 91-95, had included the mission of the apostles and calling of the Gentiles in their summaries of the Christian faith.

103. *Civ. Dei* 22.30; *Serm.* 259.2; *Enarr. in Ps.* 93 [Lt. 92].1; *Tract. in Ioh.* 9.6; 15.9.

104. Harmless, *Augustine and the Catechumenate*, 144–47.

Augustine's emphasis on the two commands to love God and love neighbour: all scripture depends on them (*Cat. rud.* 4.8); the narration of God's dealings with humanity all relate to the goal of love (6.10); the Decalogue can be reduced to these two commands (23.41); and they are the duties enjoined on Christians (27.55).[105] Augustine's concern for "steadfast faith and a good life" (*Cat. rud.* 2.5.47) prompts several warnings about the new converts being led astray by the various classes of sinners, the "chaff in the church who were Christians in name only (*Cat. rud.* 7.11; 14.21; 25.48; 27.55). His advice to close with an eschatological exhortation (*Cat. rud.* 7.11), although common enough in early Christian instruction, highlights the way in which the eschatological theme permeates the whole instruction—16.24–25 ("rest that is hoped for after this life"); 17.27–28 (eternal blessedness in the seventh age); 2.4.45 (judgment); 25.46 (defence of the resurrection); 25.47–48 (sample exhortation).

Augustine's sermons on the Psalms and on the Gospel of John were addressed to "all," including catechumens, to whom he made a number of references.[106] The sermons on John focused more on doctrine and an intellectual understanding of the faith; those on the Psalms focused on spirituality and an affective grasp of the faith.[107] Augustine saw himself as a minister of the word, whose task was to feed the [spiritually] hungry" with the bread of life. The biblical text controlled his expositions.[108] Scripture has a moral core; its purpose is to cleanse the soul for the journey home to God.[109]

Augustine repeats many themes expressed by the Greek fathers in their Epiphany sermons and their exhortations to catechumens to receive baptism.[110] After developing the common interpretation of Israel's

---

105. Raymond Canning has written a series of articles on the two commands. See his "The Distinction Between Love for God and Love for Neighbour in St. Augustine"; "Love of Neighbour in St. Augustine"; "The Augustinian *uti/frui* Distinction in the Relation between Love for Neighbour and Love for God"; "'Love Your Neighbour as Yourself'" (Matt 22:39)"; "Augustine on the Identity of the Neighbour"; "The Unity of Love for God and Neighbour."

106. E.g., *Tract. in Ioh.* 4.13, 10.10; 11.1, 2, 4. See Harmless, *Augustine and the Catechumenate*, 158–59 for *Enarr. in Psalm.* 119–33 [Lt.] and *Tract. Ioh.* 1–12, as an intertwining series of sermons preached between December and the opening of Lent, probably AD 406–7.

107. Harmless, *Augustine and the Catechumenate*, 194, 206.

108. Ibid., 160–61, 180–81.

109. Ibid., 186 with reference to *De doctrina christiana*.

110. Ferguson, "Preaching at Epiphany: Gregory of Nyssa and John Chrysostom on Baptism and the Church"; and Ferguson, "Exhortations to Baptism in the

crossing the Red Sea as a baptism in which past sins (= the Egyptians) are destroyed, Augustine challenges his hearers, "Why do you fear to come?"[111] He too contrasts Christian baptism with that of John the Baptist and explores the reasons for Christ's baptism. One purpose was to serve as an example: "If I [Jesus] have received the baptism of the servant [John], do you disdain to be baptized by the Lord?"[112]

Like his Eastern counterparts, Augustine complains that the public entertainments were more popular than church: "For there are many that live not worthily of the baptism which they have received. For how many that are baptized have chosen rather to be filling the circus than this Basilica."[113] He often complains of the many Christians who live evil lives and pull the church down.[114] One of the key themes of the sermons on Psalms and John is that Christ as the inner Teacher exhorts to ascend to the heavenly Jerusalem by good works (*Enarr. in Psalm.*, 122. [Lt 121]).[115] "The people of God are the city of God" (ibid., 125 [Lt 124.10]), so they have a foretaste of the heavenly joy; however, they remain exiles returning home (ibid., 126 [Lt 125.4]).[116]

Augustine alludes to activities of those undergoing the immediate preparation for baptism. Before coming to the water, there are fastings, tribulations, and prayers (*Enarr. in Psalm.*, 81 [Lt. 80].10). The renunciations are given a moral thrust: as well as rejecting the realm of the devil, the candidate renounced "thefts, plunderings, perjuries, manslayings, adulteries, sacrileges, abominable rites, curious arts" (ibid., 81.18). The

---

Cappadocians." There are a fair number of exhortations to baptism embedded in Augustine's various sermons and letters—Harmless, *Augustine and the Catechumenate*, 191 for a listing—but Augustine's Epiphany sermons (*Serm.* 199–204) do not treat baptism, for they follow the Western understanding of the feast as connected with the visit of the Magi to the infant Jesus.

111. *Enarr. in Psalm.* 81.8; cf. *Tract. in Ioh.* 11.4. Augustine knew the same problem of the delay of baptism by those "more fearful of future sins than present ones" (*Serm.*, 97A.3; cf. 339.8)—Harmless, *Augustine and the Catechumenate*, 187.

112. *Tract. in Ioh.* 4.12–14; quotation from 4.13. The treatment has many similarities to John Chrysostom. For literature see n. 87.

113. *Enarr. in Psalm.* 81.2. "Crowds fill the churches on feast days of the Christians which likewise fill the theaters on the ritual days of the pagans" (*Cat. rud.* 25.48); many came to church for the great feasts but at other times filled the theatres and arenas (*Sermons* 301A.8 [= Denis 17]. Cf. Gregory of Nyssa, *Bapt. Chr.* (GNO, 9, 211, 6–9, 18); and John Chrysostom, *Bapt. Chr.* 1 (PC, 49.363).

114. *Serm.*, 148; 250. Augustine lamented that those converted in appearance were greater in number than those truly converted (*In Psalm.* 40.10).

115. Harmless, *Augustine and the Catechumenate*, 207–13.

116. Ibid., 225–26.

catechumens do not eat the flesh or drink the blood of the Son of Man," for they know not what Christians receive" (*Tract. in Ioh.*, 11.3, 4). So, we turn to Augustine's Lenten instructions to the *competentes*.

In several works Augustine offered summaries of the Christian faith according to the baptismal creed. His *Enchiridion*, or *Faith, Hope, and Love*, written c.421, remains the best single introduction to his thought. The bulk of the work is a commentary on the "Apostles' Creed" (the faith: 9–113); the remainder takes up the Lord's Prayer (hope: 114–16) and the command to love (117–21)—the faith, prayer (liturgy), and love (morals) were his handbook summary of Christianity. *On Faith and the Creed* was a model explanation of the Apostles' Creed delivered while he was still a presbyter to the North African bishops in synod (AD 393). At each article, the address takes note of the false teachings refuted by the Creed. *On Christian Combat* also covers the Creed in terms of positions to be rejected (13.14—33.35). Other summaries of the creed occur in sermons addressed to the *competentes* at the occasion of the delivery of the creed to them (*traditio symboli*) two weeks before their baptism (*Sermons* 211–14 and *On the Symbol to Catechumens*) and their recitation of it (*redditio symboli*) a week before their baptism (*Sermon* 215).

Sermon 214 is much more theological than 213. Augustine's rhetorical flair for the paradoxical is evident in his characterization of the first nativity of the Son of God (from eternity) as of the Father without a mother; his second (on earth) as of a mother without a father (6). Another striking phrase is the description of the last resurrection as an end without an end (213.9). He describes the contents of the Creed as "arranged in a fixed order and condensed," so as not to tax the memory of what the initiates are accustomed to hear in scripture and in sermons in church (1).[117] As part of the *disciplina arcani*, they are admonished not to write down the Creed but to learn it by oral repetition (1; cf. 212.2).[118]

Although Ambrose and Cyril of Jerusalem interpreted the Lord's Prayer after baptism, Augustine (as Theodore of Mopsuestia) did so before baptism, delivering the text of the prayer accompanied by a sermon of instruction on the same day as the first *redditio symboli* a week before baptism. "You have been taught the Creed first, so that you may know what to believe, and afterwards the Prayer, so that you may know upon whom to

---

117. Muldowney, trans., *Saint Augustine: Sermons on the Liturgical Seasons*.

118. De Latte, "Saint Augustin et le baptême," 201, observes that in *Serm.* 212.2 Augustine bases the prohibition not on the rule of secrecy but on Jer 31:33, "written on the heart."

call ... It is the believer's prayer that is heard" (*Serm.* 56.2; cf. 57.1).[119] The first three petitions, he says, will never cease for all eternity; the remaining petitions have to do with life on this earth (19). Even these first three petitions are not for God but for one's self. For example, the prayer for the kingdom to come is a petition that it come within us so we may be found within that kingdom. It is a prayer that a person lead a good life so as to partake of the kingdom that is to come (6).

The treatise *On Faith and Works*, written in 413, refutes the error that faith and baptism alone are sufficient for salvation without good works (*Retractationes*, 2.38) and that instruction for baptism should consist only of doctrines to be believed, with morals to be taught afterwards (*Faith and Works*, 1.1).[120] The particular concern of Augustine's opponents in this treatise is adulterers, viz., those who were married to persons who had been previously married (passim, but esp. 19.35). Erroneous teaching and practice often expose the points of weaknesses that occasion the errors, and it may be that the position opposed in *On Faith and Works* grew out of the church's practice of giving more attention to instruction in the faith and little explicit attention to morals. Augustine responds that repentance requires quitting one's sins (8.12). When Paul affirmed salvation by faith, he did not mean that good works are unnecessary nor that it is enough to profess the faith and no more (14.21). Those to be admitted to baptism are those who believe in the Trinity (as in the Creed) *and* do penance for their sins (20.36). The one being prepared for baptism was to be zealous in attending instructions, exorcisms, and scrutinies (6.9). Augustine insisted that faith and morals belong together; one must have faith in order to live a good, Christian life (7.11). Those preparing for baptism are to be taught not only what to believe but also what to do in the Christian life (27.49). In practice, however, it seems that most of the moral teaching was done by way of the ceremonies of scrutiny and exorcism[121] and not by systematic exposition. Moreover, it must be said that although Augustine protested against these laxists who said to make people Christians first and then teach them how to live, his support of coercion against the Donatists and support for infant baptism had the effect of establishing that very approach. In his argument against the Donatists and Pelagians, who in different ways held to an elitist view of the church as made up of the

---

119. Kavanagh, trans., *Saint Augustine: Commentary on the Lord's Sermon on the Mount with Seventeen Related Sermons*, 57–59 also concerned the delivery of the "Our Father."

120. Lombardo, trans., *St. Augustine on Faith and Works*.

121. De Latte, "Saint Augustin et le baptême," 196–99.

pure, he began "to edge, in carefully measured ways, towards a Church of the many."[122]

Augustine, like Theodore of Mopsuestia and John Chrysostom, did not wait until Easter week to explain baptism and eucharist, for there are many explanations of its significance in the works already surveyed.[123] He gave private catecheses on the eucharist to the newly baptized on Easter Sunday morning before they received it (*Serm.*, 229 and 229A before the prayer; 227 and 272 before communion).[124] One of his Easter Sunday sermons says that he has treated the sacrament of the creed, the sacrament of the Lord's prayer, the sacrament of the font and baptism; now it is time for the sacrament of the holy altar (228.3).[125]

Augustine's sermons delivered on Easter Sunday contain many direct references to those "reborn in Christ Jesus," no longer *competentes* but now *infantes* (*Serm.* 224.1, 4; 225.4; 228.1, 2). He gave attention to sins to abstain from; adultery is prominent (224), but also mentioned is drunkenness (225.4). The older believers are admonished not to set a bad example, and the newly baptized are exhorted: "If you do not find what you may imitate, then be what somebody else may imitate" (228.1, 2).

During the Octave of Easter, eucharistic liturgies were held daily, and Augustine preached twice daily to the older and the newer believers. His sermons explored especially the meaning of the resurrection, a doctrine closely associated with the theme of the city of God. Thus, Augustine's mystagogy was not so much liturgical (as in other fourth-century representatives) as it was eschatological. To be incorporated into the church was not enough, for the church was a mix of wheat and chaff; hence Christians must keep their eyes fixed on the eschaton. A comparison of Augustine's mystagogy with that of other fourth and fifth-century teachers shows a much greater emphasis on the endtime.[126]

Hence, we have treated Augustine's catecheses as "Training to Live in the Heavenly City." This, as should be evident from even this brief survey, did not mean that Augustine had his head in the clouds. On the Sunday

---

122. Harmless, *Augustine and the Catechumenate*, 250, with reference to Markus, "Augustine: A Defense of Christian Mediocrity," in his *End of Ancient Christianity*, 51–55.

123. Harmless, *Augustine and the Catechumenate*, 306.

124. Ibid., 316–17. One of these is studied in Drobner, "Augustinus, Sermo 227."

125. For Augustine's doctrine of the real presence, see Ferguson, "The Lord's Supper in Church History."

126. Harmless, *Augustine and the Catechumenate*, 314–18, 338–39, 364–5; De Latte, "Saint Augustin et le baptême," 113.

after Easter, he concluded his instructions to new converts on a practical moral note. "You have to return to the people; you have to mingle with the faithful; beware of imitating wicked believers." Among his admonitions, the one that is elaborated on is, "Preserve your chastity"; other sins are only mentioned (*Serm.*, 260).

## CONCLUDING OBSERVATIONS

The catechumenate all along served an evangelistic function,[127] but in the course of the fourth century it became more didactic. At the beginnings of the organized catechumenate the concern seems to have been how to keep the unworthy out of the church. It established clear boundary lines, and its rituals marked the transition to a new community.[128] The fourth-century catechumenate was still concerned with boundaries in a new situation, but the principal concern seems to have become how to get the worthy into the church.

The former concern is exhibited in the *Apostolic Tradition*, which provided for a three-year catechumenate (ch. 17). Persons in certain occupations were excluded; others were told to cease their circumstances or be excluded (ch. 16). A rigorous moral examination preceded admission to the catechumenate. In the *Apostolic Tradition* the catechumens, although in the process of making a transition to the church, still in some sense belonged to the "enemy and so were subject to frequent exorcisms.[129] By the fourth century the rituals such as exorcism were still there, but the emphasis had shifted from the separation between the two realms of the world and the church to preparation for assuming a place in the church.

Maertens notes that what the *Apostolic Tradition* puts at the beginning—the moral instruction—Augustine puts at the end.[130] On Augustine's behalf, I would say that he does put a testing of motives first (*Cat. rud.* 5.9 ), and moral exhortation in the form of the two commandments to love is part of the first instruction. Nevertheless, he places the main moral instruction later. *On Faith and Works* says training in the faith and

---

127. Hinson, *The Evangelization of the Roman Empire*.

128. Finn, "Ritual Process," 69–90, finds the rituals of the carechumenate as providing a powerful influence in developing the social stamina of Christians in Rome. The social dimension of the catechesis is noted by Germain, "Baptême et education de la foi," 113.

129. Finn, "Ritual Process," 75, 79.

130. Maertens, *Histoire et pastorale*, 118.

the pattern of the Christian life goes on during the time of the catechumenate and becomes more intensive during the candidates' time as *competentes* (6.9). Elsewhere he states, "It is faith that first makes souls subject to God. Next come the precepts for right living."[131] And even in these later stages, I must observe, there is regrettably no systematic moral exposition comparable to the creedal and liturgical instructions. Daniélou explains the change in timing by saying that at the beginning of the church, moral catechesis had to come first to mark the rupture with pagan customs; in the fourth century it was at the end as the flowering of all life in the grace of the Holy Spirit.[132] Both statements are true, but the former is a sociological observation, the latter a theological affirmation. Were not morals rooted in doctrine in the second century? Was there not still a need in the fourth century to make the rupture with pagan society evident?

The space allotments in Augustine's "Handbook" (*Enchiridion*) may serve to illustrate the concerns in fifth-century teaching. One hundred and five sections discuss the creed, three sections the Lord's Prayer, and five sections charity (or love). There are likely practical considerations for this distribution, and I would not argue that it represents Augustine's ultimate priorities. Nevertheless, the disproportionate attention given to the creed over prayer and a life of love may serve as a symbol of the state of catechetical instruction in the West at the beginning of the fifth century.

The eagerness to include as many as possible in the church is illustrated by Augustine's terminology. Instead of treating catechumens as outsiders, he includes them in the name "Christian," meaning "anointed," because they were admitted to the catechumenate in a ceremony that involved being signed with the cross (*Tract. in Ioh.* 44.2). He does maintain a distinction by declaring that catechumens are servants in the household but the baptized are sons (*Tract. in Ioh.* 11.4), or in another image suggested by John 3:5, the catechumens are in the womb of the church but must be born of water and the Spirit (*Tract. in Ioh.* 11.6; 12.3). I have sometimes illustrated the changed circumstances for the church by the observation that in the third century Christian authors wrote exhortations to martyrdom; in the fourth century, exhortations to baptism. There are a number

---

131. *On Christian Combat*, 13.14, translated by Peebles, trans., *Saint Augustine*, 331. The passage continues, "When these are observed, our hope is made firm, charity is nurtured, and what before was only believed begins to be clearly understood." The same sequence of hearing, believing, hoping, and loving is found in *Cat. rud.* 4.8; cf. the related statement in *Enchiridion*, 3.8, "There is no love without hope, no hope without love, and neither hope nor love without faith."

132. Daniélou, *La catéchèse aux premiers siècles*, 126.

## Catechesis and Initiation

of these encouragements in Augustine.[133] People were glad to be identified with the church to the extent of admission to the catechumenate, but they were not eager to assume the full duties of church membership.

We have seen that the fourth century offers us examples of instruction surveying the contents of the Bible (Augustine, *Cat. rud.*), explaining the articles of the Creed (Cyril of Jerusalem, Ambrose, Augustine, and others), and interpreting the rites of initiation (Cyril of Jerusalem, Ambrose, Augustine, and others). Although there are many scattered references to moral instruction and sermons having that as the principal content, there were no catechetical instructions on morals as such and no set place in the catechumenate for giving this instruction. There was no curriculum for moral teaching comparable to that supplied by the Creed and the liturgy. Daniélou explains the lack of a separate moral catechesis in the fourth century by saying that morals were taught from the scriptures, the creed, and the sacraments,[134] and he justifies this practice as avoiding the danger of cutting off morals from their doctrinal roots.[135] Such makes the best of the anomaly. The lack of balance and consistency here, I suspect, has a great deal to do with the failure of the Christianization of the West to penetrate more deeply into the behaviour of people. At some places a balance was maintained, and some did the job of Christian formation better than others. Ambrose and Augustine certainly tried. But I am left with the (to me) disturbing impression that even in these fathers a more concentrated and thorough job was done of doctrinal and liturgical (sacramental) instruction than was done with biblical and moral teaching. The emphasis had shifted from the earlier days of the church. The new centre of gravity for catechesis in the fourth and fifth centuries perhaps reflected the prominence of doctrinal controversy in church life. Being a Christian was now defined primarily in terms of doctrine and not in terms of behaviour. It was left for the monks to maintain the witness to a distinctive Christian lifestyle. Was all this the price of becoming the church of the Empire?

---

133. See notes 110–11.
134. Daniélou, "La Catéchèse dans la tradition patristique," 19–30.
135. Daniélou, *La catéchèse aux premiers siècles*, 158.

# 3

# Christian and Jewish Baptism according to the *Epistle of Barnabas*

THE TREATISE[1] KNOWN AS the *Epistle of Barnabas* shows a Jewish community and a Christian community in contact, competition, and debate.[2] Of the three proposed dates for *Barnabas*, the time of Vespasian (69–79 CE) has few advocates,[3] the time of Hadrian (117–38 CE) has been most popular,[4] but recently the time of Nerva (96–98 CE) has gained favor.[5] With regard to provenance, although Asia Minor has been proposed[6] and Syria with better reason has supporters,[7] Egypt, and specifically Alexandria, seems more likely.[8] The author was probably a

---

1. Hvalvik, *The Struggle, for Scripture and Covenant*, 71–81, argues that *Barnabas* is a letter, specifically a protreptic letter, 158–64. Prostmeier, *Der Barnabasbrief*, 86–89, takes both options: a tractate framed as a letter.

2. Lowry, "The Confutation of Judaism in the Epistle of Barnabas."

3. Lightfoot, *The Apostolic Fathers*, Part I, vol. 2, 509.

4. E.g., Lindemann and Paulsen, *Die Apostolischen Väter*, 24; Hvalvik, *The Struggle, for Scripture and Covenant*, 17–34 (23); Prostmeier, *Der Barnabasbrief*, 111–19, specifies 130 or 131 CE (pp. 118–19).

5. Richardson and Shukster, "Barnabas, Nerva, and the Yavnean Rabbis"; Carleton Paget, *The Epistle of Barnabas*, 9–30 (28).

6. Wengst, *Tradition and Theologie des Barnabasbriefes*, 118.

7. E.g., Prigent and Kraft, *Épître de Barnabé*, 22–24.

8. Carleton Paget, *The Epistle of Barnabas*, 30–42; Prostmeier, *Der Barnabasbrief*, 119–30.

## Christian and Jewish Baptism according to the Epistle of Barnabas

Gentile convert to Christianity, a teacher, and seemingly well-known to readers (the ascription to Barnabas is secondary).[9]

The central section of *Barnabas* is a contrast of Jewish and Christian practices. Issues in the conflict include sacrifices (chs. 7–8), circumcision (ch. 9), food laws (ch. 10), baptism (ch. 11), covenant and people (chs. 13–14), sabbath (ch. 15), and temple (ch. 16). In the last group of topics the author uses περὶ τοῦ as a divider (11.1; 12.1; 13.2; 15.1; 16.1), as does the New Testament[10] and other writings. The baptismal associations in *Barnabas* are sufficiently evident that Barnard even proposed that it might be a paschal homily, and Schiller argues that the author was writing to the newly baptized and that the contents follow a catechetical scheme.[11]

This paper discusses the treatment of baptism in ch. 11. The author of *Barnabas* writes:

> (1) Let us inquire if the Lord was careful to give a revelation in advance concerning the water and the cross. It was written concerning the water with regard to Israel how they will not receive the baptism that brings forgiveness of sins but will establish [another] for themselves.
>
> (2) For the prophet says, "Be astonished, Oh heaven, and let the earth shudder even more at this, because this people did two evil things. They abandoned me, the fountain of life, and they dug for themselves a cistern of death" [Jer 2:12–13]. (3) "Is my holy mount Sinai a barren rock? For you will be as young birds fluttering about when taken from the nest" [Isa 16:1–2, LXX]. Again, the prophet says, "I will go before you; I will level the mountains; and I will break the bronze gates and shatter iron bars; and I will give you treasures lying in darkness, hidden and invisible, in order that you may know that I the Lord am God" [Isa 45:2–3; Ps 106:16, LXX].
>
> (5) And, "You will live in a high cave of a strong rock, and its water is dependable, You will see a glorious King, and your soul will cultivate the fear of the Lord" [Isa 33:16–18].

---

9. Prostmeier, *Der Barnabasbrief*, 130–34. Was the ascription to Barnabas due to his association with Mark? To my mind the most plausible hypothesis is that the author was actually named Barnabas, later confused with the companion of Paul.

10. 1 Cor 7:1, 25; 8:1, 4; 12:1; 16:1.

11. The only article known to me devoted to baptism in Barnabas is by Saber, "Le Baptême dans l'Épitre de Barnabé," [in Arabic and known to me through its French summary]. The subject is well discussed in Benoît, *Le baptême chrétien au second siècle*, 34–57; Barnard, "The Epistle of Barnabas—A Paschal Homily?" (16–21 on baptismal setting of the Epistle); Schiller, "Zur urchristlichen Tauflehre: Stilistische am Barnabasbrief."

(6) And again he says in another prophet: "The one who does these things will be as a tree planted by streams of water, which will give its fruit in its season, and its leaf will not fall off, and everything he does will prosper. (7) The wicked are not so, they are not so; rather they are like chaff, which the wind drives away from the face of the earth. Therefore, the wicked will not stand in the judgment, nor sinners in the counsel of the righteous; because the Lord knows the way of the righteous and the way of the wicked will perish" [Ps 1:3–6].

(8) Perceive how he defines the water and the cross together. For he says this: "Blessed" [Ps 1:1] are those who with hope in the cross went down into the water, because he speaks of the reward "in its season" [Ps 1:3]; at that time he says, "I will reward." For the present, what he says, "The leaves will not fall off" [Ps 1:3], means this: Every word that proceeds out of your mouth in faith and love will be for conversion and hope to many.

(9) And again another prophet says, "The land of Jacob was praised above every land" [?—the last phrase is in Ezek 20:6, 15; Zeph 3:19]. This means, he glorifies the vessel of his Spirit.

(10) Next, what does he say? "A river was flowing along on the right, and beautiful trees come up out of it. Whoever eats of the trees will live forever" [based on Ezek 47:1–12].

(11) He means this: That we go down into the water full of sins and uncleanness, and we come up bearing as fruit in our heart reverence and having hope in Jesus in our spirit. And "whoever eats from these will live forever" [Ezek 47:9; Gen 3:22] means this: Whoever, he says, hears these when they speak and believes will live forever.[12]

With this passage may he compared two other passages in *Barnabas* that without mentioning baptism contain baptismal motifs, including parallels with this chapter—6:8–19 and 16:7–10—to which we will give supplementary attention.

(6.8) What says the other prophet, Moses, to the Jewish people? Behold, the Lord God says these things: "Enter into the good land that the Lord swore to Abraham, Isaac, and Jacob that you would inherit it, a land flowing with milk and honey" [Exod 33:1, 3; Lev 20:24; Deut 1:25].

(9) Learn what gnosis says: "Hope," it says, "on Jesus who is going to be manifested to you in the flesh." For a human being is

---

12. I translate the text of Lindemann and Paulsen, *Die Apostolischen Väter*, 52, 54. There are some significant textual variants, but I will lake note of these only as they affect the discussion of baptism.

*Christian and Jewish Baptism according to the* Epistle of Barnabas

suffering earth, for the creation of Adam occurred from the face of the earth [Gen 2:7] . . .

(11) Since then he renewed us by the forgiveness of sins, he made another type [of creation], as having the soul of children, as if he were remaking us . . .

(13) Again I will show you how he speaks to us [Christians]. He made a second creation in the last days. For the Lord says, "Behold I make the last things as the first" [?]. The prophet, therefore, proclaimed with reference to this: "Enter into the land flowing with milk and honey and rule over it" [Exod 33:3; Gen 1:28].

(14) Behold, therefore, we have been remade, as again he says in another prophet: "Behold, says the Lord, I will remove from them," that is from those whom the Spirit of the Lord foresaw, "their stony hearts, and I will place in them hearts of flesh" [Ezek 11:19; 36:26], because he was going to be manifested in flesh and dwell in us.

(15) My brothers and sisters, the Lord's holy temple is the dwelling place of our heart.

(16) For the Lord says again: "In what way shall I see the Lord my God and be glorified?" [Ps 41:3, LXX; Isa 49:5] He says: "I will confess you in the assembly [church] of my brothers and sisters, and I will sing praise to you in the midst of the assembly [church] of the saints" [Ps 21:23; 107:4, LXX]. Therefore, we are those whom he led into the good land.

(17) What then are the milk and honey? [This means] that the child is given life by honey and then milk. So then also we who are given life by faith in the promise and by the word shall live and rule over the earth . . .

(19) If then this has not happened now, therefore he has spoken to us at what time, when we ourselves are perfected to become heirs of the Lord's covenant . . .

(16.7) I find then that there is a temple. Therefore, learn how it will be built in the name of the Lord. Before we believed in God, the dwelling place of our heart was corrupt and weak, like a temple truly built by hand, because it was full of idolatry and was a house of demons by reason of doing whatever was contrary to God.

(8) "It will be built in the name of the Lord" [Dan 9:24–27]. Give attention, so that the temple of the Lord may be built gloriously. How? Learn. When we received forgiveness of sins and placed our hope in his name, we became new and were created again from the beginning. Wherefore God truly dwells in us, in our dwelling place.

(9) How? His word of faith, his calling of promise, the wisdom of his ordinances, the commandments of his teaching, himself prophesying in us, himself dwelling in us, opening for us the door of the temple (which is the mouth) and giving us repentance, he leads those who were slaves to death into the incorruptible temple.

(10) ... This is the spiritual temple being built to the Lord.

"To give a revelation in advance" was important to *Barnabas* (cf. 3.6). The heading for chs. 11-12 says, "Concerning the water and the cross," subdivided into "concerning the water" in 11.1b and "concerning the cross" in 12.1. The subject of the cross is taken up mainly in ch. 12, but it is included in the quotation in 11.6-8. The water and the cross are taken up as part of the sequence of proofs that Christians understand Scripture and as another example of Jewish misunderstanding and rejection of God's intentions. The rejection of Christian baptism by the Jews was already revealed in Scripture.[13] *Barnabas* previously has taken Jewish rites as the point of departure (and he does so again in ch. 15), but here he puts the Christian rite at the center of the discussion.[14]

The association of water and the cross is made because both are related to the forgiveness of sins. *Barnabas* links the forgiveness of sins with the sprinkling of the Lord's (Christ's) blood in 5.1. This follows an extended passage on the rejection of Israel's sacrifices in ch. 2 and fasting (probably the fast of the Day of Atonement) in ch. 3.[15] Another association of wood (interpreted of the cross) and water (not mentioned by *Barnabas*) is implied in the treatment of Num 19, where hyssop is dipped in a mixture of ashes and water and sprinkled for purification from touching a dead body; *Barnabas* says those who sprinkle are "those who preached to us the good news of the forgiveness of sins" (81-83).[16] *Barnabas* connects

---

13. Wengst, *Tradition and Theologie des Barnabasbriefes*, 102. In this chapter, vv. 2 and 7 are words of judgment against Israel. On the pattern of quoting Scripture with the interpretation "this is" (= "this means"—11.8a and c; 11.9b; 11.11a and c), see Prostmeier, *Der Barnabasbrief*, 413.

14. Hvalvik, *The Struggle, for Scripture and Covenant*, 189-91.

15. See the discussion of the sequence of texts in Justin and *Barnabas* by Skarsaune, *The Proof from Prophecy*, 295-97, accepted by Carleton Paget, *The Epistle of Barnabas*, 107, noting that the rejection of cultic activity is followed by reference to remission of sins by Christ's blood. Benoît, *Le baptême chrétien au second siècle*, 36, for baptism in *Barnabas* as the subjective appropriation of the remission of sins objectively accomplished by the death on the cross with reference to Luke 12:50 and Mark 10:38.

16. Skarsaune, "Baptismal Typology in *Barnabas* 8 and the Jewish Background."

## *Christian and Jewish Baptism according to the* Epistle of Barnabas

Christ's suffering with redemption (7.2, 3, 5; 14.5).[17] The forgiveness of sins made possible by the sufferings and blood of Jesus is received in the water of baptism. The references to forgiveness of sins that makes one new in 6.11 and 16.8 are in baptismal contexts (to be developed below).[18] A number of early Christian texts associate baptism with the forgiveness of sins.[19]

Other early Christian texts in addition to *Barnabas* make the charge that Jewish washings did not procure forgiveness of sins. Especially notable is Justin, *Dialogue* 14, that Christian baptism "is alone able to purify" with the added allusion to Jer 2:13, "the cisterns that you dug for yourselves are broken."[20] Does *Barnabas* refer to Jewish washings for purification or to proselyte baptism? There was no question of forgiveness in reference to the former. The tractate in the Mishnah on "Immersion Pools" (*Mikwaoth*) lists six grades of pools of water in ascending order of purificatory efficacy.[21] As with the other tractates in the division on "Cleannesses" (*Tohoroth*), the purification was external and not internal, but nonetheless serious, and by the distinction I do not intend to be pejorative.

Neither was proselyte baptism, which may have begun not long before *Barnabas*'s time,[22] explicitly connected with forgiveness of sins. Rabbinic literature described the proselyte as not only ceremonially pure (*Pes.* 8.8) but also as separated from the grave (*Pes.* 8.8),[23] as a newborn child (*b.*

---

17. Hvalvik, *The Struggle, for Scripture and Covenant*, 145.

18. Prigent, *Les Testimonia dans le Christianisme primitif*, 86: "Il est donc clair que notre texte [6.9–19 in comparison with 16.8] parle, lui aussi, du baptême."

19. E.g., Acts 2:38; 22:16; Hermas, *Mand.* 4.3.1 [= 31.1]; Justin, *1 Apol.* 61.10; 66.1; Theophilus, *Ad Autol.* 2.16.

20. Justin, *Dial.* 14.1 and 19.2 also refer to the cisterns of Jer 2:13 in contrast to the Christian "water of life" (14.1) and "baptism of life" (19.2), and 29.1 contrasts the baptisms (the Christians' has the Holy Spirit). A contrast of Christian and Jewish baptism is also made in Pseudo-Cyprian, *Against the Jews* 10.79–82 and in the fragment of an apocryphal gospel in *Oxyrhynchus Papyri* V, #840 (translated in my *Early Christians Speak*, 3rd ed. [Abilene: Abilene Christian University Press, 1999] 31).

21. A distinction is preserved in the terminology for immersion (dipping to obtain cleansing), pouring (as in pouring water into a container to fill it 3.3), and sprinkling (as in sprinkling with the hyssop branch—4.8; cf. *Parah* 12.11).

22. Taylor, "The Beginning of Jewish Proselyte Baptism," argues for a late first-century date for its introduction. Pusey and Hunt, "Jewish Proselyte Baptism," take the reasonable position that the practice may have begun by the beginning of the first century but that the meaning developed later from its origin as a purificatory rite to a symbol of the start of a new life.

23. Does this mean separated from corpse defilement, for which idolatry was the ceremonial equivalent?

*Yeb.* 22a; 48b; 62a), as becoming a different person (*b. Yeb.* 23a), as repenting and changing life (the late *Qoh. R.* 1.8.4),[24] becoming a freed person (*b. Yeb.* 46a), and becoming an Israelite in all respects (*b. Yeb.* 47b). But these descriptions seem to refer more to legal status (*b. Sheb.* 109; *Yeb.* 112; *Hull.* 10.4) and not to entail an inner rebirth.[25] They apply to the whole process of becoming a proselyte, of which circumcision was the most important aspect, although the fact that women received only the bath led some to suggest it was more important.[26] An association with forgiveness of sins is suggested in other sources. The Jewish *Sib. Or.* 4.165–69 from the late first century says, "Wash your whole bodies in perennial rivers. Stretch out your hands to heaven and ask forgiveness for your previous deeds,"[27] but the forgiveness here appears to be connected more with prayer than with the washing.

In the translation I have taken the phrase "they will build for themselves" (ἀλλ' ἑαυτοῖς οἰκοδομήσουσιν) as a reference to another kind of baptism. If correct, that might seem to rule out ritual baptism, for it was commanded in the Law of Moses, but *Barnabas* consistently understands the Jews' literal application of the institutions in the Law as their own misinterpretations.[28] "For themselves" might only serve to reinforce the distinctions between what the Jews did and what Christians did and not point to a later institution like proselyte baptism. The literal meaning of οἰκοδομέω, "build," might suggest another meaning, not referring to baptism but to the building of the temple.[29] That has some plausibility, because the temple was the place for atoning sacrifices, and *Barnabas* maintains a recurring interest in the temple and its sacrificial system. He might be contrasting baptism with expiation at the temple even if there is not an

---

24. "She no longer lived to the world . . . and they do not return [to their evil ways]"—A. Cohen, trans., *Midrash Rabbah: Ecciesiastes*, 28–29.

25. Leipoldt, *Die urchristliche Taufe im Lichte der Religionsgeschichte*, 22.

26. *b. Yeb.* 46a-b.

27. Translation by J. J. Collins in Charlesworth, ed., *The Old Testament Pseudepigrapha*, vol. 1, 388. Contrast the reference to daily ritual washings in 3.591–93.

28. See Hvalvik, *The Struggle, for Scripture and Covenant*, 153–54, that "for themselves" is part of *Barnabas*'s charge of "man made" ordinances in contrast to what is ordained by God (cf. 14.3) and that the discussion of baptism continues the theme of the "two peoples." Prostmeier, *Der Barnabasbrief*, 420, refers also to 2.6 as a connection of "for themselves" with *Barnabas*'s stricture against what is made by human beings.

29. Suggested by Carleton Paget, *The Epistle of Barnabas*, 154, 157. He rejects (155–56), however, the further development of the idea that makes the "cistern of death" (11.2) the temple advanced by Shukster and Richardson, "Temple and *Bet ha-Midrash* in the Epistle of Barnabas," 26.

*Christian and Jewish Baptism according to the* Epistle of Barnabas

allusion to the temple in the word "build." A Jewish—Christian source preserved in the Pseudo-Clementines (*Recog.* 1.48) says that the baptism instituted by Jesus "extinguishes the fire that the high priest kindled for sins."

The collection of quotations in *Barn.* 11.2-11 is part of the evidence for collections of testimonia in early Christianity. But is the author making his own catena or is he drawing on pre-existing collections? The presence of the same texts, sometimes in the same sequence, in other authors (apparently independent of *Barnabas*) supports the view that there were previous collections.[30] The passages cited seem an unlikely collection of proof texts on baptism, even on the principle represented in other early Christian writers that every reference to water was a reference to baptism."[31] Anti-Judaism is one factor in the passages chosen: ineffective (11.2-3) or unfruitful (11.7) versus faithful or unfailing (11.5) waters. Moreover, *Barnabas* selects passages that include a negative judgment on Israel (11.2-3), passages with positive promises that can be applied to the Church ("us" and not "them" [cf. 3.1 and 3]—11.4-5, 9-11), and a passage that reinforces the distinction between the two peoples ([cf. chs. 13-14] 11.6-8).[32] The first set of passages includes a reference to rock. Although it is not cited, the unifying idea seems to be the episodes of water brought forth from the rock (Exod 17:1-7; Num 20:2-13; Ps 78:15-17),[33] a familiar scene with baptismal allusions in early Christian art.[34] Another unifying theme is that of life from the opening reference to God as the "fountain of. life" (11.2) to the closing promise whoever eats of the trees will live forever," quoted twice (11.10, 11).

The first quotation is a composite of Jer 2:13 and Isa 16:1. Jeremiah supplied the contrast between a fountain and a cistern, particularly telling in view of the Jewish preference in purifications for running water over collected water. LXX manuscripts read fountain of the water of life"

---

30. The fullest study is Prigent, *Les Testimonia dans le Christianisme primitif*, who describes *Barnabas*'s treatment in ch. 11 as "midrashic" (90-99). For *Barnabas*'s interpretation of these Old Testament texts, see also Lundberg, *La typologie baptismole dans l'ancienne église*, 178-84; and Skarsaune, *The Proof from Prophecy*, 378-79.

31. So stated by Cyprian, *Ep.* 63[62].8.

32. On this theme in *Barnabas*, see Hvalvik, *The Struggle for Scripture and Covenant*, especially 137-57.

33. Ibid., 190.

34. For the baptismal interpretation of the water from the rock, see Tertullian, *De bapt.* 9; Cyprian, *Ep.* 63[62].8; other references in Daniélou, *From Shadows to Reality*, 193-97. For Christian art, see Schlosser, "Moses" and "Quellwunder."

or "fountain of living water," the former adopted by the Latin translation of *Barnabas* and the latter by the Jerusalem manuscript. Since an explicit reference to water would have been so fitting to *Barnabas*'s purposes, the reading "fountain of life" in Sinaiticus is almost certainly original.[35] The "barren rock" of Isa 16:1[36] contrasts with the water of a "fountain of life." The quotation continues with the idea of punishment: the Jews are like lost birds.[37]

Isaiah 45:2–3 (cf. Ps 106:16, LXX) quoted in 11.4, would seem to contribute nothing to the theme of water. Lundberg appears to have pointed the way to understanding the connection *Barnabas* intended. The prophet was interpreted as speaking of Christ's death and *descensus ad inferos* when he broke the gates of the hadean world. The *Od. Sol.* 17.6–16, alluding to the same passage from Isaiah in 17.10, describes Christ's *descensus* and resurrection and the blessings of union with him. By baptism the believer shares in the benefits of Christ's death, including the safe passage through the waters of death.[38] I would add that hidden" may contain an allusion to going under the water in parallel to Christ's descensus and "treasures" may be a reference to the spiritual blessings associated with baptism.

The quotation of Isa 33:16–18 follows immediately (11.5). Here an allusion to the water from the rock in the wilderness is more obvious, although the emphasis in isaiah is on the secure dwelling place of God's people. The omission of ἄρτος (bread) from the Greek of Isaiah is

---

35. Clement of Alexandria, *Paed.* 1.9.78.2 and Tertullian, *Adv. Iud.* 13.13–15 quote the verse as "fountain of living water" in an anti-Judaic context. Justin, *Dial.* 114.5 quotes "living fountain" (cf. also 19.2); he, like *Barnabas*, quotes Jer 2:13 and Isa 16:1 as one continuous passage. This independent attestation in Justin confirms that *Barnabas* did not originate the catena. (Justin, *Dial.* 14.1 and 19.2 also refer to the cisterns of Jer. 2.13 in contrast to the Christian "water of life" [14.1] and "baptism of life" [19.2].) Even without the word "water" this anti-Judaic text was suitable for a baptismal application—Prigent and Kraft, *Épître de Barnabé*, 161.

36. *Barnabas* has substituted "holy Sinai" (Ps 67:18, ixx), a desert mountain, for the LXX's Sion perhaps to sharpen the thrust at the Jews not really water. Prigent, *Les Testimonia dans le Christianisme primitif*, 91, discusses the linking of the quotations from Jeremiah and Isaiah.

37. Kraft, "Barnabas' Isaiah Text and the 'Testimony Book' Hypothesis," 346, discusses the use of Isa 16:1–2 in *Barn.* 11.3.

38. Lundberg, *La typologie baptismole dans l'ancienne église*, 179–84, on *Barn.* 11. So, also, Prigent, *Les Testimonia dans le Christianisme primitif*, 93–95. Reicke, *The Disobedient Spirits and Christian Baptism*, esp. 233, 243–47, discusses the association of the descent with baptism through the linking of the descent with the flood, notably in *Od. Sol.* 24. Wengst, *Tradition and Theologie des Barnabasbriefes*, 40 n. 77, finds Prigent's interpretation unconvincing.

notable, since it would be so suitable to the baptismal eucharist, and may be another indication that *Barnabas* is drawing on a collection made for another purpose that he applies to baptism. In sequence to a reference to the descent, *Barnabas* is saying that the faithful find in baptism the rock that gives salvation and strength against the overwhelming flood. There they see Christ, who was glorified in victory over Satan and death. The menacing water has becom the saving water.[39]

*Barnabas* 11.6–8 introduces a quotation from Psalm 1 that combines a reference to wood and water, the "tree planted by streams of water."[40] *Barnabas* takes "wood" (ξυλόν) as meaning the cross without explanation in 5.13; 8.5; 12.7 and in 8.1 and 12.1. Justin Martyr's collection of Old Testament types of the cross includes the rod of Moses that brought water from the rock and "the tree planted by streams of waters" in Ps 1:3.[41] It is an important aspect of *Barnabas*'s baptismal teaching that the wood and water go together. Psalm 1:3 was particularly appropriate for *Barnabas*, because of the association of water with life and blessings. Psalm 1:4–6 (11.7) then served the author's anti-Judaic purpose by its words of condemnation on the wicked" The author had the whole Psalm in mind, not just vv. 3–6, for he quotes v. 1 in 10.10 and picks up the word "Blessed" from 1.1 in 11.8, and the word "meditate" in Isa 33:18 (11.5) and Psalm 12 may provide the link between the Isaiah and Psalm quotations.

The application of the quotation from Psalm 1 in *Barn*. 11.8 specifically applies the wood to the cross and water to baptism, but also makes a transition to applyng the tree to the believer. The tree is both the cross and the believer, who is rooted in baptism and now produces fruit.[42] The

---

39. Prigent, *Les Testimonia dans le Christianisme primitif*, 95; Prigent and Kraft, *Épître de Barnabé*, 162. Cf. *Od. Sol.* 11.5 for being established on a rock.

40. Vesco, "La lecture du Psautier selon l'Épître de Barnabé," classifies the treatment of Psalm 1 by *Barnabas* as a typological reading of the Psalms (14–15, 26–27).

41. Justin Martyr, *Dial.* 86.1, 4. He takes "the righteous" as Christ, who "bybeing crucified on the tree and purifying us with water, has redeemed us" (86.5); cf. *Dial.* 138 for "water, faith, and wood" saving us (with reference to Noah and the flood). The Christian *Sib. Or.* 8.245–50, also connects the water and the cross; in the New Testament note John 19:34; 1 John 5:6. *Od. Sol.* 38.16–22 alludes to Ps 1:3–6 in a context apparently baptismal (38.17 combines the ideas of being established and planted, as in *Barn.* 11.5–6). Prigent, Les Testimonia, 96, affirms that Lundberg, *La typologie baptismole dans l'ancienne église*, 182, is correct that *Barnabas* depends on baptismal *testimonia* chosen to express the conceptions of baptism attested in the *Odes of Solomon*.

42. R. A. Kraft, *Barnabas and the Didache*, 117. Kraft refers to the comparison of a person to a tree in an unknown source cited in 1 *Clem.* 23.4 and 2 *Clem.* 11.3–4.

author uses "hope" in a way other Christians used faith.⁴³ It is an important word for him: appearing as a verb for *Barnabas*'s own hope for salvation (1.3) and hopes for his writing (17.1), in a citation (6.3), for hoping in God (16.1 [instead of in a building—the temple]; 19.7), and for hoping in Christ (6.9; 8.5; 12.2, 3; 12.7 way 16.1; 16.8 [his name] and specifically Christ's cross (11.8); as a noun with reference to the vain hope of the Jews (16.2) and to hope produced in others (11.8) or with its object specified as "life" (1.4, 6), as God (6.3), as Jesus (11.11), and as the faith of Jesus (4.8). The fruit produced "in its season" is eschatologically the future "reward" to the righteous,⁴⁴ but "for the present" the tree produces other converts. The baptized believer becomes the instrument for the conversion of others. The leaves of the tree are the words⁴⁵ spoken in faith and love that produce conversion and hope in others.⁴⁶ The word spoken through the mouth connects this passage with 16.9, where the "nnouth" is the opening of the door of the spiritual temple.⁴⁷

The quotation in *Barn.* 11.9 does not correspond exactly to any known text, so it may be a composite or an interpretative quotation.⁴⁸ There is a longer discussion of the land in 6.8–19, which moves from the land representing humanity assumed by Christ in the incarnation to Christians (the Church) as the new creation brought into the good land⁴⁹ to the hope for the promised inheritance of the eschatological paradise.⁵⁰

---

43. Kraft, *Barnabas and the Didache*, 30. The fundamental character of hope is noted by Wengst, *Tradition and Theologie des Barnabasbriefes*, 94, e.g., "weil die Hoffnung geradezu Grund und Ziel des Glaubens ist." He notes that faith for *Barnabas* includes obedience (93). Prostmeier, *Der Barnabasbrief*, 425–27, notes the importance of hope and its relation to faith.

44. "Probably the resurrection" according to Carleton Paget, *The Epistle of Barnabas*, 156.

45. In the interpretation in *Barn.* 11.8 the singular "leaf" of the quotation in 11.6 becomes plural. Kraft, *Barnabas and the Didache*, 117, notes that b. *Sukka* 21b also interprets "leaf" as words, namely the conversation of scholars, and compares *Od. Sol.* 12.2.

46. Faith, love, and hope appear together also in 1.4.

47. Is that opening an allusion to preaching (teaching) or to a confession of faith?

48. *2 Barn.* 61.7 is close, but the wording can be accounted for from the canonical references given in the translation. Prostmeier, *Der Barnabasbrief*, 427, notes other passages that may lie behind the wording "praised above every land."

49. Tertullian, *De res.* 26.11–13, rebukes the Jews for considering the soil of Judaea as holy land, whereas the land ought to be interpreted as the flesh of Christ and as those who put on Christ, who are now holy by the indwelling of the Holy Spirit and truly flow with milk and honey.

50. Prostmeier, *Der Barnabasbrief*, 258–81: the christological interpretation (6.9),

*Christian and Jewish Baptism according to the* Epistle of Barnabas

That sequence offers a parallel to the development in 11.9-11. The shift from "land" to "vessel" was easy because a [pottery] vessel was made of earth.[51] The phrase "vessel of the Spirit" occurs also in 7.3, where the reference is to the body of the Son of God offered as a "sacrifice for our sins."[52] The "vessel" in 11.9, however, would seem to refer to the body of those who receive the Holy Spirit in baptism,[53] but it is just possible (in view of the subsequent verses) that the reference is more specific, to those who speak the word of the Spirit. If the former is more likely, then the "praised land" of Jacob would also be the Christian community.[54] The land appears to be at once Christ and then again the Christian, even as the tree was both the wood of the cross and the righteous person. Such was the identification of the Christian with Christ.

This land, however, is also the eschatological land of paradise. *Barnabas* 11.10 gives a quotation that condenses Ezek 47:1–12. The land of 11.9 is a fertile ("praised") land, because it has a river and trees, connecting with the earlier quotation of Ps 1.3. The description now is of a restored paradise. Ezekiel promises "everyone will live" (v. 9); the phrase "will live forever" is found in Gen. 3.22. If the latter is indeed referred to, then the intention of the citation is to describe paradise.[55] The Christian eats the fruit denied to Adam.[56] The reference to eating may have eucharistic overtones but is primarily eschatological here.[57] *Odes of Solomon* 11.12–23 may serve as a commentary on *Barn.* 11.10.

The two parts of *Barn.* 11.11 correspond to 11.10, "to come up out of" the water and "whoever eats."[58] But the verse also summarizes the dis-

---

the soteriological and ecclesiological interpretation (6.10–16), and the eschatological interpretation (6.17–18); Wengst, *Tradition and Theologie des Barnabasbriefes*, 27–29, is similar: Christology (6.9–10), ecclesiology (6.11–16), and eschatolgy (6.17–19).

51. A σκεῦος, of course, could be made of other materials, but clay was the most common. Human beings were made from the earth (Gen 2:7; 3:19).

52. Cf. *Barn.* 21.8 for "vessel" as a reference to the human body.

53. Wengst, *Tradition and Theologie des Barnabasbriefes*, 41 n. 80, for the "vessel of the Spirit" in 11.9 as the community. Clement of Alexandria, *Strom.* 3.12.86 quotes *Barn.* 11.9 in reference to those dedicated to the Lord, whether married or celibate.

54. Prigent and Kraft, *Épître de Barnabé*, 165, take the land of Jacob as the promised land that one inherits in baptism. I agree, if the land is understood as the community. The shift to the land of paradise comes in 11.10.

55. Prigent and Kraft, *Épître de Barnabé*, 165. They refer to *Od. Sol.* 11.8, a typographical error for 11.18.

56. Lundberg, *La typologie baptismale dans l'ancienne église*, 184.

57. Prostmeier, *Der Barnabasbrief*, 429.

58. Ibid., 430–32.

cussion of baptism. To "go down into the water" picks up 11.8, and "fruit" reaches back to 11.6. *Barnabas* 11.11 twice repeats the promise, "whoever eats from these [the trees of v. 10] will live forever." To live forever was an important concept for *Barnabas*.[59] The eating is explained as hearing and believing.[60] This offers a significant Johannine parallel.[61] The trees of paradise have become again the Christians of 11.8, whose leaves are the words that bring conversion. The "hope in Jesus" in 11.11 is the equivalent of "hope in the cross" in 11.8. Baptized persons are cleansed of their sins, picking up the connection with forgiveness of sins announced in 11.1, and as newly planted trees they produce fruit in their heart.

As already noted, *Barn.* 6.7–19[62] permits an elaboration of what is said more briefly in 11.9–10 about the "land praised above every land." Baptismal motifs permit other connections to be made between *Barn.* 6 and *Barn.* 11. These motifs occur in a context that emphasizes Jesus' passion (6.7), his suffering in the flesh (6.9). The discussion of the land begins with the promised inheritance of a good land "flowing with milk and honey" (6.8, a composite quotation). Milk and honey were given to the newly baptized in the baptismal eucharist.[63] *Barnabas* relates the milk and honey both to the eschatological promised land (6.13) and the food of children (6.17), and so to the new creation and the new birth,[64] both of which are connected with baptism. He identifies the new creation, being remade (6.11, 14), with the forgiveness of sins by which one receives the soul of a child.[65] To enter the promised land implies a new creation based

---

59. It appears in 6.3 (a quotation from Isa 28.16 where the modification of the LXX's "shall not be put to shame" to "shall live forever" is significant) and 8.5 (where "those who hope on Jesus will live forever").

60. Kraft, *Barnabas and the Didache*, 117, refers to *Barn.* 10.11, "The Lord circumcised our ears and hearts in order that we might understand these things."

61. John 6:35, 45–58. The wider relations of *Barnabas* and John are discussed by Carleton Paget, *The Epistle of Barnabas*, 225–30.

62. Dahl, "La terre où coulent le lait et le miel selon Barnabé 6.8–19," defends the unity of the passage. Prigent, *Les Testimonia dans le Christianisme primitif*, 84–90, discusses the passage, describing it as a midrash.

63. Tertullian, *De cor.* 3, which associates this with the food of newborn children; Hippolytus, *Ap. Trad.* 23.2, which connects the practice, as does *Barnabas*, with both the food of children and with the promised land. *Od. Sol.* 4.10 is often taken as baptismal.

64. Prostmeier, *Der Barnabasbrief*, 278–79.

65. Baptism as a rebirth is common in early Christian literature: Justin, *1 Apol.* 61; Theophilus, *Ad Autol.* 2.16; Irenaeus, *Adv. haer.* 3.17.1–2; Irenaeus, *Dem.* 3; Clement of Alexandria, *Strom.* 4.25; Tertullian, *De bapt.* 13.

## *Christian and Jewish Baptism according to the* Epistle of Barnabas

on forgiveness of sins (11.1, 11), and the new creation consists in a change of heart.[66] The Lord's incarnation made possible the change of the stony heart into a heart of flesh (6.14), which then becomes a fit dwelling place for the Spirit of God and so his temple (6.15), with perhaps the added overtone that the temple of stone is replaced by the temple of the heart. The collective hearts of those transformed by the Holy Spirit are a Church, where God is worshipped, true temple instead of the physical building.[67] The Church is further described as "brothers and sisters" (6.15), "the saints," the "good land," and the "assembly" of God's people (6.16).

The theme of the true spiritual temple connects *Barn.* 6 with *Barn.* 16. The remade people are the house [temple] of God" (16.1). The three parts of the promise quoted in 16.6—to build a temple gloriously in the name of the Lord—are interpreted in 16.7-9.[68] This building in his name takes place when hearts are purified by the forgiveness of sin (16.8), a forgiveness associated as in *Barn.* 11 with hope and being re-created. There is a strong emphasis on newness in 16.8—"new," "created again," "from the beginning." Idolatry and demons are expelled from the soul, and God then takes up his dwelling place in this spiritual temple (16.7-10; cf. 6.15). The passage quoted above begins with the individual persons as the dwelling place of God (16.7-8), but ends with the temple as something into which the individual is led (16.9), perhaps the collective group, the Church.[69] "The word of his faith" (16.9), if not a reference to confession of faith, repeats the emphasis in *Barnabas* on the necessity of speaking the word of the Lord in order to effect faith and conversion.[70]

Although the author of *Barnabas* was primarily drawing a contrast between Jewish washings and Christian baptism as part of his attempt to demonstrate the superiority of the Christian system over the Jewish system, he says enough to permit some inferences about the practice of

---

66. Prigent, *Les Testimonia dans le Christianisme primitif*, 85, 89. For baptism as a new creation in *Barnabas*, see also *Tradition and Theologie des Barnabasbriefes*, 86.

67. Ps 21:23 (LXX) is quoted also in Heb 2:12. The motifs in *Barn.* 6 are in the New Testament: milk for the new Christian (1 Pet 2:2 [cf. 1.23]); new creation (2 Cor 5:17); a responsive heart (2 Cor 3:3; Heb 3:8; 8:10); and a new temple (John 2:21; 1 Cor 3:16; 6:19).

68. Prostmeier, *Der Barnabasbrief*, 516.

69. Again we note the same themes in the New Testament: a spiritual temple in which God dwells associated with the name of the Lord (Eph 2:18-22); faith in the name (Acts 3:16—a healing); hearts purified by hope or faith (Acts 15:9; cf. Jas 1:21); opposition of the temple of God to demons and idolatry (2 Cor 6:15-16); re-creation (2 Cor 5:19); and forgiveness of sins (Acts 2:38).

70. *Barn.* 5.9; 8.3; 11.8, 11; cf. Rom 10:8, 14-17; 1 Tim 4:6.

baptism and says even more about his understanding of the meaning of baptism.[71] The express statement that "we go down into the water" and "we come up" (11.8, 11) is sufficient to indicate immersion.[72] This statement supports an implication of immersion in the association of baptism with Jesus' *descensus inferos* and receiving hidden treasures (11.4). Since *Barnabas* says much about "living" and "flowing" water, the immersion was presumably administered in running water.[73] Baptism was a response to the preaching of the gospel (5.9; 8.3; 11.8, 11). The emphasis on hope (= faith) (11.8, 11) suggests a confession of faith made at baptism, and references to the name (16.8—temple built in the name of the Lord and hope placed in his name) may refer to baptism administered in the name of the Lord.[74] *Barnabas* 16.9 refers to repentance, but there is no indication that it was ritualized this early in a verbal renunciation of Satan[75] (in spite of the next phrase referring to opening the mouth). The same verse mentions the "word of faith," which might be the preaching of the word (the following phrase speaks of "the calling of promise") or could be a confession of faith.[76] The indications point to the practice of believer's baptism.

*Barnabas* highlights the forgiveness of sins as the distinctive feature of Christian baptism (11.1). By baptism one is purified of all uncleanness (11.11; 16.7-8). This forgiveness effects a person's re-creation (6.11, 13; 16.8), a prominent theme. The new creation consists in God dwelling within (6.14; 16.8-9). This re-creation is further associated with rebirth and entrance into the promised land (6.11, 13, 16-17). By baptism one is transformed into the temple of God (6.15; 16.7-10). The association of

---

71. For sources contemporary with *Barnabas* on the practice and meaning of baptism, see Ferguson, *Early Christians Speak*, 29-64.

72. For the words καταβαίνω and αναβαίνω in reference to baptism, note Acts 8:38-39; Hermas, *Sim.* 9.16.2, 4, 6 (= 93.2, 4, 6); Cyril of Jerusalem, *Catech.* 3.12. The note in Benoît and Munier, *Le Baptême dans l'Église ancienne (Ier-IIIe siècles)*, 19 n. 4, that "Les termes: descendre—remonter, n'impliquent pas obligatoirement un rite d'immersion" is overly defensive.

73. Prostmeier, *Der Barnabasbrief*, 430, with reference to the flowing water of paradise in 11.10 and the statements in 11.2, 5, and 6 (cf. 1.3). *Did.* 7.2-3 gave preference to running water.

74. The forgiveness of sins is associated with the name of the Lord in 16.8; cf. Acts 2:38.

75. Attested in *Ap. Trad.* 21.9. Nor does the removal of a person from the realm of idolatry with a heart full of demons in 16.7 indicate exorcisms, which became a part of the later baptismal ritual, *Ap. Trad.* 20.3; 21.10.

76. See my comments preceding n. 47 and those preceding n. 70 for a similar uncertainty in regard to the door of the temple interpreted as the opening of the mouth.

ideas, furthermore, suggests that baptism brings one into the covenant of Christ, "sealed in our hearts in the hope of his faith" (4.8), so that one can describe this "covenant of Jesus the Beloved" as a covenant of forgiveness.[77]

The language of "sealing" reminds us of one thing baptism did not mean to *Barnabas*: it was not associated with circumcision.[78] The counterpart of circumcision in the flesh is circumcision of the ears and the heart by the Holy Spirit (9.1–9; 10.12). Baptism introduces one not only into the Church (6.16) but also into the eschatological kingdom (11.11). Protected from death and danger (11.4–5), the baptized person partakes of spiritual delights and is the means of bringing words of salvation to others (11.6, 8), That person, as a spiritual temple (4.11), will live a life of faith, love, reverence, and hope (11.8, 11). Preeminently, baptism is associated with life (11.2) and the promise of eternal life (11.10–11). This is so because of its association with the passion and cross of Jesus (5.1; 6.7; 11.1, 8; 12.1–11).

Most students of *Barnabas* find much traditional material in the work, but he took an original view on the covenant and exclusive Christian appropriation of it. What can we say about his baptismal doctrine? Enough parallels are referred to in the notes to suggest that much is traditional. On the other hand, certain emphases and ways of putting the material together are the author's own.

---

77. So Hvalvik, *The Struggle, for Scripture and Covenant*, 151, 153–54, calling attention to "sealed," "hope of his faith," and "the Beloved" as baptismal terminology. Note that the new covenant of Jer 31:31–34 involved the forgiveness of sins.

78. Benoît, *Le baptême chrétien au second siècle*, 57. The mention of circumcision in 10.12 followed immediately by the discussion of baptism in ch. 11 may suggest an association of circumcision with baptism, but if so, it would be because circumcision and baptism were part of Jewish proselyte initiation. Justin Martyr too mentions baptism following references to circumcision (*Dial.* 19.2; 29.1), but for him and for *Barnabas* there is no parallel between circumcision and baptism, each having its own separate counterpart in the respective Christian and Jewish institutions: Ferguson, "Spiritual Circumcision in Early Christianity," 487 and 493 on *Barnabas* and 493–94 on Justin. Hvalvik, *The Struggle for Scripture and Covenant*, 189–90, observes that circumcision of the heart equaled the gift of the Holy Spirit, and since the latter came in baptism there was a natural progression of thought from circumcision to baptism.

# 4

# Baptism according to Origen

D AVID WRIGHT HAS MADE important contributions to the study of historical theology, but he is especially known for his studies of baptism, particularly infant baptism. It seems appropriate in honoring him, therefore, to study an early Christian author who had a rich theology of baptism and made significant comments in regard to infant baptism—I refer to Origen. His voluminous writings contain abundant references to the subject of baptism.[1] I omit those bearing primarily on the ceremony of baptism, since they are incidental to other concerns and can be used to construct the liturgy known to Origen only by appealing to information provided in other sources.[2] Even with this limitation, the number of references requires some selectivity.

Origen sets the early Christian theology of baptism in his own distinctive theological system. He placed baptism, according to Crouzel, "like the other sacraments, in a series of symbolisms, corresponding to the triple distinction of the Old Testament as shadow, the temporal Gospel as image, and the eternal Gospel as reality."[3] Crouzel, and also Daniélou, explained that for Origen the baptism of John belonged with the Old Testament symbols as a shadow, baptism in the church is the image, and the

---

1. Auf der Maur and Waldram, "*Illuminatio Verbi Divini—Confessio Fidei—Gratia Baptismi*," rich in bibliographical references and references in Origen; Blanc, "Le Baptême d'après Origène"; Crouzel, "Origène et la structure du sacrement," 83–92, on baptism.

2. Kretschmar, "Die Geschichte des Taufgottesdienstes in der alter Kirche," 135–36.

3. Crouzel, *Origen*, 223.

*Baptism according to Origen*

eschatological baptism of fire and the final conforming to the resurrection of Christ are mystery.[4] Joseph Trigg understands Origen to analyze baptism in the present age of the church according to a material and a spiritual experience: water baptism for the simple believer is the beginning of the process of sanctification, and the baptism of the Holy Spirit is the higher spiritual baptism that distinguishes the spiritual Christian.[5]

Expanding and modifying these schemes, I will note the Old Testament passages in which Origen found baptismal teaching, look at the relation of water and Spirit baptism through the contrast of John's and Jesus' baptisms, add a consideration of the eschatological baptism of fire, move to descriptions of the meaning of baptism, including the place of infant baptism in his thought, consider martyrdom as a baptism of blood, and conclude with the relation in his thought of faith and repentance to baptism. We begin with the use of Old Testament passages to teach lessons about Christian baptism.

## OLD TESTAMENT FORESHADOWINGS OF BAPTISM

Origen's *Commentary on John* devotes a section to the Old Testament shadows (or types) which in Origen's allegorical exegesis become identified with Christian baptism (6.43 [26].226—48 [29].249). Origen begins the discussion by invoking Paul's comments in 1 Cor 10:1-4 about crossing the Red Sea as justification for a spiritual interpretation of Old Testament references to water, especially the Jordan river (6.43 [26].227).

Israel's crossing the Red Sea was a popular type of baptism in the early church.[6] Origen's fullest treatment of it occurs, understandably, in

---

4. Ibid., 225; Daniélou, *Origène*, 71-72, for the purely figurative baptisms of the Old Testament and John, Christian baptism as the reality signified by the Old Testament figures and itself a figure of the reality to come, and baptism with fire by which Christians are purified before they enter glory. Crouzel, "Origène et la Structure," 82-83, points out that μυστήριον for Origen refers to the spiritual, celestial, eschatological reality, and σύμβολον refers to the sensible image of that reality, a distinction not observed in Rufinus' Latin translation.

5. Trigg, "A Fresh Look at Origen's Understanding of Baptism." He perhaps exaggerates the difference, especially when he describes water baptism and the later baptism of the Holy Spirit as two rites of initiation (963—cf. Origen, *Commentary on Ephesians* 4:5, critical of the Valentinians for having two baptisms). The main thrust of Trigg's article is to distinguish two strands in Origen's thought: the perfectionist, according to which baptism carries an obligation not to sin, and the pastoral, in which baptism is the beginning and source of divine gifts but not their fulfillment.

6. Daniélou, *From Shadows to Reality*, 175-201, on "The Departure from Egypt

his *Homilies on Exodus.* "What the Jews supposed to be a crossing of the sea, Paul [in 1 Cor 10:1–4] calls a baptism; what they supposed to be a cloud, Paul asserts is the Holy Spirit" (5.1).[7] This conjunction of water and Holy Spirit, Origen says, Paul wanted to be understood in a similar manner to what the Lord taught in John 3:5, which he also quotes. The understanding of John 3:5 as the literal water of baptism was already standard by Origen's time, but in view of his usual spiritualizing exegesis is to be noted. The crossing of the Red Sea on dry land by Israel is a lesson for Christians: "That you also who are baptized in Christ, in water and the Holy Spirit, might know that the Egyptians [spiritual evils] are following you and wish to recall you to their service" (5.5).[8]

> These attempt to follow, but you descend into the water and come out unimpaired, the filth of sins having been washed away. You ascend "a new man" [Eph 2:15; 4:24] prepared to "sing a new song" [Isa 42:10]. But the Egyptians who follow you are drowned in the abyss. (5.5)[9]

The description of descending into the water and ascending is drawn from Christian baptismal practice and not from the narrative, for Israel did not actually enter the water, and would seem to reflect the practice of immersion. Baptism washes away sins so that one becomes a new person, and demonic forces are drowned in the waters.[10]

Origen's special interest in the *Commentary on John* is Israel's crossing the Jordan (Joshua 3) as an equivalent to baptism.[11] He paraphrases Paul's words about crossing the Red Sea as applicable to crossing the Jordan: "'I do not want you to be ignorant, brothers, that our fathers all

---

and Christian Initiation" in early Christian literature (185–87 on Origen's use of the motif).

7. Translation by Heine, trans., *Origen: Homilies on Genesis and Exodus,* 276. Elsewhere Origen identifies the Sea as baptism, the cloud as the Holy Spirit, the manna as the Word of God, the lamb as the Savior, and the blood as his passion (*Commentary on the Song of Songs* 2:8 on Song 1:11). He makes the following contrast: Israel's baptism was in the salty and bitter Red Sea, but the baptism of Jesus is superior, being in a river whose waters were sweet and drinkable (*Commentary on John* 6.44 [26]:229–30).

8. Ibid., 283.

9. Ibid., 283–84.

10. The contemporary application of the exodus occurs elsewhere in Origen: "Thus it is fitting, after the parting of the Red Sea, that is, after the grace of baptism, for the carnal vices of our old habits to be removed from us by means of our Lord Jesus, so that we can be free from the Egyptian reproaches" (*Homilies on Joshua* 5:9).

11. Daniélou, *From Shadows to Reality,* 261–75, on the crossing of the Jordan as a type of baptism (Origen is the principal representative of this interpretation—262–70).

passed through the Jordan, and all were baptized [ἐβαπτίσαντο] into Jesus in the Spirit and in the river'" (6.44 [26].228). This interpretation was facilitated by the equivalence in Greek of the names Jesus and Joshua.[12]

Origen develops the baptismal interpretation of Israel crossing the Jordan especially in his *Homilies on Joshua*. He connected the exodus from Egypt with the crossing of the Jordan by likening the former to entering the catechumenate and the latter to baptism that introduces one into the promised land (4.1).[13] In this passage the Latin translation of Rufinus speaks of the "sacrament [*sacramentum*] of baptism" and the "mystic [*mysticum*] font of baptism." *Sacramentum* and *mysticum* probably represent the Greek word for mystery (μυστήριον) that since Clement of Alexandria was coming into use and became the technical word in the Greek church for what the Latins came to call the sacraments.[14] In the *Homilies on Joshua* 5.1 Christians are the army of Christ, and "sacrament" is used of the soldiers' oath, implicitly compared to baptismal vows. And Origen warns of the battles that await after baptism (5.2).

The survey of events associated with the river Jordan in the *Commentary on John* next mentions Elijah and Elisha crossing the Jordan (2 Kgs 2:8, 14). Although the crossing was on dry ground, Origen calls this event too, on the basis of 1 Cor 10:2, a baptism. "Having been baptized [βαπτισάμενος], Elijah had become better prepared for his assumption" into heaven (6.46 [27].238).

Next, Origen relates the story of Naaman, the Syrian general with leprosy (2 Kings 5), who was commanded by the prophet Elisha to wash (λοῦσαι) seven times in the Jordan (6.47 [28].242-245). Origen makes more explicit the baptismal interpretation of the event in his *Homilies on Luke*. Giving a spiritual interpretation of leprosy, Origen says:

> Men covered with the filth of leprosy are cleansed in the mystery of baptism by the spiritual Elijah, our Lord and Savior. To you he says, 'Get up and go into the Jordan and wash, and your flesh will be restored to you' [2 Kings 5:10] . . . When [Naaman] washed, he fulfilled the mystery of baptism, 'and his flesh became like the

---

12. "The Jesus who succeeded Moses was a type of Jesus the Christ who succeeded the dispensation through the law with the gospel proclamation" (6.44 [26]:229).

13. A similar interpretation in *Homilies on Numbers* 26.4.

14. Marsh, "The Use of ΜΥΣΤΗΡΙΟΝ," who notes Clement's frequent use of mystery terminology but rarely with reference to the sacraments; Echle, "Sacramental Initiation as Christian Mystery."

flesh of a child.' Which child? The one that is born 'in the washing of rebirth' [regeneration—Titus 3:5] in Christ Jesus. (33.5)[15]

Origen concluded his survey of Old Testament references to the Jordan (and other rivers) with this summary of the benefits of baptism based on these passages:

> Those who come to be washed [λούσασθαι] in the Son put away the reproach of Egypt [Josh. 5:9], become prepared for assumption [to heaven] (2 Kgs 2:12), are purified from the foulest leprosy (2 Kgs 5:9), receive a double share of grace gifts (2 Kgs 2:9), and are made ready for the reception of the Holy Spirit, since the spiritual dove does not fly over any other river. (*Commentary on John* 6.48 [29].250)

A common type of baptism in the early church was the flood in Noah's day (Genesis 6–9).[16] Origen cites Gen 6:14 as spoken not only concerning the time of the flood but also "concerning the mystery of baptism. For as the apostle Peter says, just as at that time Noah was saved out of the flood, so also now by means of a similar figure those who believe shall be saved through baptism" (1 Pet 3:20–21).[17] The strong assertion of salvation through baptism is related to Noah's being saved out of the waters of the flood.

Origen could also give a baptismal interpretation to passages that were not a part of the church's usual baptismal typology. Origen understood the command to wash with water the entrails and feet of the animal for the burnt offering (Lev 1:9) as "announcing the sacrament of baptism by a figurative prophecy" (*Homilies on Leviticus* 1.4.6).[18] He explains, "For he who cleanses his conscience washes 'the inward parts'; he washes his feet who receives the fullness of the sacrament."[19] The connection of water baptism with cleansing the conscience is to be noted (cf. Heb 10:22; 1 Pet 3:21). Origen relates the latter phrase to Jesus' washing his disciples' feet

---

15. Translation from Lienhard, trans., *Origen: Homilies on Luke*, 136.

16. Daniélou, *From Shadows to Reality*, 85–102, who does not cite the passage we quote on this theme, perhaps because of its brevity, but does develop Origen's historical, mystical, and moral interpretation of the ark in his *Homilies on Genesis*—104–10.

17. *Commentary on Romans* 3.1.11. Translation from Scheck, trans., *Origen: Commentary on the Epistle to the Romans*, 184.

18. Translation by Barkley, *Origen: Homilies on Leviticus 1–16*, 36. Without mentioning baptism, Origen seems to allude to it in his comments on Num 31:21–24 (purifying booty with water and washing clothes), quoting Job 14:4 about no one is pure—*Homilies on Numbers* 25.6.

19. Ibid.

(John 13:8, 10); I take his words as meaning the complete effectiveness of the washing in reaching even the extremities.

## THE BAPTISM OF JOHN THE BAPTIST AND JESUS

Origen placed the baptism performed by John in the category of Old Testament washings and frequently contrasted it with the baptism administered by Jesus.[20] Thus, according to the *Commentary on Romans*, Jesus received John's baptism, not "the baptism which is in Christ but . . . the one which is in the law."[21] Origen understands this to be the meaning of Jesus' words in Matthew 3:15 about being baptized in order to fulfill all righteousness. "In that passage he is making known that John's baptism was a fulfillment of the old [law], not a beginning of the new [law]."[22] That is why in Acts 19:3–5 those baptized with John's baptism were rebaptized in the name of Jesus.

Origen paraphrases the words of John the Baptist in Matthew 3:11: "He will deluge you bountifully with the gifts of the Spirit, since my baptism does not give any spiritual grace (well, yes, the 'forgiveness of sins'). But he will forgive you and will give you the Spirit abundantly" (*Commentary on Matthew*, frg. 49). At his baptism Jesus received the Spirit. Quoting John 1:33, Origen comments that at his baptism Jesus "received the Holy Spirit who remained on him so that he could baptize those coming to him in that very same abiding Spirit."[23] In spite of the contrasts he made between John's and Jesus' baptism, Origen had a positive appreciation of John's baptism. He stated that the Savior sanctified John's baptism.[24]

The *Commentary on John* contrasts John's baptism with Christ's. "Christ does not baptize in water, but his disciples. He reserves for himself to baptize in the Holy Spirit and fire" (6.23 [13].125).

Origen interprets John the Baptist's testimony to Jesus (according to Matt. 3:11) to include a further contrast of the Baptist's baptism as preparatory (improving people by repentance) with Jesus' baptism:

20. Blanc, "Le Baptême d'après Origène," 116 for references on John's baptism as corporeal, having to do with the senses, and visible, and Jesus' baptism as incorporeal, having to do with the intellect, and invisible.

21. *Commentary on Romans* 5.8.6. Scheck, trans., *Origen: Commentary on the Epistle to the Romans*, 356.

22. Ibid. with my addition of law; alternatively the contrast of old and new could refer to baptisms.

23. *Commentary on John* 6.42 (25):220.

24. *Homilies on Luke* 7:1.

> [Jesus'] baptism is not bodily, since the Holy Spirit fills the one who repents and a more divine fire obliterates everything material and utterly destroys everything earthly, not only from the one possessing it but also from the one who hears those who have it. (6.32 [17].162)

The Holy Spirit and fire here appear to be two aspects of one experience in the present.[25]

Shortly thereafter Origen comments on the distinction and correlation of water and Spirit. The passage sets forth themes characteristic of Origen's baptismal thought: water, Spirit, invocation of the Trinity, the characteristics required of the one baptized, and the grace given in baptism.[26] I quote:

> [T]he bath [λουτρόν] through water is a symbol of the purification of the soul, which is washed clean from all filth of evil, and is in itself the beginning and source of divine gifts to the one who surrenders to the divine power at the invocations of the worshipful Trinity.
> ... [According to the Acts of the Apostles] the Spirit resided so manifestly in those being baptized, since the water prepared the way for the Spirit to those who sincerely approached. (6.33 [17].166–167)

The baptismal bath of water is presented here as an effective symbol. The washing of the body is a symbol of the cleansing of the soul, but it also effects what it symbolizes, being "in itself" the origin of divine gifts. The water, however, is effective only to the one who comes in faith, yielding to the divine power, and in conjunction with the invocation of the divine names. The water thus prepared for the indwelling of the Spirit, but one could receive outward baptism without an inward effect.

Origen, however, did not divorce the water from the work of the Spirit, while clearly distinguishing them. Origen notes that John's baptism was inferior to Jesus' baptism on the basis of Acts 19:2–5 (6.33 [17].168).

> The bath of regeneration [ἀναγεννήσεως] did not come with John but with Jesus through his disciples. It is called the "bath of regeneration" [παλιγγενεσίας λουτρόν] which takes place

---

25. Below one of Origen's interpretations of Luke 3:15–16 combines them eschatologically.

26. Blanc, "Le Baptême d'après Origène," 116; she notes on 117 that along with the accent placed by Origen on the spiritual reality there is the visible water in which baptism occurs.

> with "renewal of the Holy Spirit" [Tit 3:5], which Spirit is even now "borne above the water" [Gen. 1:2], since it is from God but does not intervene in everyone after the water. (6.33 [17].169)

A distinction between the Holy Spirit effecting regeneration in water baptism and his being later imparted is made in Origen's *Commentary on 1 Corinthians* 1:17. With reference to Acts 8:12–16, he says, "Philip baptized in water those being regenerated from water and the Holy Spirit, but Peter (baptized) in the Holy Spirit."

Sometimes Origen understands being baptized in the Spirit as occurring in Christian water baptism.

> The one who has died to sin and is truly baptized into the death of Christ, and is buried with him through baptism into death [Rom 6:3–4], he is the one who is truly baptized in the Holy Spirit and with the water from above [John 3:5].[27]

At other times the Spirit is given after baptism.

Hence, although Origen recognized a distinction between water baptism and Spirit baptism (and gifts of the Spirit), we should not overlook those passages where he also links the working of the Spirit with baptism.

## THE ESCHATOLOGICAL BAPTISM OF FIRE

It is not my intention here to cover all of Origen's (controversial) discussions of eschatological fire, only to mention how he brought baptismal language to bear on its purifying effect.[28] In the *Commentary on John* Origen says that as Jesus is a drink—to some water, to others wine, and to others blood—so he is "a baptism of water and Spirit, and fire, and to some even of blood" (6.43 [26].223).[29]

Origen in his *Homilies on Jeremiah* distinguishes the baptism in the Holy Spirit and the baptism in fire. "The holy person is baptized in the Holy Spirit, but the person who after believing and being counted worthy

---

27. *Commentary on Romans* 5.8.3; Schreck, trans., *Origen: Commentary on the Epistle to the Romans*, 355.

28. On the debt of sin for which even the righteous need purification after this life, see *Homilies on Leviticus* 15:3; *Against Celsus* 4:13; 5:15; *On First Principles* 2.10.4; cf. *Commentary on Matthew* 15:23 cited below. Carl-Martin Edsman, *Le baptême du feu*, dicusses the topic.

29. In the next paragraph he cites in support of the baptismal interpretation of martyrdom Luke 12:50 and 1 John 5:8 ("Spirit, water, and blood")—6:43 (26):224. See further my treatment of martyrdom as a baptism below.

of the Holy Spirit sins again is washed [λουει] in 'fire.'" "Blessed is the one who is baptized in the Holy Spirit and has no need of the baptism that comes from fire. Triply to be pitied is the one who has need of being baptized in fire" (2.3.1–2).

In the *Homilies on Luke* Origen expresses the view that even the righteous will need a "sacrament to wash and cleanse us even after resurrection from the dead" (14.6).[30] He sets forth the three baptisms in water, Spirit, and fire in his comments on Luke 3:15–16, with primary attention to the baptism in fire:

> If anyone desires to pass over to paradise after departing this life, and needs cleansing, Christ will baptize him in this river [of fire] and send him across to the place he longs for. But whoever does not have the sign of earlier baptisms, him Christ will not baptize in the fiery bath. For, it is fitting that one should be baptized first in "water and the Spirit." Then, when he comes to the fiery river, he can show that he preserved the bathing in water and the Spirit. (*Homilies on Luke* 24.2)[31]

Later, recalling this earlier interpretation, he offers an alternative view in which the fire is judgment and not purification:

> If you are holy, you will be baptized with the Holy Spirit. If you are a sinner, you will be plunged into fire. One and the same baptism will be turned into condemnation and fire for the unworthy and for sinners; but to those who are holy and have been turned to the Lord in total faith, the grace of the Holy Spirit, and salvation, will be given. (Ibid., 26.3)[32]

Baptism with the Holy Spirit and fire is here the same baptism, but with opposite effects depending on the character of the person receiving it.

---

30. Translation of Jerome's Latin by Lienhard, trans., *Origen: Homilies on Luke*, 59. In view of this statement, the subsequent words about the "rebirth of baptism" and "purified by spiritual rebirth" may apply the language of rebirth to the eschatological baptism.

31. Ibid., 103–4. *Origen's Commentary on Matthew* 15:23 appears to give another interpretation, placing the baptism of the Holy Spirit and fire at the water baptism. After citing the equivalent Matthaean text (Matt 3:11), Origen continues: "In the regeneration through the bath [Titus 3:5] we were buried with Christ, for according to the apostle, 'We were buried with him through baptism' [Rom 6:4]. In the regeneration of the bath through fire and Spirit we become conformed "to the body of his glory" [Phil 3:21] when Christ "sits upon the throne of his glory" [Matt 19:28]."

32. Ibid., 110.

## SIGNIFICANCE OF BAPTISM

Origen's treatment of the baptism of Jesus in his *Homilies on Luke* sets forth the basic gifts of Christian baptism—forgiveness of sins and the abiding of the Holy Spirit.

> The Lord was baptized. The heavens were opened and "the Holy Spirit came down upon him" [Luke 3:22]. A voice from the heavens thundered and said, "This is my beloved Son, in whom I am pleased" [ibid.]. We should say that heaven was opened at the baptism of Jesus and for the plan of forgiving sins. These are not the sins of him "who had committed no sin, nor was deceit found in his mouth" [1 Pet 2:22]. The heavens were opened and the Holy Spirit came down for the forgiveness of the whole world's sins. After the Lord "ascended on high, leading captivity captive" [Eph. 4:8], he gave us the Spirit. The Spirit had come to him, and he gave the Spirit at the time of his resurrection when he said, "Receive the Holy Spirit. If you forgive anyone's sins, they will be forgiven" [John 20:22–23]. (27.5)[33]

By Origen's time the association of baptism with the forgiveness of sins was well established, and Origen often repeats this purpose for baptism. Earlier in these *Homilies on Luke* he applied the description of John's baptism in Luke 3:3 to Christian baptism. He begins with his etymology of "Jordan" and proceeds to a ringing invitation to catechumens to repent:

> "Jordan" means "descending." But the "descending" river of God, one running with a vigorous force, is the Lord our Savior. Into him we are baptized with true water, saving water. Baptism is also preached "for the remission of sins." Come, catechumens! Repent, so that baptism for the remission of sins will follow. He who stops sinning receives baptism "for the remission of sins." For, if anyone comes sinning to the washing, he does not receive forgiveness of sins. (21.4)[34]

The premise of Origen's exhortation to catechumens to cease sinning is the association of baptism with forgiveness. He states succinctly the purpose of baptism: "You have come to Jesus and through the grace of baptism have attained the remission of sins."[35]

33. Lienhard, trans., *Origen: Homilies on Luke*, 114.

34. *Homilies on Luke* 21.3–4. For this paragraph I quote the translation from the Latin by Lienhard, trans., *Origen*, 89–90, except that I have substituted "repent" based on the shorter Greek [μετανοειν] text.

35. *Homilies on Joshua* 15:7; Bruce, trans., *Origen: Homilies on Joshua*, 150.

With the forgiveness of sins is associated the idea of cleansing. The command to Israel to wash their garments before receiving the law at Mt. Sinai (Exod 19:10–11) means that "Your garments were washed once when you came to the grace of baptism; you were purified in body; you were cleansed from all filth of flesh and spirit."[36]

The words "grace of baptism" in this quotation appear to have been a set phrase with Origen, appearing with great frequency. For example, to come to the "grace of baptism" is to be baptized into Christ's death (Rom 6:3).[37]

Receiving the Holy Spirit also was closely linked with baptism. "You who desire to receive holy baptism and to obtain the grace of the Spirit."[38] The fact that the "sons of God" are led by the Spirit of God (Rom. 8:14) makes it fitting that the Savior, "Son of God in the proper sense," after his baptism was full of the Holy Spirit and led by the Spirit (Luke 4:1).[39] The way in which Origen speaks, bringing the possession of the Spirit into his references to baptism even when his main concern is another subject, shows how natural the connection was in his mind. Nevertheless, the connection was not automatic. In addressing both catechumens and the faithful, Origen observed that there were those washed in water but not at the same time in the Holy Spirit and catechumens who were not strangers to the Holy Spirit. He cited as scriptural examples Cornelius, who before descending into the water received the Holy Spirit (Acts 10:44), and Simon, who received baptism but who approached grace with hypocrisy and was deprived of the gift of the Holy Spirit (Acts 8:13–19).[40]

Origen, moreover, frequently drew on the language of being begotten again, or born anew, based on John 3:3, 5. This experience derives from Jesus himself. By his baptism Jesus took on "the mystery of the second birth . . . He did this so that you too could wipe away your former birth and be

---

36. *Homilies on Exodus* 11:7; Heine, trans., *Origen: Homilies on Genesis and Exodus*, 365. See the quotation of *Commentary on John* 6:23 (17):166 above on the water purifying the soul. Or, again, "Through the grace of baptism you have become a clean animal"—*Homilies on Leviticus* 9:4:4; Barkley, *Origen: Homilies on Leviticus* 9:4:4. Cf. ibid., 8:3:5. Another imagery is that of the redemption of humanity through the waters of baptism—*Commentary on the Song of Songs* 2:10 on Song 1:13.

37. *Homilies on Leviticus* 2:4:6; some other passages are *On First Principles* 1:3:2; *Homilies on Exodus* 8:4 and 5; 10:4; *Commentary on Romans* 3:1:12.

38. *Homilies on Leviticus* 6:2:5; Barkley, trans., *Origen: Homilies on Leviticus*, 118.

39. *Homilies on Luke* 29:2; Lienhard, trans., *Origen: Homilies on Luke*, 119.

40. *Homilies in Numbers* 3:1.

born in a second rebirth."[41] Through a second birth the Lord Jesus Christ "wiped away the blemish of the first birth." Since it was instruction as well as birth that brought the dominion of death on human beings, Christ commanded his disciples to teach and to baptize (Matt 28:19), "so that even our mortal birth would be changed by the rebirth of baptism, and the teaching of godliness might shut out the teaching of godlessness."[42] Origen interprets John 3:3, 5 and Rom 6:3–4 as equivalent. The first earthly birth is not repeated, but a new birth from above is received.

> The one who has died to sin and is truly baptized into the death of Christ and is buried with him through baptism into death, he is the one who is truly baptized in the Holy Spirit and with the water from above.[43]

Hence, a person becomes an infant in baptism.[44]

Origen treated the new birth of 1 Pet 1:23 (ἀναγέννησις) and John 3:5 as equivalent to the regeneration (παλιγγενεσία) of Titus 3:5.[45]

> The sacrament [σύμβολον] through water given those who have hoped in Christ, which is called the "washing of regeneration." For what does rebirth signify if not the beginning of another birth?[46]

Indeed the "bath [or washing] of regeneration" was Origen's favorite phrase for baptism, not only in passages commenting on παλιγγενεσία.[47]

---

41. *Homilies on Luke* 28.4; Lienhard, *Origen: Homilies on Luke*, 116–17, with the note that the redundancy is in the Latin.

42. *Commentary on Romans* 5.2.11; Scheck, trans., *Origen: Commentary on the Epistle to the Romans*, 333.

43. *Commentary on Romans* 8.5.3; Scheck, trans., *Origen: Commentary on the Epistle to the Romans*, 355.

44. *Homilies on Joshua* 9.4; *Homilies on Exodus* 10.4.

45. See *Commentary on John* 6:33 (17):169, quoted above.

46. *On the Pasch* 4.29–36; translation from Daly, trans., *Origen: Treatise on the Passover and Dialogue with Heraclides*, 29. See also *Commentary on Matthew* 13.27; *Commentary on Matthew* 15.23 (in which note the association of Rom 6:4 with Titus 3:5; the passage also introduces the Old Testament verses (Job 14:4–5; Ps 51:5) used in support of the infant stain that justified baptizing infants.

47. *Homilies on Jeremiah* 16.5.2. A catena fragment (26) of Origen on Jeremiah interprets "water" not with the word baptism, as might be expected, but as "the bath of regeneration." Origen the realist recognized that those who received the "heavenly grace" in baptism, might nonetheless change back to the bitterness of sin—*Homilies on Joshua* 4.2—or fall into the servitude of sin—ibid., 10.3.

Origen also used the idea of dying and rising with Christ from Rom 6:3–4 to interpret the meaning of baptism.

> (T)eaching through these things that if someone has first died to sin, he has necessarily been buried with Christ in baptism. But if the person does not die to sin beforehand, he cannot be buried with Christ. For no one who is still alive is ever buried. But if one is not buried with Christ, he is not validly baptized . . .
>
> Therefore those who are hastening to baptism ought to take care as a matter of first importance that they should first die to sin . . .
>
> Now the newness of life is when we lay aside "the old man with his deeds" and "put on the new, who has been created according to God" [Eph 4:22, 24; Col 3:9–10].[48]

The moral significance of baptism which Origen gives to dying with Christ as a dying to sin and to walking in newness of life is in keeping with Paul's own point in the passage.[49] The death to sin must precede the baptism. The death to sin was the meaning of repentance for Origen. Baptism gives the Holy Spirit as a pledge, but we receive him fully when we come to perfection; in the same way baptism is a resurrection and a pledge of the perfect resurrection.[50]

As indicated in the exodus typology above, baptism was a deliverance from the devil and evil spirits.[51]

Baptism is the marriage to Christ.[52] After surveying the occasions in Scripture where spouses were met at wells, Origen finds the Old and New Testaments to be in agreement: "There one comes to the wells and

---

48. *Commentary on Romans* 5.8.2, 10, 12, 13; Scheck, trans., *Origen: Commentary on the Epistle to the Romans*, 354, 358, 359. For the use of Rom 6:3–4, see also *Commentary on John* 1.182; 10.231–32, 243; *Commentary on Matthew* 15.23 (referred to above); *Homilies on Numbers* 15.4; *Homilies on Judges* 7.2.

49. Cf. ibid., 5.9.2; 361 for baptism into Christ's death as a crucifixion of the old life of sin so that we might have hope of the likeness of his resurrection. On the motif of baptism as death and resurrection see also *Homilies on Joshua* 4.2; *Homilies on Exodus* 5.2; *Homilies on Jeremiah* 1.16.2.

50. *Homilies on Ezekiel* 2.5. For the eschatological significance of baptism, see also *Commentary on Romans* 3.1.12.

51. For Origen's vivid awareness of demonic forces and their efforts to entrap human beings, see Ferguson, "Origen's Demonology"; and Crouzel, "Diable et démons dans les homélies d'Origène." See *Homilies on Exodus* 5.4; 5.5; *Homilies on Judges* 7.2.

52. *Homilies on Judges* 8.5.

the waters that brides may be found; and the church is united to Christ in the bath of water."[53]

Origen often brings baptism into association with circumcision. Hence, Daniélou asserts that "Origen compares baptism to circumcision" and "It is the sacrament itself of baptism for which circumcision is the figure."[54] Alternatively, one could nuance the interpretation and understand the gift of the Spirit in baptism as the spiritual counterpart to physical circumcision.[55] Daniélou cites for his view Origen's *Commentary on Romans*:

> If anyone in the church who is circumcised by means of the grace of baptism should afterwards become a transgressor of Christ's law, his baptismal circumcision shall be reckoned to him as the uncircumcision of unbelief... We might say that the catechumens are the ones who are still uncircumcised, or even Gentiles, and those who are believers by means of the grace of baptism are the circumcised. (2.12.4; 2.13.2)[56]

There are other passages to the same import.[57]

In another vein, Origen could understand the second circumcsion without reference to baptism as Jesus removing the vices and cutting off every defect (*Homilies on Joshua* 1.7), or in other words his cutting off the pollution of the flesh and purging the filth of sins from the heart (ibid., 6.1). This spiritual circumcision would no doubt have been thought of as occurring in baptism, but the point is that it is not for Origen identical with baptism. This interpretation differs from seeing the baptismal circumcision as the giving of the Holy Spirit as a seal, but it accords with Origen's moral emphasis in regard to baptism as meaning that one should no longer live a life of sin.

Origen in his *Homilies on Luke* offers yet another interpretation of the circumcision of Christ that might be more nearly what Paul meant in Col 2:9–12, quoted by him in the passage. "When [Christ] died, we died with him, and, when he rose, we rose with him. So too we were circumcised

---

53. *Homilies on Genesis* 10.5; Heine, trans., *Origen: Homilies on Genesis and Exodus*, 167.

54. Daniélou, "Circoncision et baptême," 773.

55. Ferguson, "Spiritual Circumcision in Early Christianity," but with minimal use of Origen.

56. Scheck, *Origen: Commentary on the Epistle to the Romans*, 143.

57. *Homilies on Joshua* 5.5–6; Bruce, *Origen: Homilies on Joshua*, 63–64. A few paragraphs later Origen speaks more briefly of "the second circumcision of baptism" (66).

along with him" (14.1).[58] Hence, we do not need circumcision of the flesh, for his death, resurrection, and circumcision "took place for our sake."

Baptism, furthermore, added one to the church. Origen interpreted Genesis 2:15 in this way: "Those who are being begotten again [ajnagennwvmenoi] through divine baptism are placed in Paradise, that is in the church."[59]

One of Origen's pregnant thoughts, but one that he uncharacteristically does not develop, is that "By being baptized into Jesus we will know that the living God is in us" (*Commentary on John* 6.44 [26].232).

Returning to the theme of forgiveness of sins, I want to discuss Origen's thoughts on infant baptism and on martyrdom as a baptism of blood.

## INFANT BAPTISM

Origen refers to infant baptism in three interrelated passages. All three respond to questions asking for a justification of baptizing infants for the forgiveness of sins and offer a defense in terms of a stain attached to birth, citing the same Old Testament passages.

*The Homilies on Luke* were preached in Caesarea between 231 and 244.

> Christian brethren often ask a question. The passage from Scripture read today encourages me to treat it again. Little children are baptized "for the remission of sins." Whose sins are they? When did they sin? Or how can this explanation of the baptismal washing be maintained in the case of small children, except according to the interpretation we spoke of a little earlier? "No man is clean of stain, not even if his life upon the earth had lasted but a single day" [Job 14:4–5]. Through the mystery of baptism, the stains of birth are put aside. For this reason, even small children are baptized. For "Unless born of water and the Spirit one cannot enter the kingdom of heaven." (*Homilies on Luke* 14.5 on Luke 2:22)[60]

The *Homilies on Leviticus* were preached in Caesarea between 238 and 244; they survive in a Latin translation by Rufinus.

---

58. Lienhard, *Origen: Homilies on Luke*, 56.

59. *Commentary on Genesis*, Book 3, on Gen 2:15.

60. I quote the translation of Jerome's Latin version by Lienhard, trans., *Origen: Homilies on Luke*. A shortened version survives in the Greek catena, but the Greek contains the main points (translated in Ferguson, *Early Christians Speak*, vol. 1, 55).

## Baptism according to Origen

> [After quotation of Ps 51:5 and Job 14:4:] These verses may be adduced when it is asked why, since the baptism of the church is given for the remission of sins, baptism according to the practice of the church is given even to infants; since indeed if there is in infants nothing which ought to pertain to forgiveness and mercy, the grace of baptism would be superfluous. (*Homily on Leviticus* 8.3.5 on Lev. 12:2–7)

*The Commentary on Romans* belongs to Origen's mature works in Caesarea, about 246; it is preserved in the Latin translation of Rufinus.

> [After reference to Lev 12:8:] For which sin is this one dove offered? Was a newborn child able to sin? And yet it has a sin for which sacrifices are commanded to be offered, and from which it is denied that anyone is pure, even if his life should be one day long [Job 14:4–5]. It has to be believed, therefore, that concerning this David also said what we quoted above, "in sins my mother conceived me" [Ps 51:5]. According to the historical narrative no sin of his mother is revealed. On this account also the church had a tradition from the apostles to give baptism even to infants. For they to whom the secrets of the divine mysteries were given knew that there is in all persons the natural stains of sin which must be washed away by the water and the Spirit. On account of these stains the body itself is called the "body of sin." (*Commentary on Romans* 5.9.11 on Rom 6:5–6, the "body of sin")[61]

Origen reaffirms the usual Christian understanding of baptism as for the forgiveness of sins, and that understanding presented a problem for the practice of baptizing infants. Origen witnesses to questions about the practice of infant baptism and the argument that was urged against it, namely that infants had no sins to be forgiven by baptism. The subject of discussion may have been more a matter of *why* baptize infants than *whether* to do so. In response, Origen offers a modification of the earlier affirmations of the innocence of children. Before the reader jumps to the conclusion that Origen is an early witness to the doctrine of original sin (inheritance of the guilt of Adam's transgression), note should be taken of the larger context of the passage in the *Homilies on Luke*. Earlier in the same homily Origen contrasts sin (of which Jesus had none) and stain and explains that Jesus needed the purification recorded in Luke 2:22 because of the stain involved in his taking a human body (*Homilies on Luke* 14.3).

---

61. I have slightly modified the translation of Scheck, trans., *Origen: Commentary on the Epistle to the Romans*, 367.

"Every soul that has been clothed with a human body has its own 'stain'" (ibid. 14.4). Origen, therefore, is working with the category of ceremonial, bodily defilement from the Old Testament ritual law.[62] For Origen, the same impurity that attached to Jesus' birth applies to all human beings.[63] Distinguishing Origen's view from Augustine's, David F. Wright understands Origen to refer to forgiveness of the pre-cosmic fall of souls.[64] The emphasis in these passages, however, is different. The *Commentary On Romans* makes clear that Origen is applying the same understanding of "sin" as a physical "stain" in all three of the Old Testament passages to which he refers. Origen's innovation is to extend the baptismal forgiveness of sins to ceremonial impurity, particularly that associated with childbirth. As Wright correctly points out, it remained for a later age to extend the concept to inherited sin.

That the interpretation advanced in the preceding paragraph is correct and that Origen does not refer to an inheritance of Adam's sin is evident from Origen's commentary on Matt 18:2–4. There he elaborates on the condition of the child as not having tasted sensual pleasures; not having fully attained reason so not knowing anger, grief, pleasure of passions, or fear; being forgetful of evils; being humble. In these respects, being converted means an adult attains the condition of the child (*Commentary on Matthew* 13.16).

Origen's statements indicate that infant baptism preceded the justification for the practice. As has often been true in Christian history, the practice preceded its doctrinal defense.[65]

---

62. Laporte, "Models from Philo in Origen's Teaching on Original Sin," infant baptism for Origen removes the defilement resulting from birth, not Augustine's 'inherited sin' (111–13, 116).

63. Origen, *Homilies on Jeremiah* 5:14 interprets the circumcision of the heart in Jer 4:4 as meaning that everyone is born uncircumcised and so with the stain of Job 14:4–5, a passage cited in the justification for infant baptism.

64. Wright, "How Controversial Was the Development of Infant Baptism in the Early Church?"

65. Contrary to Kurt Aland's view that a change in understanding about the condition of an infant occasioned the introduction of infant baptism in the late second century—*Die Säulingstaufe im Neuen Testament and in der Alten Kirche*, 75 = *Did the Early Church Baptize Infants?*, 103–4—the reverse relationship was recognized by Joachim Jeremias, *Nochmals*, 62 (= *Origins of Infant Baptism*, 73–74), and earlier by Williams, *The Ideas of the Fall and of Original Sin*, 220–26; Didier, "Un cas typique de développement du dogme à propos du baptême des enfants," 194–200; Pelikan, *Development of Christian Doctrine*, 73–94 (87); Lukken, *Original Sin in the Roman Liturgy*, 190–200. Searle, "Infant Baptism Reconsidered," 366, observes that where sacraments are concerned, practice preceded theology.

Origen's further defense of infant baptism appealed to a "tradition from the apostles." He offers no further evidence for this claim. His citation of John 3:5 in the first passage quoted above and allusion to it in the third passage may mean that the understanding of this passage as excluding from the kingdom anyone (infants as well) who had not received the new birth was the basis of his statement. John 3:5 was a common baptismal text of the second century. The idea of apostolic origin may also be based on the baptismal interpretation of Matt 19:14 which Tertullian sought to counter. Origen's *Commentary on John* does not survive for John 3:5,[66] and his *Commentary on Matthew* 15.6–9 (on Matt 19:13–15) does not bring in baptism. Or, the claim of apostolic tradition may rest on some teaching not dependent on scriptural interpretation.

## MARTYRDOM

Jesus' passion was a martyrdom and was the greatest and the perfect baptism (*Commentary on John* 6.56 [37].290–291). His words comparing his approaching death to a baptism (Luke 12:50, quoted by Origen in this context, and Mark 10:38) provided the basis for applying baptismal concepts to martyrdom. Origen was a leading figure in defining the theology of martyrdom,[67] and that included martyrdom as a baptism.

Martyrdom brought a forgiveness of sins to the believer who had not yet received baptism and a forgiveness of any post-baptismal sins to the one who had been baptized. Origen included martyrdom as one of the seven means of obtaining forgiveness in the Christian age: baptism, martyrdom, almsgiving, forgiving others, converting a sinner, love, and repentance (*Homilies on Leviticus* 2.4.4–5).[68]

Origen in interpreting Mark 10:38 explains the relationship of martyrdom to baptism:

> Inasmuch as the one who endures [martyrdom] receives forgiveness of sins, it is a baptism. For if baptism promises forgiveness of sins, even as we have received forgiveness with reference to the baptism in water and Spirit, and if the one who endured the baptism of martyrdom receives forgiveness of sins, martyrdom

---

66. Frg. 36 from the catena is on John 3:5, but there are doubts as to its authenticity. In any case, the fragment does not apply John 3:5 to infant baptism.

67. Bright, "Origenian Understanding of Martyrdom and Its Biblical Framework."

68. His *Commentary on Romans* 2:1:2 repeats three of these: the grace of baptism, repentance, and the glory of martyrdom.

would with good reason be called a baptism. (*Commentary on Matthew* 16.6)

The key work on the subject is Origen's *Exhortation to Martyrdom*. The principal passage is this:

> Let us be mindful of our sins, because there is no forgiveness of sins without receiving baptism, and that according to the laws of the gospel it is impossible to be baptized again with water and the Spirit for forgiveness of sins, and that a baptism of martyrdom has been given us. Martyrdom is named a baptism, as is evident from [Mark 10:38 and Luke 12:50 are quoted]. (30)

It seems ironic that Origen's strongest statement on the necessity of baptism in order to receive forgiveness of sins occurs in the context of an "exception to the rule." Only Origen would not have considered the forgiveness granted in martyrdom an exception but as an extension of the Savior's death and of baptism as related to it.[69] So, he can say of the martyrs, "Being baptized in their own blood and washing away [ajpolousavmenoi] every sin at the altar in heaven" (39).

Another extended treatment occurs in the *Homilies on Judges* 7.2. Here the superiority of blood baptism is asserted, but its value is developed not in terms of the forgiveness of past sins but of preventing future sins, because few live above sin after water baptism.

## FAITH AND REPENTANCE

Auf der Maur and Waldram have emphasized the importance for Origen of the word in the preparation for baptism.[70] Origen makes many references to the *regula fidei*, "the tradition of the church and the apostles," which was the summary of what was taught.[71]

---

69. Crouzel, *Origen*, 224.

70. Auf der Maur, "Illuminatio," 52–67, 89–95. Note *Homilies on Genesis* 10:5 on "instruction in the divine books"; and *Homilies on Leviticus* 6:5:2, "The word of the law has washed you and made you clean."

71. Its essential contents pertained to God, Christ Jesus, the Holy Spirit, the nature of the soul, free will, the devil and his angels, the creation of the world, and the scriptures (*On First Principles* 1:pref:4–8). Outler, "Origen and the *Regulae fidei*." Other passages provide similar summaries of essential Christian beliefs. Origen declares that the Christian *kerygma* of Christ, which he summarizes, was well known among non-Christians (*Against Celsus* 1:7; cf. 3:15 on the rejection of idolatry). He lists the seeds of teaching as concerning the Trinity, eschatology and the scriptures: Father, the Son, the Holy Spirit, the resurrection, punishment, refreshment, law, prophets, and

The emphasis on the word and teaching had as a corollary the importance of faith. Passages already cited relate faith to baptism, and Origen's comments on the confession of faith at baptism underscore its importance.[72] "Faith properly speaking is the acceptance with the whole soul of what is believed at baptism."[73] Origen's comments on Romans 6:8–10 include the declaration that Christ by his death "freely bestowed his death of sin as if a certain reward of faith to every believer, namely to those who believe that they have died with him and have been crucified and buried together with him."[74]

Origen often refers to invoking the Trinity at baptism.[75] The *Commentary on John* (6.33 [17].166 on John 1:26) attributes the effectiveness of baptism to the "invocations of the worshipful Trinity."

Origen's emphasis on the need for repentance—to cease from sin and to reform one's life—appears in the baptismal liturgy in the renunciation of Satan[76] but also in other passages.[77] He considered the efficacy of baptism to depend on repentance, on one's own choice of manner of life. In commenting on Matthew 3:11, that John's baptism was "for repentance," Origen offers this explanation:

> By the addition of this phrase Matthew teaches that baptism has its benefit from the intentional choice of the one being baptized. This benefit comes to the one who repents, but to one who does not approach baptism with repentance the result will be more serious judgment. (*Commentary on John* 6.33 [17].165)

Origen based his call for catechumens to repent on Luke 3:7–8:

> One who remains in his original state and does not leave behind his habits and his customs does not come to baptism properly
> ...

---

in general each of the scriptures (*Homilies on Jeremiah* 5:13). The *Commentary on John* discusses God, Christ, the Holy Spirit, free will, rewards, and punishments (6:32 [15–16]:187–93). The Dialogue with Heraclides begins with Heraclides' confession of his faith, and Origen then inquires of its details.

72. *Commentary on Romans* 5:8:10; 5:10:4; *Homilies on Exodus* 8:4–5.

73. *Commentary on John* 10:43 [27]:298.

74. *Commentary on Romans* 5:10:2; Scheck, *Origen: Commentary on the Epistle to the Romans*, 368.

75. *Commentary on Romans* 5:8:7; *Commentary on Matthew* 12:20; cf. *On First Principles* 1:3:2 (only in the Latin translation of Rufinus).

76. *Homilies on Numbers* 12:4; *Homilies on Joshua* 26:2; *Commentary on Romans* 5:10:4.

77. E.g., *Homilies on Leviticus* 6:2:5.

> So, whatever [John] says to them, he also says to you, men and women, catechumens! You are arranging to come to baptism . . . Unless you expel wickedness and the serpent's venom from your hearts, [you are in danger of the wrath to come.]
>
> To you who are coming to baptism, Scripture says, "Produce fruit worthy of repentance."[78]

All this about the word, faith, and repentance might seem inconsistent with infant baptism. If Origen ever felt a tension in his thought over the question, nothing survives, but the overwhelming tenor of his remarks shows what an anomaly infant baptism was in the thought and practice of the ancient church.

I close by noting, but not developing, what was expressed in many of the quotations we have used, namely the importance Origen placed on the moral and spiritual life expected of the one who had been baptized. Baptism was central to the Christian life for Origen.[79]

---

78. *Homilies on Luke* 22:5, 6, 8; Lienhard, *Origen: Homilies on Luke*, 94–95.
79. Rahner, "Taufe und geistliches Leben bei Origenes," emphasizes this fact.

# 5

# The Doctrine of Baptism in Gregory of Nyssa's *Oratio Catechetica*

GREGORY OF NYSSA CALLS his work known as the *Oratio Catechetica* (GNO) a λόγος κατηχήσεως or simply a κατήχησις.¹ As a "word of catechesis" or "catechesis" is, the work not only expounds Christian teaching but also is concerned to answer objections to that teaching and so has an apologetic character.² In answering questions about baptism, Gregory sets the doctrine of baptism firmly in a theological context, basing it on Christology and soteriology.³ He relates baptism to the incarnation of Christ that occurred for the sake of salvation, to the

---

1. GNO 5.1 (PG, xlv , col, 9A); 102.6 (PG, xlv, col, 101B). I cite the page and lines of Mühlenberg, *Gregorii Nysseni Oratio Catechetica, Opera Dogmatica Minora, Pars IV* in *Gregorii Nysseni Opera*, III, Pars IV, supplemented with reference to the columns of Migne's *Patrologia Graeca*, xlv. My translations are from Mühlenberg. The major study of the work is now Kees, *Die Lehre von der Oikonomia Gottes*.

2. Kees, *Die Lehre von der Oikonomia Gottes*, 6, notes that the work is intended for catechists, but as aiming for conversion has an apologetic character (7), and so keeps the ones to be instructed in view (10). William Moore places the work in the category "Apologetic" writings in NPNF, 2.5, p. 47. For the association of catechesis with apologetics, see Ferguson, "Irenaeus' Proof of the Apostolic Preaching and Early Catechetical Instruction."

3. The thesis of Kees, *Die Lehre von der Oikonomia Gottes*, is that Gregory's *Oratio Catechetica* is the first work in which the methodological distinction between *theologia* and *oikonomia* is clearly worked out in its structure: the nature of God (chs. 1–4), and then God's saving activity in creation (chs. 5–8), in Christ (chs. 9—32.10), and in the sacraments (chs. 32.11—40). The individual themes are closely linked to one another (pp. 64-66, 91, 318-22).

89

death and resurrection of Christ that effects salvation, and to eschatology that consumates salvation.

Gregory introduces his discussion of baptism by referring to the divine economy or plan (οἰκονομία) in regard to the bath (λουτρόν) as part of the revealed (μυστικῶν) teachings.[4] He takes up the difficulty professed by some in seeing a connection between "prayer to God, invocation of heavenly grace, water, and faith" and the accomplishment of "the mystery of rebirth" to eternal life.[5] The subsequent discussion of baptism may be seen as taking up in turn the three requirements for Christian baptism—invocation of heavenly grace, water and faith. Prayer and the heavenly grace form the background of the argument;[6] then comes a discussion of the mystery of the water and related matters;[7] the subject of faith is introduced at the end of that section;[8] then following the discussion of the eucharist,[9] right faith becomes the theme.[10] The treatise concludes with the moral results to he expected.[11] These three requirements for baptism (divine invocation, water and faith) are related to the theological points that I have chosen to emphasize: incarnation, death and resurrection, and eschatological cleansing and salvation.

Gregory poses the question, "How do prayer and invocation (ἐπίκλησις) of divine power on the water become the cause (ἀρχηγὸς) of life to those being initiated"?[12] He responds with the analogy of the physical birth to the spiritual birth. One cannot perceive a connection between the moist seed (the sperm) and the resulting human person endowed with all the attributes of reason, yet if divine power can change that visible (τὸ φαινόμενον) underlying matter (τὸ ὑποκείμενον) into a human being, it is nothing marvellous for the divine power to bring about a "new birth through this sacramental dispensation [τοῖς διὰ τῆς ταύτης οἰκονομίας ἀναγεννωμένοις]." Others may say, "What is there in common between

---

4. GNO 82.1–5 (PG, xlv, cols. 81D–84A).

5. GNO 82.16–17 (PG, xlv, col. 84B); cf. GNO 91.19–23 (PG, xlv, col. 92B), which substitutes repentance for faith in the triad of requirements, and 92.13–25 (PG, xlv, col. 92D)—"invoke his living power . . . faith and water." Cf. Kees, *Die Lehre von der Oikonomia Gottes*, 164, 167–68.

6. GNO 82.5—86.5 (PG, xlv, cols. 84A–85D).

7. GNO 89.6—92.25 (PG, xlv, cols. 85D–93A).

8. GNO 92.11–25.

9. GNO 93.1—98.6 (PG, xlv, cols. 93A–97B).

10. GNO 98.7—102.3 (PG, xlv, cols. 97C–101A).

11. GNO 102.4—106.18 (PG, xlv, cols. 101B–105C).

12. GNO 82.20–21 (PG, xlv, col. 84B).

## The Doctrine of Baptism in Gregory of Nyssa's Oratio Catechetica

water and life?" We will say to them, "What is there in common between a moist seed and the image of God?"[13] The power of God takes the moist sperm and makes a human being; even so the power of God uses the water of baptism to make a corruptible human being into an incorruptible person. Later in his discussion, Gregory draws the reverse corollary, that even as without the divine power the moist seed is inactive (stated at this point),[14] so the material element of water alone is ineffectual in the new birth.[15]

In the midst of this argument about the power of God at work in baptism, Gregory makes his appeal to his previous discussion of the incarnation.[16] The presence of the power of God in the flesh supports the presence of that power in the baptismal waters. Gregory declares, "The evidence that the divine power was truly manifested to us in the flesh becomes the support of our present argument." The proof from the miracles that the one who appeared in the flesh was God is also a proof of "his presence in the things done every time he is invoked." Christ has "promised to be present with those who call upon him, to be among believers, to abide with them, and to live with each," and it is the property of deity not to lie. Therefore, on the basis of the truthfulness of the divine promise there is assurance that what is promised is present in the baptismal action.[17] Gregory gives great prominence to the calling (κλῆσις) upon the divine in prayer (εὐχή), either the invocation of the Spirit on the water at the beginning of the ceremony (as stated earlier),[18] the calling on the threefold divine name at the actual baptism (implicit in the following passage),[19] or both. The divine power brings about human birth, even when not asked for by the parents: "how much more in the spiritual mode of generation" will this power be effective, "since God has promised to be present in what

---

13. GNO 82.23—84.5 and 85.5—86.1 (PG, xlv, cols. 84B-D; col. 85B-C). Gregory uses the analogy of human birth and spiritual birth to the same point in *In diem luminum*: "Show me the manner of the generation according to the flesh, and I will explain the power of regeneration according to the soul"; and in regard to the question of "How"? he falls back on the incomprehensible power of God (GNO 9.227.7-26 [PG, xlvi, cols. 584B-D]). The same analogy of a moist seed making a person in reference to the resurrection is in Methodius, *Res.* 1.14 and Justin, *1 Apol.* 19.

14. GNO 83.15-16 (PG, xlv, col. 84D); and reiterated 85.9-10 (PG, xlv, col. 85B).

15. GNO 103.9-10 (PG, xlv, 101D).

16. GNO 15.16—20.25 (PG, xlv, cols. 20D-25A) and 40.6—41.8 (cols. 44C-45A).

17. GNO 84.85.3 (PG, xlv, cols. 85A-B).

18. See above n. 6.

19. GNO 86.6 (PG, xlv, col. 85D); explicit at 100.3 (PG, xlv, col. 100B), "confessing the uncreated holy Trinity."

is done and has put his own power in the work," we, according to our faith, adding our prayer and our will to what is undertaken. "Since the one who promised is God [who came in the flesh], and the miracles testify to his deity, even so there is no uncertainty about the presence of the divine in all the things done."[20]

The incarnation led to Christ's death and resurrection, and Gregory proceeds to build his case for the effectiveness of baptism from the death and resurrection of Christ. Even as he appealed to the incarnation (the presence of the divine in flesh) as parallel to the invocation of the divine power in baptism, he correlates the death and resurrection with the triple immersion. The connecting link here is *mimesis*, imitation. The imitation in baptism is the means of participation in Christ's resurrection. Where others have seen the incarnation as central for Gregory,[21] Kees sees the death and resurrection of Christ as central to the *oikonomia* in Christ,[22] and he takes imitation as the key category for Gregory's doctrine of baptism.[23]

Gregory declares, "The descent into the water and the person being immersed three times in it involves another mystery."[24] Christ brought salvation not so much by his teaching as by bringing life. When he assumed and deified flesh, he brought salvation to all that is akin to his flesh. Gregory adopts the language of Heb 2:10, "the Pioneer [ἀρχηγός] of our salvation." He uses as illustrations of being led to salvation the learning of military tactics by observing the movements of armies and the finding of the way through a labyrinth by following an experienced guide. Similarly, a method was contrived by which those who follow could imitate and so share a likeness and kinship in what was done by the leader in human salvation. To attain the goal of escape from the prison house of death, one must follow the same path as the pioneer of our salvation. He experienced death for three days and then came to life again. "What then is the plan [contrivance] through which we imitate what he did?"[25]

---

20. GNO 85.3—86.5 (PG, xlv, cols. 85B-D).

21. Bouchet, "La vision de l'économie du salut selon S. Grégoire de Nysse."

22. Kees, *Die Lehre von der Oikonomia Gottes*, 150–61.

23. Ibid., 162–78, 264–66. Hübner, *Die Einheit des Leibes Christi bei Gregor von Nyssa*, 168–75, sees the connection between flesh and spirit in regard to baptism for Gregory as imitative and not ontological.

24. GNO 86.6-7 (PG, xlv, col. 85D).

25. GNO 87.17-18 (PG. xlv, col. 88C). Cf. *Antirrheticus adversus Apollinarem* (GNO 3.1.227.4-9 [PG, xlv, col. 1260B])— "We die together with the One who died willingly, being buried through baptism in the mystical water . . . in order that the

## The Doctrine of Baptism in Gregory of Nyssa's Oratio Catechetica

Here Gregory introduces those qualities that make earth and water kindred elements: they alone of the four elements have weight, move downward, can exist in one another, and can be contained in one another. "Since then the death of him who is the Author of our life occasioned his burial under the earth according to our common nature, the imitation of his death that we perform is represented in the kindred element [of water]."[26] As Christ was three days under the earth before returning to life again, so those who are joined to him are put under the water by three successive actions in imitation of the grace of the resurrection on the third day. Gregory speaks of the person baptized as both "being poured over with water [τὸ ὕδωρ] instead of earth" and "being put under [ὑποδὺς] that element."[27] The descent into the water [κάθοδος] and coming up from [ἀναβάτες ἀπὸ] the water[28] may in one or the other or both cases refer to the action of entering and exiting the baptismal pool. The pouring over of the person with water suggests water flowing over the person's body, perhaps indicating water being scooped over the exposed part of the body while the person stood in the font; but the word for "pouring over" may have been suggested by the action in burial whereby after the body is lowered into the grave earth is "poured" over it and so refers not to what the administrator does with the water but to the water coming over the body when it was plunged into the water by the administrator. In either case the body was covered with water in imitation of a dead body buried in the earth.[29]

Death brings a dissolution of a human being. By this process, evil flows out so that at the resurrection there may be a reconstitution of the human being, purified of any evil mixture. The pioneer's death fulfilled its purpose completely. The baptismal death, burial, and resurrection of his followers is not an exact imitation; the complete likeness must await the end time. In the water of baptism there occurs "not a complete destruction but a certain rupture of the connection of evil." "What then is imitated [by baptism]? It is the bringing about by death's image in the water of the destruction of the evil mixed with our nature." The destruction is not yet

---

imitation of his resurrection might follow the imitation of his death."

26. GNO 88.2–5 (PG, xlv, col. 88C). He made the same comparison for the same purpose of connecting baptism in water with the burial of Christ in the earth in *In diem luminum* (GNO 9.228.13–26 [PG, xlvi, col. 585B]).

27. GNO 88.10–11 (PG, xlv, col. 88D); also 89.20–21 (89C), quoted below.

28. GNO 86.6 (PG, xlv, col. 85D) and 89.21 (PG, xlv, col, 89C).

29. One meaning of ἐπιχέω (in the passive) is "to be drowned." Liddell and Scott, *A Greek-English Lexicon*, 673.

complete, but two things concur in the removal of evil that breaks its continuity: "the penitence of the transgressor and the imitation of [Christ's] death." "The human being is set free from the natural inclination to evil; by penitence he advances to a hatred of evil and alienation from it, and by death he effects the destruction of evil." If the death were complete, that would be "not an imitation but an identity" so that sin would completely cease from our nature.[30] As Gregory in the discussion of the power of Christ in spiritual rebirth calls attention to prayer and faith as the human aspect, so in the discussion of Christ's death and resurrection, he calls attention to repentance and death to sin as the human aspect.

The discussion of baptism as a likeness of the death of Christ leads into the consideration of the likeness to his resurrection and so to the eschatological dimension of baptism. Gregory reaffirms his earlier comparison, shifting the emphasis now from the death to the resurrection: "Being poured over with water three times and coming up from the water, we reenact dramatically the saving burial and resurrection that took place on the third day."[31] It is in our power to be in the water and to ascend out of it; even so the sovereign of the universe "was plunged into death and departed again to his own blessedness." As a human being may come into contact with the water without danger, so it was infinitely easier for the divine power to enter death and not to be changed by it to his injury. "On account of this it is necessary for us to rehearse beforehand in the water the grace of the resurrection so that we might know that to ascend [ἀναδῦναι] again from death is equally easy for us as to be baptized in water."[32]

This connection of baptism with the resurrection makes baptism necessary for salvation. Baptism may be judged insignificant in comparison with the resurrection, just as the seed that lays down the constitution of a human being cannot be compared in glory to the resultant person; but just as the person would not exist without that seed, so "it is not possible apart from the rebirth in the bath for a person to be in the resurrection."[33] It is not only the principle of life that makes baptism necessary but also the principle of cleansing or purification. "For common sense and the teaching of the scriptures show that it is impossible for one not thoroughly cleansed of every evil spot to enter the divine presence... The salvation of

---

30. GNO 89.5–17 (PG, xlv, col. 89B).
31. GNO 89.20–24 (PG, xlv, col. 89C).
32. GNO 90.1–16 (PG, xlv, col. 89D).
33. GNO 90.16—91.5 (PG, xlv, cols. 89D–92A).

those who are in need is characteristic of the divine activity. This becomes effective through the cleansing in water. The one who has been purified will participate in Purity, and the Deity is truly pure."[34]

Water has certain properties in common with earth; it has others in common with fire. Both water and fire are capable of cleansing. This feature leads to another characteristic teaching by Gregory—the eschatological cleansing by fire resulting in *apokatastasis*, the restoration of all things to God. The rebirth in the bath looks "to the blessed and divine restoration [ἀποκατάστασις] separated from all shame." At the resurrection not all rise to the same life. "The distance is great between those who have been purified and those in need of purification. Those whose purification through the bath has preceded in this life will return to a kindred state" of purity and impassibility. But "those to whom no cleansing of their defilement was applied—no mystical water, no invocation of divine power, no correction by penitence—will be in the corresponding state" of impurity. For the latter, the proper condition is the furnace. "When the evil mixed with their nature is melted away, the pure nature is saved to God at the end of long ages. Since then there is a certain cleansing power in fire and water, those washed clean of evil's stain by the mystical water have no need of another kind of cleansing; but the uninitiated in this cleansing necessarily are purified by fire."[35]

The goal of this cleansing is a heavenly and eternal salvation, but in order to attain this, a right faith must be joined to the water.

Gregory refers once again to what a little thing baptism is, but "This which by itself is little becomes the beginning and basis of great things." It is small in the sense of the ease of accomplishment. For there is no pain in believing God is everywhere and, being present in all things, is able to effect salvation for those who call on him "You see something small and easily accomplished at the beginning—faith and water, the former lying within our free choice and the latter the habitual companion of human life—but what great good is produced from these things, to be most like to the divine himself!"[36]

In order to become like the divine, one's faith must be in truly divine beings, not in created beings. After discussing the eucharist, Gregory refers

---

34. GNO 92.8–20 (PG, xlv, cols. 92C–D). Kees, *Die Lehre von der Oikonomia Gottes*, 169–70, fails to give to purification the importance it seems to have in Gregory's treatment.

35. GNO 91.10—92.8 (PG, xlv, cols. 92B–C).

36. GNO 92.11–25 (PG, xlv, cols. 92D–93A).

again to baptism as he takes up briefly the faith in which one is baptized.[37] Here his anti-Eunomian polemic surfaces in an affirmation of the divine, uncreated nature of all three persons in the Trinity. "The one born by the spiritual rebirth should know by whom he is begotten and what sort of creature he becomes." The spiritual birth is unlike natural birth in a crucial respect. In natural birth "all things come to exist by the impulse of those who beget them, but the spiritual birth depends on the power of the one being born." In this case one has the power to choose his or her parents.[38] In another important respect, the natural and spiritual births are alike: "Of necessity what is born is of the same nature as that of the parents."[39] Gregory explicitly refers to baptism in the name of the triune God: "Since then in the Gospel are delivered the three Persons and the names through which the birth to believers occurs, the one who is begotten in the Trinity is begotten equally by the Father, the Son, and the Holy Spirit."[40] The person being baptized chooses by his or her faith the kind of birth to be received and so one's spiritual nature. "The one who confesses the uncreated holy Trinity enters into the unchanging and unalterable life," but the one who sees the Son and Spirit as created is baptized into a created Trinity and "is begotten to a changeable and alterable life."[41] The latter person places his "hope of salvation in himself and not in the divine" and "has his birth from below and not from above."[42]

The faith in which one is baptized, based on the principle that the begotten is like the begetter, has consequences for how one lives. As Gregory moves toward his conclusion, he acknowledges that his instruction is insufficient without attention to the moral implications of the new birth in baptism. "Many of those coming to the grace of baptism," Gregory complains, "overlook" the moral life that should follow, "being born only in appearance and not in reality. For the transformation of our life that

---

37. GNO 98.8–11 (PG, xlv, col. 97C). Kees, *Die Lehre von der Oikonomia Gottes*, 163–64, notes that faith for Gregory was a free rational decision (see the passage cited at the preceding note) but must also have the right content (a false doctrine cannot save one) and produce a new way of living (see below).

38. GNO 98.16—99.5 (PG, xlv, cols. 97C–D). Cf. *Vita Moysis* 11.3 (GNO 7.1.34— 8.14 [PG, xlv, col. 328B]).

39. GNO 100.7-8 (PG, xlv, col. 100B).

40. GNO 99.13–16 (PG, xlv, col. 100A).

41. GNO 100.2–7 (PG, xlv, col. 100B). Cf. *In diem luminum* (GNO 9.228.22—229.18 [PG, xlvi, cols. 585B–D]) for the argument that the baptismal formula means the equal deity of all three persons.

42. GNO 101.4-6 and 101.23—102.2 (PG, xlv, cols. 100D and 101A–B).

## The Doctrine of Baptism in Gregory of Nyssa's Oratio Catechetica

occurs through rebirth would not be a transformation if we should remain in the state in which we were."[43] It is evident to all, Gregory continues, that "the saving birth is received for the renewal and change of our nature." Yet no part of human nature in and of itself from mere baptism (here Gregory uses baptism of the water) comes to a change. The birth from above does not change the rational nature and intellectual faculties of a person (that would not be a good change); rather the "grace of rebirth" is a transformation from evil to good.[44]

At this point, Gregory moves once more from the imagery of rebirth to cleansing. "It is evident that when nature's evil features are erased the change is for the better." The mystical bath washes away the soul's evil choices, effecting a change to the better. Here I am reminded of the frequency with which earlier writers connected rebirth with sinlessness.[45] Gregory says, "But, if the bath was applied to the body, and the soul did not cleanse itself of the stains of its passions but after the initiation the life corresponds to the uninitiated life, even if it is bold to say it, I will say it and will not turn away from it, in these persons the water is water, since the gift of the Holy Spirit is in no way manifest in what occurred."[46] If the one baptized is the same after as before the baptism—guilty of anger, greed, shameful thoughts, pride, envy, arrogance, injustice, adultery—there is no change, and "what you have not become, you are not."[47] Returning to the

---

43. GNO 102.4-11 (PG, xlv, col. 101B). Gregory expresses the same concern in *In diem luminum* (GNO 9.237.23—238.11 [PG, xlvi, cols. 596A-B]). Referring to Christ as "firstborn" (see n. 55 below), Gregory makes the fact that "through the same manner of new birth through water and the Spirit we became brothers of the Lord" the basis for an exhortation to imitate his purity—*De perfectione* (GNO 8.1.203, 8.204.8 [PG, xlvi, co]s. 277A-B]). For Gregory's persistent interest in the Christian moral life see my article, "Some Aspects of Gregory of Nyssa's Moral Theology in the Homilies on Ecclesiastes," in Stuart G. Hall (ed.), *Gregory of Nyssa Homilies on Ecclesiastes* (Berlin: W. de Gruyter, 1993) 319-36.

44. GNO 102.12-24 (PG, xlv, cols. 101B-C); but *In diem luminum* says that upon receiving the power of God, "water that is nothing else than water renews a person to an intellectual rebirth (νοητὴν ἀναγέννησιν), when grace from above blesses it" (GNO 9.227.4-7 [PG, xlvi, col. 584B]).

45. E.g., Hermas, *Sim.* 9.29.1-3 = 106.1-3; *Barn.* 6.11; Theophilus, *To Autolycus* 2.16; Irenaeus, *Demonstration* 3; Clement of Alexandria, *Strom.* 4.25.160.1-2.

46. G.NO 102.24—103.10 (PG, xlv, cols. 101C-D). For the necessity of both Spirit and water, note *De Spiritu Sancto* (GNO 3.1.105.19—106.11 [PG, xlv, cols. 1324D-1325B]), which emphasizes the working of the Spirit (the "life giving power" is not in the water but in the Holy Spirit, and faith in the Lord must precede), and *In diem luminum* (GNO 9.224—25.225.14 [PG, xlvi, cols. 581A-C]), which argues for the place of water.

47. GNO 103.10—104.10 (PG, xlv, cols. 101D-104B). The examples of sins to be

imagery of new birth, Gregory makes a stirring appeal: "The child who is born of one is assuredly of the same nature with the one who begot him. If then you received God and became a child of God, show through your choices that God is in you, show in yourself the One who begot you!"[48] The *Oratio Catechetica* then closes on the eschatological note, contrasting the "unspeakable blessedness" of the wise who have followed a godly life with the torment of sinners.

Of the names used for baptism—bath, enlightenment, regeneration (παλιγγενεσία) Gregory preferred bath (λουτρόν),[49] taken from Tit 3:5, "the bath [or washing] of regeneration." In his discussions of regeneration he substitutes the language of 1 Pet 1:3 and 23, "rebirth" (ἀναγέννησις)[50] and especially of Jn 3:3-7, born from above by the Spirit.[51] Note his use of "spiritual birth"[52] and "spiritual rebirth."[53] By associating the rebirth of baptism with the resurrection to eternal life and describing the resurrection as a rebirth to life,[54] Gregory has made a creative combination of the Pauline theme of baptism as a death and resurrection (Rom 6:1-11) with

---

corrected is similar in *In diem luminum* (GNO 9,238.11-17 [PG, xlvi, cols. 596B-C]), which also cites the tax collector Zacchaeus as an example of change (GNO 9.238.20 [PG, xlvi, col. 596C]).

48. GNO 104.12-16 (PG, xlv, col. 104B). Children of God should have the characteristics of their Father—*In diem luminum* (GNO 9.239.5-8 [PG, xlvi, cols. 596D-597A]).

49. Used seven times with reference to baptism: GNO 82.2 (PG, xlv, col. 81D); 91.4-9 ("grace from the bath"—cf. *In diem luminum* [GNO 9.223.2] [PG, xlvi, col. 580A], "grace of the bath"), and 16 (PG, xlv, cols. 92A-B); 103.2, 5, and 20 (PG, xlv, col. 101D). Gregory in *In diem luminum* preferred παλιγγενεσία and ἀναγέννησις, which words he seems to have used as virtually interchangeable; see my "Preaching at Epiphany: Gregory of Nyssa and John Chrysostom on Baptism and the Church," *Church History* 66 (1997) 1-17 (3 n. 10).

50. Note GNO 91.4-5 (PG, xlv, col. 92A), where Tit 3:5 (λουτρὸν παλιγγενεσίας) is paraphrased as λουτρὸν ἀναγεννήσεως; cf. 82.17 (PG, xlv, col. 84B); 83.12 (PG, xlv, col. 84C); 85.23 (PG, xlv, col. 85C); 99.17-18 (PG, xlv, col. 100A-B); 102.9 and 24 (PG, xlv, col. 101B,C); 104.11 (PG, xlv, col. 104B) in reference to Jn 1:12-13.

51. GNO 99.14-18 (PG, xlv, col. 100A); 101.19—102.2-3, 21 (PG, xlv, col. 101A-B); cf. 104.10-12 (PG, xlv, col. 104B).

52. GNO 85.10-11 (PG, xlv, col. 85B).

53. GNO 98.18-19 (PG, xlv, col. 97C) and 100.18-19 (PG, xlv, col. 100C).

54. GNO 82.1-14; 87.12-14; 88.12-18; 91.4-5; 100.1-4 (PG, xlv, cols. 84A; 88B; 88D-89A; 92A; 100A). Note the use of the same word ἀναστοιχειόω (ἀναστοιχείωσις) "reconstitute, refashion, transform" for the resurrection (GNO 88.16-18 [PG, xlv, col. 89A1) and for the new birth of baptism (GNO 102.21-22 [PG, xlv, co1.101B]).

*The Doctrine of Baptism in Gregory of Nyssa's* Oratio Catechetica

the Johannine theme of new birth (Jn 3:3–7).[55] The language of washing is also associated with purification or cleansing in four contexts.[56]

The language of rebirth, connected with the incarnation, and of cleansing, associated with death, and their eschatological fulfillment in the resurrection to life and purity are the principal theological themes related to baptism in Gregory's *Catechetical Oration*. They correspond to the principal effects and benefits of baptism[57] that he discuses: rebirth brings life (ζωή),[58] and washing produces purification.[59] These gifts that result from invoking the divine power are received in the water, but not from the water, for they are connected with the divine activity and the faith[60] and repentance[61] of the recipient.

---

55. This is done more explicitly in *Contra Eunomium* 3.2.45-54 (GNO 2.67.64—70.18 [PG, xlv, cols. 633B–637B]) and *Refutatio Confessionis Eunomii* 79-81 (GNO 2.344.20—346.5 [PG, xlv, cols. 501B–504A]), which relate the ideas of physical birth and of resurrection with the new birth of baptism by speaking of the three births of Christians—in the body, in regeneration, and in the resurrection of the dead—as corresponding to three births of Christ, suggested by the biblical descriptions of Christ as "firstborn of creation" (Col 1:15), "firstborn among many brethren" (Rom 8:29), and "firstborn from the dead" (Col 1:18).

56. GNO 88.23—89.14 (esp. line 7) (PG, xlv, col. 89A–B); 91.14-18 (PG, xlv, col. 92B); 92.6-10, 18-19 (PG, xlv, col. 92C-D).

57. Cf. the double statement of each of these benefits of baptism in *In diem luminum*, "Baptism is cleansing of sins, forgiveness of trespasses, the cause of renewal and rebirth" (GNO 9.224.4–5 [PG, xlvi, col. 580D]).

58. GNO 82.6, 10 ("born to eternal life"), and 21 (PG, xlv, col. 84A–B); cf. 83.21 (PG, xlv, col, 84D); 88.3 (PG, xlv, col. 88C); 93.5-6 (PG, xlv, col. 93A); 100.9 and 19 (PG, xlv, col. 100C); 102.9 (PG, xlv, col. 101B).

59. See references in n. 56.

60. GNO 82.16 (PG, xlv, col. 84B); 84.18 (PG, xlv, col. 85A); 85.13–86,3 (PG, xlv, col. 85C-D); 93.4 (PG, xlv, col. 93A); 99.14 (PG, xlv, col. 100A); 100.17-22, and 101.4 (PG, xlv, col. 100C-D).

61. GNO 89.10-12 (PG, xlv, col. 89B).

# 6

# Exhortations to Baptism in the Cappadocians

THE THREE GREAT CAPPADOCIANS—BASIL of Caesarea, Gregory of Nyssa, and Gregory of Nazianzus—each delivered an exhortation for catechumens to be baptized.[1] These sermons were delivered at or immediately after Epiphany within a decade of one another—probably in 371 for Basil's sermon, 381 for the two Gregories' sermons.[2] While reflecting the distinctive emphases and settings of each preacher, the three exhortations share much in common. There would be more similarities if account were taken of other works of the three authors, but this paper will limit its comparison to these three sermons.

---

1. Basil, *Hom.* 13, *Exh. ad s. bapt.*—PG 31.424-44; Engl. trans. by T. Halton in A. Hamman, ed., *Baptism: Ancient Liturgies and Patristic Texts*, 76-87; studied by Gribomont, "Saint Basile: Le protreptique au Baptême"; and Ferguson, "Basil's Protreptic to Baptism." Gregory of Nyssa, *Adv. eos qui diff. bapt.*—G 46.416-32. Gregory of Nazianzus, *Or.* 40, *In s. bapt.*, the longest and most elaborate of the three—PG 36.359-428 and Sources Chrétiennes, vol. 358 (Paris, 1990), *Grégoire de Nazianze: Discourse 38-41*, ed. C. Moreschini and P. Gallay; Engl. trans. by C. G. Browne and J. E. Swallow in *NPNF*, Series Two, vol. 7 and by Halton in Hamman, *Baptism*, 87ff.; it figures prominently in Winslow, "Orthodox Baptism—A Problem for Gregory of Nazianzus." References to Basil will be by chapter number and Migne columns; to Gregory of Nyssa by Migne columns; to Gregory of Nazianzus by chapter numbers. I give my own translation for direct quotations.

2. For Basil, Gribomont, "Saint Basile: Le protreptique au Baptême," 71, 87-88; for Gregory of Nyssa, Quasten, *Patrology*, vol. 3, 279-80; for Gregory of Nazianzus, C. Moreschini, and P. Gallay, *Grégoire de Nazianze: Discourse 38-41*, 16-22.

*Exhortations to Baptism in the Cappadocians*

Since all three sermons are exhortations to receive baptism, they share a protreptic style. The main themes in their appeals are quite similar. Since all three were delivered early in the calendar year as the season of preparation for the Pasch, when baptism was administered, approached, all refer to the appropriate season for baptism. All times are suitable, but the day of the Pasch on which the resurrection is celebrated is most appropriate.[3] Basil and Gregory of Nazianzus use Eccl 3:1ff. on a time for everything,[4] and Basil and Gregory of Nyssa both give an explicit invitation for catechuments to turn in their names to be enrolled as candidates for baptism.[5]

The principal concern of all three preachers in their exhortations is for the hearers not to delay receiving baptism until old age or the approach of death. Basil asks the rhetorical questions, "Why are you waiting? Why do you hesitate?" He says, "I know your procrastination." Gregory of Nyssa gives the imperatives, "Do not delay." "Do not provoke the baptizer by delay." Gregory of Nazianzus too speaks of his hearers' "procrastinations" and also gives the direct command, "Do not put off grace."[6] Whatever age one is in life, that is the time to be baptized,[7] for "the funeral bier carries out every age"—the old, the one in the prime of life, the young.[8]

The uncertainty of life is prominent in the admonitions of all three sermons as a motivation for not delaying baptism. We do not know what tomorrow will bring. "Who appointed for you a fixed time of old age? Do you not see babies being seized? Those being taken in the prime of life? Life has no one appointed time."[9] "Death is not defined by the appointed times of age." Besides the misfortunes of famine and war, there may be "madness, delirium, unexpected choking, impact of winds." Death may come while one is traveling, eating, or sleeping.[10] "Every time is suitable for

---

3. Basil, *Exh. bapt.* 1 (PG 31.424C–D); Gregory of Nyssa, *Eos diff. bapt.* (PG 46.416C); Gregory of Nazianzus, *In s. bapt.* 13–14, 24.

4. Basil, *Exh. bapt.* 1 (PG 31.424A–B); Gregory of Nazianzus, *In s. bapt.* 14.

5. Basil, *Exh. bapt.* 7 (PG 31.440A); Gregory of Nyssa, *Eos diff. bapt.* (PG 46.417B). Both use the illustration of a new soldier enrolled in the army—Basil, ibid.; Gregory of Nyssa, *Eos diff. bapt.* (PG 46.429C).

6. Basil, *Exh. bapt.* 1; 5 (PG 31.425C); Gregory of Nyssa, *Eos diff.* bapt. (PG 46.417D and 421D); Gregory of Nazianzus, *In s. bapt.* 14; 24.

7. Basil, *Exh. bapt.* 5 (PG 31.342C–D); cf. Gregory of Nazianzus, *In s. bapt.* 14.

8. Gregory of *Nyssa, Eos diff. bapt.* (PG 46.420A).

9. Basil, *Exh. bapt.* 5 (PG 31.436C).

10. Gregory of Nyssa, *Eos diff. bapt.* (PG 46.417D; 420B).

your washing, since any time may be your death."[11] Gregory of Nazianzus mentions as unexpected misfortunes: war, earthquake, being snatched by a wild beast, drowning, illness, choking, drinking too much, wind storm, a runaway horse, reaction to a medicine, and human injustice.[12] Basil warns of "sudden destruction" and "disaster like a sudden storm."[13] Death comes unexpectedly as a treacherous thief.[14] "The end will come suddenly."[15]

The exhortations to baptism involve answering the excuses perceived to be the reasons given for procrastinating. Basil assumes to speak the words of the person who delays: "Let sin first rule in me; and then the Lord will rule," and the words of the Devil: "Today is mine; tomorrow is God's." Basil responds with how improper it is to bring to God a life that is no longer useful. "Continence in old age is not continence but the inability to be licentious . . . No one is righteous because of the inability to be bad."[16] Gregory of Nyssa deals with an objection by also employing prosopopoeia: "I was afraid of the inclination of our nature to sin and because of this I delay the grace of regeneration." Gregory considers the excuse specious. If one is living without sin as a catechumen, then there will be no problem afterward. If one's life is impure beforehand, it is evident that the person prefers sin. Such persons "fear baptism as the hindrance of pleasures."[17] Gregory of Nazianzus deals with the greatest number of excuses. He too takes up the fear of losing the gift of baptism by later sin as a reason why some delay the cleansing. This, he says, is the evil one's sophistry to get a person to lose Christ.[18] Another individual may protest that his life in public affairs might stain him and he should not waste God's mercy. Gregory's response is "Flee even the forum," but if that is impossible, it is "better to be stained a little by your public affairs than to be deprived of grace altogether."[19] Someone else will say, as Basil's objector did, that they will enjoy pleasure now[20] and will further use the laborers

11. Gregory of Nazianzus, *In s. bapt.* 13.
12. Ibid., 14.
13. Basil, *Exh. bapt.* 8 (PG 31.441D).
14. Gregory of Nyssa, *Eos diff. bapt.* (PG 46.428A).
15. Gregory of Nazianzus, *In s. bapt.* 24.
16. Basil, *Exh. bapt.* 5 (PG 31.436A-B); 6 (PG 31.437B).
17. Gregory of Nyssa, *Eos diff. bapt.* (PG 46.425B-D).
18. Gregory of Nazianzus, *In s. bapt.* 16. Basil too observes that "No one rejects good things for the fear of being deprived of them"—*Exh. bapt.* 7 (PG 31.441A).
19. Gregory of Nazianzus, *In s. bapt.* 19.
20. Gregory of Nazianzus, *In s. bapt.* 14: The evil one says, "give to me the present and to God the future; to me your youth, and to God old age; to me your pleasures,

## Exhortations to Baptism in the Cappadocians

in the vineyard (Matt 20:1ff.) as justification for waiting until the eleventh hour to respond. Gregory deals with the parable at length, among other things making the point that the laborers in the parable who responded at the eleventh hour still did so when they first believed.[21] Another excuse offered is that the desire for baptism will be treated by God as baptism, a position that Gregory roundly rejects. "If desire in your opinion suffices for the power of baptism," then consider in the same way that your desire for glory will be the same as attaining it.[22] A further objection is that Christ was not baptized until he was thirty years old, but Gregory draws out the differences between Christ's circumstances and ours.[23] All three thinkers give prominence to pleasure as the principal hindrance to the reception of baptism and call upon their hearers no longer to live for pleasure.[24]

There are other prominent points in common among the three addresses. These recurring themes are more or less explicitly parts of the appeal to the hearers to receive baptism. All three sermons discuss clinical or sickbed baptism and do so in such a way as to make it undesirable for a person to put off baptism until the prospect of death is imminent. The rhetorical purpose accounts for the unfavorable descriptions, but there must be some truth behind the *topos* and not simply the borrowing of a common theme. Basil has two negative descriptions of the confusion present in a person's last hours. In one he vividly describes the dying person's shortness of breath, fever, sighs, feeble voice: "Who will give baptism then?" Relatives are fainthearted, those in good health despise the sufferings, friends hesitate, the physician deceives about your condition. "It is night, and there is an absence of helpers. The baptizer is not present."[25] Gregory of Nyssa speaks of the "tumult and cry . . . There is jostling, disorder, and mournful and indistinct noise when slaves, kinsmen, friends, children, the wife are entangled with one another as if in a night battle."[26] Gregory of Nazianzus too speaks of the undesirability of receiving baptism "in distress and not freely." He calls on his hearers to respond while not yet sick in body and mind, while the tongue is not stammering or parched,

---

and to him your uselessness."

21. Ibid, 20–21.
22. Ibid., 22–23.
23. Ibid., 29–30.
24. Basil, *Exh. bapt.* 5 (PG 31.433B, 436A); Gregory of Nyssa, *Eos diff. bapt.* (PG 46.420C; 421A); Gregory of Nazianzus, *In s. bapt.* 14; 20.
25. Basil, *Exh. bapt.* 7 (PG 31.441B–C).
26. Gregory of Nyssa, *Eos diff. bapt.* (PG 46.425A).

when they can receive baptism with congratulation and not pity; before wife and children are listening for the dying words, before the physician is powerless to help, and before there is a struggle between the baptizer and the one who seeks money and there is no time for both.[27]

It is in the context of describing sickbed baptism that the most is said in these sermons relative to the ceremony of baptism. The *disciplina arcani*[28] prevented a detailed description to an audience that included catechumens, but from what is known from other sources, the reader can recognize many details. Basil speaks of the undesirability of sickbed baptism by describing what the seriously ill person cannot do: "You are not able to utter the saving words nor are inclined to hear purely, . . . , nor lift the hands to heaven nor stand upon the feet, nor to bend the knee in worship, nor to be taught profitably, nor to confess safely, nor to reach agreement with God, nor to renounce the enemy, nor to follow intelligently while being initiated."[29] Gregory of Nyssa speaks of the haste in seeking "the vessels, the water, the priest, the word that makes ready for grace."[30] Gregory of Nazianzus warns of "the tongue unable to speak the initiatory words."[31]

In incidental remarks, each preacher indicates that there was some question about the validity of clinical baptism. Basil, not very clearly, alludes to those who are present being "doubtful" and declares that "when you receive the grace knowingly, then you . . . do not threaten the activity."[32] Gregory of Nazianzus is more explicit, calling on his hearers, while they can, to be made one of the faithful "not in semblance but with open acknowledgement . . . and there is no doubt."[33] These remarks may

---

27. Gregory of Nazianzus, *In s. bapt.* 11–12.

28. Ibid., 45; Gregory of Nyssa, *Eos diff. bapt.* (PG 46.421C) for the dismissal of the catechumens prior to the "mysteries" in which "initiated" Christians participate. Gregory of Nazianzus also speaks of catechumens "at the porch of piety" (16) in contrast to being "initiated" (28).

29. Basil, *Exh. bapt.* 5 (PG 31.436C–D).

30. Gregory of Nyssa, *Eos diff. bapt.* (PG 46.425A). In other passages he speaks of the sign of the cross (417B) and all water being suitable when it finds faith in the one being baptized and receives the blessing by the priest (which is possibly the "word" in the quotation—421D).

31. Gregory of Nazianzus, *In s. bapt.* 11. Elsewhere in the sermon he speaks of the preparation for baptism (31), exorcism (27), and confession of sins (27); he further says the baptizer may be anyone of the same faith (26) and refers to the use of the Triune name (41; 44–45), the baptismal garment (25), and the psalmody and the lighting of lamps that accompanied the newly baptized's entrance into the church (46).

32. Basil, *Exh. bapt.* 5 (PG 31.436D–437A).

33. Gregory of Nazianzus, *In s. bapt.* 11.

have been rhetorical touches to emphasize the importance of receiving baptism immediately, but the way in which they are alluded to in the midst of the larger discussion without special attention being called to them would seem to indicate that, although the preachers did not refuse the practice, they were aware of doubts concerning the practice of baptizing an unconscious person, doubts they did not seek to dispel.

All of these accounts of sickbed baptism emphasize the importance of the candidate being able to speak the words of faith. This emphasis accords with the summaries of the baptismal process given by each preacher: being taught, having faith in the heart, and receiving the seal of the Spirit (Basil);[34] faith and baptism (the Nyssene);[35] "having spoken, be baptized; and being baptized, be saved" (Nazianzen).[36] This concern might seem to go counter to the practice of infant baptism, and Gregory of Nazianzus specifically addresses the issue. He urges that infants be brought for sanctification[37] and argues that if there is threat to their life "it is better to be sanctified unconsciously than to depart unsealed and uninitiated."[38] This emphasis on the objective value of the sacrament is balanced, however, by the importance of conscious understanding and confession of faith. Gregory proceeds to give his advice that parents should wait until the end of children's third year "when they are able to listen and to answer something about the mystery."[39]

These three exhortations express a rich theology of baptism, for they are full of statements about the meaning of baptism. These descriptions of what is accomplished in baptism are neatly summarized in various lists of the blessings received in baptism. Basil enumerates the benefits of baptism as "a ransom to captives, a forgiveness of debts, the death of sin, regeneration of the soul, a shining garment, an unassailable seal, a chariot to heaven, a patron of the kingdom, the gift of adoption."[40] Gregory of

---

34. Basil, *Exh. bapt.* 6 (PG 31.437A).

35. Gregory of Nyssa, *Eos diff. bapt.* (PG 46.421D).

36. Gregory of Nazianzus, *In s. bapt.* 26. Note his extensive summary of what must be believed in 45. C. Moreschini speaks of the orthodox faith as the *sine qua non* for admission to baptism according to Gregory in *Grégoire de Nazianze: Discourse 38–41*, 37.

37. Gregory of Nazianzus, *In s. bapt.* 17.

38. Ibid., 28. I have argued that this sentiment is behind the beginning of infant baptism—"Inscriptions and the Origin of Infant Baptism" (ch. 10 in this volume).

39. Gregory of Nazianzus, *In s. bapt*, 28. David F. Wright concludes his argument with this passage in "The Origins of Infant Baptism—Child Believers' Baptism?"

40. Basil, *Exh. bapt.* 5 (PG 31.433A).

Nyssa opens his address with a brief but similar summary, when he refers to the approaching "day of salvation" (the Pasch), at which "according to our custom (we) call strangers to adoption, those in need to participation in grace, those filthy in transgressions to the cleansing of sins."[41] Gregory of Nazianzus gives a lengthy and impressive list near the beginning of his discourse: "Illumination (the baptismal ceremony) is the splendor of souls, the conversion of the life, the pledge of a good conscience to God. It is the aid to our weakness, the renunciation of the flesh, the following of the Spirit, the fellowship of the Word, the improvement of the creature, the overwhelming of sin, the participation of light, the dissolution of darkness. It is the chariot to God, the dying with Christ, the bulwark of faith, the perfecting of the mind, the key of the kingdom of heaven, the exchange of life, the removal of slavery, the loosing of chains, the remodelling of the whole person . . . (It) is the greatest and most magnificent of the gifts of God."[42]

Gregory of Nazianzus follows his listing of the blessings of baptism with a list of its names: "We call it gift, grace, baptism, illumination, anointing, clothing of immortality, bath of regeneration, seal, and everything that is honorable" and proceeds to explain each of these names.[43] Illumination or enlightenment is the name with which Gregory begins his discourse, because "Yesterday we kept festival on the illustrious day of the Lights,"[44] and it continues to be frequently used throughout the sermon.[45] "Gift" is another favorite and distinctive word for Gregory of Nazianzus.[46] He also likes to speak of baptism as "grace,"[47] a common term with his colleagues as well.[48] Another important designation with Gregory is "seal," used for baptism itself, or possibly the baptismal ceremony as a whole,

41. Gregory of Nyssa, *Eos diff. bapt.* (PG 46.416C).

42. Gregory of Nazianzus, *In s. bapt.* 3.

43. Ibid., 4.

44. Ibid., 1.

45. Ibid., 1; 3; 4; 6; 10; 22; 24; 34; 36–37; 38; 46. For the theme of light in Gregory of Nazianzus, see Moreschini, *Grégoire de Nazianze: Discourse 38–41*, 62–70. Enlightenment is present in the other two works being studied—Basil, *Exh. bapt.* 1 (PG 31.424C), "Ignorance of God is the death of the soul," and "The one not baptized has not been enlightened"; and "light" in 3 (429A); cf. 7 (441B); it is expressly connected with baptism in Gregory of Nyssa, *Eos diff. bapt.* (PG 46.424B; 432A).

46. Gregory of Nazianzus, *In s. bapt.* 3; 11; 12; 16; 18; 21; 22; 23; 27; 31; 32; 34; 44.

47. Gregory of Nazianzus, *In s. bapt.* 2; 4; 7; 11; 12; 20; 24; 25; 26; 27; 28; 34; 44.

48. Basil, *Exh. bapt.* 1 (PG 31.425A); 3 (429B); 4 (432A); 5 (436A; 437A); 6 (437B); Gregory of Nyssa, *Eos diff. bapt.* (PG 46.416C; 420A,B,C—"river of grace"; 424A,B,D; 425A,B; 428A; 429B,C,D—"grace is a gift of the Master"; 432A.

and not for a separate part of it.[49] "Seal of the Spirit" is one of Basil the Great's names for baptism.[50] Although "seal" is his common term, he uses "marks" and "signs" as equivalent.[51] Gregory of Nyssa too uses "sealed" and "signed" as synonymous.[52]

All three Cappadocians associate baptism with rebirth. For Basil, it is a "spiritual rebirth" and the marvel of "how a person is born again without a mother."[53] He quotes John 3:5, "Unless one be born through water and the Spirit, he shall not enter the kingdom of heaven."[54] His brother cites John 3:3, "Unless one be born again he cannot see the kingdom of God."[55] The Nyssene adopts also the phraseology of Titus 3:5, "bath (or washing) of regeneration."[56] Gregory of Nazianzus speaks of baptism as a "birth" and "new birth" as well as a "regeneration."[57] Of the three, he makes the most use of the "bath" ("washing") or "laver."[58]

Two of the preachers make much of the imagery of Gal 3:27 and Romans 6 that baptism is being "crucified with Christ"[59] or "dying with Christ,"[60] and being buried and raised with Christ.[61]

The motif of forgiveness, cleansing, or pardon of sins occurs in all three.[62] So does the theme of freedom from imprisonment or slavery.[63] Also prominent is the use of the imagery of healing.[64] The idea of escape

49. Gregory of Nazianzus, *In s. bapt.* 4; 7; 10; 15; 17; 18; 23; 26; 28; 45.

50. Basil, *Exh. bapt.* 6 (PG 31.437A). Hence the title of Lampe's book studying the relation of the gift of the Spirit to baptism, *The Seal of the Spirit*.

51. Basil, *Exh. bapt.* 2 (PG 31.428C); 4 (PG 31.432C).

52. Gregory of Nyssa, *Eos diff. bapt.* (PG 46.424B).

53. Basil, *Exh. bapt.* 1 (PG 31.424B); 5 (433A).

54. Ibid. 2 (428A).

55. Gregory of Nyssa, *Eos diff. bapt.* (PG 46.424A).

56. Ibid. (PG 46.429C); cf. "grace of regeneration" (425B) and "benefit of the bath" (428B).

57. Gregory of Nazianzus, *In s. bapt.* 27; 2; 4; 8.

58. Ibid. 4; 10; cf. 17; 32.

59. Basil, *Exh. bapt.* 7 (PG 31.440B).

60. Gregory of Nazianzus, *In s. bapt.* 3.

61. Basil, *Exh. bapt.* 1; 2 (PG 31.424B-D; 428A); Gregory of Nazianzus, *In s. bapt.* 9; 24.

62. Basil, *Exh. bapt.* 4 (PG 31.432A-B)—whether the sins are many or few; Gregory of Nyssa; *Eos diff. bapt.* (PG 46.416C; 424B; 429C, D); Gregory of Nazianzus, *In s. bapt.* 3; 4; 7; 32; 34; 35.

63. Basil, *Exh. bapt.* 3 (PG 31.429B); Gregory of Nyssa, *Eos diff bapt.* (PG 46.417A, C; 424B); Gregory of Nazianzus, *In s. bapt.* 3; 13.

64. Basil, *Exh. bapt.* 2 (PG 31.428A); 3 (429B); Gregory of Nyssa, *Eos diff bapt.* (PG

from the devil is associated in the history of Christian thought especially with Gregory of Nyssa, but it is found in the other two Cappadocians.[65] Even more characteristic of these exhortations is the warning about the deceitfulness of the devil, who seeks to prevent one from being baptized[66] and after baptism continues to be the tempter.[67]

The community of thought among the three great Cappadocians is revealed perhaps even more than in these major themes by the incidental points they share in common. Thus all three use the example of the Ethiopian treasurer in Acts 8 with the appeal to imitate his readiness to accept baptism immediately from Philip, for nothing but the devil "hinders."[68] The parable of the talents (Matt 25:14–30) is employed by all three: being baptized is putting one's talent to work in contrast to burying it in the ground.[69] There is a common use of the "sealed" or "marked" sheep as an illustration of the identification and security of the baptized person.[70] The danger of shipwreck before reaching a harbor is another illustration in common to the Cappadocians, but the preachers allow their warning to carry them beyond Christian doctrine, for the suggestion is made that one by delay may commit sins greater than can be forgiven.[71]

Finally, it is fitting to note that all three, while exhorting their hearers to receive baptism, also lay stress on the life expected of the person baptized. The blessings of baptism are directly related to the Christian life. Gregory of Nyssa, in keeping with his moral concerns,[72] emphasizes this theme, which may be summarized by the phrase "life according to the

---

46.417A, B); Gregory of Nazianzus, *In s. bapt.* 12; 26; 34.

65. Gregory of Nyssa, *Eos diff. bapt.* (PG 46.417C); Basil, *Exh. bapt.* 2 (PG 31.428B); Gregory of Nazianzus, *In s. bapt.* 35.

66. Basil, *Exh. bapt.* 6 (PG 31.437B-C); Gregory of Nyssa, *Eos diff bapt.* (PG 46.421A); Gregory of Nazianzus, *In s. bapt.* 14; 16.

67. Gregory of Nazianzus, *In s. bapt.* 10.

68. Basil, *Exh. bapt.* 6 (PG 31.437A-B); Gregory of Nyssa, *Eos diff. bapt.* (PG 46.421C); Gregory of Nazianzus, *In s. bapt.* 26–27.

69. Basil, *Exh. bapt.* 5 (PG 31.437A); Gregory of Nyssa, *Eos diff. bapt.* (PG 46.429A-B); Gregory of Nazianzus, *In s. bapt.* 12.

70. Basil, *Exh. bapt.* 4 (PG 31.432C); Gregory of Nyssa, *Eos diff bapt.* (PG 46.417B); Gregory of Nazianzus, *In s. bapt.* 15.

71. Basil, *Exh. bapt.* 5 (PG 31.433C); Gregory of Nazianzus, *In s. bapt.* 1.1; 12. Gregory of Nyssa makes the same error but with the illustration of a long lasting illness stronger than the healing—*Eos diff bapt.* (PG 46.417B).

72. Ferguson, "Some Aspects of Gregory of Nyssa's Moral Theology in the Homilies on Ecclesiastes."

Gospel," at both the beginning and end of his sermon.[73] Basil describes the "Gospel way of life": "vigilance of eyes, control of tongue, enslavement of body, humble thinking, purity of thought, extinction of wrath; being pressed into service, do more; being defrauded, do not go to court; being hated, love; being persecuted, forbear; being blasphemed, comfort."[74] Gregory of Nazianzus devotes a long section toward the close of his sermon to an exhortation that the whole self is to be sanctified.[75]

These three exhortations to baptism, as was customary with all sermons, close with a doxology. Gregory of Nazianzus's is a fitting close of this study: When we enter inside with the Bridegroom, "We all, both those who teach these things and those who learn, will share in the more pure and more perfect teachings in the same Christ our Lord, to whom be the glory and the kingdom forever and ever. Amen."[76]

---

73. Gregory of Nyssa, *Eos diff bapt.* (PG 46.421A-B; 429B, D; 432A).

74. Basil, *Exh. bapt.* 7 (PG 31.440A-B).

75. Gregory of Nazianzus, *In s. bapt.* 38–41.

76. Gregory of Nazianzus, *In s. bapt.* 46.

# 7

# Basil's Protreptic to Baptism

MANY EXHORTATIONS TO BAPTISM were delivered in the latter half of the fourth century;[1] one of these is Basil of Caesarea's *Exhortation to Holy Baptism*.[2] This work has been less studied than another discourse attributed to Basil, *On Baptism*,[3] perhaps because of the controversy over the genuineness of the latter.[4] The only major recent study of the *Exhortation* I have found is that by Jean Gribomont.[5] Here I

---

1. In addition to the works of the Cappadocian Fathers discussed in this paper, note the following by Latin authors: Zeno, the eight *Invit. font.=tract.* 1.32, 1.49, 2.28, 1.55, 2.23, 1.23, 1.12, and 2.14 in Löfstedt, *Zenonis Veronensis Tractatus*; Max. Taur., *Ser.* 111.3 in Mutzenbecher, *Maximi Episcopi Taurinensis Sermones*; Augustine, *Ser.* 132.1 and 216.4, 9.

2. ‛Ομιλία προτρεπτικὴ εἰς τὸ ἅγιον βάπτισμα; PG, vol. 31, coll. 423–44. In the body of this paper, I shall refer to this work as the *Exhortation*; elsewhere, under the abbreviation *Exh.*, I shall cite texts from the PG first by the chapter or section number of the ancient work and then by the number and letter of the column in the printed volume. I follow, with slight revision, the translation of Halton in Hamman, ed., *Baptism: Ancient Liturgies and Patristic Texts*, 76–87.

3. Περὶ βαπτίσματος; PG, vol. 31, col. 1513–1628. In the body of this paper, I shall refer to this work as *On Baptism*; elsewhere, under the abbreviation *Bapt.* I follow, with slight revision, the English translation by Wagner, *Saint Basil: Ascetical Works*, 339–430.

4. Most scholars now seem to favor authenticity, as a result of the extensive parallels assembled in Neri's commentary to accompany his critical edition and translation, *Basilio di Cesarea, Il Battesimo*; his conclusions are summarized on 31–53. Neri's critical text is used by Ducatillon in *Basile de Césarée: Sur le Bapteme*.

5. Gribomont, "Saint Basile: Le Protreptique au Baptême." This article is wrongly assigned to *Word and Spirit* in BPatr 24/25 (1979/80) 84, #1087. There is a brief

purpose first to consider some key elements of the work—its deployment of rhetorical devices, use of Scripture, references to contemporary liturgy, and instruction in doctrinal and moral issues—and then to compare it with analogous works by Gregory of Nazianzus and Gregory of Nyssa.

Despite some ancient evidence for other attributions, the genuineness of this work seems generally accepted.[6] The *Exhortation* refers to the approach of the Pasch (1, 424D), and the occasion for the sermon is to encourage catechumens to turn in their names in order to undergo the final preparations for baptism (7, 440A). If we follow the predominant tradition in favor of Basil's authorship, the work likely comes from early in his episcopate, so the date would be prior to the paschal season in the years from 371 to 373.[7]

## RHETORICAL FEATURES[8]

Basil addresses the problem, which became common after the example of Constantine, of catechumens who delayed receiving baptism until the approach of death.[9] Basil mercilessly exposes all excuses. He exalts the advantages enjoyed by those who receive baptism (3, 429A–431A; 5, 433A), and he repeatedly warns about the dangers of delay (3, 429C; 5, 433B–C; esp. 7f., 441B–444C). Whatever one's age, one should act now, because of the uncertainties of life (5, 432C, 436C). Basil responds to the temptations to procrastinate offered by the devil (6, 437B–C) and answers objections about the supposed difficulty of the Christian life (7, 440B–D). Worthwhile human endeavors such as agriculture, commerce, marriage, and raising children carry the risk of failure, but they are not avoided (7,

---

treatment of the *Exh.* in Bernardi, *La prédication des Pères Cappadociens*, 68–70.

6. Fedwick, "The Translations of the Works of Basil before 1400," 455–56. for the attribution of this work to Chrysostom by Augustine and note 89, p. 456 for the same attribution in some Greek manuscripts. V. note 193, p. 478 for an Armenian version that assigns the work to Severian of Gabala.

7. Gribomont, "Saint Basile: Le protreptique au Baptême," says (71, 87–88) January 7, 371 or 372; Bernardi, *La prédication des Pères Cappadociens*, suggests (68) January 6 (Epiphany), 371, but acknowledges (p. 394) that the date is not certain.

8. For Basil's educational preparation, see Olbricht, "The Education of a Fourth Century Rhetorician."

9. Gregory Nazianzen (*Or.* 40, εἰς τὸ ἅγιον βάπτισμα, PG, vol. 36, col. 360B) and Gregory of Nyssa (πρὸς τοὺς βραδύοντας εἰς τὸ βάπτισμα, PG, vol. 46, col. 415f.B) also addressed this subject in discourses influenced by Basil's exhortation. V. the brief comparison at the end of this paper. In the body of this paper, I shall refer to the first work as *Or.* 40 and to the second as *Against Those Who Delay Baptism*.

441A). Though many who become catechumens spend their lives in pleasure with the idea of giving to God their old age (5, 433B, 436B), Basil urges that the present is the proper time for baptism and the acceptance of the life it entails (1, 424A–C).

As the Greek title indicates, the work is a protreptic. The rhetorical analysis by Gribomont makes unnecessary a similar undertaking on my part.[10] Gribomont notes some of the features of protreptic found in the speech: the hearers are continually addressed in the second person singular; there are, according to his counts, some fifty imperatives, seventy-six questions, and at least a dozen exclamations underlined by "Oh" (Ὦ + the genitive) or "Woe" (Αἴ με).[11]

I want to call attention to some other rhetorical features of the *Exhortation* that are recorded in J. M. Campbell's study of the style of the sermons of Basil. He mentions the frequency of redundancy and especially repetition in the *Exhortation*.[12] Campbell further notes some of the devices for achieving vivacity. Basil is fond of putting imagined speech in the first person into the mouth of the hearers (προσωποποιία).[13] Extended examples occur in chapters five (433B, 436A–B) and eight (444A–B). He often employs the rhetorical question.[14]

Metaphors and illustrations are also frequent. Campbell counts thirty-seven examples of metaphor.[15] Examples of Basil's use of metaphors common among rhetoricians are his illustrations drawn from military life (an army's use of a password, 4, 432B), medicine (a physician who promises to restore youth, 5, 432D), the sea (a ship overloaded, 5, 433C), and athletics (a crown won only by competition, 7, 44a).[16] Among the less common metaphors Basil gives some elaboration to the follow-

---

10. Gribomont, "Saint Basile: Le protreptique au Baptême," gives (pp. 73–86) this outline: Exordium (424A8–423A1), Narratio (425A1–428A15), Argumentatio I. Exempla et hypotheseis (428A15–433B1), Argumentatio II. Refutatio (433B1–440A6), Argumentatio III. Conclusio et confirmatio (440A6–444B7), Peroratio (444B7–C8).

11. Ibid., 73. V, e.g., 3, 429B–C; 8, 444A.

12. Campbell, *The Influence of the Second Sophistic*, ch. 4 and 5.

13. Ibid., 58–60. He counts (p. 60) six examples in the *Exh.*

14. Campbell's (ibid.) count (p. 52) of 35 may differ from Gribomont's ("Saint Basile: Le protreptique au Baptême") 76 interrogations (p. 73), because the latter is counting all questions and Campbell only what he considers rhetorical questions.

15. Campbell, *The Influence of the Second Sophistic*, 96–109.

16. Among the most common metaphors in rhetoric Campbell (ibid.) counts (p. 107) the following in the *Exh.*: military (3), athletics (4), hippodrome (2), sea (1), debt (3), agriculture (1), heavenly bodies (1), roads (2), court (5), personification (1), and theater (0). I have not attempted to verify these.

ing: a heifer under the yoke (1, 425C), a distribution of gold (3, 429A), a freeing of slaves (3, 429B), a cancelling of debts (3, 429C–D), objects that are sealed or marked (4, 432C), a person seeking to win another's friendship (5, 433C), a mother bird that distracts hunters from her young (7, 437C–440A), enrollment in an army, or in athletic contests, or on the citizen list (7, 440A). Campbell concludes that Basil does not use the four common metaphors of rhetors—war, athletics, the hippodrome, and the sea—as often as other speakers did, but all do appear in this work. Campbell, who uses the term "comparisons" for "similes," records fewer of these in the *Exhortation*: to the sea (2), animals (3), and war (1).[17]

Basil makes much use of a practice dear to ancient rhetoricians, comparisons (σύγκρισις), especially those involving persons of the past.[18] In the *Exhortation* he draws lessons from John the Baptist (1, 425A), Moses and Israel (2, 428B), Elijah (two different episodes: 3, 428C–429A), Eve (3, 429C), and Cain (5, 436B). The rhetorical handbooks provide parallels also to his references to the ages of life (youth, prime of life, and old age: 5, 432C, 436C)[19] and to the times and occasions suitable for different activities (1, 424C).[20]

## USE OF SCRIPTURE

As with Basil's other writings, the *Exhortation* contains frequent quotations and allusions to Scripture, both the Old and New Testaments. The persons named in his historical comparisons are biblical. Biblical, rather than secular, history provides the common history for Basil and his hearers.

The *Exhortation* begins with a quotation of Eccl 3:1–2: "For everything there is a season, and a time for every matter under heaven: a time to be born, and a time to die." This leads into the declaration that every time in man's life is a time for baptism, but especially fitting is the day of the Pasch (1, 424C–D). The application of this passage to baptism occurs first in Cyril of Jerusalem, who also anticipates Basil in suggesting that

---

17. Ibid., 110–27, esp. p. 125.

18. See Men. Rh. secc. 376–77; Russell and Wilson, *Menander Rhetor*. Subsequent reference to Menander Rhetor follows this edition.

19. See ch. 6, secc. 265f. of the *Ars rh.* passed down under the name of Dionysius of Halicarnasus; Usener and Radermacher, *Dionysii Halicarnasei quae exstant*, vol. 6: *Opusculorum*, vol. 2. Subsequent reference to ps.-D. H. follows this edition.

20. See Men. Rh. sec. 408 and ps-D. H., *Ars rh.*, ch. 3, secc. 243–44.

the reversed order, "to die and to be born," is more appropriate to baptism (*Cat. mys.* 2.4). This is one of the indications that Basil knew the work of Cyril.[21]

Basil moves into the body of his discourse by quoting four passages that had occurred in the day's Scripture readings: Isa 1:16; Ps 33:6; Acts 2:38; and Matt 11:28 (1, 425A–B). These references, appropriate to baptism and Basil's exhortation, reflect the liturgical practice of Scripture readings from the prophets supplemented by the Psalms, from the apostles (the Epistle), and from Jesus in the Gospel.[22]

## LITURGICAL MATTERS

In addition to the liturgical readings and the liturgical calendar, Basil refers to vigils of prayer, fasting, and psalmody (7, 440D). Other liturgical information, as is to be expected, has to do with baptismal practice, but nothing exceptional is revealed. Baptism was preceded by catechesis (425A).[23] For some this was a lengthy period lasting from their youth (1, 425B), even for those born into Christian families like Basil himself, since they delayed submitting to the instruction that led immediately to baptism (6, 437A). The candidate entered that period of preparation by turning in his or her name and being enrolled (7, 440A).

The allusions to the baptismal ceremony imply that the person receiving baptism was of responsible age. Repentance was required (7, 441A). The ceremony itself involved speaking "the saving words" (τὰ σωτήρια ῥήματα), lifting the hands to heaven while standing, bending the knee in worship, being taught and making confession, giving adherence to God, and renouncing the Enemy (5, 436C).[24]

---

21. Gribomont, "Saint Basile: Le protreptique au Baptême," 74. Ecclesiastes received much study in the Cappadocian theological tradition; commentaries were written by Gregory Thaumaturgos, Gregory of Nyssa, and Evagrius of Pontus.

22. Gribomont, ibid., 75. Basil prefers the phrase "kingdom of heaven" to "kingdom of God"; this indicates the influence of the Gospel of Matthew. The same preference appears in *Bapt.*, except that there ἡ βασιλεία τοῦ θεοῦ is dictated a few times by its occurrence in biblical quotations. Where Basil determines his own terminology, he chooses ἡ βασιλεία τῶν οὐρανῶν.

23. I have surveyed the different contents of catechetical instruction in "Irenaeus' *Proof of the Apostolic Preaching and Early Catechetical Instruction.*"

24. Basil, speaking to those not yet initiated, perhaps consciously does not give details or reflect the exact order, but the items to which he refers may be compared with the preliminary and initiatory ceremonies described in Cyr. Hier., *Procat.* 8–16; id., *Cat. mys.* 1–3; and *Const. app.* 7.22, 41–44, which included acts of repentance,

These allusions occur in the context of sick-bed or death-bed baptism when the person may not be conscious. Basil emphasizes how undesirable it is not to be able to follow the initiation, not to experience what is happening, and for those present to be in doubt (5, 436D–437A). Evidently clinical baptism was an accepted practice, but these remarks seem to indicate uncertainty concerning its validity. Later in the treatise, Basil refers again to the practice of death-bed baptism and warns that delay may mean the absence of anyone to administer it (7, 441C).

Basil interprets Elijah's act of pouring water three times on the altar (1 Kgs 18:33–35) as prefiguring baptism in the three-fold name of the Trinity (3, 429A). This may indicate a triple pouring in baptism, but the use of water in the biblical story was sufficient to suggest baptism, and the three-fold action of Elijah is related to faith in the Trinity, not expressly to the baptismal action. It would, therefore, be dubious to build an argument for the baptismal procedure from this allusion.[25] His references to Israel drinking from the spiritual rock (1 Cor 10:4) and eating the bread of angels (Ps 78:25) and to Christians eating "the living bread" (τὸν ζῶντα ἄρτον; cf. John 6:51) allude to the baptismal Eucharist (2, 428B).[26] There are statements about being sealed (σφραγισθεὶς, 2, 428C; τὴν σφραγῖδα, 4, 432C; 6, 437A) but not about an anointing (e.g., a form of ἀλείφω) or chrism (e.g., some such word as χρίω, χρῖσις, χρῖσμα), and the references to a seal seem to indicate the baptism itself and not a particular part of the ceremony.[27]

## DOCTRINAL POINTS

Basil in his Exhortation mentions some of the fundamentals of Christian faith: the Trinity (3, 429A), God as Creator (1, 424C; 3, 429C), salvation

---

confession of sins, renunciation of Satan, reciting the creed to associate oneself with Christ, and baptismal confession (τὴν σωτήριον ὁμολογίαν), Hier., *Cat. mys.* 2.4) at the triple immersion.

25. A triple immersion is explicit in Cyr. Hier., *Cat. mys.* 2.4 (cf. *Cat. ill.* 17.14 for immersion) and Basil, *Sp. s.* 15.35.

26. Cf. Theod. Cyr., *Qu. 27 in Ex.*; Ambr., *Sacr.* 5.1.

27. See Gribomont, "Saint Basile: Le Protreptique au Baptême," 83, 91; and see my discussion below of the seal under the doctrine of baptism. It is possible, however, that the phrases τοῖς μυστικοῖς συμβόλοις, τὸ φῶς τοῦ προσώπου Κυρίου, τὰ γνωρίσματα, πρόβατον ἀσημεῖον, and ἐὰν μὴ σημειωθῇ of 432C allude to the chrism. There were both pre- and post-baptismal anointings in the different baptismal rites of the fourth century. These were often, but not consistently, associated with the Holy Spirit; see Lampe, *The Seal of the Spirit*, esp. 215–22.

through the death and resurrection of Christ (1, 424C-D; 2, 428A), the Spirit as a seal (6, 437A), the Church as mother (1, 425A), human free will (1, 425C; 5, 432C-436C), the value of the soul (3, 429C), the human propensity to sin and its harmful effects (5, 433B, 436A), resurrection and judgment (8, 441D-444C). The greatest doctrinal value of the treatise, naturally, pertains to the importance given to baptism.

Quite basic for Basil was the idea of baptism as death to sin and resurrection to life, the thought with which he begins (1, 424B-C).[28] The benefits ascribed to baptism are numerous: illumination (1, 424C; 3, 429A, C), adoption as children of God (1, 425A; cf. 3, 429B), perfection (1, 425A), likeness or union with God (1, 425A; 3, 429A), forgiveness of sins (4, 432A), spiritual rejuvenation (5, 433A). The metaphors in chapter 3 are pertinent here: the benefits of baptism are likened to a distribution of gold (429A), a release from slavery (429B), and a forgiveness of debts (429C-D). Hence, Basil calls baptism "the grace" (v., e.g., τὴν χάριν, 4, 432A; τῆς χάριτος, τὴν χάριν, 5, 437A), a common usage in Christian inscriptions.[29] An encomium was a part of speeches on many subjects, and Basil here pronounces an encomium on baptism: "Baptism is the ransom of captives, the remission of debts, the death of sin, the rebirth of the soul, the shining garment, the unbreakable seal, the chariot to heaven, the guarantee of the kingdom, the grace of adoption" (βάπτισμα αἰχμαλώτοις λύτρον, ὀφλημάτων ἄφεσις, θάνατος ἁμαρτίας, παλιγγενεσία ψυχῆς, ἔνδυμα φωτεινόν, σφραγὶς ἀνεπιχείρητος, ὄχημα πρὸς οὐρανόν, βασιλείας πρόξενον, υἱοθεσίας χάρισμα, 5, 433A).

Inasmuch as Basil was so important for defining the doctrine of the Holy Spirit, it is fitting that he says much about the Holy Spirit in relation to baptism. This is enunciated in his opening typologies of baptism. As Israel was figuratively baptized in the cloud and the sea (cf. 1 Cor 10:2), so baptism is accomplished in the reality of water and the Spirit (2, 427B).[30] Likewise, as Elijah ascended to heaven in the chariot of fire, one can "ascend to heaven through water and the Spirit" (δι' ὕδατος καὶ Πνεύματος ἀναβαίνειν εἰς τὸν οὐρανόν, 3, 428D).[31] The subsequent language com-

---

28. Cf. his use of Rom 6:2 (7, 440B); 6:5 (2, 428A); 6:13 (436B).

29. Lampe's (*A Patristic Greek Lexicon, sub voce*, χάρις I.C.1) "almost=baptism" does not do justice to the common equation of baptism with grace. For the inscriptions see Ferguson, "Inscriptions and the Origin of Infant Baptism," 41-42 (and ch. 10 in this volume).

30. This typology was thoroughly traditional; see Daniélou, *Sacramentum Futuri*, 152-76. For Basil's treatment, see also *Sp. s.* 14.31-33.

31. This was not a common baptismal image, but cf. Cyr. Hier., *Cat. ill.* 3.5, for the

paring to baptism the water and fire on Elijah's altar at Mount Carmel may also be intended to refer to the water and Spirit. The activity of the Spirit in baptism is related to Basil's favorite imagery of the seal. One is "sealed by baptism" (σφραγισθεὶς τῷ βαπτίσματι, 2, 428C), and baptism is called "the seal" (τὴν σφραγῖδα, 4, 432C), but it is the "seal of the Spirit" (τὴν σφραγῖδα τοῦ Πνεύματος, 6, 437A). This provides the proper understanding for this statement by Basil: "A Jew does not postpone circumcision . . . But you postpone a circumcision not done by hand in the stripping off of the flesh [Col 2:11], which circumcision is performed by baptism" (ʹΟ Ἰουδαῖος τὴν περιτομὴν οὐχ ὑπερτίθεται . . . σὺ δὲ τὴν ἀχειροποίητον περιτομὴν ἀναβάλλῃ ἐν τῇ ἀπεκδύσει τῆς σαρκός, ἐν τῷ βαπτίσματι τελειουμένην, 2, 428A). Baptism is not the spiritual circumcision, as a superficial reading might suggest, but the spiritual circumcision takes place in baptism. In keeping with early Christian interpretation, Basil does not equate circumcision with baptism, but with the activity of the Spirit in baptism.[32]

## MORAL CONCERNS

One is born to the Spirit by dying to the flesh (1, 424B), a favorite description with Basil. This expresses his rigorist moral concerns, which are so evident in his discussions of baptism that the treatise *On Baptism* may be classed among his ascetic works.[33] Basil exhorts, "Take instructions, learn the constitution of the Gospels" (Μάθε, διδάχθητι εὐαγγελικὴν πολιτείαν, 7, 440A).

Basil puts into the mouth of his hearer who delays receiving baptism the following representative list of sins: "I will use my body to enjoy what is shameful, I will wallow in the mud of pleasure, I will bloody my hands, I will plunder what belongs to others, I will walk in wickedness, I will curse and swear. And I will receive baptism when I finally cease from sin" (ἀποχρήσωμαι τῇ σαρκὶ πρὸς τὴν ἀπόλαυσιν τῶν αἰσχρῶν, ἐγκαλισθῶ τῷ βορβόρῳ τῶν ἡδονῶν, αἱμάξω τὰς χεῖρας, ἀφέλωμα

explanation that Elijah crossed the Jordan before he was taken up to heaven.

32. Ferguson, "Spiritual Circumcision in Early Christianity." I remain unconvinced by Daniélou's simple and unsubstantiated equation of spiritual circumcision with baptism in "Circoncision et baptême," 755–56. For the Spirit given in baptism according to Basil, see Lampe, *The Seal of the Spirit*, 198, 211, 240. Basil, *Sp. s.* 12.28—15.35 discusses the relation of the Spirit to baptism and offers numerous parallels to the *Exh.*

33. As is done by Wagner (*Saint Basil: Ascetical Works*). For the moral teachings of the *Exh.*, see Gribomont, "Saint Basile: Le protreptique au Baptême," 88–91.

τὰ ἀλλότρια, δολίως πορυεθῶ, ἐπιορκήσω, ψεύσωμαι· καὶ τότε τὸ βάπτισμα, ὅταν λήξω ποτὲ τῶν κακῶν, ὑποδέξομαι, 5, 433B). It is especially sinful pleasures that receive strong rebuke from Basil: "Pleasure is the hook of the devil, luring us to destruction. Pleasure is the mother of sin" (Ἡδονὴ ἄγκιστρόν ἐστι τοῦ διαβόλου πρὸς ἀπώλειαν ἕλκον. Ἡδονὴ μήτηρ τῆς ἁμαρτίας, 5, 436A). Basil sees pleasure as the main reason for the delay of baptism (3, 429C), as the principal enticement of the devil for the present (6, 437C), but as causing exhaustion (7, 440C), and as bringing eternal torment (8, 444B).

Basil appeals to the fear of punishment and the hope of reward in his stirring peroration. He exhorts, "Fear hell, or strive to gain the kingdom" (ἢ τὴν γέενναν φοβήθητι, ἢ τῆς βασιλείας ἀντιποιήθητι, 8, 444B). The glory of the righteous and the grief of sinners (8, 444A) make the struggles of the Christian life worth it. Basil anticipates the modern principle, no pain, no gain: "One does not bring off the prize without running the race" (Οὐδεὶς μὴ δραμὼν ἀνείλετο τὸ βραβεῖον, 7, 440B). Moreover, the works of the devil bring their pain in this life too. "The happpiness to be enjoyed in heaven succeeds these tribulations [of the righteous], while the suffering and sorrow of hell perpetuate the pains of sin" (Ταύτας μὲν τὰς θλίψεις ἡ ἐν τῇ βασιλείᾳ τῶν οὐρανῶν μακαριότης ἐκδέχεται· τοὺς δὲ τῆς ἁμαρτίας καμάτους τὸ τῆς γεέννης ἐπίπονον καὶ σκυθρωπόν ἀναμένει, 7, 440B-C).

In one of his vivid rhetorical appeals, Basil challenges his readers: "Now think as if your soul were in a balance, drawn in opposite directions by angels and devils. To which side will you give the impulse of your heart? Who will be victorious in your regard? Carnal pleasure or sanctification of soul?" (Νῦν ὥσπερ ἐπὶ τρυτάνης ἑστάναι νόμιζέ σου τὴν ψυχήν, ἔνθεν ὑπ' ἀγγέλων, κἀκεῖθεν ὑπὸ δαιμόνων διελκομένην. Τίσιν ἄρα δώσεις τὴν ῥοπὴν τὴν καρδίας; τί παρὰ σοὶ νικήσει; ἡδονὴ σαρκός, ἢ ἁγιασμὸς ψυχῆς; 4, 432B). Although the imagery of the scale is Roman, the picture of angels and demons contending for the soul is Jewish. Having come into Christian thought, it was particularly elaborated by Origen.[34] This picture of angels and demons drawing the soul in different

---

34. For Jewish thought: *Scroll of the Rule* secc. 3-4 (a spirit of perversity and a spirit of truth allotted to each person); for Christianity: Her., *Mand.* 6.2 (an angel of righteousness and an angel of wickedness with each person) and *Barn.* 18 (plural angels of God and angels of Satan set over the two ways of life). Origen (*Prin.* 3.2.3f. and esp. 3.3.4: good spirits and evil spirits competing for control of the soul) stresses the role of free will in determining which influences one will follow. See Ferguson, "Origen's Demonology," esp. 62-64.

directions but the person choosing which influence to follow coincides with Basil's definition of virtue: "To avoid evil and do good" (ἔκκλισις ἀπὸ κακοῦ, καὶ ποίησις ἀγαθοῦ, 5, 436B).

Corresponding to Basil's list of sins is a statement of some of the qualities that constitute virtue. The way of life according to the gospel involves "vigilance of the eyes, control of the tongue, mastery of the body, humility of mind, purity of thought, and an end to anger" (ὀφθαλμῶν ἀκρίβειαν, γλώσσης ἐκράτειαν, σώματος δουλαγωγίαν, φρόνημα ταπεινὸν, ἐννοίας καθαρότητα, ὀργῆς ἀφανισμόν, 7, 440B). One must take "the narrow road [of self-control] that leads to salvation" and not "the broad road of sin" (τὸ στενὸν τῆς ἐπὶ σωτηρίαν φερούσης, τὸ εὐρύχωρον . . . τῆς ἁμαρτίας, 7, 440C).

## COMPARISON WITH ON BAPTISM

A rapid survey of some points of comparison between the two works will not reveal any decisive considerations relative to authorship nor suggest any content inconsistent with Basilian authorship of *On Baptism*. The similarities and differences of the *Exhortation* and *On Baptism* are largely accounted for by their common subject and different purposes: the *Exhortation* is a protreptic to candidates for baptism, *On Baptism* perhaps a guide for catechists who instructed candidates for baptism.[35]

Both works make extensive use of Scripture; *On Baptism* more so, for it is almost a continuous string of quotations.[36] It takes as its basis Matt 28:19, and its theme may be stated as "to live according to the Gospel" (κατὰ τὸ Εὐαγγέλιον ζῆν, 2.1, 1580C; cf. 1.2, 1565B-1569A). The terminology is different, but the idea is the same as the *Exhortation*'s "constitution of the Gospels" or "evangelical way of life" or "way of life according to the gospel" (εὐαγγελικὴν πολιτείαν, 7, 440A). Fundamental texts for *On Baptism* are Rom 6:1-11 and John 3:5 with the accompanying ideas of crucifixion, death, planting, resurrection, and newness of life or new birth. Both texts are used in the *Exhortation* (2, 428A), but the theme of death to sin is even more prominent in the longer *On Baptism*.[37] Otherwise, there is very little overlap in the scriptures cited.

---

35. See Neri, trans. and ed., *Basilio di Cesarea, Il Battesimo*, 53, who says the hearers were for the most part priests or other persons with the care of souls.

36. For the doctrine of Scripture reflected in the work, see Neri's introduction, ibid., 54-64.

37. See 1.2, 1553A, 1540B, 1541C-D, 1544A; 1.3, 1577D; 2.1, 1580C. The moral

Both works contrast the superiority of Christian baptism to the baptisms of John and Moses, but the comparison is different in each case.[38] Both works consider catechesis important; *On Baptism* says that instruction is necessary before one is worthy to receive baptism (1.2, 1525C and 1569B; cf. *Exh*. 1, 425A, B). Both *On Baptism* 1.2 (1556B–C) and *Exhortation* 5 (433A) provide lists of benefits accomplished by the death of Christ and conferred in baptism, but the contents are completely different, because the list in the *Exhortation* draws on the metaphors that precede it.[39] The use of the analogy of circumcision is similar and in both cases based on Col. 2.11.: "If one who has been circumcised in any part of the body, according to the circumcision of Moses, is a debtor to the whole law, how much greater is the obligation when one is circumcised according to the circumcision of Christ, whereby he puts off the whole body of sinful flesh." (Εἰ ... ὁ περιτμηθεὶς μέρος τι τοῦ σώματος, τὴν κατὰ Μωυσῆν περιτομὴν, ὀφειλέτης ἐστὶν ὅλον τὸν νόμον ποιῆσαι, πόσῳ μᾶλλον ὁ περιτμηθεὶς τὴν κατὰ Χριστὸν περιτομὴν ἐν τῇ ἀπεκδύσει ὅλου σώματος τῶν ἁμαρτιῶν τῆς σαρκός, 2.1,1580D; cf. *Exh*. 2, 428A). Once more, the consequences for moral living are paramount, an emphasis not inconsistent with the concerns of the *Exhortation* but not so prominent there because of its different occasion.

## COMPARISON WITH THE TWO GREGORIES

Approximately a decade later, both Gregory of Nazianzus and Gregory of Nyssa addressed the same problem as Basil, the delay of baptism, at the same season of the year, Epiphany. Nazianzen's *Or*. 40, "On Holy Baptism,"

---

teaching is similar to that of the *Exh*. and Basil's other works; see Neri, trans. and ed., *Basilio di Cesarea, Il Battesimo*, 69–97.

38. The *Exh*. contrasts John's baptism with that of Christ as only repentance instead of adoption as sons, only preliminary instead of accomplishment, only a break with sin instead of union with God (1, 425A); it contrasts Moses' baptism as type with Christ's reality (2, 428A–B). *Bapt*. presents Moses' baptism as recognizing a difference between sins and being a seal of purification; John's made no distinction among sins and offered pardon; Christ's, accompanied by the Holy Spirit, brings glory beyond all hope and a preeminence of grace (1.2, 1532C–1533C). The treatment in *Sp. s*. 14.31–15.36 is different from both.

39. *Bapt*. 1.2, 1556B–C: From the death of Christ flow λύτρωσις ἁμαρτημάτων, ἐλευθερία τοῦ ... θανάτου, καταλλαγὴ τῷ θεῷ, δύναμις τῆς πρὸς θεὸν εὐαρεστήσεως, δικαιοσύνης δωρεά, κοινωνία τῶν ἁγίων ἐν τῇ αἰωνίῳ ζωῇ, βασιλείας οὐρανῶν κληρονομία, καὶ μυρίων ἄλλων ἀγαθῶν βραβεῖον. The list in *Exh*. 5 is quoted in the text of p. 116 above.

is in scope and style much more ambitious than the related works of his fellow Cappadocians.⁴⁰ The Nyssene has two works on baptism, as does Basil, but only his *Against Those Who Delay Baptism*, a work closely approximating Basil's *Exhortation*, will be considered here.⁴¹

The discourse of Gregory Nazianzus offers several exact parallels, indicating a direct indebtedness, to that of Basil. In keeping with his fuller treatment, he elaborates the use of Ecclesiastes 3, and makes the point that every time is appropriate for the work of salvation. In the same context, he rebukes the attitude of procrastination that yields to the Evil One's enticement: "Give to me . . . the present, and to God the future; to me your youth, and to God old age" (᾿Εμοὶ δὸς τὸ παρὸν, θεῷ τὸ μέλλον· ἐμοὶ τὴν νεότητα, θεῷ τὸ γῆρας, 14, 376C; cf. *Exh*. 5, 436B; 6, 437C). Like Basil, Gregory develops the theme of the devil's deceit in inducing people to delay baptism (chh. 14, 16). In addition, the warnings about the uncertainties of life are parallel, although Gregory multiplies the specific examples (cf. 14, 376D-377A with *Exh*. 5, 436C).⁴² Gregory also deals with the concern of not living up to the requirements of the Christian life: "Do you fear the seal because of the weakness of nature?" (δέδοικας τὴν φραγῖδα διὰ τὸ τῆς φύσεως ἀσθενές, 17, 380D-381A; cf. ch. 16 and *Exh*. 7, 440B-D). Like Basil, he stresses the appropriateness of baptism for the different ages (ch. 17; cf. *Exh*. 5, 432C) and conditions of life: "There is no state of life and no occupation to which baptism is not profitable" (οὐκ ἔστιν οὐ βίος, οὐκ ἐπιτήδευμα, ᾧ μὴ τοῦτο λυσιτελέστερον, 18, 381C). Gregory too is of the opinion that pleasure is the chief deterrent to accepting baptism (e.g., 20, 384D).

Acts 8:36, "Here is water! What is to prevent my being baptized?" (᾿Ιδοὺ τὸ ὕδωρ· τί κωλύει με βαπτισθῆναι;) lent itself admirably to the needs of both preachers to encourage immediate baptism (cf. 26, 396A with *Exh*. 6, 437A). There is an incidental agreement in their use of the parable of "the Unforgiving Servant" in Matt 18:23-35 (31, 404B-C; cf.

---

40. PG, vol. 36, coll. 359-428. I cite, with occasional modification, the translation in *NPNF*, 2nd series, vol. 7 (New York, etc. 1894; rpt. 1989): *S. Cyril of Jerusalem, S. Gregory Nazianzen*, 360-77. A full-scale comparison of the three Cappadocians' works on baptism is beyond my intentions here. See Ferguson, "Preaching at Epiphany"; and Ferguson, "Exhortations to Baptism in the Cappadocians."

41. PG, vol. 46, coll. 415-32. Since this text provides no chapter divisions, reference will be solely by column, i.e., number and letter. *Cf.* note 2 above. Translations from this work are my own. The second work, "On the Baptism of Christ" = CPG, #3173.

42. Cf. *Or*. 40.13, 376A: Πᾶς σοι καιρὸς ἐκπλύσεως, ἐπειδὴ πᾶς ἀναλύσεως.

*Exh.* 3, 432A).[43] More striking is Gregory's use of the "seal" (σφραγίς, σφραγίζω) in the same sense as Basil (10, 372A; 15, 377A–B; 17, 380D), even to the detail of the unmarked sheep being easily stolen (15, 377B; cf. *Exh.* 4, 432C). Furthermore, Gregory closely approximates Basil's words about being baptized while not so sick as to be unable to say the confession.[44] Again the borrowing extends even to a detail. Elaborating the death-bed scene, he repeats the incidental comparison of the person baptized *in extremis* to the one-talent man of Matt 25:25 (11f., esp. 373B–C; cf. *Exh.* 5, 436C–437A; 7, 441C).

Gregory of Nyssa's *Against Those Who Delay Baptism* is dense with parallels to Basil's *Exhortation* but is nonetheless a work of originality. Gregory's work, while making frequent use of Scripture, has fewer explicit quotations and refers to the Bible more allusively than does Basil's *Exhortation*. The quotations offer some exact parallels to Basil's work: the combination of Ps 33:6 and Isa 1:16, but in this reversed order (417C; cf. *Exh.* 1.425A), Acts 8:27–39 (more elaborated, 421C–D; cf. *Exh.* 6, 437A), and Jn 3:5 (424A; cf. *Exh.* 2, 428A).

Basil's brother repeats his exhortation not to delay the reception of baptism (417D–420A). Death may intervene before baptism is received (417D; cf. *Exh.* 7f., 441B–444C). Life is uncertain (420B), and death may come at any age (417D–420A; cf. *Exh.* 5, 432C, 436C). Gregory too feels he must answer the objection that, because of the weakness of human nature, one may easily sin after baptism, so it is better to "delay the grace of regeneration" (πρὸς τὴν χάριν τῆς παλιγγενεσίας βραδύνω, 425B; cf. *Exh.* 7, 440B–441A). He enlarges on a strategy borrowed from Basil in order to show the speciousness of this argument: If the catechumens are living blameless lives now, there is nothing to fear from baptism; if they are living impure lives, they show that they do not want to give up the life of sin (425C–D; cf. *Exh.* 4, 432A–B).

The Nyssene uses some of the same metaphors as his brother, but not brought together in the same way. Some are less developed, and others more elaborated: release to those in bonds and settlement for debtors (417A; cf. *Exh.* 3, 429B, C–D), healing (a favorite of Gregory's, 417B; cf. *Exh.* 5, 432D), distribution of royal gifts (417B; cf. *Exh.* 3, 429A), the newly enrolled soldier (429C; cf. *Exh.* 7, 440A).

---

43. This is the title given by the editors of *The Greek New Testament*.
44. *Or.* 40.26, 396A: "Ἅρπασον τὸν καιρόν . . . καὶ εἰπών, βαπτίσθητι, καὶ βαπτισθεὶς σώθητι.

Gregory of Nyssa, like Basil, urges his hearers: "Give me your names in order that I may inscribe them" (Δότε μοι τὰ ὀνόματα, ἵνα ἐγὼ μὲν αὐτὰ ... ἐγχαράξω, 417B; cf. *Exh.* 7, 440A). Otherwise, there are fewer allusions to liturgical practice. This makes all the more striking the description—similar to those of his namesake and his brother—of the sickbed and the tumult and disorder of the last hours of life when there is the hurried search for "the sacred vessels, the water, the priest, the word that makes ready for grace" (τὰ σκεύη, τὸ ὕδωρ, ὁ ἱερεὺς, ὁ λόγος πρὸς τὴν χάριν προευτρεπίζων, 425A; cf. *Exh.* 5, 436C–437A; 7, 441C). It is better in "leisure and calmness" (ἐν σχολῇ καὶ γαλήνῃ) to make the arrangements to be numbered "in the list of those adopted as sons" (τῷ καταλόγῳ τῶν υἱοθετουμένων, 425B).

Gregory, like the other Cappadocians, refers to baptism as the "seal" and uses the analogy of the sheep that is sealed (τὴν σφραγῖδα, 417B; cf. 424B). Like Basil and Gregory Nazianzus, he also appeals to the "one talent" of Matt 25:25 in his exhortation to baptism; Gregory urges his hearers not to bury it, by deferring baptism to a last-minute decision, but to put it to work (429A–B). Like Basil, he equates baptism and grace (424D; cf., e.g., *Exh.* 4, 432A). Gregory of Nyssa gives a much shorter list of the benefits of baptism: adoption, participation in grace, cleansing of sins (416C).

Gregory of Nyssa shares Basil's concerns with the threat offered by the appeal of pleasure. He presents baptism as "a hindrance of pleasures" (ἡδονῶν κώλυμα, 425D). He tells his hearers, "Many times you gave yourself to pleasure; give also time to philosophy" (i.e., to the disciplined ascetic life; πολλοὺς χρόνους ἐχαρίσω τῇ ἡδονῇ· δὸς καὶ τῇ φιλοσοφίᾳ σχολήν, 420B–C).

## CONCLUSION

It is a measure of how far the church and its situation in society had changed that authors in the third century wrote exhortations to martyrdom, whereas preachers in the last half of the fourth century delivered exhortations to baptism. The danger to the church was no longer members who apostatized in face of persecution. Now there were those who wanted the status of Christians without the responsibilities.

# 8

# Preaching at Epiphany
## Gregory of Nyssa and John Chrysostom on Baptism and the Church

FROM AS EARLY AS 200 CE, the church made the spring paschal celebration its primary occasion for baptizing new converts.[1] A week of intense preparation climaxed for the candidates in their reception of baptism early on Easter Sunday. During the fourth century, the preliminary preparation of candidates during Lent included attendance at lectures that gave doctrinal instruction.[2] The catechumens who were ready to receive baptism at the coming Pasch turned in their names to be enrolled for the period of teaching.[3] This registration for the final period of catechetical instruction occurred near the beginning of the year, not long after the feast of Epiphany on 6 January—celebrated in the Eastern church since the fourth century as the feast of the baptism of Christ.[4] The

---

1. Evans, ed., *Tertullian's Homily on Baptism*, ch. 19.

2. Cyril of Jerusalem, *Catechetical Lectures*, may be taken as representative.

3. For a convenient outline of the fourth-century period of preparation and the initiation rites, see the introduction in Yarnold, *The Awe-inspiring Rites of Initiation*. Broader treatments are found in Riley, *Christian Initiation*; Finn, *The Liturgy of Baptism in the Baptismal Instructions of St. John Chrysostom*; and the extensive collection of sources with explanation in Finn, *Early Christian Baptism and the Catechumenate*.

4. In pre-Christian Egypt, 5 January was celebrated as a time when certain springs yielded wine instead of water, and 6 January as the birthday of Aion/Dionysus. The first evidence of an observance of the baptism of Christ in Christian circles concerns the followers of Basilides, "who hold the day of his baptism as a festival, spending

proximity of these two events—a celebration of Christ's baptism and the enrolling of candidates for baptism at the next Pasch—made the time around Epiphany a propitious time for preaching sermons on baptism. Since many catechumens in the fourth century delayed their baptism until old age, many of these sermons took the form of exhortations to baptism in order to encourage the hearers not to postpone baptism but to enroll for the immediate season.[5]

While not exhortations to receive baptism, Epiphany sermons by Gregory of Nyssa and John Chrysostom take the feast commemorating the baptism of Christ as the occasion to discuss baptism and related matters.[6] These two sermons have a proximity in space and time: Gregory preached his sermon in the province of Cappadocia in 383, and John delivered his in Antioch of Syria at Epiphany 387.[7] Gregory, called "the Philosopher," appropriately delivers the more theological of the two sermons; John, the "Golden Mouth," is the great homilist of the Greek church, and he appropriately provides the more pastoral sermon. Both sermons contain themes of importance to the church's doctrinal self-understanding and its sociological setting in the late fourth century. Baptism was the boundary line distinguishing the church from Jews and pagans. An examination of Epiphany sermons on the baptism of Christ by Gregory of Nyssa and John Chrysostom reveals not only the church's pastoral and theological preoccupations but also reinforces the centrality of baptism in the fourth-century church.

---

the night before in readings," Clement of Alexandria, *Stromata* 1.21. This passage is the point of departure for Vigne, "Enquête sur Basilide." More orthodox Christians wanted to associate the "manifestation" of Christ with his birth, but the association of 6 January with the baptism continued. On this issue, see Botte, *Les Origins de la Noël et de l'Epiphanie*; McArthur, *The Evolution of the Christian Year*, 31–76, who argues for a unified celebration of the Incarnation and the baptism before the former was associated with 25 December; Bainton, "The Origins of Epiphany" (Bainton argues for the association with the birth from the early second century); and Mossay, *Les fêtes de Noël et de l'Epiphanie d'après les sources littéraires cappadociens au IVe siècle*.

5. Examples of such exhortations include Basil of Caesarea, *Exhortation to Baptism*; Gregory of Nazianzus, *Oration* 40; and Gregory of Nyssa, *Against Those Who Delay*, which are studied in Ferguson, "Exhortations to Baptism in the Cappadocians."

6. Gregory of Nyssa's is identified as *In diem luminum* ("On the Day of Lights"), but popularly as *In baptismum Christi oratio*; John Chrysostom's is *In Homiliam de Baptismo Christi et de epiphania*.

7. Quasten, *Patrology*, vol. 3, 277; Daniélou, "La chronologie des oeuvres de Grégoire de Nysse," 164; and introductory note in Migne, PG, 49.361–62.

## GREGORY OF NYSSA

In his introduction to *On the Baptism of Christ*,[8] Gregory of Nyssa indicates that Epiphany was a popular festival when large numbers were at church: "The people that can find no place within fill the outer courts like bees" (221.6-9).[9] Parents brought their children ("I see you gathering together with your families," 222.3-4); those already baptized ("the initiated," 222.16) brought those who were not baptized in hopes of leading them "to the perfect reception of piety" (222.20-21). Gregory constantly ties his message to Scripture, and here he quotes Isaiah 60:8 (LXX) and 49:20 in reference to the growth of the church. While he celebrates the crowds present, he laments that at other times, as on "the last Lord's day" (221.18), attendance was not so large. Chrysostom elaborated even more on the contrast between the crowds present for Epiphany and the much lower attendance on other occasions. Special events were important for creating community spirit and celebrating the numerical triumph of the church (222.12).

Between the introduction and conclusion Gregory develops three main themes: the blessings of baptism, with special consideration of how material objects may be the means for spiritual blessings; Old Testament anticipations of baptism through the presence of water as a type of baptism and through prophetic passages; and the life expected of the baptized person. Gregory uses the presence of the uninitiated to lead into his first main point, the blessings of baptism. The church has a sacramental life that begins with baptism and continues to be defined by baptism. He offers this list of what can be hoped for from "the grace of the baptismal bath" (223.2): "forgiveness of things for which accused, release from bondage, close relationship to God, free boldness of speech, and in place of servile subjection equality with the angels" (222.23—223.1). Christ received baptism in order that "He might cleanse the one who has been defiled, bring down the Spirit from above, and lift up man to heaven, so that he who had fallen might be raised up and he who had cast him down might be put to shame" (223.14-16). To this summary of the accomplishments of Christ's baptism he adds the following definition: "Baptism, then, is a cleansing from sins, a forgiveness of trespasses, a cause of renewal and regeneration"

---

8. Text edited by Gebhart in GNO 9: *Sermones I*, 221-42; translation by H. A. Wilson in *NPNF* series 2, 5:518-24.

9. Direct quotations are my own renderings from GNO 9; references are to page and line. See also Chrysostom, *On the Baptism of Christ* 1 (PG 49.363), cited before note 34.

(224.4–5). Regeneration, in fact, is Gregory's favorite description of baptism in this sermon.[10] While not the explicit hortatory rhetoric found in his sermon "Against Those Who Delay Baptism," such lists of the blessings of baptism may have implicitly encouraged the uninitiated to make the decision to receive baptism. In this discussion Gregory gives prominence to a favorite motif in his doctrine of the atonement, namely the defeat of the devil, "the wicked enchanter" (223.20–21), contrasting his entering into "that creeping thing," the serpent, with Christ's assuming "perfect manhood" in order to repair the devil's "evil-doing" (223.22–25).[11]

Gregory quotes as his key text the most important baptismal text in the ancient church, John 3:5: "Except one be born of water and of the Spirit, he cannot enter into the kingdom of God" (224.27—225.1). That text introduces the topic of the use of material means and actions for a spiritual purpose. Why does God require water? Is not the Spirit alone sufficient?[12] Gregory responds that humanity is a compound of body and soul, so the combination of the sensible and the invisible is appropriate: the Spirit "blesses the body that is baptized, and the water that baptizes" (225.10–11). One should not despise the use of water as a common thing, Gregory urges. Ordinary things, when they receive the blessing and power of God, become effective for mighty and marvelous purposes other than their ordinary use. The stone of the altar, when consecrated to the service of God, becomes "a holy table," "no longer touched by all, but only by the priests" (225.18–20). The "common bread," when consecrated, "is called and becomes the body of Christ" (225.21–24).[13] This also happens

---

10. The fifteen occurrences are almost equally distributed between *anagennesis* (based on John 3:5), which appears eight times, and *palingennesia* (based on Titus 3:5), mentioned seven times. A form of *baptisma*, of course, occurs more often—twenty-one times—and because of the use of Old Testament episodes and the argument for the use of material elements, "water" is frequent—twenty-nine times (all occurrences). Other common terms in reference to baptism are *loutron* ("bath," mentioned four times), *charis* (nine times, with reference to the "grace" of baptism, although judgments on some allusions may vary), and *dorea* ("gift," three times). Chrysostom too uses regeneration frequently; see for example Harkins, *St. John Chrysostom: Baptismal Instructions*, 9.12.

11. Gregory is a leading interpreter of the atonement as a ransom from the devil's dominion over humanity; see *Catechetical Oration* 22–26; Aulén, *Christus Victor*, 62–71; and H. E. W. Turner, *The Patristic Doctrine of Redemption*, 57–61.

12. In "On the Holy Spirit" (GNO 3.1, p. 105) Gregory stresses the place of the Spirit in giving life in the water, even as in this sermon he stresses the necessity of water as the means through which the Spirit works.

13. Gregory's *Catechetical Oration* 37, starting with the description of humans as composed of body and spirit and continuing with the process of Incarnation, is

with the sacramental oil and the wine. Likewise the word of benediction transforms an ordinary man by "some invisible power and grace" into "a venerable and honorable priest" (225.26—226.8). The passage is an important contribution to the development of sacramental theology, and it is noteworthy that Gregory makes the "word of the blessing" the key element in the consecration of material objects to a new use and new power.[14]

Gregory turns from these illustrations drawn from contemporary church practice to stories from past history to further illustrate material means used for spiritual purposes (226.8—227.4). He refers to the rod of Moses that worked miracles (Exod 4:1–5) and the mantle of Elijah worn by Elisha (2 Kgs 2:6–14). The wood of the cross has a "saving function" (226.23), even as a thorn bush revealed the presence of God to Moses (Exod 3:1–6) and clay gave sight to a blind man (John 9). Water, also, "renews one to spiritual regeneration, when the grace from above blesses it" (227.5–7). Humans may not be able to understand how water does this, for God's power and wisdom lie beyond human explanation. Gregory challenges doubters to explain the physical generation of the flesh, and if they can do this, then he will explain the regeneration of the soul.[15]

Gregory then turns his hearers' attention from the unanswerable question of how God works through ordinary things to a consideration of what can be partly comprehended, "the reason why the cleansing is done by water [and not something else] and what is the need for three immersions" (228.6–7).[16] Of the four elements—fire, air, earth, and water—Gregory sets forth water as akin to earth. As Christ was buried in the earth, his followers in imitation of him are concealed in the water.[17] This

---

parallel to this section of the sermon, including the affirmation, "The bread that is consecrated by the word of God is changed into the body of God the Word."

14. This accords with the argument regarding ordination, one of Gregory's illustrations, in Ferguson, "Laying on of Hands," namely that the prayer, while accompanied by a physical action, is nonetheless the central element. For other passages in Gregory of Nyssa, see Atchley, *On the Epiclesis of the Eucharistic Liturgy and in the Consecration of the Font*, sec. 14.

15. Gregory makes the same comparison in *Catechetical Oration* 33. Here Gregory gives an incidental piece of liturgical information, citing Ps 104:24, "O Lord, how manifold are your works; in wisdom you have made them all," as a verse "sung by all" (228.1), so attesting at his time the use of this Psalm that is part of the vespers of the Greek church.

16. I consider this exposition of the theological significance of water and the practice of triple immersion (228.4—229.18) as the climax of the first main topic on material means used for spiritual blessings, but it might be treated as an independent topic or as the theological premise of the second main division of the sermon.

17. See also Gregory of Nyssa, *Catechetical Oration* 35, for baptism in water as an

is done three times to represent the resurrection on the third day. And the baptism is not done in silence, for there is spoken over the one being baptized the names of "the three holy persons [hypostases]" (228.24) in whom faith is placed. This is done according to the command of Jesus in Matt 28:19. Gregory, in passing, jabs at contemporary theological opponents whose teaching threatened ecclesiastical unity. In reference to the controversy over the deity of the Holy Spirit, he emphasizes that the Holy Spirit is equally included with the Father and the Son and that the three persons are not divided.[18]

The sermon's next major part, marked by reference to the present "festival season" (230.17), takes up anticipations of baptism in the Old Testament. The church is in continuity with Israel, and although Gregory defines it in contrast to Israel, it draws its heritage from the same Scriptures. Those Scriptures, according to Gregory, foretold baptism "by action and by word" (230.15–16), which provides the two-fold subdivision (typical actions and prophetic sayings) of this section (230.19—237.22). He, as the other church fathers, fully appropriates the "ancient scriptures" (230.11) as a Christian book.

Gregory adduces eight types of baptism from Old Testament stories involving water.[19] First, Hagar and Ishmael were shown a well of water (Gen 21:15–19): "by means of living water there was salvation for him who was perishing" (231.7–8) Gregory makes an aside against the Jewish religion, explaining the empty waterskin of Hagar as representing that "the Synagogue is not self-sufficient for life" (231.3). Second, Abraham's servant found the wife for Isaac, Rebekah, at a well (Gen 24:15–20), and Isaac dug wells (Genesis 26:18–22) that had been filled up by "foreigners," a type of the "impious men of later times" who by their opposition to Christianity "hindered the gift of baptism" (231.18–19). Third, Jacob too met his wife Rachel at a well (Gen 22:9–10), and he laid "three rods" (232.14–22) by the watering trough where the flocks mated. Introducing one of his favorite themes, overcoming the devil, Gregory interprets Laban as the

---

imitation of Christ's burial in the earth and the triple action as representing the three days in the tomb.

18. See also *On the Holy Spirit* (GNO 3.1, p. 105, line 32—p. 106, line 4) for faith in the Father first, then faith in the Lord, and finally faith in the Holy Spirit, all joined in baptism.

19. The number could be increased by two, since he relates two incidents from the stories of Isaac and Jacob respectively; or alternatively reduced by one, since the crossing of the Red Sea could be considered under the heading of Moses. Daniélou, *From Shadows to Reality*, studies the most important types employed by the church fathers; many of Gregory's types of baptism are not included.

devil and Jacob as the Christ who by baptism takes away the flock of Satan. Fourth, Moses as a babe was placed in a basket on the bank of the river (Exod 2:2–4). In two asides at the Jews, who were, he says, "close to grace" (233.2–3), Gregory declares that the Law of Moses was enclosed in a coffer and that the daily sprinklings of the Hebrews were fulfilled in baptism. Fifth, the crossing of the Red Sea "proclaimed the good news of salvation by water" (233.6–7), for the devil is defeated "in the water of regeneration" (233.9–10).[20] Sixth, Joshua's setting up twelve stones in the Jordan (Josh 4:9) anticipated the twelve apostles, "the ministers of baptism" (233.24). Seventh, Elijah, at his contest with the prophets of Baal on Mount Carmel, had water poured three times on the altar before he prayed for fire from heaven to come down on the sacrifice (1 Kgs 18:30–40). Gregory elaborates on the addition of water to the prayer (in keeping with his earlier argument for the presence of the material element along with spiritual activity), the symbolism of fire for the Spirit, and the triple application of water.[21] And finally, Elisha cured Naaman the Syrian of leprosy by washing him in the Jordan (2 Kgs 5:1–14).

Gregory turns from these indications of regeneration by baptism in "deed and act" to "the prophecies of it in words and speech" (235.13; 235.15). He quotes eight (or nine) different passages from the prophets and Psalms that refer to water or baptismal motifs, especially in a future or hortatory context.[22] Notable for the understanding of baptism are two passages cited that do not refer to water: Psalms 34:5 in the Septuagint (33:6) speaks of being enlightened (235.18–19), and Zech 3:3 speaks of removing a filthy garment and being attired with "clean and bright clothing" (236.6–7).[23] Gregory declares that his discourse would extend indefinitely if he cited every possible passage in detail. Those events and prophecies he does use represent an already well-established practice of finding in

---

20. First Corinthians 10:2 made the crossing of the Red Sea a favorite baptismal type with Christians. The destruction of the Egyptians as representing the defeat of the devil and his servants is vividly expressed by Origen, *Hom. Ex.*, in Fortier, ed., Sources Chrétiennes 16, 5.1–2; and Cyril of Jerusalem, *Mys. Catech.*, 1.2–3 (Cross, ed.).

21. Gregory's brother Basil, in reference to this episode, implies the association of fire and Spirit and makes explicit the Trinitarian typology in the triple pouring of water; see *Exh. Bapt.* 3 (PG 31.428D–429A).

22. Isa 1:16; Ps 24:5; Ezek 36:25–27; Zech 3:3; Isa 35:1–2; Pss 143:6 and 42:2, quoted together (so I have counted them as one quotation; both are glossed with quotations from John 7:37 and 4:13–14); Pss 1:4; and 29:3–4.

23. For "enlightenment" as a name for baptism, see Ysebaert, *Greek Baptismal Terminology*, 173–75.

every Old Testament reference to water some teaching about Christian baptism.[24]

In the third major section of *On the Baptism of Christ* Gregory picks up the theme of change from the first section, only now the change has to do with the changed life following baptism. The moral life defines the character of the church: "Show me, after the mystical grace, the change in your ways, and make known by the purity of your manner of life the difference of your change of character for the better" (237.25–27).[25] The theme of the kind of life expected of those who have been baptized reflects Gregory's persistent moral concern.[26]

The baptized person outwardly appears unchanged. The tokens of the new life are found in the "intentional motions of the soul" (238.6). As representative of the transformation in conduct, Gregory says that the one who was "licentious, covetous, grasping at the goods of others, a reviler, a slanderer" becomes "orderly, sober, content with his own possessions, imparting from them to those in need, a lover of truth, one who gives honor, courteous" (238.12–16). He cites biblical examples of such turnarounds: Zacchaeus, the tax collector who promised to restore fourfold to those he had defrauded (Luke 19:1–9); Matthew, another tax collector who answered the call of Jesus (Matt 9:9); and Paul, the persecutor who became an apostle (Acts 9:1–22).

Gregory points out that after receiving grace "we are called his [God's] children" (239.4). This says something about the kind of life church members should have. Children have the characteristics of their parents, so the converts should study "accurately" (239.5) the Father's characteristics and, by shaping themselves after his likeness, "may appear true children of him who calls us to the adoption according to grace" (239.7–8).[27] He cites Matt 5:44–45 about doing good to all persons, even enemies, as indicative of the kind of life that is in the likeness of the Father's goodness. This teaching from the Sermon on the Mount appears to have been part of the catechetical instruction of the church from very early days.[28]

---

24. Tertullian, *Bapt.* 3; and Cyprian, *Ep.* 62.8 [63.8].

25. The same point is developed in his *Catechetical Oration* 40.

26. Ferguson, "Some Aspects of Gregory of Nyssa's Moral Theology in the Homilies on Ecclesiastes"; and Heine, *Perfection in the Virtuous Life*. For this aspect of baptismal instruction in Chrysostom, see his *Baptismal Instructions* 4.17–33; 12.15–20.

27. See also Chrysostom, who speaks of the instruction in church enabling one to understand "with accuracy" Christian teaching (*Bapt. Chr.* 1, PG 49.365).

28. Ferguson, "Love of Enemies and Non-Retaliation in the Second Century."

On the other hand, the devil continues his "fiery temptations" after baptism (239.24). He "seeks earnestly to rob us of our second adornment, as he did of the first" (239.24-25).[29] Gregory thus continues to be concerned about the struggle with the devil. His response to the devil's challenge is to quote Rom 6:3, "We have been baptized into Christ's death." As a consequence, "Sin in us is henceforth surely a corpse" (240.4-5). The Christian's "manner of life is regulated for another life" (240.12). Paul's words in Galatians 2:20 that the world is crucified to him and he to the world are the words of one who remembers his baptismal renunciation of sin and profession of faith.[30] The church member has a distinctive moral and spiritual life, motivated by love for God.

Gregory concludes his sermon by calling attention to God and what he has done for human salvation. In a direct address to "the loving Giver" (240.23—241.1), he recalls God's saving acts, centered in the reversal of the curse for the fall and the reopening of the way into paradise. Humans may "join the angels' song" (241.19), and he calls upon his audience "to sing the hymn of joy to God" (241.21), inspired by the Spirit. "Let my soul rejoice in the Lord."[31] His closing words are a doxology to Christ, who adorns the church as a bride in fair array (242.2-3).

## JOHN CHRYSOSTOM

In his expository homilies and his sermons during the liturgical seasons, John Chrysostom addressed the concerns of himself and of his hearers, whether directly related to his text or the occasion itself. This broad approach is evident in his Epiphany sermon, *On the Baptism of Christ*.[32] The use of formal titles of address, common in the fourth century, as well as Chrysostom's close relations with the congregation, is illustrated by Chrysostom addressing his hearers throughout as "Your Love." Gregory of Nyssa and John Chrysostorn had diverse interests, preached in quite different settings (the small town of Nyssa and the metropolis of Antioch), and had no known literary connections, yet striking incidental similari-

---

29. The language of clothing may reflect the practice of clothing the newly baptized in a white garment; see Theodore of Mopsuestia, *Serm.* 4, *On the Lord's Prayer and the Sacraments*; and Ambrose, *On the Mysteries* 34.

30. For the renunciation of the devil and confession of faith at baptism, see Hippolytus, *Apostolic Tradition* 21; Cyril of Jerusalem, *Mys. Catech.* 1.2–8, 2.4; Chrysostom, *Baptismal Instructions* 2.20–21, 1 1.10–26; and Gregory, *On the Holy Spirit*.

31. He proceeds to quote Isa 61:10.

32. PG 49.363–72. I have made my own translation of the Greek.

ties exist between the two sermons in their observations and language. This probably stems from common themes and experiences supplied by a shared faith and liturgy. Chrysostom takes up three topics, all bearing on the nature and identity of the church even more directly than Gregory's sermon: attendance at church assemblies, the meaning of the feast of Epiphany, and the significance of Christ's baptism. The conclusion, more extended than Gregory's, bears on another topic of importance for the church, communion. The occasion of the sermon gives Chrysostom opportunity to talk about his concerns related to church attendance, the meaning of the festival and of baptism, and the attitudes of the people.[33]

Chrysostom begins his sermon by contrasting the joy of the people at the festival and his own feeling of pain. He, like Gregory of Nyssa, notes the "great throng" present at Epiphany and expresses his grief that the "church that gives birth to so many children is not able to have enjoyment of them at every assembly but only at the feast." "How much ... glory to God and profit for souls [there would be] if at every assembly we saw the precincts of the church so full?" People diligently engage in business and legal matters, "but meet here scarcely once or twice a year" (1.363).[34]

Chrysostom's comparison of zealous involvement in the affairs of life to sailors' efforts to cross the sea and reach the harbor provides his transition to a discussion of the importance of the church and its activities, and so of attendance at its assemblies. He compares the churches to harbors, which God provided as refuges from the storms of life.[35] "The hearing of the 'divine' scriptures" (1.363), which in the language of the time is described as an "enjoyment of philosophy" (1.363–364),[36] brings "much calm." When their message "enters into the soul of each one who hears" (1.363), the Scriptures remove anger, desire, malignancy, rebellion, love of vainglory, and all irrational passions. In another image, the church is also

---

33. We know of twelve baptismal catecheses delivered by Chrysostom, all of which are translated by Harkins, *St. John Chrysostom*. Harkins accepts the date of Lent 388 (the year after the sermon considered here) for some of these and suggests 390 for the others (p. 18).

34. Henceforth the reference for direct quotations will give only the chapter and column number from Migne, *Patrologiae Graecae* 49. Chrysostom's *Baptismal instructions* 6.1–7 complains of neophytes who deserted the church to run to the hippodrome.

35. The imagery of the church as a haven from storms was early; see Theophilus of Antioch, *To Autolycus* 2.14.

36. Malingrey, "*Philosophia*."

"the common mother of all" (1.364).[37] So the church is a harbor, a school of philosophy, and a mother.

What, Chrysostom asks, is more necessary and more useful than spending time at church? If one answers that need prevents attendance, Chrysostom says that "this excuse is not credible." The week has seven days, and God gives people six while keeping only one for himself. Yet people seize this day "that is holy and dedicated to the hearing of spiritual words" and use it for everyday affairs. And even on Sunday, the whole day is not required for the church: "As the widow cast in two obols . . . so also you, lend two hours to God and you will bring into your own house the gain of many days." Chrysostom here indicates that the Sunday service in Antioch lasted about two hours.[38] The people should beware lest God cause them to lose their material gains as, when the Jews neglected the people, he "blew away" the things gathered into their houses (Haggai 1:9). Chrysostom gives prominence to the service of the word in the Sunday assembly as a main reason why the people should be present. He is, after all, a preacher. He complains that he is unable to teach the things that need to be learned, referring again to those who "resort to us once or twice a year." He provides a list of his preaching topics: "soul, body, immortality, kingdom of heaven, punishment, Gehenna, longsuffering of God, forbearance, repentance, baptism, forgiveness of sins, this creation from above and below, human nature, angels, wicked working of demons, devices of the devil, behavior, dogmas, correct faith, destructive heresies" (1.364).

Christians *should* be able to explain these subjects to others (see 1 Pet 3:15), Chrysostom says, but they are not able to do so, since they come only incidentally "on account of the custom of the feast and not on account of piety of soul" (1.365). If they did come regularly, they would be able to understand all these things with accuracy. Chrysostom contrasts this laxity with the care given to earthly learning. People make elaborate provision for their slaves and sons to learn a trade; they have them stay with their teacher and do not allow them to return home so that nothing interrupts the learning. Why do they think that heavenly learning can be accomplished incidentally? Chrysostom then cites Scriptures about the great attention required in learning about God (Matt 11:29; Ps 34:11, 46:10) and concludes, "So there is need of much time for the one going to find enjoyment of this philosophy" (1.365). The church exemplifies itself

---

37. This image was quite early; see Plumpe, *Mater Ecclesia*.

38. See van de Paverd, *St. John Chrysostom, the Homilies on the Statues*, 185, with reference to this passage and *Hom. in Ac.* 1.2; and van de Paverd, *Zur Geschichte der Messliturgie in Antiocheia and Konstantinopel*.

in its assemblies, and there instruction in the faith occurs, so attendance at worship is important for the life and very reality of the church.

Chrysostom then turns from complaint and correction of those indifferent to church attendance to take up "the present feast" and the baptism it celebrates. He notes that "many observe the feasts and know their names" but are ignorant of their meaning: "The present feast is called Epiphany," but "What is this 'appearance' [or 'manifestation']?" Chrysostom points out that "there is not one epiphany but two: one is this present and occurring [epiphany], and the second is the coming epiphany that will occur at the glorious consummation" (2.365). The two epiphanies bracket the period of the church, which is defined by the two appearances of Christ. Earlier Christian writers had spoken of "two comings [or advents]" (παρουσίαι) of Christ, the first in humility and the second in glory, and had used this theme in polemics against Judaism.[39] Chrysostom speaks of "two epiphanies [or appearances, ἐπιφάνειαι]," but he does not use them polemically. He finds a reference to the first appearance of Christ in his earthly ministry and to the second yet to come in one of the Scripture readings of the day, Titus 2:11–13: "The saving grace of God appeared [ἐπεφάνη] to all persons," and "Expecting the blessed hope and appearance [ἐπιφάνειαν] of the glory of the great God and our Savior Jesus Christ."

Chrysostom then asks why "Epiphany" refers to the day of Jesus' baptism and not to the day of his birth.[40] When Jesus was baptized, "he sanctified the nature of the waters" (2.365–366). As "proof" of this sanctification of water, Chrysostom refers to the custom of people taking from the waters blessed at the feast of Epiphany and storing them at home, claiming that these waters remain "pure and fresh" for a year or more and are preferred to water recently drawn from the fountains. After this aside on the sacred quality of the sanctified waters, Chrysostom directly answers his question about why Christ's baptism and not his birth is called his "appearance": "Because it was not when he was born that he was revealed to all but when he was baptized. For until the day of his baptism he was unknown to many." John the Baptist declared, "Among you stands one whom you did not know" (John 1:26). And this was not remarkable, for John himself

---

39. See Ferguson, "The Disgrace and the Glory." The theme of "the two advents" is less developed in the fourth century, but in the context of baptismal instruction see Cyril of Jerusalem, *Catech.* 15.1, and Chrysostom, *Hom.* 28.1 and *In Jo.* 3.17, both of which use *parousia*.

40. Chrysostom elaborates on the distinction because only recently had the commemoration of 25 December as the birthday of Jesus been instituted in Antioch; McArthur, *The Evolution of the Christian Year*, 49–51.

said, "I did not know him" until he saw the Spirit descending on him (John 1:33), And so, "the Christ comes at baptism" (2.366).

Chrysostom now engages in a polemic against Judaism when he raises the question, "At what sort of baptism does he come?" In answer he contrasts Christ's baptism with Jewish baptism: "The Jewish baptism that removes bodily dirt did not remove the sins of the conscience" (2.366).[41] Jewish baptism was not for the removal of moral transgressions like adultery and theft but for purification from touching the bones of the dead, eating unlawful food, and contact with lepers. He quotes Leviticus in support (11:24 and elsewhere). God "made the uninitiated to be more pious through these washings and prepared them from above to be more accurate for the observance of greater things" (2.366). The contrast of Jewish and Christian baptism served to draw the lines of Christian identity, and so was important for the self-understanding of the church. We know from Chrysostom's other works that Judaism still had an appeal for Christians in late-fourth-century Antioch.[42] Gregory's comments on Jews sound more theoretical, while the prominent presence of Jews in metropolitan Antioch gave a sharper edge to Chrysostom's efforts to show the superior privileges of belonging to the Christian church.

Chrysostom expands his explanation of Christian baptism by contrasting it not only with Jewish baptism but also with John's baptism.[43] By explaining what baptism did not mean for Christ, Chrysostom indicates the meaning of Christian baptism. In distinction from Jewish purifications, Christian "purification . . . removes sins, wipes clean the soul, and gives an abundance of the Spirit."[44] "John's purification was exceedingly superior to the Jewish but was inferior to ours" (3.366). John's baptism did not concern the observance of bodily purifications but was accompanied by exhortations to change from evil to virtue. He did not call on people to

---

41. *Baptismal Instructions* 9.13–20 contrasts the washing of the baths, the washing of the Jews ("more solemn [than the secular baths] but inferior to the bath of grace" as dealing only with ceremonial uncleanness), and Christian baptism (that forgives sins and cleanses the conscience).

42. Meeks and Wilken, *Jews and Christians in Antioch in the First Four Centuries of the Common Era*; and Wilken, *John Chrysostom and the Jews*.

43. Other authors handle differently the points of contrast between the baptisms of the Jews, John, and Christians; see, for example, Basil, *Exhortation to Baptism* 1–2 (PG 31.425A, 428A–B); and *On Baptism* 1.2 (PG 31.1532C–1533C).

44. *Baptismal Instructions* 3.5–7 claims that there are ten gifts of baptism; 9.12–15 names the Christian purification as "bath of regeneration," "enlightenment," "circumcision," and "cross," and 12,6 says God gives justification, sanctity, purity, adoption, and the kingdom of heaven.

wash their clothing and bathe their body but to "produce fruit worthy of repentance" (Matt 3:8). This accompanying call for repentance and reformation of life made John's baptism superior to Jewish washings, but it fell short of Christian baptism because it "did not give the Holy Spirit, nor did it provide forgiveness through grace" (3.367), as Christian baptism does.

Chrysostom develops the limitations of John's baptism by citing the Baptist's words, "I baptize you with water; he [Christ] will baptize you with the Holy Spirit and fire" (Matt 3:11). The combination "Holy Spirit and fire" is explained by reference to the "tongues as of fire" that accompanied the coming of the Holy Spirit to the apostles on Pentecost in Acts 2:3. Chrysostom further demonstrates the incompleteness of John's baptism by quoting the episode in Acts 19:1–7, when Paul explained to those in Ephesus who had received John's baptism that "John baptized with a baptism of repentance [not of forgiveness]." When they heard Paul's explanation that the purpose of John's baptism was to prepare people to believe in Jesus who was to come, they were baptized "into the name of the Lord Jesus," and Paul laid hands on them so that the Holy Spirit might come upon them.

Chrysostom denies that John's baptism brought forgiveness and the Spirit, noting that Jesus received John's baptism—neither the older Jewish nor the later Christian baptisms—and Jesus already had a share in the Spirit and had no need of forgiveness. Christ did not require the removal of sins, for he had no sin, according to Isa 53:9 (1 Pet 2:22) and John 8:46. And Christ's flesh was not without a share of the Spirit, for it was fashioned by the Spirit (Matt 1:18, 20). By receiving John's baptism, as opposed to the Jewish or Christian baptisms, Jesus demonstrated that "he was not baptized because of sin nor as having need of the supply of the Spirit" (3.367). John the Baptist himself made clear to those present that Jesus did not come in repentance, as the rest of the people did, for he told the people to "Produce fruit worthy of repentance" (Matthew 3:8). But he said to Christ, "I have need to be baptized by you, and do you come to me?" (Matt 3:14). It seems that a dogmatic position, namely that Jesus "was much greater than the Baptist himself and incomparably purer," has controlled Chrysostom's handling of Scripture, for Mark 1:4 and Luke 3:3 state that John's baptism was "for the forgiveness of sins."[45]

---

45. Chrysostom's homilies on Matthew (dated 390) deal with Luke 3:3. John's baptism did not really bring forgiveness, he says, since the sacrifice of Christ had not yet been offered, but brought people to a consciousness of sins and to a desire to seek remission; *Hom. in Mt.* 10.2. Christ fulfilled Jewish baptism, and John's baptism lacked the Holy Spirit; *Hom. in Mt.* 12.4.

If Jesus was not baptized "for repentance, nor forgiveness of sins, nor the supply of the Spirit" (3.368), why was he baptized? Chrysostom advances two purposes: to make Christ known and to fulfill righteousness (which is to keep the commands of God).[46] The first is stated by John: "In order that he might be made known to many" (see John 1:31). This agrees with Acts 19:4: "John baptized with a baptism of repentance in order that they might believe on the one coming after him." Chrysostom suggests other means that might have been used, but they would have been difficult (going house to house or entering into the synagogue) or suspicious (since John and Jesus were kinsmen, Luke 1:36). "But when all the people poured out of every city to the Jordan and were spending time on the banks of the river" (3.368), they were all informed. And when John's testimony received "the confirmation from above by the voice of the Father which was through the manifestation of the Spirit in the form of a dove," suspicion was removed from it. John previously did not know who Jesus was (John 1:33), and so that "his testimony might not seem to be because of friendship or from relationship," the Spirit arranged for John to spend the first part of his life in the desert. John himself learned who Jesus was when the Spirit descended on him (John 1:33). The Spirit came at the baptism and remained with Christ, "as if making him known to all by a finger pointing" (3.368).

The other purpose of Jesus' baptism was expressed by Jesus himself. When John protested that he needed to he baptized by Jesus, Jesus answered, "Let it be now, for it is fitting thus for us to fulfill all righteousness" (Matt 3:15). Chrysostom asks, "What then does this mean, 'to fulfill all righteousness'?" He replies, quoting Luke 1:6, "The fulfilling of all the commandments is called righteousness" (3.369).[47] He then explains, "Since it was necessary for all people to fulfill this righteousness, but no one completed it or fulfilled it, Christ came and fulfills this righteousness" (3.369). "As then he was circumcised, offered sacrifice, kept sabbath, and

---

46. Studies of other treatments of the baptism of Christ in early Christian literature include Bertrand, *Le Baptême de Jesus*; Vigne, *Christ au jourdain*; Wilken, "The Interpretation of the Baptism of Jesus in the Later Fathers"; Doignon, "La scène évangélique du Baptême de Jésus"; and McDonnell, "Jesus' Baptism in the Jordan," who employs especially the Syriac and Armenian sources with their emphasis on the coming of the Spirit at the baptism of Jesus.

47. The same definition of righteousness occurs in his *Hom. in Mt.* 10.1 and 12.1 on Matthew 3:15. The whole treatment of the baptism of Jesus in *Hom. in Mt.* 12.1–4 parallels the treatment in the sermon under study, including the description of the dove being like a finger pointing to Christ (*Hom. in Mt.* 12.3), but with the added observation that "the Spirit comes on you at your baptism."

fulfilled the Jewish feast, so also he added this that was lacking, to yield to the prophet who was baptizing" (4.369). That it was the will of God for all to be baptized is indicated by John's words, God "sent me to baptize in water" (John 1:33) and Jesus' words that "The Pharisees and scribes set aside the will of God when they were not baptized by him" (Luke 7:30). Chrysostom adds, "If then to yield to God is righteousness, and God sent John to baptize the people, Christ fulfilled this also with all the other legal requirements" (4.369).

As he approaches the conclusion, Chrysostom, as did Gregory, reminds his hearers of what their salvation means. He relates the baptism of Christ to the atonement, and he does so with the illustration of a ransom.[48] There is a necessity for everyone to fulfill the law. The commands of the law represent our obligation to pay, but since we did not make the payment, death held us under liability. So "Christ came and found us held captive; he paid the obligation; he fulfilled what was owed; he snatched away those who do not have the means to give." Chrysostom here works with the ransom theory, as did Gregory, but puts the emphasis on the payment and the release from debt. He pictures Jesus as saying, "It is fitting for me the Master, who has, to pay out on behalf of those who do not have." He concludes, "This is the purpose of his baptism, to show to everyone to fulfill the law" (4.369).

The Spirit came down in the form of a dove because "where there is reconciliation of God, there is the dove" (4.369). This was seen when the dove brought the olive branch to the ark of Noah. As that dove symbolized God's philanthropy and the end of the flood, so the Spirit came to Jesus announcing God's mercy to the world. Here Chrysostom echoes one of Gregory's main points, namely, the kind of life expected of those baptized. The spiritual person must be "harmless, pure, and innocent" as a dove, as Jesus said: "Unless you turn and become as children, you will not enter into the kingdom of heaven" (Matt 18:3). The ark had earlier been interpreted by Christians as an image of the church,[49] but Chrysostom takes it here as an image of the "blameless and undefiled body" of Christ (4.369). This ark, instead of resting on the earth, now sits at the right hand of the Father.

The reference to the Lord's body provides Chrysostom's transition to the close of the discourse, as he anticipates the eucharistic sacrifice that

---

48. See also Aulén, *Christus Victor*, 66–67, for other images Chrysostom uses of dealings with the devil in atonement.

49. For example, Callistus in Hippolytus, *Refutation* 9.7; see also Chrysostom, *De Lazaro* 6.7 (PG 48.1037–38).

follows the sermon. He returns, as at the beginning, to complaint and rebuke. Not only is there the problem of people coming to church only at the festivals, but there were disturbances in the assembly occasioned by the early departure of many. Many come for communion since it is a feast day, but it is necessary to prepare for communion by purifying the conscience. Chrysostom stresses the theme of holiness: "to approach this holy table," "to touch the holy sacrifice," and "to partake of that holy and awesome flesh" (4.369–370). His main treatment of Christian character comes here in relation to partaking of the eucharist in a worthy manner. These "divine mysteries" or "holy mysteries" are not for the polluted and impure but for the one who "has wiped away transgressions thoroughly through repentance" (4.370). Chrysostom refers to his own policy of not admitting to communion those whose misconduct was manifest to him: "Those unknown to us, we leave to God, who knows the secrets of each one's mind" (4.370).

He then develops the attitude with which one should approach communion. It should be done with reverence and not with tumult and disorder. He contrasts the quiet and orderly behavior in the procession at the Olympic Games with the disturbances in the church. Chrysostom brings out the incongruity by allusion again to the imagery employed at the beginning of the sermon: "On the sea, [is there] calm, and in the harbor, waves?" (4.370).

Many create a disturbance by departing early from the service. But what business can compare to being where Christ and the angels are present? In the church it is time "to celebrate with angels, with whom you send up that mystical melody, with whom you offer that triumphal ode to God."[50] The noise results "because we never close the doors to you." "What are you doing, O man? When Christ is present, the angels stand by, this awesome table is set forth, your brothers are still celebrating sacred rites, do you yourself depart and start off?" A person invited to a supper, even when satisfied with food, does not depart while his friends are still reclining. "But here while the awesome mysteries of Christ are being celebrated, while the sacred rite is still occurring, do you leave and depart in the middle?" (4.370). At this point Chrysostom offers his heaviest charge.

---

50. Van de Paverd, "Anaphora, Intercessions, Epiclesis and Communion-rites in John Chrysostom," esp. 316–19 for the identification of this "canticle of victory" (his translation) as the *Gloria in excelsis*. The article includes many parallels in Chrysostom's other works to the conclusion of *On the Baptism of Christ*, notably the presence of the angels at the communion. Gregory too referred to the song at the conclusion of communion; *Bapt. Chr.* 241.19–21.

Judas at the last supper "sprang up and went out," and "These now imitate him who depart before the last thanksgiving." Judas, "if he had not gone out, would not have become a traitor; if he had not deserted his fellow disciples, he would not have perished . . . On account of this he was with the Jews" (4.371) instead of being with the disciples—another declaration of boundary definition.

Chrysostom alludes to the doctrinal meaning that he ascribed to the eucharist: Christ "gives a share of his flesh to you."[51] He also refers to the practice of an ode and prayer at the conclusion of the eucharistic liturgy. As it is fitting to conclude a meal of ordinary food with a prayer, how much more "the partaking of the spiritual food that surpasses all creation" (4.371–372),[52] Chrysostom's sermons were often greeted with applause and acclamations, and so he declares: "I say these things not in order that you may approve only nor in order that you may applaud and cry out, but in order that remembering these words in time you may show the proper good order" (4.372).

Ancient Greek religion treated the mysteries with much silence. Although the New Testament had used *musterion* in reference to the secrets of God now made known in the gospel, by the fourth century Christians used the language of the mysteries with reference to their own ceremonies. The bread and wine of the eucharist, Chrysostom says, are called "mysteries" and should be treated in the appropriate way: "Now with much silence, with much discipline, with proper reverence let us touch this holy sacrifice" (4.372; compare Gregory's use of the language of "holy mysteries" for baptism, 222.13–21). The purpose given for this behavior expresses an understanding of the act as a sacrifice by humans that wins the divine favor: "in order that we might induce God to greater goodwill and might cleanse the soul and obtain the eternal good things." However, the divine priority is reaffirmed in the closing doxology: "May it be that we all obtain those things by the grace and philanthropy of our Lord Jesus Christ, with whom to the Father together with the Holy Spirit be glory and strength and worship now and always, forever. Amen" (4.372).

---

51. Chrysostom is an important representative of the use of realist language for the eucharist; see the list of references in Quasten, *Patrology*, vol. 3, 480–81; and the collection of Greek texts with Spanish translation in Solano, ed., *Textos eucaristicos primitivos*, 1:441–664. For a recent survey see Crockett, *Eucharist: Symbol of Transformation*.

52. See van de Paverd, *St. John Chrysostom*, 186; and van de Paverd, *Zur Geschichte der Messliturgie*, 398–402, for a thanksgiving after communion.

## CONCLUSION

In their Epiphany sermons, Gregory of Nyssa and John Chrysostom revealed both theological and pastoral interests. Gregory's theological interests seem to predominate, as revealed in his understanding of salvation as the defeat of the devil (223.20-24; 232.19-22; 233.9-14), his affirmation of the fullness of Christ's manhood (223.25), his theology of baptism and the sacraments (esp. 225.1—226.8), his digression on the Trinity (229.6—230.5), his use of scriptural types and prophecies (230.19—237.22), and the concluding praise of God (240.21—242.3). Yet Gregory also spoke to the pastoral needs of his hearers, as he implicitly encouraged them to baptism (222.13—223.11), openly stressed the new moral life to follow baptism (237.23—240.20), and warned of the temptations of the devil (239.20—240.4). Chrysostom also showed theological interests (but for practical purposes) in his doctrine of the church as a harbor and a mother (1.363-364), his elaboration of the meaning of the baptism of Christ, and his reference to Christ providing a ransom (4.369). But pastoral needs predominated, as seen in his emphasis on attending church (1.363-364), his rebuke of the indifference of the people and their commotion (1.365; 4.370), discussion of righteousness and the need for purity in approaching the sacraments (4.369-370), and elementary instruction about the name of the feast and baptism (2-3.365-369).

Chrysostom centered his Epiphany sermon on the baptism of Christ, while Gregory focused on the baptism of believers, a difference that may reflect Gregory's concern over the delay of baptism. Chrysostom's focus correlates with the name "Epiphany," the manifestation of Christ; Gregory emphasizes the various names given to baptism. However, despite their different interests, both testify to the great popularity of the feast. Several factors are possible explanations for this. A pagan festival apparently was taken over by the Christian observance.[53] Chrysostom alludes to superstitions about water, necessary for life, in connection with the celebration of the festival (2.366). And the great importance attached to the rite of baptism, attested by both preachers, had something to do with Epiphany's popularity.

The Epiphany sermons of the fourth century are, as might be expected, a rich source of information for the church's understanding of baptism. They also provide valuable witnesses to the church's self-understanding—how it was defining itself against the Jews and the still largely

---

53. See n. 4 above.

pagan society, claiming superiority for itself, and struggling to establish a distinctive lifestyle for its members. Moreover, these sermons tell us much about the realities of church life in the late fourth century—liturgical customs, homiletical practices, use of Scripture, and habits and attitudes of the people. Many of those realities are still with us—both in the practices of the churches and in the responses of people.

# 9

# Spiritual Circumcision in Early Christianity

MODERN ECUMENICAL DISCUSSIONS AND liturgical reform have given new interest to the ceremonies of Christian initiation. The Reformed churches have traditionally held the view that baptism takes the place of circumcision in the economy of salvation. The interpretations of circumcision in early Christian and patristic literature would suggest a modification, or at least a nuance, to that view.

Genesis 17:11 speaks of circumcision as the "sign of the covenant" which God gave to Abraham. That understanding of the significance of circumcision continued in the language of the Jews. The Septuagint of Lev 26:11 says, "I will place my covenant in you." *Jubilees* 15:26 declares that circumcision is a sign of belonging to the Lord. Acts 7:8 records Stephen as saying that God gave to Abraham "the covenant of circumcision." The Mishnah and Talmud equate circumcision with the covenant by quoting passages about the covenant as referring to circumcision (*m. Ned.* 3:11; *b. Ned.* 32a). The bloodshed in performing circumcision is called the "covenant blood" (*b. Shabb.* 132b, 135a). The benediction prescribed at a circumcision speaks of the "covenant which thou hast set in our flesh" (*b. Shabb.* 137b).

Paul in Rom 4:11 defines the "sign of circumcision" as "the seal of righteousness."[1] "Seal" became the more common term than "sign" among Christians for religious acts.

---

1. Compare Rabbi Akiba's words about circumcision in *Mekhilta* to Exod 19:5; see

## Spiritual Circumcision in Early Christianity

In addition to the literal practice of circumcision, the Jewish Bible made frequent use of a metaphorical meaning for circumcision. The cutting off of the excess of the flesh was extended to a circumcision of the heart (Deut 10:16; 30:6; Jer 4:4). "Uncircumcision" was applied to that which was not consecrated to God or unfit for his service—the heart (Lev 26:40; Jer 9:26; Ezek 44:7, 9), lips (Exod 6:30), or ears (Jer 6:10). The circumcision of the heart continued in Jewish usage—e.g., at Qumran (1QpHab xi.13; cf. 1QS v.4-5) for cutting off evil inclinations and disobedience. Philo similarly gives the symbolic meaning of the excision of pleasure as one reason for circumcision (*Spec. Laws* 1.1-11; *Ques. Gen.* 3.48). Paul's reference to "circumcision of the heart" (Rom 2:29) assured for this phrase a rich usage in Christian literature.[2]

Origen, that "walking concordance" of the early church, brought all of these ideas, and most of the biblical passages cited above, into an allegorical interpretation of the circumcision of the heart, ears, lips, and flesh as the avoiding of evil and the doing of right with each. And then for good measure he suggested that the same principle can be applied to other members of the body (hands, feet, sight, smell, and touch), for "each of our members must be said to be circumcised if they are devoted to the service of God's commands" (*Hom. Gen.* 3.4-7).

This readiness to extend the meaning of circumcision and give a non-literal or "spiritual" interpretation to the language was a characteristic of early Christian interpretation. Sometimes this was done in very general terms without a specific content. The *Gospel of Thomas* 53 quotes Jesus, "The true circumcision in spirit has become completely profitable." Ptolemy wrote to Flora that all the typical rites of the Mosaic covenant were transformed and in their material form were taken away: "He wants us to be circumcised, not by the material circumcision of the foreskin, but by the spiritual circumcision of the heart" (Epiphanius, *Haer.* 33.5). Clement of Alexandria refers, in addition to the circumcision of the heart (*Strom.* 7.9), to the circumcision of the understanding (λογισμός—*Paed.* 2.8) and to cutting away and stripping off the passion from the whole soul (*Ecl.* 31).

A recent survey of the patristic treatments of circumcision by Hervé Savon distinguishes two main types of figurative interpretation: (1) Circumcision of the flesh was a figure of the passion of Christ and of baptism which was its application; and (2) the cutting off of a part of the flesh was

---

Lauterbach, trans., *Mekilta de Rabbi Ishmael*, vol. 2, 204.

2. In addition to passages cited in this paper note for example Tertullian, *Marc.* 5.13.7; Origen, *Hom. Num.* 6.4; Gregory of Elvira, *Tract.* 4.20. "Spiritual circumcision" is found in Tertullian, *Ad ux.* 1.2.3.

the symbol of progress of the soul and the improvement of conduct.[3] Both interpretations are found in Ambrose, *Epistle* 72. Ambrose explains that the bloodshed in circumcision lasted until the blood of Christ brought forgiveness to all. He also contrasts the inward and outward circumcision: "So there is a circumcision of the inward man, for the circumcised man has put away, like foreskin, the allurements of all his flesh."[4]

A special importance attaches to the *Epistle of Barnabas* as the earliest non-canonical Christian writer to give attention to the interpretation of circumcision. *Barnabas* follows the prophets in referring to a "circumcision of our hearing" (9.3) and of our hearing and our hearts (10.12).[5] Nevertheless, he had a particular interest in relating circumcision to the atonement in Christ. The premier example of his spiritual interpretation, according to his own self-congratulation, is finding a reference to Jesus and the cross in the 318 servants of Abraham who were circumcised (9.7). The association in Judaism of the bloodshed in circumcision with expiation[6] explains this connection. So, *Barnabas* affirms, Abraham, when he circumcised his servants, was looking forward in the spirit to Jesus. The association of the blood of circumcision with the cross was also made by Origen, *In Rom.* 2.13, who provides the link with Ambrose, *Epistle* 72.9.

Savon relates circumcision also to baptism, as the application of the benefits of Christ's death. I want to reserve discussion of that. It is preferable to include here the association of circumcision with the resurrection of Jesus along with the reference to his death. Circumcision on the eighth day (Lev 12:3) provided the connection, for the eighth day was an early designation for Sunday, the day of the resurrection. Cyprian gives an early testimony:

> For in respect of the observance of the eighth day in the Jewish circumcision of the flesh, a sacrament was given beforehand in

---

3. Hervé Savon, "Le prêtre Eutrope et la 'vraie circoncision,'" 294.

4. Ambrose, *De off.* 1.50.260 speaks of "circumcision of the Spirit." He, as other writers cited below, gives separate interpretations of the baptisms (washings) in the old covenant and of circumcision: "Just as many kinds of baptisms first took place, because the true sacrament of baptism in spirit and water which would redeem the whole man was to follow, so circumcision of many first had to take place because the circumcision of the Lord's passion was to follow." The epistle is translated as no. 16 in Beyenka, ed., *St. Ambrose Letters 1-91*, 90-100.

5. *Barnabas* quotes Jer 4:4; 9:26; Deut 10:16. Carleton Paget, "Barnabas 9:4: A Peculiar Verse on Circumcision." Tertullian, *Adv. Iud.* 3, provides another example of the Christian argument against Jewish circumcision.

6. Vermes, "Baptism and Jewish Exegesis," 310-11, 318-19; McEleney, "Conversion, Circumcision, and the Law," 333-34.

shadow and in usage, but when Christ came, it was fulfilled in truth. For because the eighth day, that is the first day after the Sabbath, was to be that on which the Lord should rise again, and should quicken us, and give us circumcision of the spirit, the eighth day, that is the first day after the Sabbath, and the Lord's day, went before in the figure. [*Ep.* 58 (64).4.][7]

Augustine seemed to like the association of circumcision with the resurrection. "We believe the commandment to circumcise infants on the eighth day was divinely given to the ancient fathers to signify the regeneration which is made in Christ, who ... on the eighth day ... rose again for our justification" (*C. Julian.* 6.7.18).[8] Methodius's reference to the "circumcision of the spiritual eighth day" (*Symp.* 7.6) may point to the resurrection of Christ.

The same passage from Methodius refers the language of circumcision also to the "passions and corruptions of men," and so it may provide a transition to Savon's second category, the moral interpretation. This was a natural extension of the biblical language and is easily the most frequent application of circumcision in patristic literature.[9] To take some random examples, Chrysostom in commenting on Rom 2:25 says there are two circumcisions, one of the flesh and one of the mind, which latter is doing all that the law requires; and on Rom 2:29 he says that the circumcision of the flesh is set aside, and the need of a good life is everywhere demonstrated (*Hom. in Rom.* 6.2). In another homily Chrysostom says that now we must circumcise not the flesh but evil thoughts (*Hom. in Joh.* 33.2). Epiphanius touches on some of the contrasts made between Christian spiritual circumcision and fleshly circumcision when he says that the perfect circumcision saves not one part of the people, but men and women, and seals not one member of the body, but the whole body, "being circumcised from sin" (*Haer.* 30.33). The presbyter Eutropius at the beginning of the fifth century, whose letter *On True Circumcision* was the occasion of Savon's

7. Cf. Ambrose, *Ps.* 118.

8. The passage continues, "Anyone with even the slightest knowledge of sacred scripture knows that the sacrament of circumcision was a figure of baptism [Col 2:10–13 quoted]. The circumcision wrought by hand, given to Abraham, is a likeness of the circumcision not wrought by hand, which is now made in Christ." The association of the resurrection with circumcision by way of the "eighth day" is also found in a recently discovered sermon of Augustine: see Étaix, "Sermon inédit de saint Augustin sur la Circoncision dans un ancien manuscrit de Saragosse," 69, with other references where the same connection is made in Augustine.

9. Savon, "Le prêtre Eutrope et la 'vraie circoncision,'" 296–301. He notes especially Gregory of Elvira, *Tract.* 4, and Zeno of Verona, *Tract.* 1 (add 1.13).

study, uses the traditional theme of the true circumcision as the cutting off of the passions to support an argument for the ascetic life.[10]

It is now time to take up the association of circumcision and baptism. The spiritual interpretation of circumcision as referring to baptism often seems to be due to the parallel of cutting off the flesh with removal of sin. Origen interpreted the reference to the second performance of circumcision in Josh 5:3 to mean that Christ "has given us a second circumcision by the 'baptism of regeneration' and purified our souls."[11] This, he explains, was because circumcision removed the opprobrium of Egypt (Josh 5:9). Lactantius gave a Christianized understanding when he said that Jesus saved the Jews by undergoing circumcision and Gentiles by baptism.[12] He proceeded to explain the fleshly circumcision as a figure of the circumcision of the heart and spirit, in which the breast is laid bare so as not to veil any shameful deed. In spiritual circumcision God has set before us repentance, for we lay open our hearts, confess our sins, and satisfy God (*Inst.* 4.17). Basil the Great spoke of performing "a circumcision in the stripping off of the flesh, performed in baptism" (*Hom.* 13.2). The removal of sins is again the connection when Epiphanius said, "Fleshly circumcision served for a time until the great circumcision, that is baptism which circumcised us from sins and sealed us to the name of God" (*Haer.* 8.6).

Some statements simply make the association of circumcision with baptism without further explanation. Isidore of Pelusium could say, "Instead of baptism the Jews made use of circumcision" (*Epp.* 1.125). Augustine, among his many interpretations, made a similar statement: "Circumcision served instead of baptism in the saints of old" (*Ep.* 187.11.34). John of Damascus's phrase, "circumcision a figure for baptism" (*Orth. Faith* 4.25) states the view that became quite common in Christianity. The interpretation that baptism takes the place in the new covenant of circumcision in the old covenant has had special significance in the Reformed tradition. Hence, Savon makes a common assertion in saying that circumcision was a figure of baptism,[13] but there is need for a closer look at the origins and basis of this interpretation.

---

10. Ibid., part 2, 391–95 and especially 400–403.

11. *Hom. Josh.* 5.5; cf. *Sel. Ps.* 118. The circumcision performed by Joshua as a type of the spiritual circumcision by Jesus/Joshua was a common Christian interpretation—see n. 25 on Justin Martyr.

12. *Inst.* 4.15. Gistelinck, "Lactance et sa théologie baptismale propre à son temps," 189.

13. Savon, "Le prêtre Eutrope et la 'vraie circoncision,'" 294.

## Spiritual Circumcision in Early Christianity

A New Testament basis for the identification of circumcision and baptism is found in Col 2:11-12.

> In him also you were circumcised with a circumcision made without hands, by putting off the body of flesh in the circumcision of Christ; and you were buried with him in baptism, in which you were also raised with him through faith in the working of God, who raised him from the dead.[14]

Two ideas relevant to the theme of spiritual circumcision in Christian thought are found in this passage. The "putting off the body of flesh" has been understood to mean that the circumcision worked by Christ removes not simply a part of the body but the whole body of flesh, the sinful nature.[15] This interpretation corresponds with the patristic comparison of fleshly circumcision to the cutting off of the passions and emphasis on spiritual circumcision as involving not just one member but the whole body. The other idea is the understanding of the death of Christ as itself figuratively a circumcision. This interpretation supports the connection between the blood of circumcision and the blood of the cross.[16] Both ideas, the removal of sin and the death of Christ, are associated with baptism. However, the sequence of thought in Colossians 2 does not require a direct identification of circumcision and baptism. The circumcision of Col 2:11 is done "without hands," so is not simply the outward act of baptism. Rather, baptism seems to be the occasion or to be connected in time or in thought with the spiritual circumcision. This suggestion is to be pursued later.

A further connection of baptism with circumcision may be seen in the common designation of baptism as the "seal."[17] G. W. H. Lampe in his book *The Seal of the Spirit* set out to refute the argument of Gregory Dix, L. S. Thornton, and others that confirmation was the Christian equivalent of circumcision.[18] He was correct in his refutation and in his contention that baptism and not confirmation was the central rite of initiation into

---

14. The argument of Gardner, ""Circumcised in Baptism—Raised Through Faith," that *en ho* in 2:12 refers to "in Christ," not "in baptism" does not affect our concerns.

15. Lightfoot, *Saint Paul's Epistles to the Colossians and to Philemon*, 183-85. For a sample patristic text see Basil, *Bapt*. II. Q.1, "the circumcision of Christ, whereby the entire body is despoiled of the sins of the flesh" (PG 31.1580D).

16. Vermes, "Baptism and Jewish Exegesis," 318-19, argues that the sacrificial significance of the bloodshed in circumcision (above at note 6) accounts for Paul's conjunction of baptism and the sacrificial death of Christ in Col 2:11-12.

17. *II Clement* 6.9; 7.6; 8.6; 14.3-5; Hermas, *Sim.* 9.16.3-4; 9.17.4; Irenaeus, *Proof* 3.

18. Lampe, *The Seal of the Spirit*, x, 306ff.

the new covenant. However, Lampe overstated the identification of baptism and circumcision: "The evidence is clear that it was *Baptism* which was believed to have been foreshadowed by the circumcision which it superseded."[19] At other times Lampe nuances his statements in a way that gives greater accuracy. For instance, in commenting on Col 2:11-12. he says, "The real correspondence to which St Paul points is between the Christian's possession of the Spirit . . . and the inward 'circumcision of the heart'" (p. 5). That which permitted Dix to arrive at his theory was the frequent identification of circumcision with the gift or activity of the Holy Spirit. Greater attention to this by Lampe, although he quotes some of the sources accurately in this matter, would have kept him from some inaccurate or careless statements about the teachings of some ancient writers.

The association of baptism with circumcision is actually secondary and, I think, derived from the identification of the seal with the Holy Spirit. The earliest texts associate the seal of the new covenant with the gift of the Holy Spirit and do not identify baptism with circumcision. We have noticed that Paul equates the language of "sign" and "seal" (Rom 4:11). When he earlier in Romans (2:29) spoke of circumcision of the heart, he said it was done "spiritually," or should we render "in" or "by" the Spirit? He elsewhere uses the verb form "to seal" as equivalent to receiving the Holy Spirit: "He has put his seal upon us and given us his Spirit in our hearts as a guarantee" (2 Cor 1:22). The Epistle to the Ephesians twice makes a similar use of the verb: "[You who] have believed in him were sealed with the promised Holy Spirit" (1:13); and "Do not grieve the Holy Spirit of God, in whom you were sealed for the day of redemption" (4:30). Paul also says that "We [Christians] are the true circumcision, who worship God in Spirit" (Phil 3:3).[20]

Post-canonical literature continued this association of circumcision with the activity of the Holy Spirit, and this topic Savon does not include in his survey. The *Odes of Solomon* 11:2-3. says God "circumcised me by his Holy Spirit."[21] Irenaeus repeated the language of circumcision as a sign and affirmed that the circumcision of the flesh typified that after the Spirit, followed by a citation of Col 2:11 about a circumcision made without hands (*Adv. haer.* 4.16.1-2). Origen with a characteristic turn, but here in agreement with the normal association of the Spirit with the Word of God,

---

19. Ibid., 84. Similar statements on 169, 245.

20. On the correct interpretation of these passages about sealing, see Lampe, ibid., 5-6; and Beasley-Murray, *Baptism in the New Testament*, 174.

21. Lampe, *The Seal of the Spirit*, 85, strangely cites 11.10, "I stripped [folly] off," for circumcision equaling baptism, perhaps because of (symbolic) water in 11.6-7.

says that the sword by which the people of God were circumcised is the word of God.[22] Cyril of Alexandria likewise, after pointing to circumcision as a type of the purification of the heart, refers to the one "who receives circumcision in spirit by the evangelical preaching."[23] Chrysostom's comments on the New Testament texts about the seal identify it with the Holy Spirit: "For the Jews had circumcision for a seal, but we, the earnest of the Spirit" (*Hom. 2 Cor.* 3.7) and "The Israelites also were sealed, but that was by circumcision . . . We too are sealed, but it is as sons, 'with the Spirit'" (*Hom. Eph.* 2.2).

*Barnabas* is often cited for the circumcision/baptism analogy,[24] but in fact, as shown above, he does no such thing. The contention fails to observe the structure of *Barnabas*' argument. His discussion of baptism (ch. 11) takes up a new subject. It has nothing to do with circumcision and is contrasted with the ceremonial washings of the Jews.[25]

The earliest author to connect baptism with spiritual circumcision was Justin Martyr. And in his case we are given a clue as to what brought about the shift from circumcision = gift of the Holy Spirit to circumcision = baptism: namely, that the Spirit was given in baptism. Justin's very extensive discussion of circumcision in his *Dialogue with Trypho* incorporates almost, if not all, the themes to be found in early Christian discussions of circumcision.[26] For instance, circumcision is a covenant (10.3), a sign (Justin stresses its purpose of keeping the Jews separate—16; 19). Christians have a circumcision of the heart (92; cf. 19). The moral interpretation is given an anti-pagan/intellectual turn connected with the removal of the error of idolatry as well as of every kind of wickedness (47.1; 113.6f.; 137.1; 114.4). This "good and useful circumcision" (28.4) is effected by the preached word of the apostles (114.4). Circumcision is also connected with the death and resurrection of Christ. "The blood of [Jewish] circumcision is obsolete, and we trust in the blood of salvation" (24.2). Circumcision on the eighth day was a type of the true circumcision through Jesus who rose from the dead on the first day after the Sabbath (41.4). Our special interest

22. *Hom. Gen.* 3.6.

23. *Hom. Pasch.* 6; PG 77.520C–521C. He continues, "The power of circumcision is not in the flesh but in will to do what God enjoins."

24. Lampe, *The Seal of the Spirit*, 84, 104. Cf. Wilken, *Judaism and the Early Christian Mind*, 12: *Barnabas* argued "circumcision was only a temporary institution and is replaced by baptism" (9.4; 11.1).

25. The same is done in Ambrose, *Ep.* 72.9 in n. 4.

26. Surveyed in Otranto, "La tipologia di Giosué nel 'Dialogo con Trifone ebreo' di Giustino."

now is those passages where Justin associates circumcision with baptism. "God bids you to be washed in this laver [Isaiah 1] and be circumcised with true circumcision" (18.2). Are these the same? I would suggest that the two are brought together because proselytes were circumcised and baptized. Justin says that Christians are baptized with the Holy Spirit, so they do not need Jewish circumcision and Jewish baptism (29.1; cf. 19). I understand the "baptism with the Holy Spirit" to be water baptism in which the Holy Spirit is received.[27] That brings us to the key text for this discussion: "And we who have approached God through [Christ] have received not carnal but spiritual circumcision ... And we have received it through baptism" (43.2).[28] Baptism is not circumcision itself for Justin, but the occasion when it is received.

That view is found in many other writers. Cyril of Jerusalem states it precisely:

> And then, following upon our faith, we receive like [Abraham] the spiritual seal, being circumcised by the Holy Spirit through baptism, not in the foreskin of the body, but in the heart. (*Cat.* 5.6.)

Chrysostom, as a good exegete, normally identified the seal with the Holy Spirit but in dealing with Col 2:11 brought the Spirit as the seal into relation with baptism:

> No longer is the circumcision with the knife, but in Christ himself: for no hand imparts this circumcision, as is the case there, but the Spirit. He circumcises not a part, but the whole man. It is the body both in the one and the other case, but in the one it is carnally, in the other it is spiritually circumcised; but not as the Jew, for you have not put off flesh, but sins. When and where? Baptism. And what he calls circumcision, he again calls burial. (*Hom. Col.* 6.2)

In the light of this precision of the relation of circumcision (= gift of the Spirit) to baptism, those passages which refer to circumcision in close proximity to baptism may not be making as close an identification of the two as is often assumed. Notice the way Asterius expresses the relation:

> If the circumcision of the Jew was given early and quickly, immediately after swaddling clothes, to the infant, how much more

---

27. Lampe, *The Seal of the Spirit*, 84–85.

28. Cf. Gregory of Elvira, *Tract.* 4.28, "In baptism every man is circumcised as well as reborn."

ought the circumcision of Christ, which is by baptism, be given more quickly to the infant for safety. (*Hom. 12 in Psalm 6* [Richard, 83])[29]

In some cases, the Jewish context may indicate that the conjunction of circumcision and baptism for proselytes accounts for their being brought together and so would indicate that two different and not two similar or parallel acts were meant. This I think is clearly the case in the Pseudo-Cyprian sermon *Against the Jews* 10.79–82. Of the Jewish converts to Christ it is said, among other things, that they "are dipped who used to 'baptize,' and are circumcised who used to circumcise."[30] In the *Didascalia Apostolorum* 24 it is said:

> But sufficient for the faithful is the circumcision of the heart, (which is) spiritual, as He said . . . [Jer 4:3–4 and Joel 2:13 are quoted]. And as for baptism also one is enough for you, even that which has perfectly forgiven you your sins.[31]

Here, as in *Barnabas*, circumcision and baptism are two separate acts from the Jewish heritage which each have different counterparts in the Christian dispensation. In Chrysostom's *Hom. John* 14.1 the Old Testament counterparts to Christian items include baptismal washings compared to Christian baptism and fleshly circumcision compared to spiritual circumcision.[32]

At other times, the pairing of circumcision with baptism may be due to the working of the Spirit in baptism, without this being expressly stated. Aphrahat is a special case, for one of his *Demonstrations* (11) is entirely devoted to circumcision.[33] After an extended polemic against literal circumcision, Aphrahat comes to talk about the Christian equivalent: "They find life who are circumcised in their hearts and who circumcise themselves a second time on the true Jordan, the baptism of the forgiveness

---

29. See also his *Hom. 6*.

30. Van Damme, *Pseudo-Cyprian Adversus Iudaeos*.

31. The rewriting in *Apostolic Constitutions* 6.14.5 and 6.15 misses the original Jewish context, for after urging that the circumcision of the heart by the Spirit suffices, the compiler applies the injunction to one baptism as a counsel against rebaptism instead of a contrast with the repeated purifications of the Jews.

32. The same in Cyprian, *Test.* 1.8 and 12.

33. Neusner, *Aphrahat and Judaism*; and Neusner, "The Jewish-Christian Argument in Fourth Century Iran." Duncan, *Baptism in the Demonstrations of Aphraates*, I.2 on baptism as spiritual circumcision interprets the Spirit as the equivalent of circumcision. The *Hymns for Epiphany* attributed to Ephraim the Syrian make the anointing that preceded baptism (3.1) equivalent to circumcision (3.4 and 13).

of sins" (11.11). Since the true circumcision is of the heart, it is possible to take the reference to baptism as an explanation of the Jordan and so as a separate act and not the second circumcision. In an extensive Joshua/Jesus typology Aphrahat makes a statement which seems to preclude this interpretation:

> Joshua [Jesus] our redeemer a second time circumcised the people who believed in him with the circumcision of the heart, and they were baptized and circumcised with "the knife" which is his word ... [Heb 4:12] ... Joshua our redeemer promised the land of the living to whoever passed through the true Jordan, believed, and circumcised the foreskin of his heart ... Blessed are those whose hearts are circumcised from the foreskin and who are born through water, the second circumcision, for they are inheritors with Abraham. (11.12)[34]

Aphrahat does not preserve the same sequence of events in each recounting of Joshua's deeds, so it may be that he is thinking of a complex of events rather than a sequence. In that case we may have a juxtaposition of circumcision and baptism in which spiritual circumcision and baptism occur together but are not counterparts.

It may be recalled that those passages which make circumcision in some sense the equivalent of baptism begin to appear later than those which identify circumcision with the Spirit. In the early writers the counterpart of circumcision is not baptism but what happens in baptism. The progression of thought would be as follows: (1) the Spirit as the seal of the new covenant on the analogy of circumcision as the seal of the Mosaic covenant, (2) the Spirit given in baptism, an extension natural enough and perhaps present from the beginning but reinforced by the association of both the covenant and baptism with the death of Christ, which inaugurated the new covenant, (3) baptism as the counterpart of circumcision. If that be a correct analysis, then the understanding presented gives more precision to the relation of baptism to circumcision than has customarily been observed, i.e., baptism as the time or occasion of the spiritual circumcision, and it offers a greater degree of consistency to the still quite varied application of the imagery of spiritual circumcision in patristic literature.

---

34. On the Joshua typology cf. Tertullian, *Adv. Marc.* 3.15.

# 10

# Inscriptions and the Origin of Infant Baptism

JOACHIM JEREMIAS GAVE CONSIDERABLE attention to the inscriptional evidence in presenting his history of infant baptism in the early church.[1] Kurt Aland's reply to Jeremias showed that the inscriptions add nothing to what is known from literary sources concerning the time when infant baptism began. Christian inscriptions commence in the third century and by that time infant baptism is already attested.[2] Aland appears to have confirmed the judgment of early twentieth-century critical scholars that there is no certain evidence for the practice of infant baptism before the late second century.[3]

Aland argued that the introduction of infant baptism is to be attributed to a belief in original sin. A change in attitude toward children from regarding them as innocent to regarding them as tainted with sinfulness can be seen in Origen and Cyprian.[4] This change combined with a decline

---

1. Jeremias, *Die Kindertaufe in den ersten vier Jahrhunderten*, 49–50, 59–60, 88–95, 100–101, 105–7; ET = *Infant Baptism in the First Four Centuries*, 41–42, 55–56, 75–80, 85, 89–90. Some points are reaffirmed more briefly in Jeremias, *Nochmals*, 42–46; ET = *Origins of Infant Baptism*, 49–53.

2. Aland, *Die Säuglingstaufe im Neuen Testament und in der Alten Kirche*, 48–53; ET, *Did the Early Church Baptize Infants?*, 75–79.

3. Jeremias acknowledges that there is no direct *provable* evidence before Tertullian—*Nochmals*, 5 (ET = *Origins*, 9–10).

4. Aland, *Säuglingstaufe*, 75 (ET = *Did the Early Church*, 103–4).

in eschatological expectations that the Lord would return before children passed from an age of innocence made baptism a necessity.[5]

Aland's theological explanation of the origin of infant baptism, however, has not held up as well as his historical arguments. Why the retreating eschatological expectation did not affect the practice of baptism until late in the second century is not clear. The eschatological outlook was the strongest in North Africa where infant baptism had its earliest and most widespread acceptance.[6] More significantly, the eschatological atmosphere could be argued as working in the opposite direction. Jeremias suggested that it was the understanding of baptism as an eschatological sacrament which made it plausible for children as well as their parents to receive this sign of salvation before the imminent overthrow of the present world order.[7]

The relationship between infant baptism and original sin appears, as Jeremias noted, to be the reverse of that stated by Aland.[8] The practice of infant baptism was an argument for infant sinfulness rather than infant guilt being the basis for infant baptism (at least in the early sources). The argument of Augustine in this regard is well known. The practice of baptizing infants was by his time general and was one of his strongest points against the Pelagians:

> The inevitable conclusion from these truths is this, that, as nothing else is effected when infants are baptized except that they are incorporated into the church, in other words, that they are united with the body and members of Christ, unless this benefit has been bestowed upon them, they are manifestly in danger of damnation. Damned, however, they could not be if they really had no sin. Now, since their tender age could not possibly have contracted sin in its own life, it remains for us, even if we are as yet unable to understand, at least to believe that infants inherit original sin.[9]

Cyprian and Origen introduced the idea of a stain or pollution attaching to birth and did so in the context of a consideration of infant baptism.

---

5. Ibid., 77–78; *Taufe und Kindertaufe*, 37–39.

6. Frend, *Martyrdom and Persecution*, 418.

7. Jeremias, *Kindertaufe*, 28 (ET = *Infant Baptism*, 23); *Nochmals*, 69–72 (ET = *Origins*, 83–84).

8. Jeremias, *Nochmals*, 62 (ET = *Origins*, 73–74).

9. *De pecc. mer. et rem., et de bapt. parv.* III. 39; cf. I. 23, 28, and 39; III. 2; *C. Julian. Pel.* III. 5. 11; *De gratia Chr. et de pecc. orig.* II. 2–4.

*Inscriptions and the Origin of Infant Baptism*

Cyprian speaking for the North African bishops in favour of conferring baptism immediately after birth and not waiting until the eighth day says:

> If forgiveness of sins is granted, when they afterwards come to believe, even to the worst transgressors and to those who have previously sinned much against God, and if no one is held back from baptism and grace; how much less ought an infant to be held back, who having been born recently has not sinned, except in that being born physically according to Adam, he has contracted the contagion of the ancient death by his first birth. He approaches that much more easily to the reception of the forgiveness of sins because the sins remittted to him are not his own, but those of another. (*Ep.* lxiv [lviii].5)

The line of argument is that if baptism is not denied to the worst of sinners, it should not be denied (or delayed) to the new born. Cyprian recognizes that they have no sins of their own; therefore, he can only refer the forgiveness to the sins of Adam. By his birth the infant contracts the death which Adam's sins brought into the world, and so in a sense the infant is in touch with Adam's sins.[10] Origen more explicitly indicates that the idea of baptizing infants raised the question, "For the forgiveness of whose sins?" His answer does not move much beyond the idea of a ceremonial or physical impurity associated with birth:

> I take this occasion to discuss something which our brothers often inquire about. Infants are baptized for the remission of sins. Of what kinds ? Or when did they sin ? But since "No one is exempt from stain," one removes the stain by the mystery of baptism. For this reason infants also are baptized. For "Unless one is born of water and the Spirit he cannot enter the kingdom of heaven."[11]

The movement is clearly from the existing practice to the doctrine and not from the doctrine to the practice.[12] Whatever influence the doctrine of original sin had in establishing a fairly uniform practice after Augustine's

---

10. Pelikan, *Development of Christian Doctrine*, 79–87. It is usually assumed that Cyprian is talking about normal practice, but in view of the evidence presented below one may raise a question whether this is a discussion only about the age for emergency baptism.

11. *Hom. Luc.* XIV. 5. Cf. *Hom. Lev.* VIII. 3 with reference to Job 14:4 and Ps 51:5 and *Comm. Rom.* V. 9 with reference to Lev 12:8 and Ps 51:5 in justification for baptizing infants for the remission of sins.

12. Williams, *The Ideas of the Fall and of Original Sin*, 220–26.

time, it seems not to have been the reason for the introduction of infant baptism.

If we are convinced by Aland that there is no sure evidence for infant baptism before Tertullian, and if we agree with Jeremias that original sin was not the explanation for its origin, then we are obligated to offer an alternative explanation. One who is not willing to use theology to fill in the blanks left by history will not be satisfied to stop where the researches of Jeremias and Aland have left us.

It is here that the inscriptions may offer assistance. Although most of the inscriptions are difficult to date and those which carry dates are later than the time for which there is literary testimony to the practice of infant baptism, they do reveal the popular Christian religious sentiments. They indicate the motives operative in infant baptism. They give a specificity and scope of evidence which the surviving literary records do not provide.

The collection by Ernst Diehl affords an excellent instrument by which to study the Latin evidence.[13] The Greek Christian inscriptions do not yet have a comparable corpus, so the same comprehensiveness is not possible in studying them.[14] A consideration of the inscriptions as a whole leaves some unmistakable impressions. Moreover, they suggest a specific setting in which infant baptism took its rise and which is consistent with the surviving literary evidence.

Only those inscriptions which undeniably refer to baptism and state when it was conferred permit definite conclusions. Inscriptions employing the terms "in peace," "innocent," and "believer" have not been found especially helpful in themselves for determining the age of baptism. *In pace* has often been appealed to as an indication that the person was baptized and so died "in the peace" of the church. There are many cases where this is likely,[15] but if one assumes the sinlessness or innocence of children, there is no reason why *in pace* would not be used of children apart from baptism. That there was no necessary connection between dying or resting "in peace" and baptism may be seen from Diehl no. 1509B: "Boniface, a

---

13. *Inscriptiones latinae christianae veteres.* Numbers will be to this edition unless otherwise stated.

14. See the collections on this subject by Didier, *Le Baptême des enfants dans la tradition de l'église*; and H. Kraft, *Texte zur Geschichte der Taufe, besonders der Kindertaufe in der alten Kirche.*

15. Notably is this the case where a *fidelis* is said to have lived in peace (*vixit in pace*) for a given period of time—nos. 1346, 1348, 5349, 1349A, 1351, 1372, 1381A, et al. *Fidelis in pace* was characteristic of North Africa (LeBlant, *Rev. Arch.*, 1881, 240).

## Inscriptions and the Origin of Infant Baptism

hearer in peace, who lived 1 year and 4 months." The child evidently had been enrolled as a catechumen, died unbaptized, but "in peace."

The word "innocent" (*innocentia*) had no necessary suggestion of sinlessness. As well as being used of children from infancy on,[16] it is even used of quite elderly persons: "more or less 50 years" (no. 3444, A.D. 397), 36 years old (no. 461), and even 80 years old (no. 2932). Did these persons die recently baptized? More likely the meaning is "blameless," "upright."

"Believer" or "faithful" (*fidelis*, πιστός) means "baptized" and is used of persons of varying ages: an infant (no. 3160), 4 year old (1334), 8 year old (1349), 33 year old (1347), etc.[17] Unless specifically stated, no firm conclusions can be drawn as to when the person became a "believer." The wording of an inscription like 1366 (near Aquileia) makes one think of an emergency baptism, but this is not explicit:

> To the divine dead. For the well-deserving son Covoideonus who lived 9 years, 2 months, 7 days. Buried December 28. He departed a believer in peace. His grieving parents made this according to a vow.

No doubt attaches to the important 1549, now in the Louvre and dated c. AD 314:

> Her parents set this up for Julia Florentina, their dearest and most innocent infant who was made a believer. She was born a pagan on the day before the nones of March before dawn when Zoilus was censor of the province. She lived eighteen months and twenty-two days and was made a believer in the eighth hour of the night, almost drawing her last breath. She survived four more hours so that she entered again on the customary things. She died at Hybla in the first hour of the day on September 25 . . .[18]

Little Julia was baptized clearly because she was on the point of death, and that accords with the information in a great many inscriptions.

The word baptism is rare, but the ceremony is referred to by such expressions as "made a believer" (*fidelis facta*, as in no. 1549 above), "received grace," and neophyte. One of the earliest dated inscriptions to

---

16. No. 3489 has a brother 11 years old and a sister 2 years old, whose "innocent souls deservedly went to God, assured of eternal life."

17. The word "Christian" is rarer than "believer" and I have not found it applied to children.

18. See observations by Mohrmann, "Encore une fois: *paganus*," 113–14.

allude to baptism is quite typical of the later inscriptions: no. 3315, dated AD 268, from the catacomb of Callistus:

> Pastor, Titiana, Marciana, and Chreste made this for Marcianus, a well-deserving son in Christ the Lord. He lived 12 years, 2 months, and ... days. He received grace [*crat(iam) (sic) accepit*] on September 20 when the consuls were Marinianus and Paternus the second time. He gave up (his soul) on September 21. May you live among the saints in eternity.

From Diehl's numbers 1523–43 the following are pertinent:

- 1523 (Salona, late 4th century)—For Flavia, dearest infant, who with sound mind obtained the grace [*gratiam consecuta*] of the glorious font on Easter day and survived after holy baptism five months. She lived 3 years, 10 months, 7 days. The parents, Flavian and Archelais, for their pious daughter. Burial on the 18th of August.

- 1524 (Rome, early 4th century)—ΙΧΘΥC N(εοφωτιστων?) Postumius Eutenion, a believer, who obtained holy grace the day before his birth day at a very late hour and died. He lived six years and was buried on the 11th of July on the day of Jupiter on which he was born. His soul is with the saints in peace. Felicissimus, Eutheria, and Festa his grandmother, for their worthy son Postumius.

- 1525 (Capua, AD 371)—Here is laid Fortunia, who lived more or less 4 years. The parents set this up for their dearest daughter. She obtained (grace) on July 27 ... and died on July 25 [*sic*, evidently the workman exchanged the dates]. Gratian for the second time and Probus were the consuls.

- 1527 (Rome)—The boy Maurus, age five years and three months, was buried on the nones of August. He obtained grace at two or three.

- 1528 (North Africa)—... obtained (the grace) of God on December 5 and lived in this world after the day of obtaining until December 7 and died ...

- 1529 (Rome)—For the well-deserving Antonia Cyriaceti who lived 19 years, 2 months, 26 days. Received (the grace) of God and died a virgin on the fourth day. Julius Benedictus her father set this up for his sweet and incomparable daughter. November 20.

## Inscriptions and the Origin of Infant Baptism

- 1530 (Rome)—Blessed Crescentine, my dear sweet wife, who lived 33 years, 2 months. She received (grace) on June 29 and was buried on October 27. Well-deserving.

- 1531 (Rome, Catacomb of Priscilla, third century)—Sweet Tyche lived one year, 10 months, 15 days. Received (grace) on the 8th day before the Kalends... Gave up (her soul) on the same day.

- 1532 (Rome, Catacomb of Priscilla, third century)—Irene who lived with her parents 10 months and 6 days received (grace) on April 7 and gave up (her soul) on April 13.

- 1535 (Rome)—To the divine dead. For Euphrosune, dear wife of Kampano, who lived with him 12 full years, 2 months, 5 days. She passed away in her 35th year. After the day of her receiving (grace) she lived 57 days.

- 1536a—For the well-deserving Simplicius who lived 51 years and after his reception (of grace) 27 days. Buried on February 1 in peace.

- 1539 (Rome, Catacomb of Domitilla, AD 338)—In the consulship of Ursus and Polemius the girl named Felite, more or less 30 years old, obtained (grace) on March 26 and died in peace after April 29 on the day of Mercury at the 9th hour.

- 1540—Euphronia, daughter of Euphronius and her mother, killed in a shipwreck. Born November 1, obtained (grace) April 11, died May 1.[/BL]

Diehl's numbers 1477–1507, as well as many others, use the word "neophyte" ("newly baptized") for the deceased. Where ages are given they are mostly young. A few examples may be cited:

- 1477 (Rome, St. Agnes outside the walls, AD 348)—Flavius Aurelius, son of Leo, marvelously endowed with the innocence of generous goodness and industry, who lived 6 years, 8 months, 11 days. A neophyte, he rested (in peace) on July 2 in the consulship of Julius Philip and Sallias...

- 1478 (Rome, AD 370)—For the well-deserving Perpetuus in peace, who lived more or less 30 years... Buried April 13, died a neophyte...

- 1478A (Rome, A.D. 371)—For Romanus, well-deserving neophyte, who lived 9 years, 15 days. May he rest in the Lord's peace. Flavius Gratian Augustus for the second time and Petronius Probus consuls.

- 1480 (Rome, AD 385)—In the consulship of Flavius Arcadius and Baudone on the 22nd of June died Leontius a neophyte who lived more or less 28 years, 5 months, 15 days. Well-deserving, in peace.
- 1481 (Rome, AD 389)—Aristo, an innocent child, who lived 8 months, a neophyte, departed on June 4, Timasius and Promotus being consuls.
- 1484 (Rome, Catacomb of Callistus)—Innocentius a neophyte lived 23 years.
- 1484B (Rome, Cemetery Cyriacae)—For Paulinus, a neophyte, in peace, who lived 8 years.
- 1484C (Ravenna)—For Proiectus, an infant neophyte, who lived 2 years, 7 months.
- 1485A (Rome, Catacomb of Pontianus)—For Domitian, innocent neophyte, who lived 3 years, 30 days. Buried May 24.
- 1485B (Rome, Catacomb of Praetextatus)—Mercury a neophyte is buried here. He lived 42 years, 2 months, 15 days. Eugenia while she lived made this.
- 1485C (Rome, Catacomb of Praetextatus)—Pisentus, an innocent soul, who lived 1 year, 8 months, 13 days, a neophyte, buried on September 13 in peace.
- 1485D (Rome, Capitoline Museum)—For the dear son Casiacinus who lived six years and 3 days, a neophyte, buried on May 5. Well-deserving, in peace.
- 1487—For Zosimus, who lived 5 years, 8 months, 13 days, neophyte in Christ. Donatus his father and Justa his mother for their well-deserving son.
- 1488B (Naples)—For the well-deserving Eugenia of happy memory who lived not 19 years, a neophyte.
- 2764 (Rome, Catacomb of Callistus)—For Felix, a well-deserving son, who lived 23 years, 10 days. He departed a virgin with reference to the world and a neophyte in peace. His parents made this. Buried August 2.[/BL]

Neophytes could come in all ages: from 24 days (no. 1497) or 80 days (4462B) to 42 years (1483) or 59 years (3352).

A few of the deceased are described as catechumens instead of neophytes. Diehl's no. 1508 (dated AD 397) is a 60-year-old catechumen. No.

1509A from Rome reads, "Lucilianus for his son Bacius Valerius who lived 9 years, 8 months, 22 days, a catechumen." Note 1509B quoted above about a "hearer" who died in peace.

The Greek inscriptions which have been brought into the discussion yield the same picture.

- CIG IV. 9810—Achillia, a neophyte, fell asleep in her first year, fifth month, on February 24.
- CIG IV. 9855—Here lies Macaria, daughter of John of the village Nikeratos. She lived 3 years, 3 months, 16 days. She died a believer on the 24th of the month Sandikou in the 11th consulship of Honorius Augustus and of Constantius.[19] [/BL]

It is noteworthy that all of the inscriptions which mention a time of baptism place this near the time of death. The explicit inscriptional evidence is not an argument for infant baptism as the normal practice. Rather, the evidence points to the opposite conclusion. The inscriptions do not tell the whole story, but as far as they go they provide an argument that in the third and fourth centuries infant baptism was abnormal. All of the above cited examples may be considered cases of "emergency baptism." Death was near, and the person received baptism "on his death-bed" as it were. Jeremias has pointed to the practice of the delay of baptism in the fourth century,[20] but the third-century inscriptions show the same practice. Why is baptism not mentioned except when it was administered near death? Any effort to argue from silence will be subjective. Instead of trying to fill in the silence in the archaeological record with conjectures (as has been done with the literary record), we should listen to what the existing evidence is saying. The newborn were not routinely baptized in the period of our early inscriptions. Baptism was administered before death, at whatever age. This fact offers the most plausible explanation of the origin of infant baptism. One early inscription says it explicitly:

---

19. The other Greek inscriptions introduced by Jeremias do not help: the Zosimus inscription (*Kindertaufe*, 59 [ET = *Infant Baptism*, 56]) actually gives no information on the time of baptism, and the Dionysius inscription (*Kindertaufe*, 90 [ET = *Infant Baptism*, 77]) gives no indication of baptism.

20. Jeremias, *Kindertaufe*, 102–7 [ET = *Infant Baptism*, 87–91]. Jeremias argues that the third-century examples (nos. 1611C, 1343, 3891C, 1531, 1532, 3315) are children of non-Christians. This seems unlikely: why then were they baptized and buried in a Christian cemetery? At least the parents would have been catechumens. We may leave this question aside as we look for the motivation.

> Sacred to the divine dead. Florentius made this monument for his well-deserving son Appronianus, who lived one year, nine months, and five days. Since he was dearly loved by his grandmother, and she saw that he was going to die, she asked from the church that he might depart from the world a believer. (Diehl, no. 1343, from the Catacomb of Priscilla, third century)

The discussion centering on the likelihood that the father was a pagan and the bearing of this on the baptism has diverted attention from the most important thing which this inscription has to say, namely the desire that the child die a "believer," i.e., "baptized." Why was there this strong desire, reflected in all the "emergency baptisms" above, even though baptism was not administered earlier?

Since the inscriptions are epitaphs, reception of baptism must have been considered an important preparation for the afterlife. As the inscriptions indicate, the approach of death was the occasion for the baptism. Many children must have died unbaptized, and so the urge for baptism soon after birth became strong. I would suggest that John iii. 5 (cited by Origen above) supplied the biblical basis for the Christian concern about children in the after-life. This logion was the favourite baptismal text of the second century.[21] John Chrysostom continued to defend infant baptism in terms of its positive benefits while rejecting a doctrine of original sin:

> You have seen how numerous are the gifts of baptism. Although many men think that the only gift it confers is the remission of sins, we have counted its honors to the number of ten. It is on this account that we baptize even infants, although they are sinless, that they may be given the further gifts of sanctification, righteousness, filial adoption, and inheritance, that they may be brothers and members of Christ, and become dwelling places for the Spirit.[22]

John 3:5 has remained a prooftext for infant baptism in the Catholic tradition. The universal understanding of baptism as for the remission of sins gave impetus to the doctrine of original sin which then in turn became the theological basis for infant baptism.

John 3:5 could be thought as debarring any unbaptized person from heaven. Baptism was the rite which assured a blessed hereafter. The request

---

21. Hermas, *Sim.* IX. xvi. 3; Justin, *Apol. I*, 61; Theophilus, *Ad Autol.* II. xvi; Irenaeus, *Adv. Haer.* III. xvii. 1f.; Clement of Alexandria, *Strom.* IV. xxv; Tertullian, *De bapt.* 12.

22. *Bapt. Lect.* III. 6. Cf. Gregory Nazianzus, *Carmina* I. i. 9, lines 87–92; his *Or.* XL. xxviii supports the interpretation advanced in this article.

from parents (or a grandparent, as above) for baptism for a gravely sick child would be natural and would be hard to refuse. Even an opponent of infant baptism like Tertullian appears to allow for emergency baptism as a regular practice:

> It follows that deferment of baptism is more profitable, in accordance with each person's character and attitude, and even age; and especially so as regards children. For what need is there, if there really is no need, for even their sponsors to be brought into peril. (*De bapt.* 18.4)

Tertullian stood at the point where there was pressure from some to extend the emergency measure to other circumstances. It is not uncommon for emergency procedures to become regular practice. That is, I submit, what happened here. If baptism was a necessary precaution before death, it would be easy to make the precautionary measure normal, especially as it gained the support of powerful theological reasons. The initiative in infant baptism, therefore, lay with parents of sick children who asked of the church that they might not die unbaptized. These parents then gratefully recorded the fact of the baptism at the burial site.

The practice of baptism before death exerted an influence in two directions. The association of baptism with the time of death might cause baptism to be put off until the end of life, so that its saving benefits could be applied to the entire life. Thus occurred the delay of baptism which became a problem in the fourth century. Baptism in adult years when there was no immediate threat of death, to be observed in the lives of several prominent church leaders in the fourth century, however, was not the same thing as the death-bed baptism of Constantine and others. On the other hand, the desire to die baptized, or to have one's children die baptized, could exert an influence in the opposite direction. The high mortality rate of infants in the ancient world, to which the Christian inscriptions are a powerful if mournful witness, would encourage the practice of giving baptism soon after birth as insurance no matter what might happen. The inscriptions say that it was in such natural, human feelings that we are to find the real origin of a practice which later acquired such significant theological support.

# 11

## The Disgrace and the Glory
### A Jewish Motif in Early Christianity

DURING THE PASSOVER MEAL, as described in the Mishnah, "the son asks his father . . . , 'Why is this night different from other nights?' . . . And according to the understanding of the son his father instructs him. He begins with the disgrace and ends with the glory."[1] The theme of disgrace followed by glory (or the hope of glory) is broadly represented in Jewish history.

When Jewish believers in Jesus came to the Passover and reflected on the experience of Jesus at that season of the year, they would certainly see the crucifixion and resurrection as another, and climactic, expression of the history that leads from disgrace to glory. They would tell their own story according to the pattern they had learned at Passover. Eduard Schweizer has shown how deeply embedded in the New Testament is the Jewish theme of the Righteous One who suffers humiliation and is rewarded with exaltation (see Luke 24:26).[2] A New Testament passage of special interest for this paper, because it connects the theme with Old Testament prophecies, is 1 Pet 1:11—"[The prophets] predicted the sufferings of Christ and the subsequent glory."[3] The passion and resurrection of

---

1. *Pesachim* 10.4.

2. Schweizer, *Erniedrigung und Erhöhung bei Jesus und seinen Nachfolgern*; ET = *Lordship and Discipleship*.

3. Danker, "Lexicographical Hazards, Pitfalls, and Challenges, with Special Reference to the Contributions of John Edward Gates," 236, argues that the sufferings are by Christians for Christ rather than the sufferings of Christ. This is grammatically

*The Disgrace and the Glory*

Jesus has quite naturally continued to be told by Christians according to the pattern of disgrace (humiliation) and glory (exaltation). The contrast permitted many different formulations. As random selections from the period covered by patristic literature, I note one of the Christian additions to the *Testaments of the Twelve Patriarchs* (probably second century), "I know how humble he shall be on earth and how glorious in heaven,"[4] and from four hundred years later [Ps.] Gregory the Great, the "disgrace of his death and the glory of his power against death."[5]

The motif of disgrace followed by glory early received another application in Christianity. There occurred a shift of the humiliation/exaltation pattern from death/resurrection to the two comings of Christ. The origin and function of this secondary application of the motif of humiliation and exaltation will be considered in this paper.

The New Testament hints at the language of two comings: Acts 1:11 quotes the angels at the ascension, "This Jesus . . . will come in the same way as you saw him go into heaven" and Heb 9:28 declares, "Christ, having been offered once to bear the sins of many, will appear a second time, not to deal with sin but to save those who are eagerly waiting for him." The theme of "two comings of Christ" may have been "traditional" by the time of Justin Martyr[6] (and I think it is), but the first literary expression of the theme of the two comings occurs in him. Justin expresses the pattern of humiliation and glory almost as a formula: "For the prophets proclaimed beforehand two advents of Christ: the one, which is already past, as a dishonoured and suffering man; and the second, when, according to prophecy, he shall come from heaven with glory."[7] It is not simply the idea of a second coming which is of concern here but the specific formulation of two comings, the first in humility and the second in glory.[8]

---

possible, but he loses the forest in looking at a tree: the subject of the passage is the grace that brings salvation to the readers, and that must have come through the sufferings and glory of Christ. The pattern of sufferings leading to glory is found in 1 Peter also in 4:13; 5:1, 10; this pattern agrees with the paschal themes found in the book—Cross, *1 Peter, A Paschal Liturgy*.

4. *Test. Benj.* 9.3(4).
5. *Dial.* 2.8.
6. Prigent, *Justin et l'Ancien Testament*, 80.
7. *1 Apol.* 52.
8. Osborn, *Justin Martyr*, 187–88, notes that Justin is the first to speak of Christ's second coming, but he quotes the passages with little comment; cf. Barnard, "Justin Martyr's Eschatology," 87–89. Trakatellis, *The Pre-Existence of Christ in Justin Martyr*, studies Justin's basic scheme of pre-existence, incarnation, exaltation and concludes that Justin makes more of the pre-existence leading to the humiliation of the

This scheme of two comings according to Justin is covered in Oskar Skarsaune's recent book *The Proof from Prophecy: A Study in Justin Martyr's Proof-Text Tradition*.[9] Skarsaune states some of the conclusions to which I had come independently, so I will take his study as a basis for this communication. The theme of two comings is not a major concern of his important study, and a broader look at the theme may substantiate some of his points.

Justin sets the motif of two comings at the forefront of his concerns in the *Dialogue with Trypho*: "Of these and such like words written by the prophets . . . some were spoken concerning the first advent of Christ, in which he has been preached to appear as inglorious, without comeliness, and mortal; but others had reference to his second advent, when he appears in glory and above the clouds."[10] Justin uses the two comings to answer Trypho's objections that Jesus did not correspond to the expectation of a royal Messiah. In reply to Trypho's argument that the Jews awaited the Messiah of Daniel 7, Justin explained that there are "two advents—one in which he was pierced by you; a second, when you shall know him whom you have pierced, and your tribes shall mourn" [Zech 12:10-14].[11] Again, he says, "If scripture compels you to admit that two advents of Christ were prophesied to take place—one in which he would appear suffering, dishonoured, and without comeliness; but the other in which he would come glorious and judge of all," then there is an answer to the objection that Elijah had not come by placing that event before the second coming.[12] The two comings became, as Skarsaune says, "a hermeneutical key to Old Testament messianic prophecies."[13] Jacob's blessing of Judah in Gen 49:8-12 was understood as a prophecy "that there would be two advents of Christ, and that in the first he would suffer."[14] Justin's main texts were Isaiah 53 for the first coming, Daniel 7 for the second, and Zechariah 12 and Psalm 110

---

incarnation than he does of the humiliation leading to exaltation (cf. 178, "The picture of the righteous one who is humiliated but who finally is vindicated by God is absent").

9. Skarsaune, *The Proof from Prophecy*.

10. *Dial.* 14.8.

11. *Dial.* 32.2; cf. 33.2 ("He shall be first humble as a man, and then exalted") and 34.2 ("liable to suffering at first . . . and coming again with glory"). Dom Jean Leclercq sets the theme of the two comings in the context of "L'idée de la royauté du Christ dans l'œuvre de Saint Justin," esp. 87-91.

12. *Dial.* 49.2. Cf. Gregory of Nyssa, *Test. adv. Iud.* 17, "That Elijah will come before the second advent of the Lord [Mal 4:5]."

13. Skarsaune, *The Proof from Prophecy*, 156.

14. *Dial.* 52.1.

*The Disgrace and the Glory*

for both. As Justin moved toward the conclusion of the *Dialogue*, invoking Micah 4, he brought a ringing charge against the Jews: "O unreasoning men! understanding not what has been shown by all these passages, that two advents of Christ have been announced: the one, in which he has been preached as suffering, inglorious, dishonoured, and crucified; but the second, in which he shall come from heaven with glory."[15] The two comings became a comprehensive scheme for interpreting the Old Testament, which provided not only prophecies but symbols of the two advents.[16] *Dialogue* 111 refers to two of these types: the two goats on the day of atonement (Leviticus 16) and Moses stretching forth his hands (representing the cross) while Joshua in the battle against Amalek (Exod 17:8–13) conquered (representing the victorious second coming). The two goats received fuller treatment in chapter 40: "The two similar goats which were commanded to be offered during the fast, of which one was sent away as the scapegoat and the other sacrificed, likewise declared the two appearances of Christ: the first, in which the elders of your people and the priests, having laid hands on him and put him to death, sent him away as the scapegoat; and his second appearance, because in the same place in Jerusalem you shall recognize him whom you have dishonoured and who was an offering for all sinners willing to repent."[17]

The theme of two comings, one in disgrace and the other in glory, receives full development first in Justin Martyr. Did it originate with him, and what was its original context? Justin's use of the idea suggests four possible settings.

1. As part of a creedal summary of the career of Christ. Skarsaune points to the remarkably constant terminology and constant group of biblical references as indicating that "we have to do with a stereotyped scheme attached to the 'creed' sequence of testimonies."[18] Justin treats the two comings especially in the collection of testimonies bearing on the career of Jesus which Skarsaune designates as his "Kerygma Source."[19] In

15. *Dial.* 110.2.

16. *Dial.* 52.4.

17. The basis of the interpretation was the requirement that the two goats be alike—*Yoma* 6.1—and be chosen in Jerusalem—*Yoma* 3.9. *Barnabas* 7 had already given a Christological interpretation of the two goats, the sacrificed goat associated with the crucifixion and the scapegoat with the second coming (the reverse of Justin's interpretation), but stopped short of expressly speaking of two advents, so Justin represents a second stage of reflection on Jewish Christian exegesis.

18. Skarsaune, *The Proof from Prophecy*, 156.

19. Ibid., 260.

support of this suggestion may be cited the Muratorian Fragment, which concludes its kerygmatic summary of the Gospel facts about Jesus with the statement that the one Spirit declares in all the Gospels Jesus' "double advent, the first in humility when he was despised, which has been; the second in royal power, glorious, which is to be."[20] Against this suggestion that the motif of two comings originated in summaries of the apostolic preaching is Justin's use outside his kerygmatic section and the absence of the motif from other statements of the rule of faith.[21]

2. As a heading in the arrangement of Old Testament *testimonia* to Jesus. Early collections of testimonies were drawn on in presenting the argument for the different character of the two comings, and Justin had sources for his presentation.[22] I think it is doubtful, however, that the *testimonia* originated the scheme; the arrangement of the testimonies according to this pattern would be secondary. At any rate, the later collections of *testimonia* did not preserve the motif in their arrangement. Cyprian appears to have known the language, but he preserves it only in connection with the first coming: "That Christ was to come in low estate in his first advent," citing Isaiah 53; 50:5-7; 52:2-4; Psalms 22; Zechariah 3; and Philippians 2.[23] The absence is particularly notable in the *Pseudo-Epiphanius Testimony Book*,[24] which arranges the prophecies according to the career of Jesus.

3. As an anti-Marcionite argument. Justin is known to have written a work against Marcion,[25] and Prigent includes the treatment of the two comings in the *Dialogue* among the material which he claims Justin took

20. Lines 24-25; cf. Justin, 1 *Apol.* 42: Ps. Clem., *Recog.* 1.69.

21. Irenaeus, *Proof* 48, finds the two comings in Ps 110:7 ("He shall drink of the torrent in the way: therefore shall he lift up the head") as Justin, *Dial.* 33 does, and says. "He is referring to the exaltation with glory, after his human nature, and after his humiliation and ingloriousness." This passage is part of a catechetical summary of the career of Jesus but is incidental to the whole development of the instruction. More directly attached to the kerygma is the phrase in the statement of the *regula fidei* in *A.H.* 1.10.1, "the Holy Spirit proclaimed through the prophets . . . the advents," according to the Greek, but the Latin has the singular: in either case there is no express connection with the humility/exaltation theme.

22. Skarsaune in Part II of his book seeks to delineate Justin's sources more closely than has been accomplished before.

23. *Ad Quirinum* II.13; see *Patience* 23-24, "Although he came first shrouded in humility, yet he shall come manifest in power," as part of an exhortation to patience, for God will punish evildoers. Cf. note 12 for Gregory of Nyssa preserving the language in reference to the second coming.

24. Hotchkiss, ed. and trans., *Pseudo-Epiphanius Testimony Book*.

25. Irenaeus, *Against Heresies* 4.6.2.

from his earlier (lost) work against heresies.[26] Marcion followed the Jewish interpretation of the Messiah of the Old Testament in arguing that Jesus was not the Messiah of the Old Testament and that the Father of Jesus was not the God of the Old Testament. The scheme of two comings would have been an effective reply in affirming the continuity between the Old Testament and the New and the same God in both. Even so, Irenaeus, although he made minimal use of the scheme, applied it against Marcion (but with reference to Jewish misunderstanding). His one explicit statement seems to be based on Justin, but alludes to more texts than he: "All the prophets announced his two advents: one indeed in which he became a man subject to stripes [Isa 53:3; Zech 9:9; Ps 118:22; Isa 53:7; Exod 17:11] . . . ; but the second in which he will come on the clouds [Dan 7:13; Mal 4:4; Isa 11:4]."[27] Tertullian also uses the theme against Marcion: "We affirm that the two descriptions of Christ set forth by the prophets signified beforehand the same number of advents; one, and that the first, in humility . . . These signs of degradation correspond to his first advent, even as those of majesty to the second."[28] Nevertheless, the scheme of two comings does not seem central to the anti-Marcionite polemic, and in any case Marcion's argument is based on the Jewish interpretation,[29] and Tertullian's statement is introduced as an explanation of the errors of the Jews. Therefore, it appears that the anti-Marcionite use, like the kerygmatic and testimony uses, is a secondary application.

    4. As part of anti-Jewish polemic. Justin expressly puts the two comings of Christ in an anti-Jewish context. Skarsaune notes that in the *Apology* the emphasis is that since the prophecies of the first coming have been fulfilled in detail, we can be sure that those of the glorious second coming will be too; in the *Dialogue* the scheme of the two parousias is an answer to the Jewish argument that Jesus did not fulfill the triumphant messianism of the Old Testament.[30] He concludes that the use of this scheme to answer Jewish complaints that the lowly Jesus does not correspond to the messianic hope of the Old Testament points to an original Judeo-Christian provenance.[31] Another pointer is the presence of the same scheme in the Pseudo-Clementines. It is stated almost as a formula in a description of

26. Prigent, *Justin et l'Ancien Testament*, 78–88.
27. *Against Heresies* 4.33.1.
28. *Adv. Marc.* 3.7.1.
29. *Adv. Marc.* 3.6.2ff.: 3.8 1.
30. Skarsaune, *The Proof from Prophecy*, 156.
31. Ibid., 285–87.

what James supposedly said in conversation with Caiaphas: "[He] taught that two advents of [Jesus] were foretold: one in humiliation, which he has accomplished; the other in glory, which is hoped for to be accomplished, when he shall come to give the kingdom to those who believe in him and who observe all things which he has commanded."[32] The same teaching is ascribed to Peter: "[Moses][33] therefore indicated that he should come, humble indeed in his first coming, but truly glorious in his second. And the first has indeed already been accomplished, since he has come and taught, and he the judge of all has been judged and slain. But indeed at his second coming he shall come to judge and he shall indeed condemn the wicked but shall take the pious into a share and association in his kingdom . . . The Jews therefore have erred concerning the first coming of the Lord; and between them and us there is disagreement only on this point. For they themselves know and expect that Christ will come; but that he has come already in humility, even this one who is called Jesus, they do not know."[34] Both passages belong in the section of the *Recognitions* (1.33–71) assigned by Georg Strecker to the Jewish-Christian source AJ II (*Anabathmoi Iakobou*, "Ascents of James") to be dated between 135 and 200.[35] Skarsaune, furthermore, refers to several modern authors, who without giving an extensive discussion say the theme of two comings was an answer to Jewish objections: Marcel Simon,[36] Per Beskow,[37] and B. Z. Bokser.[38] A surprising omission is Jean Daniélou, whose *Theology of Jewish Christianity* does not discuss the two comings. He does consider the two angels, two spirits, and two ways; if the position taken here is correct, he should have added the two advents.

I think other references to the two comings in early Christian literature confirm its origin in the Jewish and Christian debate. The same themes and texts of scripture employed by Justin are found in the treatise *Adversus Iudaeos* attributed to Tertullian. *Adversus Iudaeos* 14 is nearly identical in many places word for word, with *Adversus Marcionem* 3.7. The two characters of Christ shown forth by the prophets correspond to two

---

32. *Recog.* 1.69.
33. Gen 49:10 is alluded to later in the passage.
34. *Recog.* 1.49–50.
35. Strecker, *Das Judenchristentum in den Pseudoklementinen*, 221–54; new edition (Berlin, 1981). See now Van Voorst, *The Ascents of James*. Segal puts it in book 7 of *Kerygmata Petrou* ("Jewish Christianity," 345).
36. Simon, *Verus Israel*, 190–92.
37. Beskow, *Rex Gloriae*, 98–99.
38. Bokser, "Justin Martyr and the Jews," 109.

advents. Isaiah 53; Ps 38:17; Isa 8:14; Pss 8:5; 22:6 describe the first advent in humility; Dan 2:34ff. and 7:13–14; Ps 8:5–6; and Zech 12:10, 12 speak of the second advent. The two kinds of garments—"filthy garments" and "rich apparel"—of the priest Joshua (Jesus) in Zech 3:1–5 represent the two comings of Jesus. The two goats of the Day of Atonement are another type of the two comings, as in Justin's interpretation. "Therefore, since the first coming was obscured by many figures and debased with every dishonour, while the second was to be manifest and worthy of God, they were easily able to understand and believe the second and to look intently on the second coming alone, which is in honour and glory, and they were not unexpectedly deceived about the more obscure, seemingly unworthy first coming. And so even today they deny that their Christ has come, because he did not come in majesty, while they are ignorant that he was first to come in humility."[39] If we accept the arguments of Säflund and Tränkle for the authenticity of *Adversus Iudaeos* and its precedence to *Adversus Marcionem*, our case is strengthened.[40] Even if the treatise is not authentic, or only its second half, the presence of the same material from *Adversus Marcionem* 3.7 in a treatise against the Jews supports the indications of the *Adversus Marcionem* itself that its original context is the debate between Jews and Christians.

As Justin had referred to the two comings in his *Apology* to pagans, so also did Tertullian. Even when used in an apology to pagans, the reference to the two comings occurs in the context of Christian differences from Jews. "The Jews knew that Christ was to come, since the prophets spoke to them. And even now they look for his coming; nor is there any greater conflict between us and them than that they do not believe him already to have come. Two comings were predicted for him—a first, which has been fulfilled, in the humility of human form, a second, which is imminent at the end of the world, in a majestic display of divinity. By not understanding the first, the Jews considered the second, which they hope for as more openly foretold, to be the only one. It was the merited punishment of their

---

39. *Adv. Iud.* 14.10.

40. Säflund, *De Pallio and die stilistische Entwicklung Tertallians*, Part V, esp. 143, 178–79, 193ff., 201. The work is a careful refutation of the influential dissertation by Akerman, "Über die Echtheit der letzten Hälfte von Tertullians *Adversus Iudaeos*." Hermann Tränkle, ed., *Q.S.F. Tertulliani Adversus Iudaeos*. Cf. the argument of Hugo Koch, "Tertullianisches," 462–69 that *Adv. Iud.* 8 and 9 are from the same hand. Viciano, "Principios de hermenéutica biblica en el tratato 'Adversus Iudaeos' de Tertuliano," 637–44, esp. 638–39.

sin not to understand the first coming."[41] Tertullian's dependence on Justin is well recognised.[42] His statement focusing the differences between Jews and Christians on the first coming of the Messiah establishes a point of contact also with the *Ascents of James II* in the Pseudo Clementines,[43] and so once more with the Jewish-Christian conversation.

Origen uses the theme of two comings likewise in the context of the debate between Jews and Christians. Celsus had introduced the arguments of a Jew against Jesus being the Christ. Origen's reply states, "Now it escaped the notice of Celsus, and of the Jew whom he has introduced, and of all who are not believers in Jesus that the prophecies speak of two advents of Christ—the former characterised by human suffering and humility . . . , and the latter, distinguished only by glory and divinity, having no element of human infirmity intermingled with its divine greatness."[44]

The motif of the two comings was remembered and continued to be invoked in relation to the Jewish rejection of Jesus. Lactantius states: "Now his humility gave the Jews boldness for this deed. For when they read with what power and glory the Son of God was going to come from heaven, yet they saw Jesus humble, of low condition, and without comeliness, they did not believe him to be the Son of God, being ignorant that two comings of his had been predicted by the prophets: the first obscure in the humility of the flesh, and the second manifest in the power of his majesty."[45] He proceeds to quote Psalms 72 and Isaiah 53, favorite texts on this theme. Lactantius' repetition of the charge of ignorance by the Jews connects his words with Tertullian's formulation of the tradition.

As the living debate with Jews receded into the background of the church's concerns, the scheme of one coming in humility and a second in glory became less frequent. The theme had found a place in the church's catechesis as a way of teaching the economy of salvation, now divorced from the anti-Judaic polemic but employing the same prophetic texts.[46] Cyril of Jerusalem preserves one of the rare later uses of the motif: "We preach not one advent only of Christ, but also a second much more glori-

---

41. *Apol.* 21.15.

42. Skarsaune, *The Proof from Prophecy*, 435–45.

43. *Recog.* 1.50.

44. *C. Cels.* 1.56.

45. *Inst.* 4.12, 14, 16. Eusebius, *Dem. ev.* 4.16; 9.17 also uses the two comings in refutation of the Jewish interpretation of the prophecies.

46. Augustine, *De catech. rud.*, although suggesting biblical history as the framework of instruction, does not use the two comings. Cf. 17.28, "Ancient saints were saved by believing he would come, as we are by believing he has come."

## The Disgrace and the Glory

ous than the former. For the former showed his endurance, but the second brings the crown of a divine kingdom. For the most part, all things pertaining to our Lord Jesus Christ are twofold: a twofold generation . . . his descents twofold: one, the unobserved [Ps 72:6], a second, manifest, which is to be."[47]

The texts formulating the two comings according to the disgrace/glory pattern occur with great consistency in relation to the interpretation of Old Testament prophecy. The pattern functioned apologetically to answer Jewish objections to Jesus as the Messiah and exegetically as a scheme to interpret the scriptures. The Jewish motif of humiliation leading to exaltation was applied first to the death and resurrection of Jesus. A shift occurred to apply the humiliation to the first coming of Jesus and the exaltation to the second coming. The texts seem to indicate that the impetus for this shift was the Jewish polemic against Jesus as not meeting the qualifications of the Messiah. The theme of two comings provided a comprehensive scheme for interpreting the Old Testament and so could be used as part of the general apologetic argument from the fulfillment of prophecy, not only in response to the Jewish argument that Christians did not read the prophecies correctly, but also in response to Marcionites and pagans, who relied on the Jewish interpretations for their own purposes. The occasional incorporation of the pattern into the kerygma led to its use in catechesis and so allowed some continued life for the idea apart from its original setting.[48]

---

47. *Cat.* 15.1–2. Other fourth-century texts are Eusebius, *Prophetical Extracts* (pp. 4, 5); Chrysostom, *Hom. Jo.* 28.1 on John 3:17; Chrysostom, *De bapt. Chr.* 2 (PG 49.365); Jerome, *Ep.* 121.

48. Other early texts include Hippolytus, *Antichrist* 44; Victorinus, *Comm. Rev.* 1.7.

# 12

# The Kingdom of God in Early Patristic Literature[1]

WHETHER THE KINGDOM OF God is future or present has dominated discussion of Jesus' proclamation since Albert Schweitzer.[2] The treatment of the early patristic usage of the terminology of the kingdom must be set in the broader terms of the discussion of the meaning of kingdom in the New Testament. Although the temporal question may not always be the most helpful category to apply to the New Testament material, it does seem to have been a significant concern in the early Christian development. Most of the second-century references to the kingdom of God can be classified according to a temporal outline. The principal options may be outlined as follows:

I. The Kingdom as Present—Realized Eschatology

    A. Interior—the kingdom within the believer

    B. Soteriological/Ecclesiastical—the kingdom as meaning salvation or realized in the church

II. The Kingdom as Future—Consistent Eschatology

---

1. This contribution is a rewriting of a paper read at the Eighth International Conference on Patristic Studies at Oxford in 1979. Parts of that paper incorporated in this article are reprinted with permission from *Studia Patristica* XVIII (ed. E. A. Livingstone), Copyright 1982, Pergamon Press—E. Ferguson, "The Terminology of the Kingdom in the Second Century," 669–76.

2. A history of research and selections from some major interpretations may be found in Chilton, ed., *The Kingdom of God*.

A. Millennial—the kingdom as earthly before the end

B. Heavenly—the kingdom as the world to come

III. The Kingdom as Both Present and Future—Inaugurated Eschatology

In Process of Being Realized—the present kingdom as leading to consummation

IV. Symbolic—the kingdom as a literary symbol

These views are not mutually exclusive. Some examples of kingdom in each of these senses may be found in second-century Christian literature, but the great majority of passages will be found to represent a consistent eschatological reference.

The basic meaning of kingdom in biblical usage was kingship, "reign." From this came the secondary meaning of realm, kingdom in its modern sense.[3] The secondary sense definitely predominates in early patristic literature, but is not the exclusive meaning. This shift in emphasis from the active sense of kingly power to the static sense of realm illustrates the shift in thinking from the dynamic biblical concepts to the more static concepts of Greco-Roman thought. In that regard the patristic view of the future and heaven differed from the consistent eschatology advocated by Schweitzer in interpreting the New Testament texts.

## BIBLICAL CITATIONS AND ALLUSIONS

Many occurrences of the word kingdom in early patristic literature are found in biblical quotations and allusions. These have been largely omitted, for reasons of space, from the collection of quotations in the appendix. Some observations, however, are in order because of the insights which these quotations give to the concerns of the authors.

The use of a particular verse was sometimes thrust upon an author by reason of special circumstances. The refutation of Gnosticism by Irenaeus, bishop of Lyons (ca. 180–200), required extensive treatment of 1 Cor 15:50.[4] Paul's statement that "Flesh and blood cannot inherit the kingdom of God" accorded well with the Gnostic dualism of body and soul, with its corollaries of the salvation of the soul and denial of a resurrection of the flesh. Irenaeus interpreted "flesh and blood" as referring to the sinful works of the flesh, the flesh without the Spirit of God.

3. Schmidt, "βασιλεύς"; Klappert, "King, Kingdom."
4. *Against Heresies* 5.9–14; cf. 1.30.13.

W. H. Lampe, "Some Notes on the Significance of *Basileia Tou Theou, Basileia Christou* in the Greek Fathers," *JTS* 49 (1948) 60 makes a generalization which holds for the second century when he says that patristic usage differs from the Synoptic Gospels in that kingdom bears a less "dynamic" meaning and as a rule does not suggest the irruption of the divine into human history. Exceptions to this generalization will be noted in the discussion below.

Treatments of the kingdom of God in the post-canonical literature are not nearly so numerous as those dealing with the Bible, but in addition to works cited in the notes following mention may be made of A. Robertson, *Regnum Dei* (London, 1901); Robert Murray, *Symbols of Church and Kingdom* (London: Cambridge Univ. Press, 1975); and the works cited in John E. Groh, "The Kingdom of God in the History of Christianity: A Bibliographical Survey," *Church History* 43 (1974) 257–67.

Irenaeus' eschatological understanding of the kingdom is shown in his special fondness for Matt 25:34.[5] Likewise other authors indicate their viewpoint by their favorite texts. Irenaeus' eschatological understanding was reinforced by Daniel 2 and 7; Dan 7:27 was important also to Justin Martyr (ca. 150–160) in his argument against Judaism. Daniel 7:27 (supported by 2 Sam 7:12–16; Ps 132:12; cf. 2 Pet 1:11) furnished him with the set phrase "eternal kingdom" in order to contrast Christ's kingdom with the temporal kingdom of Israel.[6] Justin, as other Christians, also found Ps 45 useful in exalting Jesus as the anointed King.[7] From the New Testament, Justin quotes Matt 8:11–12 with some frequency.[8] Clement of Alexandria (ca. 190–200) most frequently cites Matt 11:12 (Luke 16:16), emphasizing the human effort which must be exerted in order to enter the kingdom.[9] The Pseudo Clementine *Recognitions* show their moral concern by the special interest in Mt 6:33.[10]

The biblical phrases which really caught the attention of the second century were "inherit the kingdom of God" (1 Cor 6:9; Gal 5:21; cf. Eph 5:5; Matt 25:34; James 2:5) and especially Jesus' "enter the kingdom of heaven [God]" (frequently in Matthew and Luke), phrases occurring too often to cite examples and both understood the same way—eschatologically.

5. *Against Heresies* 4.18.6; 28.2; 40.2; 5.27.1.
6. *Dialogue* 31; 79.2; 118:2; 68.5; 76.1; and see 65.
7. *Dialogue* 56; 63; 86.
8. *Dialogue* 76.4; 120.5–6; 140.2.
9. *Miscellanies* 4.2; 5.2; *Who Is the Rich Man that Is Saved* 21; 31.
10. Appendix No. 109; *Recognitions* 2.21; 46; 3.20; 37; 41.

## FACTORS INFLUENCING CHRISTIAN USAGE

### Debate with the Jews

The polemic against Judaism made it necessary for Christians to affirm that the kingdom had been taken from the Jews and that the followers of Jesus were its true heirs (Nos. 55, 62, 64, 75; Matt 8:11–12 was important here). Thus Justin declares that the eternal kingdom belongs to Jesus (No. 49; cf. 46 and 48 and Tertullian, *Against Marcion* 4.33), and Irenaeus asserts that Christ has the eternal kingdom (Nos. 65, 69, 72). Of course, neither Jews nor Christians in the second century were permitted a "political" expression of their kingdom claims.

### Political Situation

"Kingdom" occurs occasionally in second-century Christian literature as a neutral term for the secular kingdoms in human history (Nos. 11, 20, 57, 58; cf. 56). Of more significance was its use for the Roman Empire in conscious relation or even contrast to God's kingdom. The *Martyrdom of Polycarp* (155 ?) employs a dating formula at its conclusion which deliberately substitutes a reference to the eternal reign of Christ in place of the year of the reigning emperor (No. 27; cf. 24 and 25). The Apologists were particularly aware that the biblical word for "kingdom" was the ordinary word for the empire (Nos. 45, 58) or any kingship (No. 68). They stressed that the source of earthly rule was God (No. 58; cf. 11 and Justin, *II Apology* 2.19 for God as king in contrast to the emperor) and could even make a parallel between the origins and growth of Christianity and the development of the Roman Empire (No. 59). More typically, Christians made a contrast between the earthly human kingdoms and the heavenly kingdom of God (Nos. 45, 106; cf. John 18:36). Hegesippus summed up the characteristic second-century understanding of the kingdom of God saying that it was no threat to Rome because it was heavenly, angelic, and altogether future (No. 61).

### Controversy with Gnosticism

The Gnostics emphasized the present realization of the blessings of salvation and the immediate passage of the soul at death into the heavenly realm. Therefore, their emphasis was on the interior kingdom (Nos. 113,

114).[11] The debate between the Gnostics and their opponents within the church may be seen in the contrasting interpretations of a saying attributed to Jesus found in the *Gospel of Thomas* 22 (No. 112) and *2 Clement* 12 (No. 16).[12] According to the wording of the latter, the saying was this: "Whenever the two shall be one, and outside as the inside, and the male with the female, neither male nor female." The *Gospel of Thomas* does not offer an interpretation of the saying but formulates it in terms of conditions for entry into the kingdom. The interpretation of the saying as referring to the interior kingdom is explicit in the Naassenes (Ophites), who used a variant of this logion. Hippolytus sandwiches his quotation of this saying among the Naassenes between two other sayings which expressly interpret the kingdom as within, a treasure hidden inside a person waiting to be discovered (Nos. 113, 114). *Second Clement* puts the logion attributed to Jesus in the context of the question of the time when the kingdom comes. The author gives a consistently moral interpretation to the several parts of the saying. This moral interpretation and the eschatological understanding of the time of the coming of the kingdom were characteristics of the second-century "orthodox" and were in marked contrast to Gnostic understandings.[13]

---

11. Cf. *Gospel of Thomas* 3, 113. In some passages from Nag Hammadi the kingdom appears to be heavenly without being eschatological—e.g., *Tripartite Tractate* (1,5) 96, 17-37; 101, 29-102, 22; 131, 35-132, 20; *Eugnostos* (V,1) 8, 19-23; (III,3) 81, 13-16; (III,3) 85, 15-17; 85, 21—86, 2.

12. It may be deduced from Clement of Alexandria, *Miscellanies* 3.13.92; 6.45; and 9.36 that the quotation comes from the *Gospel of the Egyptians*. A similar statement is found in the *Martyrdom of Peter with Simon* 9, 94. The passage in *2 Clement* 12 is discussed in Donfried, *The Setting of Second Clement in Early Christianity*, 73-77, 152-54, who sees in *2 Clement* 12 an anti-gnostic polemic, and by Baarda, *Early Transmission of Words of Jesus*, 261-88, who concludes that *2 Clement* 12 preserves the earliest form of a saying independently attested also in the *Gospel of the Egyptians* and in the *Gospel of Thomas* 22. For the kingdom in *Gospel of Thomas* see Cerfaux, "Les paraboles du royaume dans l'Evangile de Thomas"; Mueller, "Kingdom of Heaven or Kingdom of God?"; Miller, "Study of the Theme of 'Kingdom.'"

13. *Second Clement* also gives an eschatological interpretation to 1 Cor 2:9 (No. 15), a statement which appears as a saying of Jesus in *Gospel of Thomas* 17. This accords with the general eschatological usage of kingdom in *2 Clement* (Nos. 12-17).

## INTERPRETATIONS OF THE KINGDOM OF GOD

### Apostolic Fathers

Some of the earliest noncanonical documents seem to preserve a duality of present and future that may be interpreted along the lines of inaugurated eschatology. The *Epistle of Barnabas* 8:5f. (No. 7) refers to the reign of Christ from the cross and says that "in his kingdom there will be evil and foul days in which we will be saved." Similarly, ch 4 (No. 5) may be understood as present. The section at the end, based on the "Two Ways" (No. 8), however, speaks in eschatological tones, and the reference in ch 7 (No. 6) is apparently future.

Ignatius, bishop of Antioch at the beginning of the second century, implies, along with a future kingdom (Nos. 18, 21), a present dynamic kingdom by declaring the old kingdom of evil destroyed at the coming of Christ (No. 19). He seems to make a Johannine-like association of kingdom and eternal life (No. 19).

Hermas, a prophet at Rome in the first half of the second century, has a clearly future view of the kingdom (Nos. 32, 33), and he emphasizes the ethical conduct required in order to enter it (Nos. 30, 31, 33, 35). Although he does not make the kingdom present, his thought brings the church and kingdom more closely together than does that of any of his contemporaries.[14] Hermas had a great fondness for the phrase "enter the kingdom of God," and from Jn 3:5, or some statement behind that verse, associated entrance into the kingdom with baptism and taking the name of the Son of God (Nos. 30, 32). The church and the kingdom are in close association, for through Christ one enters the kingdom, and Christ is the rock on which the church (tower) is built (No. 30), so that entrance into the church is entrance into the kingdom and failure to enter the church excludes one from the kingdom.

The other earliest noncanonical documents have a predominantly futuristic understanding of the kingdom.[15] The *Didache* (from Syria, perhaps ca. 100) includes two prayers for the church to be gathered into the (eschatological) kingdom (Nos. 2, 3). The petition for grace to come and this world pass away (No. 3) is equivalent to a prayer for the kingdom to come.[16] Is it significant that this document, which provides the earliest

---

14. Frick, *Die Geschichte des Reich-Gottes-Gedankens*, 32.
15. Ibid., 27ff.
16. Ibid., 47.

attestation for the addition of the doxology to the Lord's Prayer (No. 1; cf. 3), does not include "Yours is the kingdom"?

Clement of Rome (ca. 96 CE) transferred the proclamation by Jesus of the coming kingdom, as reported in the Synoptic Gospels, to the apostles after the resurrection (No. 9), only without the sense of imminence and urgency. The kingdom of God (No. 9) and the kingdom of Christ (No. 10) appear to be the same, as is common in early Christian writings.[17]

Papias of Hierapolis in the early second century gave expression to the hope for a millennial kingdom on earth (No. 36).

## Apologists

The Apologists of the second century, in writings addressed to pagans, made infrequent use of kingdom terminology.[18] The *Epistle to Diognetus* refers to God sending his Son as a king (No. 41), but his kingdom is placed in heaven (No. 43), so the kingdom which Christians enter through the power of God (No. 42), although not unambiguous, is probably to be understood also as in heaven. The other references in the Apologists (Nos. 44, 58) or writings influenced by apologetic concerns (No. 60) also follow a futurist understanding.

Among the Apologists, Justin Martyr (mid-second century) made the most frequent use of the word kingdom (Nos. 45–55), but most of these occurrences are in the *Dialogue with Trypho*, which records the Christian debate with Jews. Although Justin most often speaks of the "eternal kingdom," he also believed in an intermediate millennium.[19] His kingdom language puts the emphasis on eschatology.[20]

---

17. Schmidt, "βασιλεύς," 581; Herrick, *The Kingdom of God in the Writings of the Fathers*, 10, 105.

18. Frick, *Die Geschichte des Reich-Gottes-Gedankens*, 35ff.

19. *Dialogue* 80, without use of the word kingdom.

20. Herrick, *The Kingdom of God in the Writings of the Fathers*, 21. Barnard, "Justin Martyr's Eschatology," 87–88, states that Justin preserves the "already" and "not yet" of New Testament eschatology. I would agree with this as a general assessment, but it is not true of his kingdom terminology. Dal Covolo, "'Regno di Dio' nel Dialogo di Giustino con Trifone Giudeo."

## Irenaeus

Irenaeus has the most fully articulated doctrine of the kingdom of any second-century author. For him "kingdom" was equivalent to heaven in a routine way (Nos. 66, 70, 73, 78, 82, 83), and his usual phrase was "kingdom of heaven" (Nos. 63, 71, 76, 77, 80, 85), not "kingdom of God" (but cf. Nos. 66, 76, 84). Irenaeus also believed there would be an earthly millennial kingdom at the second coming of Christ before the worthy entered into their abode in heaven (Nos. 79, 86–92). Irenaeus integrated this millennial kingdom into his total theology by presenting it as a time when the righteous become accustomed to partake of God's glory (Nos. 87, 90).

Although Irenaeus' use is predominantly eschatological, either millennial ("earthly kingdom") or heavenly, there are exceptions. After all, God possesses a kingdom without end (No. 70) and has committed the kingship of all that is to Christ (No. 65). Thus the heavenly kingdom is not altogether future: Those who die in innocence go immediately into the kingdom (No. 73). This thought may be a corollary of Irenaeus' identification of the kingdom and heaven. The meaning of kingship is preserved in the statement that even the law of Moses showed that death did not properly have the kingship (No. 74). The context of some passages where the prevailing usage of Irenaeus might make one think of the future kingdom (Nos. 76, 82, 84) at least implies the possibility of a present understanding of the kingdom.[21] In these passages the kingdom is in some sense the state of salvation.[22]

## Miscellaneous Writings

*Fifth Ezra* 2.38 says, "called you to heavenly kingdoms." The *Epistle of the Apostles*, in opposing Simon and Cerinthus, repeatedly associates the kingdom with heaven (12, 19, 21, 26–28, 32, 42).

Poetic language is often ambiguous, and the *Odes of Solomon*, conventionally dated to the early second century,[23] share that characteristic.

---

21. Jossa, *Regno di Dio e Chiesa*, 246–48, finds the kingdom of God purely future in Irenaeus.

22. Herrick, *The Kingdom of God in the Writings of the Fathers*, 22–23; however, the "earthly kingdom" in Irenaeus is the millennial kingdom, not the church, as Herrick supposes.

23. A third-century date has been argued by Drijvers, "Facts and Problems in Early Syriac-Speaking Christianity," 166–69.

The *Odes* preserve the Semitic meaning, "kingship" (Nos. 38, 40). In one passage the kingdom may be equivalent to the church (No. 39).

The apocryphal *Acts of John* (No. 111) speaks about "joint-heirs and partners in the kingdom." It is not clear whether the gospel ministry or heaven is the meaning.[24]

The Pseudo-Clementines have a striking formulation of "two kingdoms"—the kingdom of the kings of the earth and the kingdom of heaven, the devil's kingdom and God's kingdom, the present kingdom and the future kingdom (Nos. 106, 107). Although there are passages where the idea of "kingship" is present (as *Recognitions* 1.42.1, "the preaching of the blessed kingdom of God"), the prevailing usage is future (*Recognitions* 1.55.4, those without baptism deprived of the kingdom of heaven; Nos. 108, 109).[25] The Jewish-Christian *Epistle to James* has a beautiful picture of the church as a ship bearing people through the storms of life into the kingdom (No. 110).

The *Sentences of Sextus* (No. 105) draws on the Stoic principle that the wise person is the true king in order to affirm that "the wise person shares in the kingdom of God." The philosophical background indicates that the kingdom in this statement is present and interior. This metaphorical, philosophical sense is symbolic but unlike either the biblical image or the Gnostic usage.

## Clement of Alexandria (late second century)

For an author so influenced by Greek thought it is notable that Clement's use of kingdom "is limited to the eschatological sense and depends on biblical conceptions of entrance into the kingdom."[26] For Clement kingdom was primarily a biblical word, and that part of the biblical usage which

---

24. Chapter 78 carries a variant reading "his kingdom" for "his own rest and renewal of life." The association of kingdom and rest is to be noted; cf. Nos. 12, 86, and in Gnosticism the *Tripartite Tractate* (I,5) 101, 29–102, 22, and *Second Apocalypse of James* (V,4) 56, 2–5.

25. Herrick, *The Kingdom of God in the Writings of the Fathers*, 31–34 concludes that the kingdom is always eschatological in the *Homilies* whereas the *Recognitions* wavers as to whether the righteous are now in God's kingdom. My impression is that one sees the "kingship" idea in the *Homilies* and the meaning "kingdom" with reference to the future more in the *Recognitions*. The different layers in this literature from different dates, now extremely difficult to determine, make pursuit of this question unprofitable.

26. Frick, *Die Geschichte des Reich-Gottes-Gedankens*, 92, who gives a sympathetic treatment of Clement's kingdom ideas.

he appropriated was the future, heavenly aspect (Nos. 93–95, 97–98, 101–4). Clement was concerned with the moral life, and he emphasized the connection between inheriting or entering the kingdom and present moral conduct and spiritual qualities (Nos. 93, 95, 102). Clement's identification of "seeing God" with entering the kingdom (No. 102) has a parallel in *Gospel of Thomas* 27. At one place Clement associates the church with the kingdom without identifying them: the earthly assembly is a copy of the heavenly church (No. 96).[27]

## Origen (185–254)

Origen marks the change in Christian usage of "kingdom" to the interior meaning of the rule of God in the heart.[28] He was able to integrate the "Gnostic" dimension of the kingdom, the inward rule of God in the soul, into his total thought (No. 115). Origen frequently used future language for the kingdom, but the kingdom's eschatological character allowed room for the immanent also. Luke 17:21 and 1 Cor 15:24 were favorite verses with him. In the deepest sense what Origen meant by the kingdom of God was the rule of the divine Spirit in the world of spirits. This rule is not only at the beginning and end of the development but continues throughout. The creation awaits the fulfillment not as a sudden breaking-in, but as the inner progress of the kingdom growing within.[29]

Origen's interpretation of the Lord's Prayer prepared the way for later fathers to emphasize the reign of God in the soul.[30] This understanding of the kingdom permitted Origen to speak more frankly of the kingdom in his apologetic work *Against Celsus* (No. 116) than did other apologists, unless Celsus' comments on the kingdom in the Gospels made a response necessary. Accompanying the interiorization of the kingdom was a change in emphasis from a general eschatology to an individual eschatology, also evident in Gnosticism. Origen achieved a synthesis of the present and future, the dynamic and static features of the kingdom, but he did so in

---

27. Herrick, *The Kingdom of God in the Writings of the Fathers*, 26.

28. Lampe, *The Seal of the Spirit*, 58–73, and see n. 30.

29. Frick, *Die Geschichte des Reich-Gottes-Gedankens*, 95–103. Nigg, *Das Ewige Reich*, 61–77 notes the importance of Origen in building up a new theology to take the place of apocalyptic.

30. Herrick, *The Kingdom of God in the Writings of the Fathers*, 26. Actually Tertullian had already combined the eschatological interpretation of "thy kingdom come" with an inward interpretation, "come in us"—*On Lord's Prayer* 5. But Tertullian's references to kingdom are on the whole eschatological and Origen's not so much so.

the framework of a philosophy and world view quite different from the thought world of Jesus and the earliest church.

## SUMMARY AND EVALUATION

Apart from the Gnostics (Nos. 112–14), the interpretation of the kingdom as an interior, present possession hardly occurs before Origen (Nos. 105, 115). There are a few passages in early noncanonical Christian literature which relate the kingdom to the present salvation or the church (Nos. 7, 19, 30, 32, 39, 82, 84). The affirmation that the kingship belongs to Jesus could be understood to support this view (Nos. 49, 65, 69, 72). Inaugurated eschatology might be invoked to account for the kingdom seeming to be both present and future in the same author (Nos. 5–8, 18–21, 65–66), and one might even cite an occasional instance of a symbolic meaning (Nos. 105, 41). Otherwise, the overwhelming usage of "kingdom" in second-century Christian literature is eschatological. G. W. H. Lampe states that although the variety of meanings given the phrase "kingdom of God" in patristic literature is great, most common of all is the idea of the kingdom as a present spiritual reality.[31] This may be true for patristic literature as a whole, but it is clearly wrong for the second century, where this meaning is rare. The kingdom for second-century authors is almost uniformly future (Nos. 2, 3, 9, 10, 12, 15, 78 ,106, 108, 109, etc.), heavenly (Nos. 29, 58, 63, 67, 71, 77, 95, 106, etc.), and eternal (Nos. 26, 44, 47, 48. 51, 52, 53, 70, 106, etc.). For several writers in the second century the future kingdom will be earthly and millennial: Cerinthus (No. 37), Papias (36), Justin (*Dialogue* 80), Irenaeus (Nos. 79, 86–92), and others. The Montanist movement had as one of its characteristics an expectation of the imminent appearance of the kingdom.[32]

Corollaries of the eschatological perspective were emphases on the conduct necessary to gain entrance into the heavenly kingdom (Nos. 13–15, 18, 21, 31, 33–35, 44, 63, 85, 98–100, 107) and upon the kingdom as a reward for such conduct (Nos. 8, 12, 80, 103, 109). This very strong correlation of the kingdom with moral conduct may be seen as a reflection of the meaning of the "rule of God." It was characteristic of the

---

31. Lampe, *The Seal of the Spirit*, 62. The article is similar to the entry in Lampe, *Patristic Greek Lexicon*, 289–92, although I find the classification and especially the references chosen to illustrate it unsatisfactory.

32. Nigg, *Das Ewige Reich*, 47ff. on early writers in general and pp. 78ff., on Montanism. Millennialism, however, is not attested for early Montanism—Hill, "The Marriage of Montanism and Millennialism."

## The Kingdom of God in Early Patristic Literature

second century to emphasize that aspect of the Gospels' account of Jesus' proclamation which demanded conduct worthy of the kingdom. Nevertheless, some authors did not fail to remind their readers that the kingdom is God's gift and activity, and entrance into it is by grace (Nos. 24, 26, 42, 43, 66, 71, 94).

The debate with Jews could have favored an emphasis on the church as a replacement of Judaism as the realm in which God's kingship is presently exercised. The references to the kingdom of Christ (or Christ possessing the kingdom) occur primarily in an anti-Judaic context. On the other hand, since the Jews no longer had a kingdom and Christians were in a precarious political situation in the empire, the debate with Judaism could also have shifted attention to the heavenly nature of the kingdom.

The other principal factors influencing Christian thought in the second century—the external difficulties from the "kingdom" of Rome and internal controversies with Gnosticism—definitely favored an eschatological interpretation of the kingdom. The church's troubles with the Roman Empire gave it reason to play down the kingdom idea, especially any indication of its present manifestation. Thus in political contexts Christians emphasized that Christ's kingdom is otherworldly and heavenly (Nos. 45, 61).

The controversy with Gnosticism was also a significant factor in the church choosing to focus on the eschatological nature of the kingdom. The Gnostics emphasized the present aspect of the New Testament teaching about the kingdom. A radically realized eschatology was already encountered in the New Testament (1 Corinthians 15; 2 Tim 2:18). The second-century Gnostics seem to have gone further in interiorizing the kingdom. Just as New Testament authors drew on apocalyptic ideas to counter an overly realized eschatology (cf. 2 Thessalonians 2), so the second-century church emphasized a future eschatology.

The kingdom terminology was no longer capable in the second century of carrying as much freight as it did in the New Testament. Of course, history and human beings rarely stay in neat compartments; in the same way, the alternatives are not absolute in the second century, but the broad outline seems clear: The "orthodox" church took the futuristic side of the New Testament proclamation of the kingdom, and the "Gnostics" took the present aspect.

## APPENDIX: KINGDOM LANGUAGE IN THE SECOND CENTURY[33]

1. "Your kingdom come" quoted from the Lord's Prayer (*Did.* 8:2).

2. "May your church be gathered from the corners of the earth into your kingdom" (*Did.* 9:4).

3. "Remember, Lord, your church to deliver her from all evil and to perfect her in your love, and to gather her from the four winds when she has been sanctified into your kingdom which has been prepared for her. Yours is the power and the glory for ever. May grace come and this world pass away" (*Did.* 10:5–6).

4. "'I am a great king, says the Lord'" (*Did.* 14:3 quoting Mal 1:11, 14).

5. "Let us never relax on the basis of being the elect and fall asleep in our sins, lest the wicked ruler gain power over us and thrust us out from the kingdom of the Lord" (*Barn.* 4:13).

6. "'Even so,' he says, 'those who want to see me and touch my kingdom must receive me through tribulations and suffering'" (*Barn.* 7:11).

7. "Why was the wool put on the wood? Because the kingdom of Jesus is on the wood, and because those who hope on him shall live forever."[34] "Why are the wool and the hyssop together? Because in his kingdom there will be evil and foul days in which we shall be saved" (*Barn.* 8:5–6).

8. "He who does these things shall be glorified in the kingdom of God, and he who chooses the others shall perish with his works" (*Barn.* 21:1).

9. "The apostles went forth in the assurance of the Holy Spirit preaching the good news that the kingdom of God is going to come" (*1 Clem.* 42:3).

10. "Those who have been perfected in love according to the grace of God have a place among the pious who shall be manifested at the visitation of the kingdom of Christ" (*1 Clem.* 50:3).

11. "You, Master, gave the authority of kingship to rulers and governors" (*1 Clem.* 61:1).

---

33. I have been greatly assisted in compiling these passages by Herrick's list, *The Kingdom of God in the Writings of the Fathers*, 109ff., but his list is no longer sufficient.

34. Based on a variant reading of Ps 96:10; cf. Justin, *Dialogue* 73:1; *1 Apology* 41.4.

12. "The promise of Christ is great and marvelous and is the rest of the coming kingdom and of eternal life" (2 *Clem* 5:5).

13. "If we do not keep our baptism pure and undefiled, with what confidence shall we enter into the royal house [kingdom] of God?" (2 *Clem* 6:9).

14. "Let us love one another in order that we all may enter into the kingdom of God" (2 *Clem* 9:6).

15. "If we do righteousness before God, we shall enter into his kingdom and receive the promises 'which ear has not heard nor eye seen nor entered into the heart of man'" (2 *Clem* 11:7).

16. "Let us then wait for the kingdom of God hour by hour in love and righteousness, since we do not know the day of God's appearing. For when the Lord himself was asked when his kingdom would come, he said: 'Whenever the two shall be one, and the outside as the inside, and the male with the female, neither male nor female.' 'The two is one' when we speak the truth to each other and one soul may be in two bodies with no insincerity. And 'the outside as the inside' means this: he calls the inside the soul and the outside the body. In what way your body appears, even so let your soul be manifest in good works. And 'the male with the female, neither male nor female' means this: when a brother sees a sister he thinks nothing concerning her femaleness nor does she think anything concerning his maleness. 'When you do these things,' he says, 'the kingdom of my Father will come'" (2 *Clem.* 12).

17. "Unbelievers shall be astonished when they see the royal house (kingdom) of the world in Jesus" (2 *Clem* 17:5).

18. "Those who corrupt families 'shall not inherit the kingdom of God'" (Ignatius, *Eph.* 16:1). (Cf. 1 Cor 6:9–10; Eph 5:5.)

19. "The old kingdom was destroyed, for God was manifest as man for the newness of eternal life" (Ignatius, *Eph.* 19:3).

20. "The kingdoms of this age will profit me nothing. It is better for me to die in Christ Jesus than to rule over the ends of the earth" (Ignatius, *Rom.* 6:1).

21. "'Be not deceived,' my brothers, if any one follows a schismatic, 'he shall not inherit the kingdom of God'" (Ignatius, *Phld* 3:3).

22. "Theirs is the kingdom of God" quoting Matt 5:10 (Luke 6:20) (Polycarp, *Phil.* 2:3).

23. "Shall not inherit the kingdom of God" (Polycarp, *Phil* 5:3, referring to Gal 5:17–21).

24. "How can I blaspheme my king who saved me?" (*Mart. Pol.* 9:3).

25. "We rightly love the martyrs as disciples and imitators of the Lord on account of their unsurpassable affection to their king and teacher" (*Mart. Pol.* 17:3).

26. "To him who is able to bring us all by his grace and gift into his eternal kingdom" (*Mart. Pol.* 20:2).

27. "When our Lord Jesus Christ was reigning for ever" (*Mart. Pol.* 21:2).

28. "In whose footsteps may we be found in the kingdom of Jesus Christ" (*Mart. Pol.* 22:1 = Epilogue 1).

29. "In order that the Lord Jesus Christ may gather me with his elect into his heavenly kingdom" (*Mart. Pol.* 22:3 = Epilogue 5).

30. "'What is the rock and the gate?' 'This rock and the gate,' he said, 'is the Son of God.' 'How is it, Sir,' I said, 'that the rock is old but the gate is new?' 'The Son of God is older than all his creation . . . therefore the rock is old . . . Because he was manifested at the consummation of the last days the gate is new, that those who are going to be saved may enter through it into the kingdom of God . . . No one shall enter into the kingdom of God unless he take his holy name . . . A man is not able to enter into the kingdom of God otherwise than through the name of his Son who was beloved by him . . . Whoever does not receive his name shall not enter into the kingdom of God.' I said, 'What is the tower?' He said, 'This tower is the church.' 'And what are these maidens?' He said, 'These are holy spirits, and a man cannot be found in the kingdom of God in any other way except they clothe him with their clothing. For if you receive the name alone but do not receive the clothing from them, you will benefit nothing'" (Hermas, *Sim.* 9.12.3, 4, 5, 8; 13.1, 2).

31. "He who bears these names [faith, self-control, power, longsuffering, etc.] and the name of the Son of God will be able to enter the kingdom of God . . . The servant of God who bears these names [unbelief, impurity, disobedience, etc.] shall see the kingdom of God but shall not enter it" (Hermas, *Sim.* 9.15.2, 3).

32. "'They had need,' said he, 'to come up through the water that they might be made alive, for they could not otherwise enter into the kingdom of God unless they put away the mortality of their former life. So these also who had fallen asleep received the seal of the Son of God and entered into the kingdom of God. For before a man bears the name of the Son of God he is dead. But when he receives the seal he puts away mortality and receives life. The seal then is the water. They go down then into the water dead and come up alive. This seal, then, was preached to them also, and they made use of it to enter into the kingdom of God'" (Hermas, *Sim.* 9.16.2–4).

33. "The rich cleave with difficulty to the servants of God, fearing that they will be asked for something by them. Such with difficulty enter into the kingdom of God. For just as it is difficult to walk with naked feet among thistles, so it is also difficult for such men to enter into the kingdom of God" (Hermas, *Sim.* 9.20.2, 3).

34. "Such then shall live without doubt in the kingdom of God, because by no act did they defile the commandments of God but remained in innocence all the days of their lives" (Hermas, *Sim.* 9.29.2).

35. "This world and the vanities of their riches must be cut away from them, and then they will be suitable for the kingdom of God. For it is necessary for them to enter into the kingdom of God . . . Therefore not one of this kind shall perish" (Hermas, *Sim.* 9.31.2).

36. "[Papias] says that there will be a millennium after the resurrection of the dead, when the kingdom of Christ will be set up in material form on this earth" (Eusebius, *Church History* 3.39.12).

37. "Cerinthus . . . says that after the resurrection the royal house of Christ will be on earth" (Gaius of Rome from Eusebius, *Church History* 3.28.2).

38. "Because his kingdom is firm" (*Odes Sol.* 18:3).

39. "And the foundation of everything is Thy rock. And upon it Thou hast built Thy kingdom, And it became the dwelling-place of the holy ones" (*Odes Sol.* 22:12).

40. "And with it, was a sign of the kingdom and of providence" (*Odes Sol.* 23:12).

41. "As a king sending a son, he sent him as King, he sent him as God" (*Diog.* 7:4).

42. "When we made it plain that we were unable to enter the kingdom of God by ourselves, we became able through the power of God" (*Diog.* 9:1).

43. "To mankind God sent his only Son, to them he promised the kingdom in heaven, and he will give it to them who loved him" (*Diog.* 10:2).

44. "This is the way of the truth which leads those who travel therein to the everlasting kingdom promised through Christ in the life to come" (Aristides, *Apology* 16; late Greek text only, missing from the Syriac, so probably not original).

45. "You, when you heard we expected a kingdom, uncritically understood us to say a human when we speak of the one with God ... If we were expecting a human kingdom, we should also deny our Christ that we might not be killed" (Justin, *I Apology* 11).

46. "Trypho said, 'These and such like scriptures, sir, compel us to wait for him who, as Son of man, receives from the Ancient of days the eternal kingdom." (Justin, *Dialogue* 32). (Daniel 7 quoted in ch 31; cf. chs 76 and 79.)

47. "Christ is preached as first made subject to suffering, then returning to heaven, and coming again with glory and having the eternal kingdom" (*Dialogue* 34). (Cf. selection 108.)

48. "Trypho replied ... 'That the Christ is to come again in glory and to receive the eternal kingdom of all the nations when every kingdom is subjected to him is sufficiently shown by the scriptures recounted by you'" (*Dialogue* 39).

49. "The eternal kingdom is Jesus" (*Dialogue* 46).

50. Jesus preached, "that the kingdom of heaven is near" (*Dialogue* 51; cf. Ps. Clement, *Homilies* 1.6; *Recognitions* 1.6).

51. "If we keep his commandments, he has promised to provide an eternal kingdom" (*Dialogue* 116).

52. "He shall raise all men from the dead and appoint some to be incorruptible, immortal, and free from sorrow in the everlasting and imperishable kingdom, but he shall send others away to the everlasting punishment of fire" (*Dialogue* 117).

53. "Those worthy of the eternal kingdom to come" (*Dialogue* 120).

## The Kingdom of God in Early Patristic Literature

54. "All powers and kingdoms feared his name" (*Dialogue* 121; same in 131).

55. "They deceive themselves and you supposing that the eternal kingdom will be given to those of the dispersion who are of Abraham after the flesh, although they are sinners, faithless, and disobedient towards God" (*Dialogue* 140).

56. "The brothers of Zeus, who shared the kingdom with him . . . Kronos was ejected from his kingdom. . . .. How, too, can he give kingdoms who no longer reigns himself?" (Tatian, *Oration* 9).

57. Earthly kingdoms as chronological periods—four times in *Oration* 39.

58. "May you, by considering yourselves, be able to have the heavenly kingdom also. For all things are subservient to you . . . who have received the kingdom from above" (Athenagoras, *Plea* 18). (He uses 'kingdom' for the kingship of the Roman emperor in 1.3; 6.3; 37.1 [twice].)

59. "If you protect the philosophy which grew up with the empire [kingdom] and began with Augustus . . . Our doctrine flourished for good along with the empire in its beginning" (Melito, *Apology*, from Eusebius, *Church History* 4.26.7, 8).

60. "And I pray thee, let me rest a little from my song, Holy Giver of manna, king of a great kingdom" *(Sib. Or.* 2:347, in the context of describing the parousia and judgment).

61. "[The grandsons of Judas, the brother of Jesus according to the flesh] were asked [by the authorities] concerning the Christ and his kingdom, its nature, origin, and time of appearance, and they explained that it was neither of the world nor earthly, but heavenly and angelic, and it would be at the end of the world, when he would come in glory to judge the living and the dead" (Hegesippus, from Eusebius, *Church History* 3.20.4).

62. "Tell my people that I will give to them the kingdom of Jerusalem which I would have given to Israel . . . The kingdom is already prepared for you: watch!" (*4 Ezra* 2:10–13).

63. "The former road leads to the kingdom of heaven by uniting man with God" (Irenaeus, *Proof of the Apostolic Preaching* 1).

64. Many prophecies written "about our Lord Jesus Christ and about the people and about the calling of the Gentiles and about the kingdom" (*Proof of the Apostolic Preaching* 28).

65. To Christ God "has committed the kingship of all that is" (*Proof of the Apostolic Preaching* 41; cf. 36).

66. Jesus "takes us and bears us into the kingdom of the Father" (*Proof of the Apostolic Preaching* 46).

67. Gen 49:10f., "For 'whom lies in store' a kingship in heaven ... He is the 'expectation of the nations' ... because we expect him to re-establish the kingdom" (*Proof of the Apostolic Preaching* 57).

68. Herod was frightened lest he be ousted by Christ from the kingship (*Proof of the Apostolic Preaching* 74).

69. The Jews denied the eternal king and acknowledged the temporal Caesar as king (*Proof of the Apostolic Preaching* 95). (On Christ as eternal king cf. 47; 52; 56; 58; 61; 64; 84.)

70. God "possesses a kingdom without end" (Irenaeus, *Against Heresies* 2.28.3).

71. The covenant "which renovates man, and sums up all things in itself by means of the Gospel, raising and bearing men upon its wings into the heavenly kingdom" (*Against Heresies* 3.11.8).

72. Christ "has received from his Father an eternal kingdom in Israel" (*Against Heresies* 3.12.13).

73. (Referring to the slaughter of the innocents in Matthew 2) "He suddenly removed those children belonging to the house of David, whose happy lot it was to have been born at that time, that he might send them on before into his kingdom" (*Against Heresies* 3.16.4).

74. The law of Moses "did truly take away death's kingdom showing that he was no king but a robber" (*Against Heresies* 3.18.7).

75. Jeconiah and his descendants were "excluded from the kingdom" (*Against Heresies* 3.21.9 [twice]).

76. "Those who frame the idea of another God besides him who made the promises to Abraham are outside the kingdom of God ... setting at naught and blaspheming God, who introduces through Jesus Christ Abraham to the kingdom of heaven" (*Against Heresies* 4.8.1).

77. "For God shall be seen as Father in the kingdom of heaven" (*Against Heresies* 4.20.5; cf. 5.33.2).

78. "Abraham believed in things future as if they were already accomplished, because of the promise of God; and in like manner do we also, because of the promise of God, behold through faith that inheritance in the kingdom" (*Against Heresies* 4.21.1).

79. "He shall at his second coming first rouse from their sleep all [righteous persons] and shall raise them up, as well as the rest who shall be judged, and give them a place in his kingdom" (*Against Heresies* 4.22.2).

80. "They who believe in him . . . shall receive the kingdom of heaven" (*Against Heresies* 4.24.2).

81. "In order that both the sower and the reaper may rejoice together in the kingdom of Christ" (*Against Heresies* 4.25.3).

82. Solomon "prefigured the kingdom of Christ." "We ought to fear lest . . . we obtain no further forgiveness of sins but be shut out from his kingdom" (*Against Heresies* 4.27.1, 2, citing a "certain presbyter").

83. "The beauty and splendor which exist in his kingdom" (*Against Heresies* 4.33.11).

84. They are ignorant "of the ineffable Father, of his kingdom, and of his dispensations" (*Against Heresies* 4.34.3).

85. "Inasmuch, then as in this world some persons betake themselves to the light, and by faith unite themselves with God . . . on this account he says that those on the right hand are called into the kingdom of heaven" (*Against Heresies* 5.28.1).

86. "Bringing in for the righteous the times of the kingdom, that is the rest, the hallowed seventh day, and restoring to Abraham the promised inheritance [the kingdom]" (*Against Heresies* 5.30.4 [which clarifies the similar statement in 4.16.1; cf. also 5.33.2]).

87. "They are ignorant of . . . the [earthly] kingdom which is the commencement of incorruption, by means of which kingdom those who shall be worthy are accustomed gradually to partake of the divine nature" (*Against Heresies* 5.32.1).

88. "The predicted blessing, therefore, belongs unquestionably to the times of the kingdom, when the righteous shall bear rule upon their rising from the dead" (*Against Heresies* 5.33.3).

89. The promise of the Old Testament indicates "the feasting in the kingdom of the righteous which God promises that he himself will serve" (*Against Heresies* 5.34.3).

90. "The righteous shall reign on earth . . . and shall become accustomed to partake of the glory of God the Father, and shall enjoy in the kingdom association and communion with holy angels" (*Against Heresies* 5.35.1; called "the times of the kingdom" in 5.35.3).

91. "For in the times of the kingdom the righteous man who is upon the earth shall then forget to die" (*Against Heresies* 5.36.2).

92. "John foresaw the first resurrection of the just and the inheritance in the kingdom of the earth . . . For the Lord also taught these things, when he promised that he would have the mixed cup new with his disciples in the kingdom . . . The same God the Father . . . fulfills at the resurrection of the just the promises for the kingdom of his Son" (*Against Heresies* 5.36.3).

93. "Then shall he be deemed worthy to he made his heir, then will he share the kingdom of the Father with his own dear Son" (Clement of Alexandria, *Exhortation* 9).

94. "And they shall rejoice in the kingdom of their Lord forever. Amen" (*Exhortation* 10).

95. "By his blood and by the word he has gathered the bloodless host of peace and assigned to them the kingdom of heaven . . . Both [work and grace] are necessary that the friend of Christ may be rendered worthy of the kingdom and counted worthy of the kingdom" (*Exhortation* 11).

96. "He who eats of this meal [righteousness, peace, joy] shall possess the kingdom of God, fixing his regards here on the assembly of love, the heavenly church" (Clement of Alexandria, *Instructor* 2.1).

97. "Wealth, when not properly governed, is a stronghold of evil, casting their eyes about which many will never reach the kingdom of heaven" (*Instructor* 2.3; cf. 3.7).

98. "He who has this wealth [the true riches of the Word] shall inherit the kingdom of God" (*Instructor* 3.7).

99. "If we are called to the kingdom of God, let us walk worthily of the kingdom, loving God and our neighbor . . . When the kingdom is worthily proved, we dispense the affection of the soul by a chaste and

closed mouth, by which gentle manners are expressed" (*Instructor* 3.11).

100. "The good man who has become an heir of the kingdom" (Clement of Alexandria, *Miscellanies* 2.19).

101. "This is he who is blessed by the Lord, and called poor in spirit, a meet heir of the kingdom of heaven" (Clement of Alexandria, *Who Is the Rich Man That Is Saved?* 16).

102. "Becoming pure in heart you may see God, which is another way of saying 'enter the kingdom of heaven" (*Who Is the Rich Man That Is Saved?* 19).

103. "The kingdom of heaven is [the apostles'] recompense" (*Who Is the Rich Man That Is Saved?* 21).

104. "Spare not perils and toils that you may purchase here the heavenly kingdom . . . This kingdom God will give you" (*Who Is the Rich Man That Is Saved?* 32).

105. "The wise person shares in the kingdom of God" (*Sentences of Sextus* 311). (Cf. Clement of Alexandria, *Miscellanies* 2.4 on the Stoic principle that the wise man possesses kingship.)

106. "God appointed two kingdoms and established two ages, determining that the present world should be given to the evil one . . . but he promised to preserve for the good one the age to come, as it will be great and eternal . . . Two kingdoms have been established—the one called the kingdom of heaven and the other the kingdom of those who are now kings upon earth" (Ps. Clement, *Homilies* 20.2).

107. "God instituted two kingdoms and has given to each man the power of becoming a portion of that kingdom to which he shall yield himself to obey" (Ps. Clement, *Recognitions* 5.9; see 8,10–12 and cf. 1.24).

108. "For two advents of him are foretold: one in humiliation, which he has accomplished; the other in glory, which is hoped to be accomplished, when he shall come to give the kingdom to those who believe in him and who observe all things which he has commanded. And when he had plainly taught the people concerning these things, he added this also: That unless a man be baptized in water in the name of the threefold blessedness . . . he can neither receive remission of sins nor enter the kingdom of heaven" (*Recognitions* 1.69). (Cf. on the two comings 1.49 and on baptism 6.9; *Homilies* 11.26; 13.21.)

109. "The first duty of all is to inquire into the righteousness of God and his kingdom; his righteousness that we may be taught to act rightly, his kingdom that we may know what is the reward appointed for labor and patience, in which kingdom there is indeed a bestowal of eternal good things upon the good" (*Recognitions* 2.20).

110. "For the whole business of the church is like a great ship bearing through a violent storm men who are of many places and who desire to inhabit the city of the good kingdom" (Ps. Clement, *Epistle to James* 14).

111. "My brethren . . . joint-heirs and partners with me in the kingdom of God" (*Acts of John* 106; cf. 8 and 22).

112. "Jesus saw infants being suckled. He said to his disciples, 'These infants being suckled are like those who enter the kingdom.' They said to him, 'Shall we then, as children, enter the kingdom?' Jesus said to them, 'When you make the two one, and when you make the inside like the outside and the outside like the inside, and the above like the below, and when you make the male and the female one and the same, so that the male not be male nor the female female; and when you fashion eyes in place of an eye, and a hand in place of a hand, and a foot in place of a foot, and a likeness in place of a likeness; then will you enter" (*Gospel of Thomas* 22).[35]

113. "A happy nature which, the Naassene says, is the kingdom of heaven to be sought for within a man" (Hippolytus, *Refutation of All Heresies* 5.2).

114. "[The Naassene said the miracle at Cana] manifested the kingdom of heaven. This is the kingdom of heaven that reposes within us as a treasure, as leaven hidden in the three measures of meal" (*Refutation of All Heresies* 5.3; cf. also 5.4).

115. "It is evident that he who prays that the kingdom of God should come prays with good reason that the kingdom of God should spring up and bear fruit and be perfected in him. For every saint who takes God as his king and obeys the spiritual laws of God dwells in himself

---

35. Other references to the kingdom in *Gospel of Thomas* include logia 3, 20, 27, 46, 49, 54, 57, 76, 82, 96–99, 107, 109, 113, 114. See nn. 10 and 11. For "kingdom" in the Nag Hammadi texts see my "The Terminology of the Kingdom in the Second Century" referenced at the beginning of the article; Hodgson, "The Kingdom of God in the School of St. John," 166–74; Hedrick, "Kingdom Sayings and Parables of Jesus in the *Apocryphon of James*."

as in a well-ordered city, so to speak. Present with him are the Father and Christ who reigns with the Father in the soul that has been perfected . . . But every sinner is under the tyranny of 'the prince of this world.' . . . As we advance unceasingly the kingdom of God that is in us will reach its highest point when [1 Cor 15:28] . . . The kingdom of God cannot co-exist with the kingdom of evil. If therefore it is our will to be under the reign of God, let not sin in any wise reign in our mortal body" (Origen, *On Prayer* 25).

116. "But we desire not only to understand the nature of that divine kingdom of which we are continually speaking and writing, but also ourselves to be of those who are under the rule of God alone, so that the kingdom of God may be ours" (Origen, *Against Celsus* 8.11).

# 13

## Was Barnabas a Chiliast?
An Example of Hellenistic Number Symbolism in *Barnabas* and Clement of Alexandria

ABRAHAM J. MALHERBE HAS demonstrated the influence of Hellenistic popular philosophy, especially in moral exhortation, on the New Testament writings. This influence extends to the non-canonical writings, including those that show the greatest concern with Jews and Judaism. A case in point is the *Epistle of Barnabas*. A feature of Hellenistic number symbolism will shed some light on a problematic text in *Barnabas*.

### THE CHILIASTIC INTERPRETATION OF *BARNABAS*

When I was a child, I heard my paternal grandmother express her belief that the world would come to an end in the year 2000. She explained that God created the world in six days and rested on the seventh; a day with the Lord is as a thousand years (2 Pet 3:8; Ps 90:4), so the world will last for six thousand years. Accepting the chronology that placed Creation about 4000 BC, she placed the end at about 2000. My grandmother was not an educated person and had few intellectual contacts. As far as I know, she figured this out for herself. If so, she has not been the only one to make such calculations. When I grew older and began reading in patristics, I was amazed to learn what an impressive list of thinkers could be claimed for the view that the world would last for six thousand years. Although still not convinced, I gained new respect for my grandmother's theological understanding.

The names of those who in some way use the equation of one day with a thousand years for chronological speculation or who calculate the duration of the world on the basis of the Creation week include Justin Martyr,[1] Irenaeus,[2] Tertullian,[3] Hippolytus,[4] Lactantius,[5] Methodius,[6] Commodian,[7] Victorinus of Pettau,[8] Bardesanes,[9] and for a time Augustine.[10] With most of these, the chronology includes God's rest on the seventh day, producing a specifically premillennial framework: Jesus Christ was born during the sixth millennium and will return at its close; then will come the thousand-year Sabbath rest (the seventh millennium), followed by the eternal world. Irenaeus provides the first full exposition of this scheme.[11]

---

1. Justin Martyr, *Dialogue* 81 explains that Adam did not live a thousand years, because he died in the "day" in which he sinned; chap. 80–81 refer to the millennial reign in Jerusalem followed by the general resurrection and judgment.

2. Irenaeus, *Against Heresies* 5.28.3 gives six thousand years for the world on the basis of the six days of Creation, quoting 2 Pet 3:8; *Against Heresies* 5.33.2 identifies the subsequent millennial kingdom as the true Sabbath; cf. 5.23.2.

3. Tertullian, *On the Soul* 37 implies the millennium as 7 and Heaven as 8; *Against Marcion* 3.24 speaks of the millennial kingdom.

4. Hippolytus, *Commentary on Daniel* 4.23–24 uses the six thousand years to calculate that the second coming of Christ will not be until about AD 500. The Sabbath is a type of the millennial kingdom of rest.

5. Lactantius, *Epitome* 72 is clearest on the millennium, but *Divine Institutes* 7.22, 24, 26 contain the calculations giving a total duration of the world as seven thousand years, including the millennium.

6. Methodius, *Symposium* 9.1 gives the same 6 + 1 scheme as Lactantius but bases it on the description of the tabernacle in the Law.

7. Commodian, *Instructions* 43, 44, and 80—the earth will last six thousand years.

8. Victorinus of Pettau, *On the Creation of the World*, presents the seventh millennium as the true Sabbath, followed by the eighth age.

9. Bardesanes, *On Fate*, at the end says that the world will last for six thousand years.

10. Augustine, *City of God* 20.7; 22.30 keeps the scheme without a literal millennium.

11. *Against Heresies* 5.23.2; 28.3; 33.2. Cf. *Didascalia* 6.18 for the Sabbath as a type of the final rest, the seventh thousand-year period; the ogdoad, or last day, is the first day.

Jean Daniélou has analyzed the forms that millenarian thought took in the early church.[12] Some early Jewish Christians looked for an earthly reign of the Messiah when the saints would be at rest. The Asiatic type of millenialism (typified by Papias) added to the earthly messianic reign the expectation of material fecundity and a human life span of a thousand years. The Syriac type of millennialism, on the basis of astrological calculations of a cosmic week of seven millennia representing the seven planets, saw the seventh millennium as corresponding to the seventh day of Creation, on which God rested. Alexandrian thought, in contrast, connected the hebdomad with the world of time in contrast to the ogdoad, which is the world of eternity, a cosmological rather than a chronological perspective.

Daniélou saw *Barnabas* as an early representative of the Syrian type of millennialism whose originality lay in relating the early idea of the eschatological rest to speculations on the cosmic week. *Barnabas* brought together the Jewish idea of rest on the seventh day with the Hellenistic idea of seven millennia.[13] When one reads in *Barnabas* 15 the combination of the six days of Creation, a day with the Lord as one thousand years, and the Lord's judgment at the completion of six thousand years, it is easy to fill in, as Daniélou does, "the archaic doctrine of the earthly reign of Christ"[14] during the seventh millennium, with the result that *Barnabas* belongs in the premillennial camp.

It is not surprising, therefore, to find *Barnabas* claimed by modern adherents of an Adventist, or premillennial, view.[15] It is more significant to find other scholars accepting this interpretation of *Barnabas*. Johannes Quasten writes, "The author is a follower of chiliasm." After the judgment "will dawn the sabbath of the millennial kingdom."[16] James A. Kleist, in *Ancient Christian Writers*, links the author of *Barnabas* with Papias as the first Christian writers to advocate chiliastic ideas, with *Barnabas*'s contribution the dividing of history into six millennia typified by the six days of Creation and followed by eschatological rest. Kleist charts the chronology as follows: days 1 through 5 were past for *Barnabas*, day 6 is the present

---

12. Daniélou, "La typologie millenariste de la semaine dans le christianisme primitif"; Daniélou, *The Theology of Jewish Christianity*, 376–404, esp. 396–403.

13. Daniélou, *The Theology of Jewish Christianity*, 396–98. Daniélou is followed by Blum, "Chiliasmus II," 730.

14. Daniélou, *The Theology of Jewish Christianity*, 398.

15. Shea, "The Sabbath in the Epistle of Barnabas."

16. Quasten, *Patrology*, vol. 1, 89.

era, day 7 will be the millennium, and "day" 8 will be eternity.[17] W. Rordorf concludes that we should regard *Barnabas* 15 as a unity with a natural progression, so that the seventh millennium in 15:8 is followed by the eighth day, a new aeon.[18]

At one time I agreed with these scholars in their reading of *Barnabas*, so it will not be understood as disrespectful if I now argue for another interpretation. Some commentators set forth the chiliastic parallels to *Barnabas* but are more cautious about saying what *Barnabas* does not say. P. Prigent warns that in spite of the one thousand years attributed to each day, *Barnabas*'s speculations must not be confounded with millennial hopes, which, he says, were not based on the cosmic week but on the expectation of a return to Paradise.[19] Prigent distinguishes 15:1–5, which draws on an earlier source, from 15:6–9, which expresses *Barnabas*'s Christianizing interpretation. In particular, 15:8 makes the eighth day, and not the seventh (as in 15:5), the type of a new world. Nevertheless, Prigent marks the parallel from Augustine, *City of God* 22.30.5, according to which we are now in the sixth day; the seventh will be the great Sabbath of God, and the eighth day the eternal day of God.[20] In his later commentary for *Sources Chretiennes*, Prigent still sees 15:1–5 as coming from another source in preference to Rordorf's view of the chapter's unity, which has received strong support from Klaus Wengst.[21] I would point out that separate sources would make unnecessary an effort to reconcile the two parts of the chapter by proposing a millennial scheme of 6 + 1 + 1. I will later attempt a nonmillennial interpretation based, however, on the unity of the chapter. Prigent notes further that as against millennialism in the technical sense, *Barnabas* refrains even in 15:5 from explicitly interpreting the seventh day as a seventh millennium and puts at the end of the sixth or the beginning of the seventh day events that are placed in Revelation 20 after the millennium.[22] Robert Kraft does take the "rest" period as "an interim between the old and new worlds"[23] but cautions that "it might be

---

17. Kleist, *The Didache, the Epistle of Barnabas*, 179.

18. Rordorf, *Sunday*, 93–94.

19. Prigent, *Les Testimonia dans le Christianisme primitif: L'Épître de Barnabé I–XVI et ses sources*, 67.

20. Ibid., 70.

21. Prigent and Kraft, *L'Epître de Barnabé*, 182–88; Wengst, *Tradition und Theologie des Barnabasbriefes*, 48–51.

22. Prigent and Kraft, *L'Epître de Barnabé*, 186.

23. R. A. Kraft, *Barnabas and the Didache*, 129.

considered strange if Pseudo-Barnabas or his tradition interpreted the 'six thousand years' literally."[24]

## THE ARGUMENT OF *BARNABAS* 15

Chapter 15 of *Barnabas* occurs in the body of the treatise, which takes up the central practices or institutions of Judaism and gives what may be described as an allegorical, spiritual, or Christian interpretation of these: sacrifice (chapters 7–8), circumcision (chapter 9), food laws (chapter 10), washings (chapter 11), covenant (chapters 13–14), and temple (chapter 16). Chapter 15 deals with the Sabbath. It begins with three quotations, only the third of which can be definitely identified: "Now also concerning the sabbath, it has been written in the Ten Commandments, which God spoke on Mount Sinai to Moses face to face: 'Sanctify the sabbath of the Lord with pure hands and a pure heart.' And in another place he says: 'If my sons will keep my sabbaths, then I will place my mercy upon them.' The sabbath is mentioned at the beginning of creation: 'And God made the works of his hands in six days, and he completed them on the seventh day and rested on it and sanctified it'" (15:1–3).

The first quotation, although cited as coming from the Decalogue, is more like a conflation of Jer 17:22 and Ps 24:4. Several passages might suggest the thought of the second quotation, but the closest verbal parallels are provided by a combination of Exod 31:13–17 with Isa 44:3. Both the first and the second quotations are paraphrases similar to Targumim.[25] The third quotation is close to Gen 2:2–3 but follows the Hebrew Massoretic Text and the Aramaic Targum Onqelos in reading "He completed on the seventh day," rather than the Septuagint, Syriac, and Samaritan Pentateuch in reading "He completed on the sixth day." That latter reading is followed in *Barnabas*'s next verse: "Observe, children, what it says: 'He completed [his work] in six days.' This means that in six thousand years the Lord will complete all things. For a day with him signifies a thousand years. He bears me witness by saying, 'Behold the day of the Lord will be as a thousand years'" (15:4). If *Barnabas* has followed a testimony collection in the first three verses, the change to "sixth day" may be a correction

---

24. Ibid., 128.

25. Prigent, *L'Epître de Barnabé*, 66. Prigent and Kraft, *L'Epître de Barnabé*, 183, give references for the Decalogue interpreted in a spiritual sense; this may have been the intention behind the original testimony collection, but *Barnabas*'s use is different. The fullest commentary is Windisch, *Der Barnabasbrief, Die Apostolischen Väter*.

to agree with the Greek text of Genesis or, more significantly, to avoid the idea of God's completing his work on the seventh day.[26] (If *Barnabas* was conscious of the variant, it might have contributed to his collapsing the numbers 6 and 7, and 7 and 8, which will be discussed below.) The scriptural support for his eschatological interpretation of the Creation account is apparently Ps 90:4, but the wording is actually closer to 2 Pet 3:8.

The purpose of this eschatological interpretation is indicated by these further comments: "'And he rested on the seventh day.' This means, when his Son comes, he will bring to an end the time of the lawless one, will judge the ungodly, and will change the sun, moon, and stars; then he will truly rest on the seventh day" (*Barn.* 15:5). The Second Coming of Christ will bring to an end the six thousand years of this world. The future tense rules out the possibility that the reference is to the first coming; moreover, the terminology is the usual eschatological description for the end time. Only when lawlessness is overthrown will God truly be able to rest. The true meaning of the Sabbath, in *Barnabas*, is the eschatological rest. The chiliastic language of 15:4 is here seen to be used not for a chronological purpose per se but to remove the Creation account as a basis for the literal observance of the seventh day.

Next, *Barnabas* gives another reason why the Jews are wrong in taking the Sabbath command literally, a reason designed to remove the Decalogue command as a basis for Sabbath observance. It is humanly impossible to keep the Sabbath as intended: "Moreover, he says: 'Sanctify it with pure hands and a pure heart.' If, then, anyone, by being pure in heart is able now to sanctify the day which God sanctified, we have been in every way deceived. See, therefore, that at that time when we truly rest, we will sanctify it, when we shall be able, since we will have been justified and will have received the promise, there being no more wickedness and all things being made new by the Lord. Then we will be able to sanctify it, we ourselves having first been sanctified" (*Barn.* 15:6–7). The repetition of the quotation in 15:1 changes the plural to the singular, bringing it closer to the form of the Decalogue and preparing for the individualized interpretation that follows. *Barnabas*, unlike others, concludes that no one now is able to sanctify the Sabbath, so it is not to be observed. The seventh day is eschatological. As in the Epistle to the Hebrews 4:9, "there remains a sabbath rest for the people of God"—the world to come.[27] Only when

26. R. A. Kraft, *Barnabas and Didache*, 127, on the reading; Prigent and Kraft, *L'Epître de Barnabé*, 184, for parallels in Philo; also Hermans, "Le Pseudo-Barnabe est-il millenariste?" 863–64.

27. Barrett, "The Eschatology of the Epistle to the Hebrews," 369–71.

God's people have been completely sanctified and lawlessness no longer exists will it be possible genuinely to rest. *Barnabas* elsewhere affirms that complete justification before God must await the future.[28]

Having argued that the Creation Sabbath is really the eschatological Sabbath and that it is impossible for sinful human beings to sanctify the Sabbath day, the author reverts to his usual approach[29] of quoting the prophets' condemnation of Israel's ritualistic observances: "Moreover, he says to them: 'I cannot endure your new moons and sabbaths.' See, now he says, 'The present sabbaths are not acceptable to me, but that [Sabbath] which I have made, in which when I have rested in everything, I will make the beginning of the eighth day, which is the beginning of another world'" ( *Barn.* 15:8). The quotation of Isa 1:13 is identical with that in 2:5, where the preceding context is included in the quotation. "Your [Jewish] sabbaths" are the Sabbaths of the present era,[30] in contrast to God's eschatological Sabbath. The author words his interpretation in the first person, as if a quotation from God, and the wording may have been influenced by some source.[31] The important point for our purposes is the shift from the seventh to the eighth day to describe this eschatological rest. Rabbinic thought interpreted the Sabbath as a figure of the world to come,[32] as the author had done in *Barn.* 15:5. *Barnabas* now, however, takes the eighth day instead of the seventh day as representative of the world to come. More attention will have to be given to the significance of this shift, but for the moment it may be noticed that it was prompted by thought of the Christian's special day, called "the eighth day" perhaps under the influence of its relation to the eschatological day: "Wherefore we keep the eighth day for rejoicing, in which also Jesus arose from the dead and when he was manifested ascended into heaven" (15:9).

Instead of using the terminology of the first day of the week, or Lord's day, *Barnabas* "trumps" the Jewish exaltation of the seventh day as the climax of Creation by connecting the day of Christian celebration with the new world of eternity. The Christian Sunday does not fit a typology of the week culminating in the seventh day, so a different eschatological

---

28. *Barn.* 4:10; 6:19; cf. 21.

29. For example, *Barn.* 2; 3; 9; 16.

30. Kleist, *The Didache, the Epistle of Barnabas*, 179.

31. Prigent, *L'Epître de Barnabé*, 69; Prigent and Kraft, *L'Epître de Barnabé*, 186–87. The closest parallel is *2 Enoch* 33:1, which may itself be a Christian interpolation—so Rordorf, *Sunday*, 235. The eighth-day symbolism occurs in *Sibylline Oracles* 7.140.

32. *Tamid* 7.4; *Mekhilta* on Exod 23:13.

symbolism is introduced, that of the ogdoad.[33] The reference to Jesus' Resurrection and Ascension emphasizes the eschatological significance of the eighth day.[34] Whether or not *Barnabas* means to say that the Ascension occurred on the day of the Resurrection,[35] the author does seem to put the Ascension also on an eighth day,[36] which becomes a prophecy of the new creation. As Kleist observes, *Barnabas* uses "eighth day" in two senses: for the day of eternity (the other world [15:8]) and for the first day after the lapse of the preceding week (15:9). Because Jesus arose on the eighth day in the second sense, we commemorate on it, by anticipation, the eighth day in the first sense.[37]

## THE ESCHATOLOGY OF *BARNABAS*

Rordorf argues for the seventh millennium's being an interim between the six thousand years and the eighth age, since otherwise we must assume that two eschatological ideas have been forcibly yoked, with both the seventh and eighth days as the new aeon.[38] *Barnabas* may indeed have drawn on two different eschatological traditions,[39] and the whole treatise shows how little the author was interested in consistency. Whatever served to make a point could he brought in. The scheme of seven ages in the early part of the chapter relativizes the weekly Sabbath for him, and the imagery of the number 8 in the latter part of the chapter connects with the Christian's special day. The two symbolisms serve different functions in the argument, so there was no need to harmonize them. Neither serves the purpose of periodization.

To quote C. K. Barrett, "The only point that is really clear here is perhaps the only point that *Barnabas* really wished to make: the Jews with their Sabbaths are in the wrong, the Christians with their Sundays are in

---

33. Riesenfeld, "Sabbat et Jour du Seigneur," 215–16. Daniélou affirms the Christian origin of the "eighth day"—*The Theology of Jewish Christianity*, 397–98; Daniélou, *The Bible and the Liturgy*, 256.

34. Justin Martyr, *Dialogue* 41, uses the eighth day in an anti-Jewish sense, connected with circumcision.

35. As in *Gospel of Peter* 13.56; cf. Tertullian *Against the Jews* 13.

36. Rordorf, *Sunday*, 235.

37. Kleist, *The Didache, the Epistle of Barnabas*, 180.

38. Rordorf, *Sunday*, 93–94.

39. Daniélou, "La Typologie millenariste," 1–8; Windisch, *Der Barnabasbrief*, 383–84.

the right."⁴⁰ As the present survey of *Barnabas* 15 shows, the author was not interested in chronological calculation. He still lived in the early Christian expectation of an imminent end of all things (chapter 4). He drew on chiliastic traditions,⁴¹ but he was not interested in them for their own sake. He subordinated chiliastic thought to another purpose—to eliminate the weekly Sabbaths, particularly the support the Creation account and its eschatological reapplication might seem to give them.

Albert Hermans has most thoroughly argued the case that *Barnabas* was not millennialist.⁴² He shows that the Christian millennialists (Irenaeus, Lactantius, Victorinus, and Methodius) do not know a succession of two eschatological Sabbaths. The millennium may be called a Sabbath, but the celestial world to follow it is not so called; hence it is most unlikely that *Barnabas* speaks of a double final Sabbath, one during the seventh, and the other during the eighth, period.⁴³ Hermans advances three further arguments against the interpretation of *Barnabas* as millennialist: (1) the author's vocabulary identifies the consummation and rest at the end of the sixth period with the inauguration of the heavenly world; (2) the description of the events of the end allows only one series of future events and makes no provision for anything to bring a supposed seventh millennium to an end; and (3) the argumentation of chapter 15 sets up a correspondence between the divine rest after the first creation to the Jewish Sabbath and the divine rest of the new creation to the Christian observance of the eighth day.⁴⁴

The second of Hermans's arguments has been strongly urged by D. H. Kromminga to establish the same point. Kromminga, as well as others, has noticed that in the usual apocalyptic scheme,⁴⁵ the judgment follows the millennial "rest." *Barnabas* 15:5 puts the judgment of the ungodly and the cosmic changes at the beginning of the seventh day, not at the end of the millennium, where they occur in the usual premillennial outline.⁴⁶

Hermans's first and third arguments mean that for *Barnabas* the seventh and eighth ages are identical and not sequential. William H. Shea has

---

40. Barrett, "The Eschatology of the Epistle to the Hebrews," 370.

41. Rordorf, *Sunday*, 93–94.

42. Hermans, "Le Pseudo-Barnabas," 849–76.

43. Ibid., 859–60.

44. Ibid., 861–75. I take exception to Hermans's designation of the eighth day as the "Christian sabbath" (868).

45. Cf. *4 Ezra* 7:30.

46. Kromminga, *The Millennium in the Church*, 32; Prigent and Kraft, *L'Epître de Barnabé*, 186; Windisch, *Der Barnabasbrief*, 385.

argued against the interpretation that the seventh age is the same as the eighth, because, he says, that would mean that the Christians are keeping the Sabbath, "which is exactly what he [Barnabas] opposes."[47] Shea's reasoning should be reversed. What he says might have some force if the eighth were understood as a Sabbath, but not if the eighth superseded the seventh. Here the two forms of text at Gen 2:2–3 may have a further significance. The seventh day marks the completion of the six days of work, so the literal seventh day is joined to the sixth day as part of the created order.[48] Yet, in another sense, the seventh-day rest is really the creation of a new world and so belongs to the eighth period, the new order. *Barnabas* is so anti-Jewish that it prefers the eighth-day terminology over the seventh day for the eschatological rest. If the eighth day (*Barn.* 15:8), which is the beginning of another world, means an eighth millennium, this is inconsistent with 15:5–7, where the seventh millennium is the time when sin is overcome.[49] Moreover, *Barnabas*'s doctrine of the Sabbath really precludes the chiliastic reading of his text. Continued observance of the Sabbath amounts to a denial of our present sinfulness.[50] It is hard to see how the author's negative view of the weekly Sabbath would allow for an intermediate seventh millennium to be a time of perfection.

Another question should be raised: Is it even proper to read *Barnabas* in the light of Justin, Irenaeus, and Hippolytus and their chiliastic tradition? Is that *Barnabas*'s intellectual lineage? It is true that *Barnabas* shares with Justin similar combinations and applications of biblical texts, but this comes from a shared use of early Christian collections of testimonia.[51] On matters of fundamental doctrinal outlook, there is little in common beyond the basics of Christian faith. On such key matters as the covenant, the understanding of Old Testament history, and the method of biblical interpretation, *Barnabas* has a completely different approach from Justin and Irenaeus.[52]

---

47. Shea, "Sabbath," 168.

48. Cf. R. A. Kraft, *Barnabas and the Didache*, 127–28.

49. Barrett, "The Eschatology of the Epistle to the Hebrews," 370; Windisch, *Der Barnabasbrief*, 383–84.

50. Kromminga, *The Millennium*, 34–35; Wengst, *Tradition and Theologie*, 74; Prigent and Kraft, *L'Epître de Barnabé*, 186.

51. The most recent treatment is by Skarsaune, *The Proof from Prophecy*.

52. Ferguson, "The Covenant Idea in the Second Century."

## CLEMENT OF ALEXANDRIA AND BARNABAS

*Barnabas* belongs to another tradition in the early history of Christianity, an Alexandrian tradition[53] that led to Clement of Alexandria and Origen. The first attestation of *Barnabas* comes from Clement, who was clearly indebted to its author and held him in high regard. I count eight quotations in Clement's *Stromata* from *Barnabas*, the author of which is called an "apostle," companion of Paul, and one of the seventy disciples.[54] Indeed, it was reading Clement that led me to reexamine the passage in *Barnabas* and suggested another way of interpreting its author. The parallels between *Barnabas* and Clement are duly noted by the commentators but are not then pursued as to *Barnabas*'s meaning.[55] These parallels show how an early reader of the treatise reconciled the tension between 7 and 8 as types of the eschatological rest.

Before looking at the relevant section in Clement, I should explain that for Clement, 6 is the number associated with this world and the natural order, and 8 is associated with the heavenly realm. Of course, 7 is the day of rest, according to the OT.

Clement's interpretation of the Sabbath commandment in *Strommata* 6.16 will confirm Hermans's first and third arguments about the equivalence of 7 and 8 for *Barnabas*. Clement begins with the equivalence of the seventh day to a new beginning: "The seventh day, therefore, is proclaimed a rest—an avoidance of evils—preparing for the original day, our true rest; which, in truth, is the first beginning of light, in which all things are perceived and inherited."[56] Clement, however, is aware that Christians gave superiority to the eighth day, and he is able to accommodate that fact to the OT text: "For one may venture to say that the eighth is properly the

---

53. In support of this view, see Barnard, *Studies in the Apostolic Fathers and Their Background*, 46, and literature cited there.

54. Clement of Alexandria, *Stromata* 2.6, 7, 15, 18, 20; 5.8, 10; 6.8. There may be an unreferenced allusion to *Barnabas* in *Stromata* 6.16, the chapter I see as giving a clue to *Barnabas*'s symbolic use of numbers: "By following him, therefore, through our whole life, we become impassible; and this is to rest." If *Barnabas*'s "perfected" (chap. 6) and "justified" (chap. 15) were understood by Clement as "impassible," the result would be the statement he gives.

55. Hermans, "Le Pseudo-Barnabe est-il millenariste?" 864–65, for instance, cites Clement only as an illustration of how the author's mind might have worked; Kraft, *Barnabas and Didache*, 129; Prigent and Kraft, *L'Epître de Barnabé*, 184.

56. Clement is borrowing from Aristobulus, a passage preserved in Eusebius *Preparation for the Gospel* 13.12.9–11. Aristobulus identified the first day and the seventh day. Prigent and Kraft, *L'Epître de Barnabé*, 185.

seventh, and the seventh actually the sixth; that is the eighth is properly the sabbath, and the seventh a day of work."[57] After notices of occurrences of the number 6 in the natural order of the world, Clement observes that for the Pythagoreans, the number 7 is "motherless and childless." He connects this statement with Jesus' declaration that in the coming rest, those who are resurrected "neither marry nor are given in marriage" (Luke 20:35). The association of the number 6 with the world is illustrated by the account of the Transfiguration, where Jesus was the sixth person present (but by the Resurrection became the eighth), indicating that he was "God in a body of flesh" (*Strom.* 6.16).

Then comes the comment to which I would like to draw special attention: "For in the order of numbers six is included in the list, but the sequence of the letters employs the symbol digamma that is not used in writing. In this regard, each letter is kept in its position for the numbers themselves only up to seven and eight, but in the number of the letters of the alphabet *zeta* is six and *eta* seven. Yet when the symbol *digamma* was inserted (I know not how) into writing, if we should follow it out thus, six becomes the seven and seven the eight" (*Strom.* 6.16). The basis for this not-clearly-stated explanation is that the numeral 6 in Greek was the letter *digamma*, which had dropped out of the alphabet and was used only for the numeral or as a contraction. If one did not count the *digamma*, then the letter that stood for 7 (*zeta*) was actually the sixth letter in the alphabet, and the letter that stood for 8 (*eta*) was the seventh. With this explanation made, Clement can proceed to an extended praise of the number 7 in the nature of things, as supported by many pagan writers. His premise seems tobe that the seventh day of the Law was to be identified with the Christian's first (eighth) day. Not that Clement advocated keeping the first day in the way Jews kept the seventh day, as later Christian Sabbatarians would: he has in mind "abstinence from evil"[58] and especially the eschatological rest. That puts him in the tradition of the Epistle to the Hebrews (4:1–11) and, I would add, the tradition of *Barnabas*.

Clement's identification of 8 with 7, by way of the peculiar relation that obtained between the Greek alphabet and Greek numerals, may give an explanation for *Barnabas*'s apparent inconsistency in combining two different eschatological schemes as if they were one. What appears to us as,

57. Cf. a similar play in *Stromata* 4.25.

58. The spiritual interpretation of the prohibition of work on the Sabbath as meaning an abstinence from evil was common in the early church—see Bauckham, "Sabbath and Sunday in the Post-Apostolic Church," 265–69, for metaphorical interpretations of the Sabbath command.

at worst, a chronological contradiction or as, at best, a sample of muddle-headedness was of no concern to the author. And that fact itself separates him from a chiliastic mentality. There is no intermediate millennial kingdom in *Barnabas*. The seventh age of heavenly rest, according to one set of terms, was also the eighth period according to another terminology. And the difference is one of terminology, not of eschatological schemes.

Having delivered *Barnabas* from the chiliasts, have we delivered him to the Gnostics?[59] After all, many of them were connected with Alexandria. Clement was likely acquainted with the numerical speculations of the Valentinian Gnostic Marcus.[60] The latter refers to the intervention of Jesus (whose name in Greek has six letters) in transforming the hebdomad (represented by Anthropos and Ekklesia) into the ogdoad (represented by Logos and Zoe).[61] But there is nothing to connect *Barnabas*, who was earlier, with these speculations. *Barnabas*'s gnosis has little, if anything, in common with the Gnosticism of a Basilides or a Valentinus. Moreover, the number symbolism in *Barnabas* has a quite different significance. For the Gnostics, the number 7 (the hebdomad) stood for the seven planetary spheres, in contrast to the fixed stars of Heaven above (the ogdoad).[62] The number 7 represented the world of time, and the ogdoad was the world of eternity. Gnostics gave the numbers a cosmological significance; *Barnabas* gave them an eschatological significance (but not in the same way as chiliasts). Although chronology as such was not his main concern, the six thousand years remained a chronological concept.

No, *Barnabas* was not a chiliast, nor was he a Gnostic. There were other options possible in the mixture of Jewish and Hellenistic traditions available to early Christians.

---

59. As Robert Grant perceptively asked on hearing a first reading of this paper.

60. Clement *Strom.* 6.16 (cited above) makes the same reference as Marcus (Irenaeus, *Adv. haer.* 1.14.6) does to Jesus as one of six persons on the mount of Transfiguration.

61. Irenaeus *Adv. haer.* 1.14.5. Cf. Daniélou, *The Theology of Jewish Christianity*, 399.

62. Daniélou, *The Bible and the Liturgy*, 259; cf. Daniélou, *The Theology of Jewish Christianity*, 403.

# 14

## Millennial and Amillennial Expectations in Christian Eschatology
### Ancient and Medieval Views

As we approach the year 2000, it is well to be reminded that 2000 is the last year of the second millennium, not the first year of the third millennium. The year 1 was the first year of the first decade of the common era. There was no year zero, so the year 10 was the last year of the first decade, and 11 was the first year of the second decade. The year 100 ended the first century; the second century began with 101. Similarly, the year 1000 ended the first millennium, while 1001 began the second millennium. But this dating was meant to begin with the incarnation, to count time from the coming of Christ, Anno Domini (AD). Historians now generally agree that Dionysius Exiguus in the sixth century miscalculated the year of Jesus' birth by four to six years. So, if we really are counting time from the incarnation, we are already living in the third millennium.

Eschatological hope was strong and central to early Christian existence.[1] I will focus on only one aspect of Christian eschatology: the question of millennial and amillennial expressions of this hope. This topic is

---

1. Daley, *The Hope of the Early Church*. Froom, *The Prophetic Faith of Our Fathers*, vol. 1, collects texts in translation for the ancient and medieval periods. His interests are broader than the millennium and the commentary reflects Adventist perspectives.

intimately connected with other aspects of eschatology, but these related matters will be explored primarily as they relate to the question of millennialism. Although the word *millennialism* is used in sociological studies in a broad sense of hope for a coming perfect age, I will confine my interest to the specific meaning of a thousand-year rule by Christ over an earthly kingdom related in some intimate way to his second coming. Hence, I use *millennialism*, from the Latin, and *chiliasm*, from the Greek, as synonymous. Bernard McGinn brought clarity and precision to terminology that is often employed in confusing ways by distinguishing eschatology, apocalypticism, and millennialism.[2] Eschatology, "the doctrine of last things," is the general word for all aspects of thought related to the end time. Apocalypticism is a narrower term for a specific expectation of a three-stage drama that McGinn characterizes as crisis, judgment, and vindication. It was usually characterized by speculation on an imminent unfolding of these events. Millennialism and chiliasm refer to the expectation that the vindication of the righteous involves a one-thousand-year period of blessedness in this world that is connected with the return of the Messiah.[3] Postmillennialism expects the return of Christ after the millennium, and premillennialism expects the return of Christ before the millennium.

Christian eschatology, whether apocalyptic or nonapocalyptic, did not necessarily entail a literal millennium before or after the return of Christ.[4] There are other misconceptions to be laid aside as we enter into our survey. Apocalyptic eschatology, both Jewish and Christian, was a learned product. It was not necessarily a lower-class phenomenon.[5] Apocalypticists were more often passive than active. Some did take up arms or acted in some aggressive manner to hasten the action in the divine drama, but most expected God to take care of things. They only wanted to understand what was happening, and sometimes when and how.[6]

2. McGinn, *Visions of the End*, xvi–xvii, 1–36.

3. Hill, *Regnum Caelorum*, 5. Hill includes Jewish texts for which the 1,000-year duration was not normative, offering this definition: "Chiliasm or millennialism as used here will signify belief in a temporary, earthly, Messianic kingdom to be realized sometime in the future: temporary, for, whereas it covers an extended period of time, it is not viewed as the ultimate state of things; earthly, as it takes place on this earth, typically with Jerusalem as its capital; and Messianic, as an individual deliverer(s) plays a central role in it."

4. For example, the fifth-century text, *The Revelation of the Holy Theologian John*, describes a time of great productivity followed by the appearance of the anti-christ, but no millennium. See McGinn, *Visions of the End*, 54–55, for a translation.

5. McGinn, *Visions of the End*, 32.

6. Ibid.

## Millennial and Amillennial Expectations in Christian Eschatology

Two patterns of eschatological hope found expression early on. These patterns shaped two different perspectives with reference to the millennium.[7] Millennial and amillennial expectations have existed side-by-side throughout Christian history. Eschatological expectations are often associated in contemporary thought with premillennialism, but it has not always been so. Eschatological fervor can be nonmillennial. Similarly, apocalypticism is often equated with millennialism, but the historical record does not confirm this connection. Moreover, it is often thought that premillennialism dominated the first two hundred years or so, even as it has in evangelical and conservative Protestant circles in the late nineteenth and twentieth centuries. I hope to show that premillennialism was not as dominant in the early centuries as often claimed and that an alternative eschatology from the early years contributed to the negligible place it occupied in the Middle Ages.[8] Christian truth, of course, is not determined by counting a show of hands, but I think it is correct that the majority of Christians throughout history have been amillennial. This was true even in the first three centuries, contrary to what one reads in some influential reference works.[9]

## JEWISH APOCALYPTICISM IN THE GRECO-ROMAN PERIOD

Jewish apocalypticism set the background for many Christian expectations.[10] Not all eschatological hopes among the Jews included a messiah, and where they did, this messianic figure is variously depicted as prophet, priest, king, or supernatural man.[11] Where an interim messianic kingdom was included in the speculation, its length varied from 40 to

---

7. Hill, *Regnum Caelorum*, 178–80, 194–95.

8. For the first three centuries, I follow Hill, *Regnum Caelorum*, whose conclusions on the distribution of chiliastic views are summarized on pp. 181–84. A more generous estimate of the extent of premillennialism in the early church is found in Bietenhard's dissertation, "Das tausendjährige Reich: Eine biblisch-theologische Studie," which I know through his article, "The Millennial Hope in the Early Church."

9. E.g., Harnack, *History of Dogma*, vol. 1, 167–70; Schürer, *The History of the Jewish People in the Age of Jesus Christ (175 B.C.—A.D. 135)*, vol. 2, 547.

10. For introduction, see Collins, ed., *Semeia 14: Apocalypse*; Collins, *The Apocalyptic Imagination*; D. S. Russell, *Divine Disclosure*; Collins, ed., *Encyclopedia of Apocalypticism*, vol. 1: *The Origins of Apocalypticism in Judaism and Christianity*.

11. Ferguson, *Backgrounds of Early Christianity*, 3rd ed., 551–54. See the bibliography there, to which add Fitzmyer, *The One Who Is to Come*; and Porter, ed., *The Messiah in the Old and New Testaments*.

365,000 years.[12] Rabbi Aqiba said that the days of the Messiah would be forty years.[13] Fourth Ezra, which is contemporary with the book of Revelation, puts the messianic era at 400 years (7:28). Also contemporary with the book of Revelation, Rabbi Eliezer ben Hyrcanus (ca. 80–120), arrived at various figures, including 400 years[14] and 1,000 years.[15] *Second Baruch* 26–30 has a period of tribulation followed by an interim messianic age of abundant and plenty that ends with the general resurrection and judgment.

Various views about the afterlife were current in Judaism at the beginning of the Christian era.[16] Among these was the belief that the souls of the righteous would await the resurrection in the underworld. Although the ideas of an interim messianic kingdom before the last judgment and of an interim abode in the underworld before the resurrection were widely recognized in Jewish sources, the combination of these two ideas is found principally in Fourth Ezra and *Second Baruch*, both roughly contemporary with the book of Revelation.[17] Jewish thoughts on the messianic kingdom and the world to come provided the material with which early Christian teachers developed their thoughts. When put together in sequence, the combination of an interim state of the dead in the underworld and an interim earthly messianic kingdom contributed decisively to the development of Christian chiliasm, which settled on the 1,000 years as the duration of the interim kingdom under the influence of Rev 20:4, 6.

Another factor was the fusion of the interpretation of 1,000 years as one day (based on Ps 90:4; 2 Pet 3:8) with a cosmic week chronology. The result was a paralleling of the week of creation in Genesis 1 with the length of time that the world would exist. For some, this meant that after 6,000 years there would follow 1,000 years of rest, peace, and plenty. Some Christians in this line of development identified the heavenly existence as

---

12. Rabbinic evidence is collected in Strack and Billerbeck, *Kommentar zum Neuen Testament aus Talmud and Midrasch*, 3:823–27. Cf. also Prigent, "Le Millénium dans l'Apocalypse johannique," 148–50. Prigent notes that all the variant numbers represent biblical periods applied by typological exegesis to the coming messianic age.

13. *Pesiqta Rabbati* 1.7 (4a); cf. *b. Sanhedrin* 99a.

14. *Pesiqta Rabbati* 1.7 (4a).

15. *Tanhuma* 7b; *Midrash on Psalm* 90:17. Cf. also R. Eliezer ben Jose Hagelili (ca. 150)—*Pesiqta Rabbati* 1.7 (4a). The *Testament of Isaac* 8:6 has a "millennial banquet," but places this in the "kingdom of heaven." In its present form the work is Christian and may be dated to the second century CE, but it may come from Egyptian Judaism.

16. See Ferguson, *Backgrounds of Early Christianity*, 554–55, for various views of the afterlife.

17. Hill, *Regnum Caelorum*, 57.

the eighth period. Others saw the world as ending after 6,000 years and the Sabbath rest as representing eternal life.[18]

## THE CONNECTION OF PREMILLENNIALISM WITH THE INTERMEDIATE STATE OF THE DEAD

Charles Hill has established certain associations of ideas that permit an identification of authors as premillennialists or amillennialists even when they do not speak specifically to the question of a 1,000-year earthly reign by Christ. On the basis of Irenaeus especially, it is clear that premillennialists believed that the souls of the righteous awaited the millennial kingdom in subterranean vaults. Orthodox nonchiliasts, on the other hand, believed that the souls of the righteous at death entered the divine presence. For both positions, the period after death was an intermediate state. But for premillennialists the coming earthly kingdom was preparatory to entering the divine presence, whereas for nonmillennialists, souls in the heavenly circumstances awaited reunification with their bodies in the resurrection. For these nonmillennialists their "heavenly, post-mortem existence *takes the place of the millennium*" and makes it "redundant."[19]

Some unorthodox "Gnostic" nonchiliasts were antagonistic to the salvation of the flesh, but orthodox nonchiliasts did not reject the resurrection of the body. Belief in a bodily resurrection did not automatically place one in the chiliast camp. Also, some orthodox nonchiliasts shared with chiliasts a sense that the world would soon end. An expectation of an imminent parousia did not necessarily mean one was a chiliast.[20] Those who looked forward to a heavenly intermediate state with the Lord did not in the early period of Christianity show any indication of accepting an intermediate earthly kingdom. On the other hand, belief in a subterranean intermediate state did not necessarily signify expectation of a millennial kingdom, but all chiliasts did believe in an infernal resting place as part of their eschatology.[21]

---

18. Daniélou, "La typologie millenariste de la semaine dans le christianisme primitif"; Daniélou, *The Theology of Jewish Christianity*, 396–403. Christian periodizations of history are set in a broad context in Luneau, *L'Histoire du salut chez les Pères de l'Église*.

19. Hill, *Regnum Caelorum*, 17–18.

20. Ibid., 182–83.

21. Ibid., 154.

On Hill's showing, the New Testament is not premillennial—not even the book of Revelation! In Revelation the righteous dead are already in heaven awaiting the final judgment (Rev 6:9–11; 12:10–12; 15:2–4; 18:20; presumably the same applies to Rev 20:4). In a sense, Satan is already bound (Rev 12:9–12; cf. Matt 12:29). Moreover, the kingdom in Revelation is present to the author and his recipients (Rev 1:6, 9; 5:10; 12:10). The "reign" of Revelation 20 uses the same language and would likewise appear to be present.[22] Moreover, a nonchiliastic exegesis of Revelation 20 existed in the early church, as can be discerned in Hippolytus, Origen, Cyprian, and Dionysius of Alexandria, alongside the chiliastic exegesis of Justin Martyr, Irenaeus, and Tertullian.[23]

The so-called delay of the Parousia seems not to have been as big a problem as some make it.[24] A few texts speak about what might be described in this way, but by and large the texts do not reflect a great concern. If this factor was as crucial to the early development of Christianity as some think, one would expect the problem to be addressed more significantly than it is.[25]

## PREMILLENNIALISTS IN THE PERIOD BEFORE CONSTANTINE

The only apostolic father known to have been a premillennialist was Papias, bishop of Hierapolis in the early second century. The church historian Eusebius had access to his now-lost writings. He said that Papias

> adduces other accounts, as though they came to him from unwritten tradition, and some strange parables and teachings of the Savior, and some other more mythical accounts. Among them he says that there will be a millennium after the resurrection of the dead, when the kingdom of Christ will be set up in

---

22. Prigent, "Le Millénium dans l'Apocalypse johannique," concludes that the 1,000 years in Revelation 20 symbolizes paradise because after the birth of Christ and his earthly ministry, the Seducer is conquered and the new paradise is opened. On the other hand, Otto Böcher finds indications of a chiliastic eschatology in Revelation and other parts of the New Testament; Böcher, "Chiliasmus I. Judentum and Neues Testament," 724, 727–28.

23. Hill, *Regnum Caelorum*, 120, 136–37, 142, 149–50, 188–92.

24. Notably, Werner, *The Formation of Christian Dogma*.

25. Cf. the judicious observation of Daley that the "delay of the Parousia" caused no more of an upheaval for Christians of the first and second centuries than it does for modern believers; Daley, *The Hope of the Early Church*, 3.

## Millennial and Amillennial Expectations in Christian Eschatology

material form on this earth. I suppose that he got these notions by a perverse reading of the apostolic accounts, not realizing that they had spoken mystically and symbolically. For he was a man of very little intelligence, as is clear from his books. But he is responsible for the fact that so many Christian writers after him held the same opinion, relying on his antiquity, for instance Irenaeus and whoever else appears to have held the same views.[26]

Irenaeus himself cited Papias in confirmation:

> The elders who saw John, the disciple of the Lord, related that they had heard from him how the Lord used to teach in regard to these [millennial] times and say: "The days will come in which vines shall grow, each having ten thousand branches, and in each branch ten thousand twigs, and in each true twig ten thousand shoots, and in each one of the shoots ten thousand clusters, and on every one of the clusters ten thousand grapes, and every grape when pressed will give twenty-five metretes of wine. And when any one of the saints shall lay hold of a cluster, another shall cry out, 'I am a better cluster, take me; bless the Lord through me.' In like manner that a grain of wheat would produce ten thousand ears, and that every ear should have ten thousand grains, and every grain would yield ten pounds of clear, pure, fine flour; and that all other fruit-bearing trees, seeds, and grass would produce in similar proportions; and that all animals feeding on the productions of the earth should become peaceful and harmonious among each other and be in perfect subjection to man."[27]

The Christian teacher multiplies by ten a similar description of the abundance of the messianic age by a Jewish teacher in *2 Baruch* 29:5 (cf. *1 Enoch* 10:19).

The first unfolding of a millennial eschatology to survive is found in Justin Martyr's *Dialogue with Trypho* 80–81 in the mid-second century.[28] Justin has not fully systematized his material, for in many passages he reflects aspects of a nonchiliastic eschatology. One possible reconciliation of his varied statements is that Justin began with a chiliastic eschatology

---

26. Eusebius, *Church History* 3.39.11–13.

27. Irenaeus, *Adv. Haer.* 5.33.3-4.

28. Barnard, "Justin Martyr's Eschatology," esp. 92–95 on the resurrection and the millennium.

shortly after his conversion but moved away from it later.[29] However that may be, his millennial program emphasizes two points: "a resurrection of the dead and a thousand years in Jerusalem, which will then be built, adorned, and enlarged" (*Dial.* 80.5). The thousand years is confirmed by appeal to Isa 65:17-25. Verse 22 is read as "according to the days of the tree of life" and interpreted as referring to a thousand years, since a day of the Lord is as a thousand years (Ps 90:4) and Adam was told that in the day he ate of the tree he would die (Gen 2:17) and he did not live a thousand years.[30] Justin further appeals to John, "one of the apostles of Christ," who "prophesied in the Revelation that those who believed in our Christ would have one thousand years in Jerusalem" (Rev 20:4-6). "After these things there will occur the general and eternal resurrection of all persons together at once and the judgment" (*Dial.* 81.4). Justin expresses the key points of classical chiliasm: a resurrection (of the righteous), a thousand years in the earthly Jerusalem,[31] then the general resurrection, and finally the judgment.

The fullest and most systematic early expression of millennial eschatology occurs in Irenaeus, *Against Heresies* 5.31-36. There is some indication that Irenaeus moved from a nonchiliastic to a chiliastic eschatology in the course of writing his great polemical work,[32] but we will focus on his final exposition. In Irenaeus we see for the first time in Christian literature the scheme of 6,000 years for the world's history to be followed by 1,000 years of the earthly kingdom of Christ. He sees a large number of scriptural texts (mainly from the prophets) as applying to the earthly kingdom, which will be initiated by the resurrection of the righteous. He argues that these texts are to be taken literally and not allegorized. Irenaeus adds to the basic points in Justin the coming of antichrist and destruction of all nations under his rule before the resurrection of the righteous, who will reign with the Lord. And he adds texts that he applies to the heavenly kingdom after the judgment.

The millennial kingdom has an important polemical purpose for Irenaeus. An earthly, material kingdom enjoyed by the righteous in their

29. Hill, *Regnum Caelorum*, 20-24.

30. He lived only 930 years, according to Gen 5:5; cf. *Dial.* 81.1-3. *Jubilees* 4:29-30; 23:27 has a similar exegetical argument. Daniélou thinks Justin used *Jubilees* (*The Theology of Jewish Christianity*, 391-93). The Jewish background of the argument is noted by Prigent, "Le Millénium dans l'Apocalypse johannique," 150-53.

31. On the importance of Jerusalem in early chiliasm, see Heid, *Chiliasmus und Antichrist-Mythos*.

32. Hill, *Regnum Caelorum*, 184-85.

resurrected bodies was a powerful anti-heretical thrust against those who denied a fleshly resurrection and took a negative view of the created world.[33] Moreover, the millennial kingdom had a positive function in Irenaeus's sweeping scheme of salvation history. The millennium serves to prepare physical bodies for the spiritual life of a heavenly existence. Human beings truly rise from the dead and "receive practice beforehand for incorruption. [They] improve and flourish in the times of the kingdom in order to be capable of receiving the glory of the Father."[34]

Irenaeus's chiliasm is quite distinctive. He does not emphasize the thousand-year duration. The purpose of the millennial kingdom is not expressed as reward to the faithful for their service but as preparation for partaking of the divine glory. For Irenaeus, the kingdom does not intervene between the old and new creation and between the provisional and the definitive defeat of evil; rather, the earthly kingdom is integrated into his view of recapitulation and constitutes the restoration of creation to its pristine condition as an earthly paradise. This theology of creation is fundamental to Irenaeus's doctrine of recapitulation and to his "chiliasm."[35]

In North Africa in the early 200s, Tertullian also found the literal millennial kingdom congenial to a defense of the Jewish heritage of Christianity and of the resurrection of the flesh. Tertullian's eschatology stands on its own as a separate argument and is not integrated into the context of salvation history as it is by Irenaeus. Moreover, Tertullian articulates more clearly than his predecessors and contemporaries the interim state of the deceased in the underworld.[36] To accommodate the biblical passages, especially in Revelation, about the righteous in heaven, he developed the view that the martyrs were the only ones exempt from a stay in the subterranean world, for one of their privileges was to go immediately to the presence of the Lord.

Following Justin, Tertullian accepted the millennium but ignored the 7,000 years for the earth's existence. His millennial view is expressed in *Against Marcion* 3.24. Marcion understood the Jewish messiah to promise to the Jews a recovery of their country. But Tertullian says, "We do confess that a kingdom is promised to us upon the earth, although before heaven, only in another state of existence, inasmuch as it will be after the

---

33. Daley, *The Hope of the Early Church*, 232 n. 10.

34. *Adv. Haer.* 5.35.2; see also 5.32.1.

35. C. R. Smith, "Chiliasm and Recapitulation in the Theology of Irenaeus."

36. Daley, *The Hope of the Early Church*, 35-37. See especially Tertullian, *On the Soul*, 55; cf. also 37.11; 58.1, 8.

resurrection for a thousand years in the divinely built city of Jerusalem 'let down from heaven'" (*Against Marcion* 3.24). This city is a recompense to the saints at their resurrection for all they have despised or lost because of service to God. The resurrection of the saints occurs in shifts during the millennium, those with the greater merits arising sooner and others later. At the end of the millennium occurs "the conflagration of all things at the judgment." The righteous are changed in a moment into the substance of angels. Tertullian distributes the blessings promised in Scripture—some to the earthly kingdom, some to the subsequent heavenly kingdom.

At the turn to the fourth century, we see three important chiliast authors, each with a distinctive twist. Lactantius, whose *Divine Institutes* book 7 is devoted largely to Christian eschatology, represents traditional chiliasm. Chapter 24 is a "vivid and detailed presentation of apocalyptic expectations" about the renewed world in the millennium.[37] On his chronology, the world would last no more than another 200 years (7.25.5). The 6,000 years plus 1,000 years represent six epochs plus one. The millennial epoch follows the devastation of the world, its cleansing from all defilement, and the restoration of the souls of the righteous to their renewed bodies (7.14, 22–23). The righteous then serve as judges under the rule of Christ and produce an infinite multitude of offspring to enjoy the rich productivity of the earth. Some of the nations are left, subjected to perpetual slavery. The devil is bound, but at the end of the millennium he is loosed, after which is the second and last judgment and the heavenly world.

Victorinus of Pettau wrote the oldest surviving commentary on the book of Revelation. He presented a materialistic millennial kingdom, but allegorized many of the features in Revelation. To get around the difficulty of Rev 6:9–11, where the souls of the martyrs await the judgment under the heavenly altar, Victorinus placed this altar under the earth in Hades.[38]

Methodius sets forth a fully spiritualized millennium.[39] The souls of the righteous await the resurrection in the presence of God, as in non-chiliast eschatology.[40] The millennium, the seventh 1,000 years corresponding to the seventh day, is characterized by rest, with no begetting or being born (9.1). This seventh millennium of rest begins on the day of the resurrection, which is also the day of judgment (9.3; 9.5). So the millennium does not precede the judgment as in traditional chiliasm. Methodius

---

37. Daley, *The Hope of the Early Church*, 67.
38. Ibid., 65–66; cf. Hill, *Regnum Caelorum*, 34–37.
39. Methodius, *Banquet* 9.
40. Methodius, *On the Resurrection* 3.2.5; *Banquet* 8.2.

may have understood the 1,000 years as one day, the day of resurrection and judgment. The body changed during "the thousand years" moves smoothly into the greater and better things of the house of God above the heavens. Methodius kept the traditional language of chiliasm but employed it according to the pattern of a nonchiliast eschatology.[41]

Missing so far in this survey of second- and third-century proponents of chiliasm is a reference to Montanism, the prophetic movement that began in Asia Minor shortly after the middle of the second century. Although nearly every reference work attributes a central place to chiliasm in fueling the "New Prophecy," this omission is intentional. Although there is evidence for some intense eschatological interest among Montanists, the evidence for millennialism is slender and late.[42]

The village of Pepuza in Phrygia was important in the beginning of the movement and was called "Jerusalem," but the interpretation that Montanists expected the "Jerusalem from above" to descend there occurs only in Epiphanius in the late fourth century (*Panarion* 48.14). The descent of the heavenly Jerusalem is described in Revelation 21, after the reference to the 1,000 years in Revelation 20, not before the millennium in the usual chiliastic scenario. If Epiphanius is right that Montanists expected the new Jerusalem to descend in Pepuza and was not reporting a conjecture based on calling Pepuza "Jerusalem" (Eusebius, *Church History* 5.18.2), then this claim represents a permutation in the chiliastic expectation.[43]

I have also only mentioned Cerinthus because the patristic sources give contradictory descriptions of his teaching as Gnostic or chiliast. A plausible new proposal is that the chiliastic views ascribed to Cerinthus were not his own views but his interpretation of Jewish expectations, in much the same way as Marcion had said that Jewish expectation of an earthly Messiah was the correct interpretation of the Old Testament.[44]

---

41. Hill, *Regnum Caelorum*, 32–34.

42. Hill, "The Marriage of Montanism and Millennialism."

43. Another proposal is that the imagery of Sirach 24 is the basis for the claim that Wisdom now has an earthly dwelling in Pepuza (not a millennial eschatology)—Poirier, "Montanist Pepuza-Jerusalem and the Dwelling Place of Wisdom."

44. Hill, "Cerinthus and Johannine Christianity."

## AMILLENNIALISTS IN THE PERIOD BEFORE CONSTANTINE

The three principal early witnesses to chiliasm in the church—Justin, Irenaeus, and Tertullian—also testify to the existence of orthodox believers who were not millennialists They distinguish these from those they considered heretics, who denied a literal bodily resurrection. Justin affirmed that he and other "right-minded Christians" believed that Jerusalem would be rebuilt and the resurrected righteous would live there 1,000 years. But he acknowledged that "many who belong to the pure and pious faith and are true Christians think otherwise." Different were "some who are called Christians, . . . who say there is no resurrection of the dead and that their souls, when they die, are taken to heaven" (*Dial.* 80.5, 2, 4).

The testimony of Irenaeus is particularly important because he shows that "the stumbling block to chiliasm" was the belief that Christians on their death went to the presence of the Lord. This made return to an earthly existence, however pleasant, superfluous, even a "retrogression."[45] Irenaeus notes the existence of "some who are reckoned among the orthodox" and are ignorant "of the kingdom that is the commencement of incorruption by means of which those who shall be worthy are accustomed gradually to partake of the divine nature" (*Adv. Haer.* 5.31.1; 32.1). These, Irenaeus says, have been influenced by heretical opinions that "immediately upon their death they shall pass above the heavens." Irenaeus does not charge these orthodox with a denial of the resurrection, as he does the heretics, but rather with ignorance of "the order of the resurrection," and the function of the first resurrection in "training beforehand for incorruption" (*Adv. Haer.* 5.31.1).

Tertullian also had orthodox opponents on the subject of where the righteous go at death. He wrote against those who believed in the resurrection, yet said at death that "the soul shall mount up to heaven where Christ is" (*De an.* 55). They used kingdom for the heavenly post-mortem state. Tertullian insists that all except the martyrs must wait in Hades, a deep space in the interior of the earth, until this world passes away and the kingdom of heaven is opened.

Who were among these orthodox believers in the resurrection of the body who rejected an earthly millennium at the Lord's coming? They include some of the other most honored figures in the early history of the church. Indeed, this nonmillennial eschatology is found in early Jewish

---

45. The term *retrogression* is Hill's, *Regnum Caelorum*, 13 and 17.

*Millennial and Amillennial Expectations in Christian Eschatology*

Christianity among the very relatives of the Lord. In the later second century, Hegesippus tells of an incident a century earlier. Grandsons of Judas, one of Jesus' brothers, were brought before the emperor Domitian, who was afraid of the coming of the Messiah. He asked them about Christ and his kingdom. "They gave answer how it would be neither of the world nor of the earth, but heavenly and angelic, and will be at the consummation of the world, when he will come in glory and judge the living and the dead, and will render to each according to his conduct."[46] The only future kingdom they knew was not millennial or earthly, but heavenly. And this heavenly kingdom would occur at the second coming and the last judgment.

Among the Apostolic Fathers, Clement and Hermas of Rome, Ignatius of Antioch, and the author of *2 Clement* fall within the pattern of a nonmillennial eschatology.[47] Polycarp of Smyrna is particularly important as the connecting link between the New Testament John and Irenaeus. Polycarp's letter to the *Philippians* indicates that those who live in faith and righteousness go to be with the Lord at their death (*Phil.* 9.2; cf. 12.2). A similar conviction is expressed in the letter his church wrote after his death, the *Martyrdom of Polycarp*.[48] Its record of Polycarp's prayer expresses the hope to "join the whole race of the righteous who are living in your [God's] presence" and "today to be received in your presence." The church was convinced that Polycarp, now "crowned with the incorruptible crown," was "rejoicing with the apostles and all the righteous" in their praise of God and Christ, who bring "us all into the heavenly kingdom."[49]

The *Epistle of Barnabas* is often included in the millennial camp. The basis for this judgment is that the author assigns 6,000 years according to the six days of creation to the existence of this world, to be followed by the seventh day of rest. However, *Barnabas* 15 is not interested in chronological calculation, but uses the cosmic week to remove the support of the creation account for the Jewish observance of the Sabbath. For *Barnabas*, the judgment occurs at the end of the 6,000-year period, not after the seventh millennium on the usual chiliastic scheme. Moreover, the seventh-day rest is identified by the author as equivalent to the heavenly rest on the eighth day. No intervening millennial rest occurs between the close of this age and the world to come.[50]

---

46. Quoted by Eusebius, *Church History* 3.20.4.
47. Hill, *Regnum Caelorum*, 66-78, 80-89.
48. Ibid., 78-80, 105-7.
49. *Martyrdom of Polycarp* 14.1-2; 17.1; 19.2; 20.2.
50. Ferguson, "Was Barnabas a Chiliast? An Example of Hellenistic Number

The Alexandrian theological tradition offered a nonmillennial eschatology. Clement of Alexandria believed in a heavenly intermediate state, accepted the resurrection of the body, and left no room for an earthly millennium in his eschatology.[51] The "gate of death" for martyrs "is the beginning of true life," for honors come after death to those who have lived holy lives, but punishments to those who have lived unrighteously (*Str.* 4.7.45.1). To follow in the Master's footsteps is to "join those who are to be enrolled in the heavens" (*Quis dives* 21.6). "The church meditating on the resurrection of the dead" is the interpretation offered of the praise to God by striking on the stretched skin of the timbrel in Psalm 150:4 (*Paed.* 2.4.41.4). The resurrection occurs "at the end of the world," when "the heavens shall receive into the celestial abodes those who truly repent; and before all the Savior himself goes to meet them, . . . conducting them to the Father's bosom, to eternal life, to the kingdom of heaven" (*Quis dives* 42.15). "The end is reserved until the resurrection of those who believe," and this represents the arrival of eternity and the end of time (*Paed.* 1.6.28.3).

Origen's teaching on the spiritual nature of the resurrection body—or at least the way it was understood by many—was rejected by most of his contemporaries and subsequent generations in the church. But his rejection of chiliasm and his alternative view of the state of the soul after death were not found objectionable. To the contrary, on these matters the Greek tradition overwhelmingly followed the thinking of the Alexandrian school, on which Origen gave the most explicit statement up to his time. Leaving aside the controversial aspects of his eschatology, I will concentrate on his witness to a pattern of eschatology that preceded him and that was to become the dominant view in the Greek church.[52]

Origen took a strongly negative view on millennial expectations. He gives a detailed account of the earthly kingdom expected after the resurrection as the "views of those who, while believing in Christ, understand the divine scriptures in a sort of Jewish sense, drawing from them nothing worthy of the divine promises." "Those, however, who receive the representations of scripture according to the understanding of the apostles" interpret the promises spiritually (*De princ.* 2.11.2–3). For example,

---

Symbolism in Barnabas and Clement of Alexandria" (ch. 13 in this volume).

51. Hill, *Regnum Caelorum*, 120–27.

52. For all aspects of Origen's eschatology, see Daley, *The Hope of the Early Church*, 48–59. For the specific topic of his refutation of chiliasm, see Hill, *Regnum Caelorum*, 127–41.

prophecies about Jerusalem refer to the heavenly Jerusalem.[53] Origen concludes, in what he understands to be the agreed-on apostolic teaching, that the soul "after its departure from the world shall be rewarded according to its deserts, being destined to obtain either an inheritance of eternal life and blessedness, if its actions shall have procured this for it, or to be delivered up to eternal fire and punishments, if the guilt of its crimes shall have brought it down to this." Then "there is also to be a time of resurrection from the dead" (*De princ.*, pref. 5). He speculates that "all the saints who depart from this life will remain in some place situated on the earth, which holy scripture calls paradise, as in some place of instruction, and, so to speak, class-room or school of souls."[54] Elsewhere Origen is indefinite on the location: "bosom of Abraham," "Paradise," or "God knows what place" where "the soul enters into possession of the very inheritance promised to the fathers" (*Hom. Num.* 26.4). For Origen, this postdeath paradise serves a function comparable to Irenaeus's earthly millennial kingdom in preparing souls for their heavenly existence.[55] The souls of the just are with Christ in paradise, awaiting the resurrection. Origen sought to refute the view that the soul remained with the body in the tomb. Rather, he affirmed, "Before the resurrection the righteous man is with Christ and in his soul he lives with Christ."[56]

The surviving writings by Origen hint of an exegesis of Revelation 20 consistent with this eschatology. The "first resurrection" is the rising of the soul to paradise in the intermediate state. The faithful, especially the martyrs, reign with Christ during this intermediate state. Since the binding of Satan occurred at the crucifixion and resurrection of Jesus, the millennium has begun.[57]

Later in the third century, Dionysius, bishop of Alexandria, is important for writing against the views of Nepos that there would be a "millennium on this earth devoted to bodily indulgence" and for successfully winning over his followers to a nonmillennial understanding. Unfortunately, we know Nepos's views only from Dionysius, and we know Dionysius's two books *On Promises* only from excerpts in Eusebius.[58] Dio-

53. *On First Principles* 4.1.22; cf. *Against Celsus* 7.28-30.

54. *On First Principles* 2.11.6. On educational imagery in Origen's thought, see Ferguson, "Divine Pedagogy" (ch. 16 in this volume).

55. *On First Principles* 2.11.6-7.

56. Chadwick, trans., *Dialogue with Heraclides*, 452; cf. also *Exhortation to Martyrdom*, 47.

57. Hill, *Regnum Caelorum*, 132-39.

58. Eusebius, *Church History* 7.24-25.

nysius is best known in biblical studies for his argument that the author of Revelation was a different John from the apostle John who wrote the Fourth Gospel and the Letters of John. Nevertheless, he regarded the author as "a holy and inspired person."[59] Dionysius reflects the acceptance by the Alexandrian church's hierarchy of Origen's spiritualizing interpretation of Revelation and of the millennium.

In the transition from the Greek East to the Latin West in the third century, we take Hippolytus, an author who wrote in Greek but lived in Rome. Ascertaining the views of Hippolytus on eschatology is complicated by determining which of the works ascribed to him are actually his.[60] Many traditional themes of apocalyptic concern are evident in the *Commentary on Daniel*, *On Christ and the Antichrist*, and *On the Cause of the Universe*, but *Refutation of all Heresies* speaks the language of deification and seems to contemplate passing from this life into the celestial kingdom (10.30). The author of the works with more apocalyptic coloring accepts the world-week chronology that the world lasts for 6,000 years, but he uses that to quiet concerns for an imminent end of the world. On his chronology, the Parousia would not come until 500 years after the birth of Christ, so it was still some 300 years away.[61] "After 6,000 years comes the Sabbath ... The Sabbath is a type and figure of the future kingdom of the saints, when they will reign with Christ after his coming from heaven, as John recounts in Revelation" (*Comm. Dan.* 4.23). But he does not draw the conclusion of an earthly millennium for this seventh day.

Although many assume that meaning, several other statements are inconsistent with such a conclusion. The kingdom given to the saints when Christ returns is the eternal, heavenly kingdom and follows the general resurrection and judgment.[62] The *Commentary on Daniel* 4.58 lays out the sequence that the Judge descends from heaven, the resurrection of the dead occurs, the eternal kingdom is given to those who are worthy, and never-ending fire is kindled for the impious. The "kingdom of Christ" began with his ascension to the Father and is not temporary or earthly.[63] At his resurrection, Christ effected the release of the righteous dead from

---

59. Ibid., 7.25.7.

60. For the conflicting views in regard to eschatology, note Hill, "Hades of Hippolytus or Tartarus of Tertullian?"

61. Dunbar, "The Delay of the Parousia in Hippolytus."

62. *Commentary on Daniel* 4.10.1–2; 4.23; *On Christ and Antichrist* 65.

63. *Commentary on Daniel* 4.11.4; *On Christ and Antichrist* 61.

Hades,[64] and thereafter the "first resurrection" is the resurrection of the souls of the righteous, "prophets, martyrs, and apostles, who have entered into their rest in the kingdom of Christ."[65]

After the third century, millennial hopes were entertained more often in the West than in the East, but the most important third-century Latin bishop, Cyprian of Carthage, was not a millennialist.[66] Cyprian declares that "the one dedicated to God and Christ desires not earthly but heavenly kingdoms" (*Or. Dom.* 13). All the faithful, not just the martyrs, are admitted to heavenly beatitude immediately after death. Revelation 20:4–6 is interpreted, "All live and reign with Christ, not only those who have been slain, but even whosoever, standing in firmness of the faith and the fear of God have not worshipped the image of the beast."

> What a security it is ... in a moment to close the eyes with which men and the world are looked upon and at once to open them to look upon God and Christ! Of such a blessed departure how great is the swiftness! You shall be suddenly taken away from earth to be placed in the heavenly kingdoms.[67]

## THREE TRENDS

Three trends related to eschatological expectations may be noted. First, kingdom language became focused on the future and heavenly kingdom. In the New Testament, kingdom of God and related terms applied to the present rule of God, to its manifestation in the imminent future, or to the heavenly kingdom in the indefinite future. I have elsewhere studied the shift in usage in the second century, where God's kingdom is seldom used in a present sense and almost always in a future sense. I attributed this shift to the excessively realized eschatology of those heretics usually termed Gnostics who led the mainstream of the church to emphasize present

---

64. *On Christ and Antichrist* 45.

65. Ibid., 59; *Commentary on Daniel* 1.21.4–5; 2.37.3–4; 3.31.3. On these points and on the various works ascribed to Hippolytus, see Hill, *Regnum Caelorum*, 111–20. Luneau, *L'Histoire du salut chez les Pères de l'Église*, 211–13, also doubts the usual description of Hippolytus as a premillennialist.

66. Daley, *The Hope of the Early Church*, 42–43; cf. Hill, *Regnum Caelorum*, 143–53.

67. *To Fortunatus on Martyrdom* 12; 13. Cf. *On Mortality* 26: "Let us greet the day that assigns each of us to his own home, that snatches us hence and sets us free from the snares of the world, and restores us to paradise and the kingdom."

experience of the future aspects of the kingdom.[68] What is relevant to the question of chiliasm is the predominant reference to a heavenly as over against an earthly kingdom. This is sometimes interpreted as an apologetic attempt to allay fears by the governing authorities that Christianity was a disloyal revolutionary movement. But that consideration accounts for only a small number of the texts. The use of kingdom language in reference to heaven did not of itself exclude an earthly millennial kingdom, but in most cases it made no allowance for such.

A second trend, subsequent to the first, was a shift of focus from either an earthly or a heavenly kingdom to the present political kingdom.

The spread of Christianity in the third century brought into the church numbers of people with a concern for the affairs of state and society. The change in government policy under Constantine and his successors focused even more attention on the kingdom of this world. Eusebius of Caesarea saw the rule of Constantine as a foretaste of the eternal kingdom.[69] He followed Origen's theology but added his own emphasis on God's saving work in history. He held millenarians in contempt.[70] The seventh day represents repose in God after the resurrection of Christ, and the 1,000 years of Ps 90:4 is the period between the construction of the temple and the coming of Christ.[71] Not all were as enthusiastic about Constantine as Eusebius, but he does illustrate the changed situation of the fourth-century church.

A third trend represents a difference in degree. While a few apocalyptic works continued to be written, those of the fourth and fifth centuries were interested in the circumstances of individuals at death more than in the end of the cosmos.[72] The *Apocalypse of Paul* has the 1,000-year reign, but this is not its center of interest.[73] Thus the trend toward an individual in place of a communal eschatology was not incompatible with chiliasm, but it does correspond to the general pattern of nonchiliast eschatology that prevailed in the East and West, but especially in the East.

---

68. Ferguson, "The Kingdom of God in Early Patristic Literature" (ch. 12 in this volume).

69. Eusebius, *Life of Constantine* 1.3; *Praise of Constantine* 3.5.

70. Eusebius, *Church History* 3.39.11–13 on Papias and 7.24.1–2 on Nepos.

71. Eusebius, *Commentary on Psalms* 91.2–3; 90.4.

72. Luneau, *L'Histoire du salut chez les Pères de l'Église*, 110; Daley, *The Hope of the Early Church*, 120.

73. *Apocalypse of Paul* 21–22, which includes a description of the productivity of the earth similar to that in Papias.

*Millennial and Amillennial Expectations in Christian Eschatology*

## AUGUSTINE: HIS SETTING AND INFLUENCE

Augustine of Hippo (354–430) was a decisive influence on Western theology, including eschatology. He offered a nonchiliast interpretation of Revelation that became the majority view in the West. Some of his predecessors may be singled out for brief comment.[74] Hilary of Poitiers (ca. 315–ca. 367) accepted the chronology that counted the world's history as a "week" of 6,000 years, but he was no millennialist.[75] In contrast, although Ambrose disagreed with limiting the world's history to 6,000 years,[76] he thought the end of the world to be near. He followed Origen and other Eastern interpreters as well as Cyprian in taking the millennium of Revelation 20 as an allegory of the "interim" state between death and the general resurrection.[77] Jerome took apocalyptic predictions of the end of history as referring primarily to an individual's confrontation with death or to the ascetic's anticipation of death in controlling the passions.[78] So instead of six or seven ages, he distinguishes only two—the era here below and the blessed afterlife. His *Commentary on Daniel*[79] took apocalyptic themes more literally, but he pronounced a literal millennium a fable, though he granted that if shorn of materialistic Jewish hopes, it had a venerable tradition in the church.[80] He took Revelation 21 as referring to the historical church.[81] Particularly important for Augustine was the schismatic Donatist, Tyconius. He anticipated the eschatology of Augustine by applying Rev 20:1–6, as he did all biblical passages, to the time of the church, from the passion of the Lord until his second coming. The church reigns with Christ until the end of the world.[82]

---

74. Luneau, *L'Histoire du salut chez les Pères de l'Église*, 235–45, on Hilary of Poitiers; 247–61, on Ambrose; and 263–80, on Jerome.

75. Daley, *The Hope of the Early Church*, 94.

76. *Commentary on Luke* 7.7.

77. *On Psalms* 1.47–48. Daley, *Hope*, 97–100, discusses Ambrose.

78. See Daley, *The Hope of the Early Church*, 101, with reference to his *Commentary on Zephaniah* 1.14 and *Commentary on Isaiah* 6.14.1.

79. Archer, trans., *Jerome's Commentary on Daniel*; Braverman, *Jerome's Commentary on Daniel*; Daley, *The Hope of the Early Church*, 101–4.

80. For his opposition to millennialism, see *Commentary on Daniel* 7.17: "The saints shall never possess an earthly kingdom, but only a heavenly. Away, then, with the fable about a millennium"; and 7.25; *Commentary on Isaiah*, book 18, preface; *Commentary on Jeremiah* 19.10–11 and 31.38ff.

81. *Commentary on Ezekiel* 11.36.

82. Daley, *The Hope of the Early Church*, 127–31. For Tyconius and Augustine, see Fredriksen, "Tyconius and Augustine on the Apocalypse."

At the time of Augustine, there were many premillennialists in the Latin church, such as Gaudentius of Brescia and Hilarianus.[83] In his early career in the church, Augustine himself identified the "Sabbath to come" with the millennial kingdom of Revelation 20, and he considered this interpretation unobjectionable if the joys of the saints would be spiritual and not carnal.[84] By the time he wrote *City of God,* book 20, he had adopted the ecclesiological interpretation of the millennium, not in order to exalt the church but to clarify Christian eschatology. This identification of Rev 20:4–6 with the age of the church differed from the nonchiliastic Eastern interpretation that understood the 1,000 years as referring to the time between the soul's departure from the body and the return of Christ.

Augustine's interpretation of the first resurrection differs from the chiliast interpretation of the resurrection of the righteous when Christ returns at the beginning of the millennium, and from the interpretation found sometimes in Hippolytus and Origen that it refers to the resurrection of the souls of the righteous at their death. According to Augustine, the first resurrection is the spiritual resurrection in this life, and the second resurrection is at the end of the world for judgment.[85] The binding of Satan occurred with the work of Christ, and the 1,000 years has two possible interpretations. It refers either to the remaining years of the sixth millennium (which is now in progress and will be followed by the seventh day that has no evening and constitutes the endless rest of the saints) or to all the years to elapse to the end of the world, since 1,000 refers to perfection and marks the fullness of time.[86] At the end of this period, Satan will be loosed for three years and six months.[87] "The church is already now the kingdom of Christ and kingdom of heaven," and the saints (including the faithful dead) reign with Christ during the 1,000 years in which Satan is bound, although in a different way from the reigning in the world to come, when there will be no enemy.[88] For Augustine, the souls are judged at death but receive only a hint of their full destinies until the last judgment. The direct contemplative vision of God comes after the resurrection.[89] Some of those consigned to punishment at death may be helped by the

---

83. Daley, *The Hope of the Early Church,* 124, 127.
84. Augustine, *City of God* 20.7; *Sermon* 259.
85. *City of God* 20.6.
86. Ibid., 20.7; 22.30 on the seven ages.
87. Ibid., 20.8.
88. Ibid., 20.9.
89. Ibid., 22.29.

*Millennial and Amillennial Expectations in Christian Eschatology*

prayers of the faithful so that they are delivered after a period of time from torment.[90]

Augustine's influence meant that literal hopes for a 1,000-year earthly reign of Christ faded, and most persons avoided making predictions of the date of the end. In the period from 400 to 1000, visions of heaven and hell remained popular, current crises were sometimes seen as signs of an imminent end of the world, and the threat of the last judgment was still a powerful incentive for mission work and moral reform.[91] Gregory the Great, for instance, felt keenly that the end of the world was near, but he resisted apocalyptic calculations. The sense of an imminent end gave urgency to his preaching, works of charity, and interest in missions.[92]

Although Augustine came to have tremendous influence on Western thought, his authority did not put an end to millennial interpretations of Scripture and certainly not to apocalyptic expectations. He had no influence in the Greek East, where other influences diminished chiliasm but did not completely subdue it.

## THE BYZANTINE EAST AND MEDIEVAL WEST

The earliest-known extant Greek commentaries on Revelation were written in the sixth century. Current opinion assigns priority in date to the commentary by Oecumenius. He rejects a literal millennium and interprets the 1,000 years of Rev 20:1–7 as the "day" of Christ's first parousia. At the crucifixion of Christ, the devil is loosed to do his work. Nonetheless, new disciples are won, and their receiving life from the Holy Spirit is the "first resurrection."[93] The homilies on Revelation by Andrew of Caesarea in Cappadocia (563–614) became the standard commentary on the book in the Greek church. He notes various opinions on the 1,000 years, agreeing with Augustine that it is a symbol of completeness referring to the indefinite length of the period of preaching the gospel between the resurrection of Christ and the coming of antichrist.[94] Oecumenius and Andrew, each in his own way, plotted a moderate middle course be-

90. Cf. Daley, *The Hope of the Early Church*, 131–50, on all aspects of Augustine's eschatology.

91. McGinn, "The End of the World and the Beginning of Christendom," 62–64.

92. Ibid., 69–70.

93. Daley, *The Hope of the Early Church*, 180; Lamoreaux, "The Provenance of Ecumenius' Commentary on the Apocalypse."

94. Daley, *The Hope of the Early Church*, 198–99.

tween the eschatologies of Origen and of the chiliasts. Oecumenius was closer to Origen and Andrew more crtical of Origen, but both shared his rejection of a literal millennium. The state of theological thought in the East is shown by John of Damascus (ca. 650–ca. 749). When he wrote his *Exposition of the Orthodox Faith*, his discussion of eschatology treats only the antichrist and the resurrection, with no mention of the 1,000 years of Revelation.[95]

Art provides a further testimony to the prevailing nonchiliastic eschatology of the Greek East. Portrayals of the resurrection of Christ in middle Byzantine and later mosaics and frescoes take the form of the "Harrowing of Hell." As Christ comes from the tomb, he brings with him the faithful of the Old Testament. This artistic representation follows the earlier dogmatic interpretation that Christ in his resurrection broke the gates of Hades and released the souls of the righteous from Hades to accompany him to paradise.[96] This accords with the nonchiliastic eschatology that the righteous are in the presence of Christ, awaiting the great resurrection and judgment, and contradicts the chiliast eschatology that places the souls of all in Hades before the resurrection of the righteous, when Christ returns and inaugurates his earthly kingdom.

Times of crisis could bring a rebirth of apocalyptic speculation, and such a crisis was the Muslim invasion of the seventh century. A notable example is the book of *Revelations* from the latter half of the seventh century, attributed to the Methodius of the early fourth century and so known as Pseudo-Methodius.[97] The author wrote in Syriac, but his work was translated into Greek, Armenian, Arabic, and Slavonic. His work came to be well-known in western Europe in the Middle Ages through a Latin translation. His contributions to medieval apocalypticism include the incorporation of the legend of Alexander the Great into the apocalyptic timetable, his response to the Muslim crisis, and his expectation of the Last World Emperor. This apocalyptic work included the seventh millennium within present world history. In this final period of history, the "seed of Ishmael," the Muslims, will wipe out the Persian empire and bring Syria and Egypt under their yoke. A coming emperor would defeat these enemies of Christ, restore Roman glory, and surrender his crown to God. The antichrist would then rise, followed by the return of Christ. The idea

---

95. *Exposition of the Orthodox Faith* 4.26–27.

96. Schiller, *Ikonographie der christlichen Kunst*, Vol. 3, *Die Auferstehung and Erhöhung Christi*.

97. I follow McGinn, *Visions of the End*, 70–76.

of a Last World (or Roman) Emperor was often picked up in apocalyptic works, and hopes for his victory over the forces of evil substituted for the millennial expectations of a time of earthly goodness.[98]

Pseudo-Methodius illustrates how changing events forced a revision of eschatological interpretations in order to include in their timetables new historical circumstances. Richard Landes has shown how the passing of time brought revisions in eschatological timetables.[99] The first Christian chronological writings by Theophilus of Antioch and Clement of Alexandria in the second century were unconcerned with a Sabbath millennium. Hippolytus and Julius Africanus in the early third century established a chronology based on the "year of the world" (*annus mundi*) that placedced the incarnation 5,500 years after the creation. Hippolytus used this chronology in his *Commentany on Daniel* to argue that since the world will end in the year 6000, the end was still approximately 300 years away. He was opposing a certain Judas, who argued on the basis of Daniel that the appearance of antichrist was imminent. The persecution under Septimius Severus gave encouragement to this concern.[100] Eusebius's chronology put the beginning of Christ's ministry at the year of the world 5228. However, he did not conclude that the end was 500 years away because he did not accept the idea of a 6,000-year history for the world. After the fall of Rome, the Eusebian chronology gained currency over the soon-to-be-outdated Hippolytan chronology.

Theologians of the early Middle Ages continued to use chronological calculations to oppose apocalyptic fears, but they were committed to a calculation of the age of the earth that became more dangerous as the years went by.[101] Bede (673–734) produced new figures based on the Hebrew text of the Old Testament, which had lower numbers than the Greek version. In doing so he followed Jerome's translation based on the Hebrew, although Jerome had not used this information to revise Eusebius's *Chronicle* when he translated it into Latin. Bede placed the incarnation in the year of the world 3952, giving the world another 1,200 years. Only with the passing of the year 6000, according to the Eusebian calculation, did this new chronology of Bede's become the commonly accepted one. The crowning of Charlemagne in 800 occurred in the year 6000 of the world.

---

98. McGinn, "The End of the World and the Beginning of Christianity," 78.
99. Landes, "Lest the Millennium Be Fulfilled."
100. Eusebius, *Church History* 6.7.
101. Landes, "Lest the Millennium Be Fulfilled," 171.

Thus the renewing of the Roman empire in the West had eschatological significance.

Bede himself divided world history into six ages, but denied that this meant 6,000 years. Furthermore, he warned against those who believed the seventh period of 1,000 years would be an earthly one, arguing that no text supported the Sabbath millennium. Bede's *Commentary on Revelation* represented a moralized reading of Revelation dependent on Augustine.[102] The strategy of recalculating the age of the earth had the effect of keeping apocalyptic hopes alive while postponing their fulfillment.

This historical experience reminds me of a personal experience. When people learned that I was majoring in church history, they came to me with questions about the interpretation of the book of Revelation. They assumed that Revelation laid out Christian history in prophetic form. Thus, someone informed in church history should be able to tell what different passages were describing. The history of the interpretation of Revelation shows how this way of reading the book has led people of every age to revise the understanding of Revelation to accommodate new historical developments, typically placing themselves somewhere near the climactic closing chapters. The conversion of Constantine, the expansion of Islam, the rise of the western monarchies, the rule of Frederick II, and the Mongol invasion were among the prominent historical events accommodated to the framework of apocalyptic thought. With these observations, we turn to a few soundings of developments in the Western Middle Ages.

A major source for our knowledge of Tyconius's commentary on Revelation was the commentary written about 786 by Beatus (ca. 750–798), a Spanish monk. Beatus compiled excerpts from earlier Latin writers, especially Tyconius, and followed the Tyconian/Augustinian line of interpretation. His became the most influential medieval commentary on Revelation. It was the most widely copied work among the illuminated manuscripts produced in Spain from the ninth to thirteenth centuries (32 copies) and so is important not only in the history of interpretation of Revelation, but also in iconography.[103]

---

102. Ibid., 175–77; McGinn, "The End of the World," 70–71.

103. See McGinn, *Visions of the End*, 77–79, and references in his notes; to which add Matter, "The Apocalypse in Early Medieval Exegesis," 45–46; and for the illustrations, Klein, "Introduction: The Apocalypse in Medieval Art," 186–88 (Beatus Manuscripts and Related Cycles); and Williams, "Purpose and Imagery in the Apocalypse Commentary of Beatus of Liebana."

## Millennial and Amillennial Expectations in Christian Eschatology

The year 1000 seems not to have occasioned as much eschatological excitement as some have thought.[104] The common people were not greatly aware of the year. For those who were conscious of chronology, the age of the world gave no significance to the year 1000. Only if one followed literally Augustine's interpretation of 1,000 years as the age of the church would the year potentially have had significance. But devoted followers of Augustine knew that he took the number as symbolic of perfection and not as the literal length of the church period. The surviving literature from this time provides only a small base of data from which to draw conclusions, so there may have been more excitement than we can confirm. Yet the concern was mainly with turning millennial symbolism to the support of the institutions of society, and eschatological thought gave more attention to the expected coming of the antichrist than to Christ's second coming.[105]

Eschatological views developed in an amillennial framework. Church leaders argued that even after the antichrist was slain, "No one knows how great a space of time there may be . . . until the Lord comes to judge."[106] Gerhoh of Reichersberg (ca. 1092–1169) saw the 1,000 years beginning with the passion of Christ as significant, but his application of antichrist language to current events involved a reinterpretation of eschatological imagery. He noted that more than 1,000 years had elapsed from the passion of Christ, when Satan was bound, before he was loosed in the form of the opposition of King Henry IV to the papacy in the later eleventh century. He viewed the antichrist as a collective of all who had opposed the righteous since the time of Cain, but he found special manifestations in the worldly church and in the imperial enemies of the church.[107] A late twelfth-century apocalyptic text, The Erythraean Sibyl, declared that the Last Judgment would follow the antichrist.[108] Anselm of Havelberg (ca. 1100–1158) placed the seventh age after the judgment and collapsed it into the eighth day.[109]

---

104. For the evidence, see Fried, "Endzeiterwartung um die Jahrtausendwende."

105. McGinn, *Visions of the End*, 88–90.

106. Adso, *Letter on the Origin and Life of the Antichrist*, written ca. 950; quoted in McGinn, *Visions of the End*, 87. From comments made by Jerome, later writers speculated about the length of time and purpose of the period after the defeat of Antichrist, sometimes describing it in terms related to earlier millennial thought. See Lerner, "Refreshment of the Saints."

107. McGinn, *Visions of the End*, 96–97, 99–100.

108. Ibid., 124.

109. *Dialogues*, book 1, quoted in McGinn, *Visions of the End*, 114, 116.

Medieval Western art also testifies to an amillennial eschatology by showing the fusion of the present reign of Christ in glory with the last judgment, not allowing for an earthly interval. This had been evident in earlier sculpture, but found grandiose expression in the triumphal arches adorning the entrances to Romanesque and Gothic churches.[110]

Hildegard of Bingen (1098–1179), German abbess and prophetess, saw both the empire and the papacy failing as the time of crisis unfolded.[111] Christ was incarnate in the sixth age, as Adam was created on the sixth day, a parallel also made by Augustine. The world in her time was in its seventh age, "approaching the end of time."[112] The seventh age is a Sabbath that may be indefinitely prolonged. She put no timetable on her visions. The time of trouble had begun with the attacks of Henry IV against the church in the eleventh century. Hildegard described five ferocious epochs to come. The career of the antichrist is a parody that reverses the career of Christ. At an unspecified time after the fall of antichrist, the last judgment will come and history will end. Before the end of the world, the devil will perish and "the Son of Man will be brilliantly and beautifully seen in the Catholic faith. The truth will be plainly shown in Him."[113] She had no chiliastic thoughts. The end-time sequence is the resurrection, the Son coming in human form to judge, and God receiving the elect while hell swallows up the damned. In addition to salvation history, her visions concerned the torments and joys of the afterlife.

Robert Lerner affirms that the first medieval commentator to take the 1,000 years of Revelation 20 literally was Alexander Minorita (a German Franciscan), whose commentary on Revelation in 1235 applied the 1,000 years to the time between the triumph of Christianity under Constantine and the last judgment, expected about 1326.[114] Thomas Aquinas

---

110. See, for example, the pictures in Williamson, *Gothic Sculpture 1140-1300*, *passim*. Christe, "The Apocalypse in the Monumental Art of the Eleventh through Thirteenth Centuries," argues that imagery from Revelation was ecclesiological rather than eschatological before the mid-thirteenth century, when it began to focus on the end of time and the last judgment. Cf. in the same work, Klein, "Introduction: The Apocalypse in Medieval Art," 162–64.

111. McGinn, *Visions of the End*, 97. Cf. Hart and Bishop, trans., *Hildegard of Bingen: Scivias*. Pages 493–521 translate book III, chap. 11, on "The Last Days and the Fall of Antichrist"; and chap. 12, on "The New Heaven and the New Earth." A summary of these chapters begins on p. 42.

112. Hart and Bishop, trans., *Hildegard of Bingen: Scivias*, 42.

113. Ibid., 496–70.

114. Lerner, "The Medieval Return to the Thousand-Year Sabbath," 60.

spoke for scholastic theology in maintaining a strict Augustinian view of eschatology. He judged chiliasm to be a heresy.[115]

## JOACHIM OF FIORE AND HIS SUCCESSORS

An unexpected blending of Augustinian views on the age of the church with millennial apocalyptic interpretations produced a postmillennial scheme, but without its terminology or the expectation of a literal 1,000 years. Joachim of Fiore in Calabria (southern Italy; ca. 1135–1202) turned eschatological thought from the Tyconian/Augustinian framework back to an emphasis on historical sequence.

Joachim was one of the most original thinkers of the Middle Ages and one of the most disturbing influences in the apocalyptic fervor of the later Middle Ages. We will simplify here a complex and sometimes contradictory system of thought.[116] Joachim offered a Trinitarian scheme of history. The first age, the age of the Father, was the period of marriage under the Law of Moses. The second age, the age of the Son, was the period of the clergy under grace that was to last 1,260 years. The third age, the age of the Spirit, will be the age of the monks, who having the mind of the Spirit, would live in liberty without the mediation of the church. The last age would see the rise of new religious orders that would convert the world and usher in the Church of the Spirit. Joachim's word was actually not age but the Latin *status*. It is conventionally described as an "age" because it does represent a periodization. The word might better be thought of as referring to a "condition" or "constitution" that leads to a "climax."

In interpreting Revelation historically, Joachim broke with the allegorical interpretation of the book, but he viewed history as evolutionary, not revolutionary. The three periods or conditions are organically connected. The first began under Adam and flourished under the Law. The second period had its germination in the time of king Uzziah (in the forty-second generation since Adam), but flourished under the Gospel of Christ. The third period had its beginning with Benedict, the founder of

---

115. *Summa contra Gentiles* IV, 83; *Summa Theologiae* III, Supp. ques. 77, art. 1 (posthumously edited), both with reference to Augustine.

116. The literature on Joachim and his followers is considerable. For orientation, see Reeves, *Joachim of Fiore and the Prophetic Future*; and McGinn, *The Calabrian Abbot*. For this brief treatment I follow esp. McGinn, *Visions of the End*, 126–41. Note also the contributions by Lerner, "The Medieval Return to the Thousand-Year Sabbath," 57–60; and Daniel, "Joachim of Fiore: Patterns of History in the Apocalypse," 72–88; both in *The Apocalypse in the Middle Ages*, ed. Emmerson and McGinn.

the Benedictine monks (in the forty-second generation since Uzziah). Its surpassing excellence will flourish near the end of the forty-second generation from Christ, when the defeat of antichrist will occur. "After the destruction of this Antichrist there will be justice on earth and an abundance of peace," during which time the dragon "will be imprisoned in the abyss"[117] until his release before the final conflict. Joachim, therefore, applied the 1,000 years of Revelation 20 to the time between the antichrist and the end, a future earthly sabbath of spiritual delights that would be short in duration, not a literal 1,000 years. Joachim's own time was the fortieth generation of the second status, but he did not think it was possible to calculate the length of the last two generations, for they might be quite short in time.[118]

Joachim differed from the papal view of the church in that his expectations of an angelic pope did not match the image of the institutional papacy. His view of history and eschatology differed from Augustine's inasmuch as he expected a new and better church on earth before the Lord comes. Nor was his expectation of a spiritual age a revival of earlier millenarianism, for he looked for a renewed church and not the biblical kingdom of God on earth.[119] He did not consider the 1,000 years to be literal and did not expect Christ himself to reign during that time. But Joachim's views were related to each. The spiritual church germinates from the papal church. His vision of the future may be seen as an outgrowth of Augustine's spiritual view of the age of the church. His third condition is in two respects a kind of transposition of ancient millennialism—from material prosperity on the earth into a spirituality lived on this earth, and from the time after to the time before the return of Christ. His third status of the Holy Spirit is the symbolic 1,000-year kingdom of Revelation of indefinite but short duration, and is itself followed by another assault from Satan unloosed again. In this regard, one could speak anachronistically of a kind

---

117. Quoted by McGinn, *Visions of the End*, 138. See Joachim's *Book of Concordance*, book 2, part 1, chap. 4–5, translated in McGinn, *Apocalyptic Spirituality*, 124–25.

118. Joachim had various formulations of the three status. *Figurae* suggests a somewhat different scheme of germination, growth, and fructification: The first status began with Adam, was in sterility until the time of Abraham, and reached fecundity with John the Baptist. The second status springs from the "node" formed by Hagar, was sterile until John, but the church was conceived in Elizabeth and is fecund until the (Joachim's) present. The third status springs from the "node" of Elizabeth, but the church of the Holy Spirit was conceived in Mary and is sterile until the (Joachim's) present. See Reeves and Hirsch-Reich, *The* Figurae *of Joachim of Fiore*, 164–65.

119. McGinn, *Visions of the End*, 146.

of postmillennialism, but of shorter duration and without the optimistic secular features of modern postmillennialism.

Did Joachim replace Christ as the goal of Christian expectations with the Holy Spirit, and thus give the Holy Spirit a significance greater than Christ in his scheme? This was not his intention, but if such was the effect, he was not the first nor the last to flirt with this enchantment. He certainly did have the effect of reducing the significance of the institutional church. His prophecies could be read as optimistic about the future, based on biblical assurances of the victory of God over evil; or as pessimistic, critical of the existing institutional church. It was in the latter sense that his influence was to be felt. His description of the "spiritual men" of the last age fired the imagination of those who saw themselves as the forerunners of the Church of the Spirit. Joachim's prophecies had great influence on apocalyptic speculations of the late Middle Ages.[120]

After the Fourth Lateran Council (1215) condemned Joachim's attack on the trinitarian theology of Peter Lombard, the followers of Joachim became increasingly anti-papal. They did what he did not do, setting the year 1260 as the date for the beginning of the new age. Greater expectancy was associated with this year than had been with the year 1000. Joachim's ideas gained entrance into the Franciscan order, and John of Parma (their minister general, 1247-1257) identified their founder, Francis of Assisi, as the angel of the sixth seal of Revelation 7:2.[121] Bonaventura, the next minister general of the Franciscans (1257-1274), divided the history of the church into seven ages. His own time belonged to the sixth age, for he followed John of Parma in identifying Francis with the sixth angel of Revelation 7:2, but he saw this sixth age as running together with the seventh. The seventh age is of indefinite length but has characteristics that belonged to earlier premillennial expectations and so represents a kind of postmillennialism without the time frame.[122]

In the late thirteenth and early fourteenth century, there was a sharp conflict within the Franciscans between the Conventuals and the Spirituals. The Conventuals modified the practice of mendicancy and accommodated to the other religious orders and the wishes of the papacy. The Spirituals, however, insisted on a rigorous interpretation of Francis's ideal of poverty. They saw the practice of "apostolic poverty," which they understood to have been the lifestyle of Jesus and the apostles, as not only

---

120. Ibid., 147.
121. Ibid., 159-60.
122. See the quotations of Bonaventura in McGinn, *Visions of the End*, 197-200.

the distinctive essence of their order, but also as what qualified them as the "spiritual men" who would lead the church in the impending last days predicted by Joachim.

A notable thinker among the Spiritual Franciscans was Peter John Olivi (ca. 1248–1298), active in southern France. He saw the fifth and sixth ages of the history of the church as overlapping, a time in which he located himself. The carnal church of the fifth age is renewed by the spiritual revival of the sixth age, during which the persecution by the antichrist is also unleashed. The seventh period of peace and spirituality precedes the coming of Gog and the coming of Christ for the last judgment.[123] He found three different interpretations for the binding of Satan that begins the millennium: the death and resurrection of Christ, the expulsion of idolatry in the time of Constantine, and the death of antichrist in the seventh age.[124] Olivi differed from Joachim in expecting the age of the Spirit to be lengthy and in considering, because of the persecution of the Spirituals, a false Pope (Boniface VIII) as potentially the image of the beast and one manifestation of antichrist (a hesitancy no longer observed by the later Spirituals of his order). He placed the seven ages of the church before the return of Christ. The seventh is Joachim's third age of the Holy Spirit, a sabbath time of peace and participation on earth in the future heavenly glory, beginning about the year 1300, lasting until the year 2000, and leading into the other life of the general resurrection. Olivi not only reduced the period from a literal 1,000 years, but he also specifically excluded the premillennial interpretation, for this is the age of the Holy Spirit, not of Christ's kingdom.[125] In placing all seven ages, including the "millennium" of whatever length, before the coming of Christ, Olivi was followed by other Spirituals like Ubertino of Casale (ca. 1259–ca. 1330).[126]

In the later Middle Ages, the heads of the two great institutions of the medieval world, the emperor and the pope, figured in contradictory ways in eschatological expectations, depending on one's political and religious loyalties. The emperor might be viewed as the "Good Emperor,"

---

123. McGinn, *Visions of the End*, 204–5; Lerner, "The Medieval Return to the Thousand-Year Sabbath," 61–66; Lewis, "Peter John Olivi," 222–40.

124. Lewis, "Peter John Olivi," 234–35; Froom, *The Prophetic Faith of Our Fathers*, 775 and 780, for the same options in Ubertino of Casale.

125. Lewis, "Peter John Olivi," 234, 238–39.

126. McGinn, *Visions of the End*, 212. Lerner, "The Medieval Return to the Thousand-Year Sabbath," 67, reports that in 1349, John of Rupescissa calculated that after antichrist came in 1366 and was destroyed in 1369, a Sabbath of a literal 1,000 years would follow.

## Millennial and Amillennial Expectations in Christian Eschatology

God's instrument for bringing in the good times to come; or he might be seen as the "imperial antichrist," a forerunner of the Antichrist. The pope might be viewed as the "Angelic Pope," or he might be accused as the "papal antichrist."[127] The latter judgment came not only from the Spiritual Franciscans but was also voiced by Dante.

By the end of the Middle Ages, the three principal options regarding the place of a millennium in Christian eschatology—amillennialism, premillennialism, and postmillennialism—had found advocates.[128]

---

127. McGinn, "Angel Pope and Papal Antichrist." The term antichrist had been applied to an unworthy Pope already by Arnulf, bishop of Orleans, at a synod at Rheims in 991, and later by Robert Grosseteste (ca. 1170–1253). In the thirteenth century, Emperor Frederick II called Pope Gregory IX antichrist. Gregory returned the favor, calling him the "beast from the sea"; Froom, *The Prophetic Faith of Our Fathers*, 541–42, 624, 795–96.

128. For brief historical overviews of the different options, note Bauckham, "Millennium," 428–29; Clouse, "Millennium, Views of the."

# 15

# Number Symbolism in the Ancient World

NUMBER SYMBOLISM WAS VERY important in the ancient Mediterranean world, but because it is foreign to modern ways of thinking, students and scholars often miss its significance. This paper will highlight a few features of the cultural background and give some examples of early Christian use of number symbolism in order to highlight the importance of this neglected aspect of early Christian thinking.

I am using number symbolism and numerology as equivalent terms. By number symbolism or numerology I refer to the practice of using numbers to express hidden realities, or (in reverse) finding meanings in numbers beyond their bare numerical value. These hidden realities or meanings often were seen to explain the secrets of the universe. Roots of this practice lie in the ancient Near East, but it was among the Greeks that the practice achieved full development. The early Christians drew on both backgrounds when they used numbers to express esoteric meanings.

In ancient Egypt four, as a round number, was a holy number. The holiness of eight and later sixteen (in the Greco-Roman period) was dependent on their relation to the number four. After four, seven was the most common holy number, and it later replaced four in importance. Special significance was given to other numbers as well. Both four and seven continued to be the most important holy numbers in the Egyptian magical papyri (in Greek and in Demotic).

## Number Symbolism in the Ancient World

In Babylonia seven indicated the whole and so was considered a perfect number. Its components, three and four, also had significance—three as a superlative and an expression of completeness, and four to refer to all sides and so what was universal. These meanings in themselves indicated no special number symbolism but opened the way to ascribing a mystical value to numbers.

In the Old Testament some numbers were important—e.g., ten (ten plagues on Egypt and ten commandments), twelve (twelve patriarchs and twelve tribes of Israel) and forty as a round number for periods of time (in days, Moses on Mt. Sinai; and years, Israel's wandering in the wilderness). But no number rivals seven in frequency of occurrence and importance And only for seven can symbolic significance be claimed in some cases. It was the preeminent holy number. Seven stood for completeness or wholeness, as in Babylonia, although not in every case of its use. Seven had continued importance for Jewish thinkers. Philo, for instance, devoted extended treatment to the meaning and prevalence of the number seven, a number in which "Nature takes delight," he says (*Leg. All.* 1.8–20; *Op. Mund.* 89–128).

Astronomical observations in Babylonia and Egypt combined with the use in the Old Testament of seven for a full period of time and seventy for an extended and self-contained period fed apocalyptic speculations among Jews. The numbers seven, ten, and twelve occur frequently in apocalyptic literature. The accounts of heavenly phenomena and periodization of history gave numbers in apocalyptic literature a symbolic significance that goes beyond their importance in the scriptures. The "Book of the Heavenly Luminaries" (*1 Enoch* 76–77) has a concentration of symbolic numbers—twelve openings for the winds, four directions, seven mountains, and seven rivers. The "Apocalypse of Weeks" has seven periods of history (seven "weeks"), the last a time of apostasy followed by the messianic age of righteousness (*1 Enoch* 93.2–10). In *1 Enoch* 91.12–17 from the same apocalypse, there are ten weeks, the last of which is judgment. Seven visions structure the book of *4 Ezra*. The number eight appears as a symbol for eternity, unending in contrast to the periods of time, according to *2 Enoch* 33.1–2, but that passage is possibly a Christian rewriting.

Among the Greeks, Pythagoras was particularly important in the development of number symbolism. Pythagoras observed that musical intervals could be expressed by arithmetic ratios. This led to his understanding of numbers as the primary reality and the key to the universe (Aristotle, *Metaphysics* 1.5.1–2, 985b–986a). Furthermore, he or his followers discovered that the same relationships existing in musical intervals existed between the position of the planets in heaven. Hence, the Pythagoreans correlated musical harmony with the movements of the planets to produce what was known as the "music of the spheres." Both music and the movements of the heavenly bodies could be expressed by mathematical formulas.

Pythagoreans considered the number ten as especially sacred, but they also called attention to the importance of seven. There were seven vowels in the Greek alphabet, seven notes to the musical scale, seven stars in the constellation Pleiades, seven heroes attacked Thebes. Pythagoreans then went further to suggest that things with the same number are in some way the same (Aristotle, *Metaphysics* 14.6.3–5, 1093a-b).

The use in Greek of letters of the alphabet to stand for the cardinal numbers (*alpha* = one, *beta* = two, etc.) facilitated the development of number symbolism among the followers of Pythagoras and others. The use of letters to stand for numerical values by the Hebrews and Romans seems to have been borrowed from the Greeks.

The widespread influence of Pythagorean number symbolism by the beginning of the Christian era is seen in the "Dream of Scipio" recorded by Cicero. The numbers seven and eight, for different reasons, were considered perfect numbers (*Resp.* 6.12). The universe consists of nine spheres: Heaven, the circuits of the seven planets (Saturn, Jupiter, Mars, Sun, Venus, Mercury, Moon), and the sphere of the Earth (6.17). Human music imitates the music of the spheres, and the number seven is the key to almost everything (seven notes in the musical scale, seven planets, seven vowels in the alphabet—6.18).

Significant for religious history is that Mithraism took over this world view and had seven stages of initiation corresponding to the seven planets (Origen, *C. Cels.* 6.22).

The magical papyri show influence from Egyptian, Babylonian, Jewish, and Greek ideas. Elements from all these cultures appear in magic and contributed to the frequency of certain numbers like three, seven, and twelve in the formulas and practices in the magical papyri. The instructions often call for reciting spells seven times or three times (e.g., *PMG* IV.955–60; XXIIB.26). Several spells invoke the god whose name has seven letters (ΙΑΩ ΟΥΕΗ) in harmony with the seven sounds of the planets (*PMG* XII. 252–53). This occurs in a prayer for consecration of an Abrasax ring and elsewhere (XIII.775–79; XXI.10–12). A Coptic Christian book of healing spells instructs: "Make seven strings, . . . , bind them and make seven knots, and look toward the east and say seven times, "Lord Gabriel,

## Number Symbolism in the Ancient World

lord Gabriel, lord Gabriel, heal the patient" (Michigan 136; Meyer and Smith, 85).

I have mentioned the use of letters of the alphabet to stand for numbers. The Greeks knew two systems of using letters for numbers. The *thĕsis* or straight-line system gave a numerical value to letters by their position in the alphabet. The Milesian system was more common: it included three additional signs to the twenty-four letters of the alphabet and beginning with *iota* the letters stood for ten and its multiples and beginning with *rho* stood for the hundreds.

This use of letters to stand for numbers gave rise to gemátria and isopsephy. Gemátria is the adding of the numerical values of the letters of a word or name and designating that word by the numerical total. Isopsephy is substituting one word for another when two or more words have an equal numerical value. I will note examples of each of these practices as I proceed.

A common example of gematria—that is, a number and a name as identical—is the name Abrasax, the name given to the god of the year, identified by Egyptians with the sun, their great god. The numerical value of Abrasax, by totaling the number equivalents of each letter in the name, is 365 (the number of days in a year). In this case, instead of the name coming first and the numerical equivalent standing for the name, it is probable that a name was devised to stand for the numerical total. In other words, the symbolism is the explanation for the giving of the name. An invocation in the magical papyri reads, "You are the number of [the days of] the year, Abrasax" (*PGM* XIII.156; VIII.49). One spell prescribes making 365 knots in a thread while saying, "Abrasax, hold her fast" (*PGM* IV.330–32).

Abrasax also offers an example of isopsephy—that is, two names with the same numerical value identified with each other. One spelling of Mithras (Meithras) also gave the number 365. So Mithras was identified with Abrasax. Jerome gives us the information: "Basilides called the omnipotent God by the more fantastic name Abrasax, and that name he said contains, according to the Greek letters, the number of the course of the year in the circuit of the sun. The pagans under the same number by other letters call him 'Meithras'" (*In Amos* 1.3.9–10).

Another example of isopsephy from the magical papyri occurs in the invocation, "I call your name Horus [=Helios], which is in number equivalent to those of the Moirai [Fates]" (*PGM* I.455; also I.325; IV.1985).

Magical gems carrying the name Abrasax and depicting a composite creature with snake feet, human torso, and varied heads (a cock, a dog, an ass) may or may not be attempts to personify Abrasax.

A curious example comes from magical papyri and gems used as amulets that employ letters whose numerical equivalent is 9,999. "You [the most great and mighty god] have given me as a gift the knowledge of your most great name [and so the power to compel the god's action], of which the number is 9,999 [followed by a string of letters]" (*PGM* II.126-31). This text, like several in the magical papyri, employs Jewish divine names.

With this perhaps overly long introduction, which I thought necessary in order to set the historical and cultural context, I move to Christian texts. But I make the transition by referring first to those texts describing the people called Gnostics. Christian anti-heretical writers fastened on the extensive use of number symbolism by those whom they labelled "Gnostics."

Irenaeus gives a lengthy treatment to the symbolic value given to letters and numbers by Marcus the Valentinian (*A.H.* 1.14-16) and Valentinians in general (*A.H.* 2.20-25). The Pleroma (divine fullness) of the Valentinians comprised thirty aeons, symbolized by Jesus' age of thirty at his baptism (*A.H.* 1.1.3; 1.3.1; 2.22.1, 4-5). The thirty aeons were grouped as a decad (represented by *iota*, the first letter of Jesus' name and standing for ten—*A.H.* 1.3.2), a duodecad (symbolized by Jesus' teaching at the age of twelve, the woman with a hemorrhage for twelve years, and the twelve apostles—*A. H.* 1.3.2; 2.20-21), and two tetrads (groups of four). The word Pleroma itself, according to the *thĕsis* system of assigning numbers to letters in their alphabetical order, equalled 88. The ogdoad (eight) was particularly important in Gnostic thought. Irenaeus says that for them it was "the root and substance of all things" (*A.H.* 1.1). Eight represented the eternal realm outside this world (cf. the eighth heaven in *Hypostasis of the Archons* from the Nag Hammadi library—NHC II 95,34). Thus it was significant that the name Jesus in Greek according to the usual or Milesian system of assigning numerical values to letters was 888 (*A.H.* 1.15.2; 2.24.1; Hippolytus, *Ref.* 6.45). This was a fact appreciated even by a writer not associated with heretical views—in the Christian *Or. Sib.* 1.324-29. Basilides included in his system 365 heavens, at the head of which, as noted above and according to his earlier opponents Irenaeus (*A.H.* 1.24.3, 7) and Ps.-Tertullian (*Adv. omn. haer.* 1), was Abrasax.

Other Christians also made use of number symbolism. Some numbers in the New Testament seemed to have been employed for their

## Number Symbolism in the Ancient World

symbolic significance. It is generally recognized that Jesus chose twelve apostles (Luke 6:13; Matt 19:28) as symbolic of the reconstituted Israel. It has been plausibly suggested that Matthew arranges the genealogy of Jesus in three groups of fourteen generations (Matt 1:17), because the name David in Hebrew (דָּוִד) has the numerical total of fourteen, so there is gemátria with a theological motif. The number of the beast, 666, in Rev 13:18 is stated to be the number of a person, so an instance of gemátria. If we have a name, it is easy to calculate the numerical equivalent; the reverse is not so easy, for many letter combinations will give the desired total, so the passage has challenged commentators through the centuries. The number of 1,000 years for the period of the binding of Satan and the reign of the saints (Rev 20:2–4, 6) must have been chosen for some significance of its own, since we do not encounter this period for the messianic kingdom in previous apocalyptic literature.

A curious detail is the 153 fish caught by the disciples after the resurrection of Jesus (John 21:11). Why not a round number, 150? Indeed, why any number at all, for no numbers are recorded in other miraculous catches of fish (Luke 5:6). An ingenious modern interpretation employs an ancient interpretative device known as *atbash*. This technique employs writing the letters of the alphabet in reverse direction and substituting the letter that falls in the equivalent position. It is suggested that John 21:11 uses *atbash* to create gemátria. If the Greek alphabet is written in reverse (Semitic order) without the three added letters used in the normal Greek numerical system, Ι becomes 70, Χ becomes 3, and Θ becomes 80. The total is 153. These are the first letters of Jesus, Christ, God. And so we have a hidden confession of faith. The 153 fish represent Christians, identified with Christ. A further step in interpretation sees this symbolism in John as the origin of the fish acrostic and fish symbolism in early Christianity, by which ΙΧΘ expanded to ΙΧΘΥΣ, "Jesus Christ, God's Son, Savior," elaborated by Tertullian that Christians are little fishes in relation the Christ, the Great Fish.

Early Christian writers wrestled with the meaning of some of these numbers in Scripture. Irenaeus thought the name designated by 666 (he rejected the alternative reading 616) to be insoluble before the appearance of Antichrist, but he noted the possibility of *Lateinos* (Latin) as the name for the last of the four kingdoms of Daniel 2 and *Teitan* (Titan) as the name for a ruler who brings vengeance. He thought the triple sixes indicated the full extent of apostasy (*A.H.* 5.29.2–30.4). Methodius analyzed the figures in the total 1,260 days (Rev 12:6) for their symbolic significance (*Banq.* 8.11).

Chiliasts, like Justin (*Dial.* 80.5) and Irenaeus (*A.H.* 5.31–36), took the 1,000 years of Revelation 20 literally as the period of Christ's reign on earth after his second coming. Amillennialists, like Origen (*Princ.* 4.1.22; 2.11.6–7; *Dial. Heracl.*) and Augustine (*Civ. Dei* 20.6–9), understood the binding of Satan and the 1,000 years to have begun with the death and resurrection of Jesus and so to be symbolic of the Christian age or of the completeness of Christ's victory.

Augustine's mind was attuned to number symbolism. He began his interpretation of the 153 fish by noting the presence of seven disciples, standing for the end of time. He analyzed the 153 into ten (=the law) and seven (=Holy Spirit); the two together are seventeen, and if one adds all the digits from one through seventeen the total is 153. This represents all who share in the grace of the Holy Spirit. His fertile mind further suggested that the three stood for the Trinity, fifty for Pentecost, then multiplied by three; fifty was also seven times seven plus one for the Holy Spirit who gives seven gifts to humanity (*Tract. Ioan.* 122.6, 8).

I'll take some examples now according to some early Christian writings.

The *Epistle of Barnabas* found the heart of the gospel in a most unlikely place to our way of thinking—the 318 servants of Abraham whom he circumcised (Gen 14:14; 17:23). Eighteen was written *iota* and *ēta*, the first two letters of Jesus' name in Greek (Irenaeus, *A.H.* 1.14.4, noted Gnostic use of these letters), and 300 was *tau* (the shape of a cross). So the number 318 gave Jesus and him crucified (9.7–9). This symbolic interpretation occurs more extensively in Clement of Alexandria, *Str.* 6.11; also Ps. Cyprian, *Pasch. comp.* 10. The rabbis took an interest in this number 318 also and found in it the name Eliezer (*Midrash Rabbah Genesis* 4.3.2). The power of this symbolism became evident in the Trinitarian controversy of the fourth century when the significance of 318 was the decisive consideration for later writers in determining the number of bishops who approved the Nicene creed in AD 325 (Hilary, *Synod.* 86; Ambrose, *Fide* 1. prol. 3, 5; 1.18.121). Earlier writers had given smaller round figures, but 318 became the canonical figure and indeed the shorthand for referring to the decisions at Nicaea.

*Barnabas* was the first to designate the day of Christian meeting as the "eighth day" (first day of the week or Sunday) instead of the Jewish seventh day (Sabbath). There is for him the further symbolism that the six days of creation stand for 6,000 years, after which the Lord returns, and the eighth day stands for the beginning of another world (15.1-9). This is not a millennial scheme, as many assume, for *Barnabas* does not have an intermediate seventh age. He collapses seven into eight for the periods of the world in a similar manner to the way eight supersedes the Jewish seventh day.

The apologist Theophilus of Antioch found a Christian meaning in the six days of creation. The first three days were types of the "Triad of God, his Word [Christ], and his Wisdom [Holy Spirit]" (*Ad Autol.* 2.15). This is our first surviving use of the language of a triad, or Trinity, for the three divine persons.

Irenaeus considered his four-Gospel canon to be the only possible number of Gospels because four coresponded to the four zones of the world, the four winds, and the four living creatures of Rev 4:7 (*A.H.* 3.11.8). Modern scholars, not appreciating the significance of number symbolism for the ancients and misunderstanding how it worked, have scoffed at Irenaeus's argument. But it would be to misapprehend the situation to imagine that Irenaeus thought that his examples of fours were the reason he determined four Gospels to be canonical. It was because he had four Gospels that he saw the appropriateness of this number. The appeal to four in the structure of the world and in the heavenly beings would have had more persuasive force to his readers than to us, but regardless, we should not mistake the historical sequence as to which was causative: his argument from symbolism is secondary to his testimony of having four Gospels.

Clement of Alexandria drew on his acquaintance with philosophical and poetic writings to make frequent use of number symbolism. Ten is "the perfect number," he says (*Str.* 6.11). He reports that some interpreted the dimensions of the Tabernacle—300 by 50 by 30 cubits—so that the 300 was a symbol of the Lord's sign (the cross—*tau*, or T, you remember is 300), 50 the hope of forgiveness offered at Pentecost (Acts 2), and 30 the preaching of the gospel, since the Lord preached in his thirtieth year (or on the variant reading of twelve, then the preaching of the twelve apostles) (*Str.* 6.11). His commentary on the Decalogue is introduced by the comment, "That ten is a sacred number it is superfluous to say," and the suggestion that perhaps the two tables may be a prophecy of the two covenants. His discussion of the Sabbath commandment occasioned considerable treatment of the numbers six, seven, and eight (*Str.* 6.16).

Now a few words about particular numbers. The number seven continued to be meaningful for Christians, as it was for Jews. Contrary to some authors, for whom seven in the periodization of history stood for the present sinful time, seven had for Irenaeus and Tertullian a positive eschatological sense as standing for the millennial kingdom (Irenaeus, *Haer.* 5.30.4; Tertullian, *An.* 37.4). Cyprian has an extensive listing of sevens in the Bible (*Test.* 1.20). Jerome says concerning his interpretations of Scripture: "Without adhering to everything literally, we leave untouched the secrets of numbers. For the Sabbath certifies that the number seven is sacred" (*In Amos* 2.5.3). This continuing importance of seven may be seen in a perhaps unexpected way. The number seven was important in early Christian letter collections. Revelation was addressed to seven churches (Rev 1:11). Paul wrote to seven churches (we overlook this fact because there are two letters each to the Corinthians and the Thessalonians), and the *Muratorian Fragment* pointed out that by writing to seven churches he and John in Revelation were writing to all the churches (lines 56–59; Cyprian, *Test.* 1.20 also points out that Paul and the Apocalypse addressed seven churches). This feature was a factor in delineating the canon. There were seven letters also in the collection of Ignatius's letters.

The number eight, as indicated above, was important as standing for the eternal realm (in Gnosticism) and the world to come (in apocalypticism), and it became the most important symbolic number for early Christians. The resurrection of Jesus on the Jewish first day of the week (the Roman Sunday), which by the inclusive method of counting was also the eighth day (John 20:1, 19, 26) appears to have been decisive for the development of the Christian symbolism of eight as representing resurrection, eternal life, and the world to come. This symbolism was related to other biblical occurrences of the number eight (circumcision on the eighth day after birth—Lev 12:3; Luke 2:21 and the eight persons saved on the ark of Noah—Gen 7:13; 1 Pet 3:20-21 in a baptismal context). The number eight trumped the Jewish adherence to the number seven. For Origen seven, standing for the seven-day week, is the time of the present life, but eight is the world to come, for on it is received the purified flesh by the resurrection (*Lev. hom.* 8.4). He expressed the symbolism succinctly, "As eight is the symbol of the world to come, containing the power of the resurrection, so seven is the symbol of this world" (*Sel. Ps.*).

Hence, eight assumed architectural significance in the octagon, a common shape for baptisteries and martyria. For Christians, spiritual circumcision, resurrection to new life, salvation from sin, and hope for the world to come were received in baptism; hence the octagonal shape was especially prominent in baptisteries and baptismal fonts. Mausolea and funerary memorials sometimes took a circular shape in the Roman world, but the association of eight with resurrection and the world to come made the octagon common in Christian memorial buildings in honor of martyrs.

On the system of assigning numerical value by the position of letters in the alphabet the Christian symbol of Chi-Rho with the letters Alpha and Omega within a circle (which itself stood for 36) totalled 100. So too did the abbreviation for "Jesus (ΙΣ) Christ (ΧΣ) conquers (ΝΙΚΑ)"; and also the word-cross for "life" (ΖΩΗ) and "light" (ΦΩΣ).

Permit me to close with a word of exhortation. Do not do as I did for so long, that is, as I was reading texts to skim over or ignore the numbers contained in them. Sometimes the mention of numbers can be skimmed over. But it is well to pause and ask, why is this number mentioned? Does it have some significance beyond the surface meaning? Often, it does.

# 16

# Divine Pedagogy
## Origen's Use of the Imagery of Education

LeMoine G. Lewis has been preeminently a teacher—a scholarly teacher, a teacher of scholars, but always a teacher. His doctoral dissertation was on "The Commentary: Jewish and Pagan Backgrounds in Origen's Commentaries." Origen, too, was preeminently a teacher. One of his students, Gregory Thaumaturgus, paid tribute to him as a teacher in his *Panegyric to Origen*.[1] In this volume in which his former students pay tribute to LeMoine Lewis as a teacher, it is appropriate to examine Origen's use of the imagery of education in expounding his world view and understanding of salvation.

Origen's life was lived primarily in the school and classroom. In a chapter that seems to be in part autobiographical, or at least based on personal experience, he says that man, as a rational animal, "must always be engaged in some movement or activity." This ceaseless activity may be that of satisfying bodily pleasures, engaging in political activity for the public good, or may be intellectual:

> But if there be a man who can discern something better than these activities, which appear to be connected with the body, and can give diligent attention to wisdom and knowledge, he will undoubtedly direct all his efforts towards studies of this sort, with the object of learning, through inquiry into truth,

---

1. Translation by Metcalfe, *Gregory Thaumaturgos: Address to Origen*; Slusser, *Life and Works*.

what are the causes and reason of things. As therefore in this life one man decides that the highest good is the pleasure of the body, another the service of the State, and another devotion to studies and learning, so we seek to know whether in that life which is the true one, the life which is said to be "hid with Christ in God," that is, in the eternal life, there will be for us any such order or condition of existence.[2]

There is no doubt that Origen put himself in the third class. The restless energy of his life was expended in constant study and teaching, whether by the spoken word or in writing. Origen was a man of books, widely read and studious. Here the parallel to LeMoine Lewis continues. It will come as no surprise to my readers that I had to borrow the books for research on this paper which the university library did not have from LeMoine Lewis' personal library. Origen was an intellectual, and his was the life of the mind.

> Now when our eye sees the works of the craftsman, if it observes an article which has been made with unusual skill, immediately the mind burns to discover of what sort it is and how and for what uses it was made. Much more, and beyond all comparison, does the mind burn with unspeakable longing to learn the design of those things which we perceive to have been made by God. This longing, this love has, we believe, undoubtedly been implanted in us by God; and as the eye naturally demands light and vision and our body by its nature desires food and drink, so our mind cherishes a natural and appropriate longing to know God's truth and to learn the causes of things.
>
> Now we have not received this longing from God on the condition that it should not or could not ever be satisfied; for in that case the "love of truth" would appear to have been implanted in our mind by God the Creator to no purpose, if its gratification is never to be accomplished. So when even in this life men devote themselves with great labor to sacred and religious studies, although they obtain only some small fragments out of the immeasurable treasures of divine knowledge, yet they gain this advantage, that they occupy their mind and understanding with these questions and press onward in their eager desire. Moreover they derive much assistance from the fact that

---

2. *On First Principles* II.11.1. I quote the translation of Butterworth, *Origen On First Principles*.

by turning their mind to the study and love of truth they render themselves more capable of receiving instruction in the future.[3]

Origen placed his intellectual interests at the service of the church. Both he and LeMoine Lewis have been not only men of books but also men of piety.

Origen's career as a teacher began at an age when most are still students. After the martyrdom of his father when Origen was not yet seventeen, he supported his mother and six younger brothers by teaching grammar.[4] At eighteen he was asked by bishop Demetrius of Alexandria to take charge of the catechetical instruction of candidates for baptism, persecution having disrupted the normal instructional program of the church.[5] The demands of teaching made him realize the need for more advanced study and instruction, so he gave the elementary instruction to Heraclas and devoted himself to more advanced teaching.[6] Thus he began a new enterprise, a private school along the lines of Pantaenus and Clement earlier.[7] Origen was something of a walking encyclopedia, and he personally gave a university education with a major in philosophy and theology.[8] When he moved to Caesarea in 230, he set up the same kind of school there, as we know from Gregory's panegyric. Although Origen was active as a writer, preacher, and consultant to distant churches on theological matters, the principal setting of his career was the school.

In these circumstances it was natural that pedagogy provide an imagery for Origen's view of religion. Hal Koch indeed saw this as a key to Origen's whole system of theology.[9] Eugène de Faye, whose massive study of Origen Koch considered his work as supplementing because of inadequate attention to the themes of providence and pedagogy, recognized the importance of the motif of education in Origen.[10] In the popular summary of his research, which has been translated into English, de Faye said: "In

3. *On First Principles* II.11.4.
4. Eusebius, *Church History* VI.2.15.
5. Ibid., V1.3.
6. Ibid., VI.15.
7. Daniélou, *Origen*, 9ff.
8. Eusebius, *Church History* VI.18–19.

9. Koch, *Pronoia und Paideusis*. He affirms that a fundamental thought recurs in Origen: the education of fallen intellectual beings through providence. God is the great teacher who in every way leads and educates souls so that without losing their free self-determination they are led back to their heavenly origin (p. 18).

10. De Faye, *Origène*, 3.214-23. De Faye distinguishes Origen from the Gnostics on this point.

the final analysis, education is the method of redemption as understood by Origen. It consists essentially in divine training and guidance. The God of Origen, as we have seen, is an educator; the salvation he wills can be nothing else than an education."[11] Werner Jaeger has adopted Koch's viewpoint: "There are certain motifs that occur again and again and determine the nature of the questions [Origen] raises. Among them the paideia concept of the Greeks is of fundamental importance."[12] Daniélou also acknowledges the importance of the educational theme in Origen but differs from Koch in finding it of biblical and ecclesiastical derivation and not philosophical in origin.[13] Our study will be much more modest in scope than Koch's effort to interpret all of Origen's theology in terms of this motif. We will not attempt to trace the philosophical background nor to give a comprehensive treatment of Origen's references to education.[14] Rather we shall call attention to some passages where the educational process provides the imagery for explaining the divine plan and the means for attaining it. Not only was this imagery central to his understanding of reality, but Origen used it to explain some of the key features of his theology.

Origen shared with the philosophical thought of his time the view that "education is the way to virtue,"[15] but he differed as to the content of that education, finding the true knowledge of God in Christianity. Moreover, Christ is the Savior of the intelligent and of the simpleminded, and Christianity showed its power in being able to improve all persons, not just the educated. Indeed, this was one of Origen's chief arguments against the pagan critic Celsus, recurring throughout the *Against Celsus*.[16]

---

11. *Origen and His Work*, 128. De Faye places this in the context of Origen's emphasis on moral freedom, which means that souls may be saved only by persuasion. Consequences of this view of salvation are that it will take a long time (requiring a plurality of worlds), it will be moral and intellectual in nature, and will result in universal salvation. It may be added as another consequence that punishment has a disciplinary role. For these points see further below.

12. Jaeger, *Early Christianity and Greek Paideia*, 69.

13. Daniélou, *Origen*, 269-70, 276-89.

14. As a sample of what could be done, Origen's *Commentary on the Song of Songs* Prologue 3 understands the three books of Solomon (Proverbs, Ecclesiastes, Song of Solomon) as covering respectively the three branches of learning—ethics, physics, and theoretics (or theology). English translation by Lawson, trans., *Origen: The Song of Songs Commentary and Homilies*.

15. *Against Celsus* III.49, on which this paragraph is based. I quote the translation of Chadwick, *Origen: Contra Celsum*.

16. Koch, *Pronoia und Paideusis*, 55-56, 310; Chadwick, "The Evidences of Christianity in the Apologetic of Origen."

Some references to the teaching work of Christ may not be understood in any distinctive sense, in view of the prominence given in the Gospels to Jesus as a teacher; yet it seems characteristic of Origen to see the influence of Jesus in this way: "We admire Jesus who changed our thoughts from considering all objects of sense, not only everything corruptible but also what will be corrupted, and who led us to honor the supreme God with upright conduct and prayers."[17] Christ was a different kind of king from Herod, because "he would bestow no moderate and indifferent benefit, so to speak, upon his subjects, but by truly divine laws would educate them and lead them on."[18] And the church Origen rather casually calls "the school of Christ." As Koch observes, for Origen the church was what the philosophical schools were for other scholars of the time.[19]

Some general statements point to the more distinctive concerns of Origen's theology:

> I verily believe that God orders every rational soul with a view to its eternal life, and that it always maintains its free will, and of its own motion either mounts ever higher and higher until it reaches the pinnacle of virtue, or on the contrary descends through carelessness to this or that excess of wickedness.[20]

Human training or discipline was necessary for receiving the gift of prophecy:

> Holy and stainless souls, when they have devoted themselves to God with entire affection and entire purity and have kept themselves apart from all contact with daemons and purified themselves by much abstinence and have been steeped in pious and religious exercises, acquire thereby a communion with the divine nature and win the grace of prophecy and of the other divine gifts.[21]

According to Origen God created souls before he created the material world. These souls fell into sins of various kinds. They were assigned different bodies as punishment according to the kind of transgression. In their bodily states they are disciplined until they are liberated and return

17. *Against Celsus* III.34.

18. Ibid., I.61.

19. *Commentary on Matthew* XII.16. I quote the translation by John Patrick in *Ante-Nicene Fathers* 10. Koch, *Pronoia und Paideusis*, 79.

20. *On Prayer* XXIX.13. I quote the translation by Oulton in *Alexandrian Christianity*.

21. *On First Principles* III.3.3.

## Divine Pedagogy

to God. The world, thus, was created as a training ground of souls, and souls "undergo discipline" or training in the world.[22] Human beings were put here as in "a place of affliction"[23] in order to educate them to return to their Maker. God will bring all beings into subjection to himself. Origen illustrates how this is done by the training given to a slave, employing both threats and reasonable persuasion:

> But this subjection will be accomplished through certain means and courses of discipline and periods of time; that is, the whole world will not become subject to God by the pressure of some necessity that compels it into subjection, nor by the use of force, but by word, by reason, by teaching, by the exhortation to better things, by the best methods of education, and also by such merited and appropriate threatenings as are justly held over the heads of those who contemptuously neglect to care for their own salvation and advantage and their spiritual health. For even we men, in training slaves or children, restrain them by means of threats and fear so long as their age renders them incapable of listening to reason; but when they have acquired an understanding of what is good, profitable and honorable then the fear of blows may cease and they can be persuaded by word and by reason to acquiesce in everything that is good.[24]

Origen makes much of the educational value of punishment. Ancient writers who spoke about education frequently referred to the liberal use of the rod by schoolmasters.[25] This frequent association of education with disciplinary punishment in the ancient world may have something to do with Origen's interpretation of sufferings and evils in the world in terms of an educational purpose. "To punish" (κολάζειν) is almost synonymous with "to educate" (παιδεύειν, hence "to discipline").[26] "Having been disciplined, you may be saved."[27] God uses sufferings to cancel and purge sin, to warn others, and to instruct and improve the wrongdoer himself.[28] *Against Celsus* IV.99 well summarizes the educational and saving value of punishment:

---

22. Ibid., III.5.4.
23. *Against Celsus* VII.50.
24. *On First Principles* III.5.8.
25. Marrou, *A History of Education in Antiquity*, 220–22, 366–67.
26. *Against Celsus* V.31.
27. *Homilies on Jeremiah* X11.3. Translation my own.
28. Koch, *Pronoia und Paideusis*, 135–38.

> And providence will never abandon the universe. For even if some part of it becomes very bad because the rational being sins, God arranges to purify it, and after a time to turn the whole world back to Himself. Furthermore, he is not angry because of monkeys and flies; but He inflicts judgment and punishment upon men, seeing that they have gone against the impulses of nature. And He threatens them through prophets and through the Savior who came to visit the whole human race, in order that by means of the threat those who hear may be converted, while those who neglect the words aimed at their conversion pay penalties according to their deserts. It is right that God should impose these according to His will to the advantage of the whole world upon people who need healing and correction of this kind or of such severity.

One passage brings together the pains inflicted by parents, pedagogues, and physicians:

> Just as when, to speak loosely, we understand as evils the pains inflicted on those who are being educated by fathers and teachers and schoolmasters, or by doctors on those who undergo operations or cauterizations in order to cure them, we say that the father does evil to his sons or that the schoolmasters or teachers or doctors do so, and yet do not regard those who inflect the beating or perform the operation as doing anything reprehensible; so also if scripture says that God inflicts pains of this nature in order to convert and heal those who are in need of such punishment, there can be no ground for objection to what the Bible says ... The distress itself is inflicted for remedial purposes ... For he creates physical and external evils to purify and educate those who are unwilling to be educated by reason and sound teaching.[29]

This point that what is painful may often serve a good purpose for the benefit of another is most often made by Origen (and his predecessors and contemporaries) in terms of medical imagery: the physician must inflict pain in order to heal, and similarly God must punish in order to improve.[30] Origen in one passage, however, makes a distinction between the roles of the physician and the teacher: the physician is for the sick, but the teacher is for the well. "The divine Logos was sent as a physician

---

29. *Against Celsus* VI.56.

30. As a sampling note *Against Celsus* III.61; VII.60; *On First Principles* II.10.6; III.1.13.

## Divine Pedagogy

to sinners, but to those already pure and no longer sinning as a teacher of divine mysteries."[31] This passage turns from the corrective role of the pedagogue to the positive instructional role of the teacher who leads his pupils to greater things.

Origen explains that God is altogether love. References to God's anger or similar expressions in Scripture are not to be taken literally, for they express his practice of applying punishment for a corrective and benevolent purpose.[32]

> God is good and merciful. If enforcing penalties against sinners were not useful for their conversion, he would never requite sins with punishment. He is like a good father who corrects his son to teach him a lesson or like a master who has the great foresight to put on a severe face and administer correction to his pupil, for fear the child should go to the bad through realizing that he is loved ... All the bitter-seeming things God sends turn out to be educative or medicinal. God is a Healer and a Father, a kind and not a cruel Master ... They were punished in their lifetime so that there should be no need to punish them afterwards.[33]

Origen sees references to God's wrath as an illustration of God "deceiving" men (Jer 20:7): "For his wrath is not without fruit; but as his word educates [παιδεύει], so also does his wrath. For those not educated by word, wrath educates."[34] Even punishments, therefore, are not a matter of force but of persuasion; "wrath" is but an expression of love.

God suits his punishments and instructions to the level of development reached by an individual or by the human race. With reference again to Jer 20:7 Origen comments:

> He said it when he had discovered the deceit, and he implied that it was by deceit that he had been taught the rudiments and given his first lessons. He could not have learned the rudiments or gained knowledge enough of the truth to realize that he had been deceived, had it not been for that preliminary deceit. An example bearing on the subject will be enough to show you what I mean. When we talk to children, we behave like children ourselves. We do not talk to them as we talk to grown persons; we treat them as children who need teaching. We deceive children;

---

31. *Against Celsus* III.62.
32. Koch, *Pronoia und Paideusis*, 131–45.
33. *Homilies on Ezekiel* 1.2. I quote the translation in Daniélou, *Origen*, 277–78.
34. *Homilies on Jeremiah* XX.1. Cf. *Commentary on Matthew* XV.11.

we frighten them to make them docile. We frighten them with the sort of lies that are effective at that age, in the hope that our lies will instill fear enough into them to make them attend school regularly and do what children must if they are to make due progress. God looks on us all as children, and we all need the sort of education children receive. Hence, out of pity for us, God deceives us. He does not let us become aware of the deception until the proper time, because he wants us to learn from these fictions of his; he does not want us to get our schooling from reality, as though we had outgrown our childhood.[35]

One may disagree with the pedagogy described here but nonetheless recognize its employment by others and so understand Origen's use of it as an illustration. His basic idea is that God's accommodative language and corrective actions may involve an apparent falsehood or deception, or at least give the wrong impression, when compared to God's real nature or ultimate will. Origen defends the medicinal use of falsehood for a corrective effect. In terms of our theme we may compare the inadequate words of the elementary teacher to what Origen calls the deceit used by physicians in order to heal their patients:

> Do you not say, Celsus, that sometimes it is allowable to use deceit and lying as a medicine? Why, then, is it unthinkable that something of this sort occurred with the purpose of bringing salvation? For some characters are reformed by certain doctrines which are more false than true, just as physicians sometimes use similar words to their patients ... But further, there is nothing wrong if the person who heals sick friends healed the human race which was dear to him with such means as one would not use for choice, but to which he was confined by force of circumstances. Since the human race was mad, it had to be cured by methods which the Word saw to be beneficial to lunatics that they might recover their right mind.[36]

The idea of God's accommodative language accords with the sound pedagogical principle of suiting instruction to the age and development of the student. As we adapt our language to the age of the children to whom

---

35. *Homilies on Jeremiah* XVIII.15. I quote the translation in Daniélou, *Origen*, 281–82, which gives this reference. The passage is found in Nautin, trans. *Origène: Homélies sur Jérémie* as XIX.15.

36. *Against Celsus* IV.19.

*Divine Pedagogy*

we speak, so God has adapted his language in revelation to our nature and our capacity to understand.[37]

> For example, if Plato had wished to help by sound doctrines people who spoke Egyptian or Syriac, he, being a Greek, would have taken pains to learn the language of those who were to be his hearers and, as the Greeks say, to speak like a barbarian for the sake of improving the Egyptians and Syrians rather than, by remaining a Greek, have no power to say anything helpful to either of them. Similarly, the divine nature, which cares not only for those supposed to have been educated in Greek learning but also for the rest of mankind, came down to the level of the ignorant multitude of hearers, that by using the style familiar to them it might encourage the mass of the common people to listen. After they have once been introduced to Christianity they are easily able to aspire to grasp even deeper truths which are concealed in the Bible.[38]

The educational principle of the adaptation of teaching to the age and spiritual development of the pupil recurs in several forms in Origen.[39] The appearances of the Logos likewise were accommodated to the state of development of those to whom he came.

> There are, as it were, different forms of the Word. For the Word appears to each of those who are led to know him in a form corresponding to the state of the individual, whether he is a beginner, or has made a little progress, or is considerably advanced, or has nearly attained to virtue already, or has in fact attained it.[40]

The sequence of the educational curriculum suggested to Origen the proper understanding of the relation of the law and prophets to the gospel. The former are related to the latter as the rudiments are to advanced instruction:

> For as every man who is going to be wise in the words of truth must first be taught the rudiments, and further pass through the

---

37. *Homilies on Jeremiah* XVIII.6, translated in Tollinton, *Selections from the Commentaries and Homilies of Origen*, 19–22.

38. *Against Celsus* VII.60.

39. Cf. *Homilies on Genesis* 1.7 and *Homilies on Numbers* XXVII.1, translated in Tollinton, *Selections from the Commentaries and Homilies of Origen*, 260–62, 180–84; and *On Prayer* XXVII.9, "Each of those who are nourished, in proportion as he has offered himself to the word." The idea of the growth of the human race from infancy in Adam to maturity in Christ was suggested by Irenaeus, *Against Heresies* IV.38.1.

40. *Against Celsus* IV.16.

> elementary instruction, and appreciate it highly but not abide in it, as one who, having honored it at the beginning but passed over towards perfection, is grateful for the introduction because it was useful at the first; so the perfect apprehension of the law and the prophets is an elementary discipline for the perfect apprehension of the Gospel, and all the meaning in the words and deeds of Christ.[41]

For this idea, as for most of his teaching, Origen found good biblical support: "Every soul, therefore, which comes to childhood, and is on the way to full growth, until the fullness of time is at hand, needs a tutor" (or pedagogue; cf. Gal 3:24–25; 4:1–4). There is a knowledge which is partial and is replaced when that which is perfect comes (1 Cor 13:9–10); so other forms of knowledge, including those of the law and prophets, are surpassed by the knowledge of Christ.[42]

The educational imagery similarly enters into the justification for the allegorical interpretation of Scripture, Origen's fundamental exegetical tool.[43] Those who belong to the church, Origen explains, "are made wise and are educated by mystical contemplation of the law and the prophets."[44] In other words, the member of the church does not stop with the legal or literal sense of the Old Testament. The literal understanding of scripture is for children. It has its relative justification for a certain stage of development which serves to lead the person to seek a deeper knowledge.[45] The literal or historical sense of Scripture was to be preserved, as elementary instruction was; but the scribe of the kingdom of heaven goes on to the spiritual meaning:

> And one is a scribe "made a disciple to the kingdom of heaven" in the simpler sense, when he comes from Judaism and receives the teaching of Jesus Christ as defined by the church; but he is a scribe in a deeper sense, when having received elementary knowledge through the letter of the scriptures he ascends to things spiritual, which are called the kingdom of the heavens.[46]

Educational imagery further enters into Origen's explanation of the relationship of grace and free will. Free will is one of the fundamental

---

41. *Commentary on Matthew* X.10.
42. Ibid. X.9.
43. Hanson, *Allegory and Event*; Grant, *The Letter and the Spirit*.
44. *Against Celsus* II.6.
45. Koch, *Pronoia und Paideusis*, 60 and our n. 41 above.
46. *Commentary on Matthew* X.14.

*Divine Pedagogy*

principles from which Origen's whole theology was built up.[47] In order to say with Scripture that all is of grace yet maintain free will, Origen compares an ignorant person who gives himself (an act of free will) to a teacher for instruction (hence all that is learned is a grace from the teacher). He comments on Ezekiel 11:19-20 as follows:

> But if God promises to do this, and if we do not lay aside our "stony hearts" before he takes them away, it is clear that it is not in our power to put away wickedness. And if we ourselves do nothing to implant within us the "heart of flesh," but it is the work of God, then to live a virtuous life will not be our work, but something due entirely to the divine grace.
>
> Now this is what will be said by the man who, arguing from the bare words, which destroy our free will. We, however, shall reply that these words must be understood in the following manner. It is as when a man who suffers from ignorance and want of education, and becomes conscious of his personal defects either from the exhortation of his teacher or from his own reflection, entrusts himself to one whom he believes to be capable of leading him on to education and virtue. When he so entrusts himself, his instructor promises to take away his lack of education and to implant in him education, not as if it counted for nothing in regard to his being educated and escaping from his ignorance that he should have brought himself to be cured, but because the instructor promises to improve one who desires improvement.
>
> So the divine word promises to take away the wickedness which it calls a "stony heart," from those who come to it, not if they are unwilling, but if they submit themselves to the physician of the sick . . . This then is the way by which the word of God promises to implant knowledge in those who come to it, taking away the stony and hard heart, which signifies wickedness, to enable them to walk in the divine commandments and to keep the divine ordinances.[48]

As this passage briefly indicates ("not if they are unwilling"), Origen knew from Scripture (Jer 5:3) and his own experience that "the teacher may do

---

47. Noted in all studies of Origen's theology: Völker, *Das Vollkommenheitsideal des Origenes*, 25-44; de Faye, *Origène*, 3:179-98; Koch, *Pronoia und Paideusis*, passim; Daniélou, *Origen*, 203-19, 285-88; Jackson, "Sources of Origen's Doctrine of Freedom."

48. *On First Principles* III.1.15.

everything in his power to transmit knowledge, but the student refuse to receive the lessons."[49]

Most characteristic of Origen's system as a whole is the thought of souls receiving progressive stages of education through successive worlds. Since education is a slow, gradual process, God's work with souls is not complete in one lifetime. Extending the relation of the Old to the New Testament to apply to a more perfect heavenly understanding after this life and using Gal 3:24 as a point of departure, Origen says:

> It seems to me, therefore, that as in this earth the law was a kind of schoolmaster to those who by it were appointed to be led to Christ and to be instructed and trained in order that after their training in the law they might be able with greater facility to receive the more perfect precepts of Christ, so also that other earth, when it receives all the saints, first imbues and educates them in the precepts of the true and eternal law in order that they may with greater facility accept the precepts of heaven which are perfect and to which nothing can ever be added. And in heaven will truly exist what is called the "eternal gospel" and the testament that is always new, which can never grow old.
>
> This, then, is how we must suppose that events happen in the consummation and restitution of all things, namely, that souls, advancing and ascending little by little in due measure and order, first attain to that other earth and the instruction that is in it, and are there prepared for those better precepts to which nothing can ever be added . . . [Christ] himself will instruct those who are able to receive him in his character of wisdom, after their preliminary training in the holy virtues, and will reign in them until such time as he subjects them to the Father.[50]

The most extended use of the educational imagery comes in Origen's grand vision of the souls of the departed in a classroom:

> I think that the saints as they depart from this life will remain in some place situated on the earth, which the divine scripture calls "paradise." This will be a place of instruction and, so to speak, a lecture room or school for souls, in which they may be taught about all that they had seen on earth and may also receive some indications of what is to follow in the future.[51]

---

49. *Homilies on Jeremiah* VI.2.
50. *On First Principles* III.6.8f.
51. Ibid., II.11.6.

Those who are "pure in heart and of unpolluted mind and well-trained understanding" will make rapid progress. They will learn the nature of the stars, the reasons for the works of God, the causes of things, and the power of God's creation. Then they will ascend to the invisible things and then to perfect knowledge.[52] The intellectual nature of Origen's system is clearly expressed in the climax of the passage:

> And so the rational being, growing at each successive stage, not as it grew when in this life in the flesh or body and in the soul, but increasing in mind and intelligence, advances as a mind already perfect to perfect knowledge, no longer hindered by its formal carnal senses, but developing in intellectual power, ever approaching the pure and gazing "face to face," if I may so speak, on the causes of things. And it attains perfection, first that perfection by which it rises to this condition, and secondly that by which it remains therein, while it has for the food on which it feeds the problems of the meaning of things and the nature of their causes. For as in this bodily life of ours we grew first of all bodily into that which we now are, the increase being supplied in our early years merely by a sufficiency of food, whereas after the process of growth has reached its limit we use food not in order to grow but as a means of preserving life within us; so, too, I think that the mind, when it has come to perfection, still feeds on appropriate and suitable food in a measure which can neither admit of want nor of superfluity. But in all respects this food must be understood to be the contemplation and understanding of God, and its measures to be those that are appropriate and suitable to this nature which has been made and created. These measures will rightly be observed by every one of those who are beginning to "see God," that is, to understand him through "purity of heart."[53]

One may quarrel with various aspects of Origen's system, but it is indeed an apt statement, hardly to be improved on from another way of conceiving reality, to say that the food of the mind is contemplation of God.

For the present, however, created beings must accept with humility Origen's caution: "For however far one may advance in the search and make progress through an increasingly earnest study, even when aided

---

52. Ibid., II.11.7.
53. Ibid.

and enlightened in mind by God's grace, he will never be able to reach the final goal of his inquiries."[54]

There seems to be sufficient justification for Daniélou's statement, following Koch: "It might be said that being a *didaskalos* [teacher] himself, Origen regarded his God as a *Didaskalos* too, as a Master in charge of the education of children, and looked on God's universe as a vast *didaskaleion* [school] in which every single thing contributed to the education of the free human beings at school there."[55]

---

54. Ibid., IV.26.
55. Daniélou, *Origen*, 276.

# 17

# Early Christian Martyrdom and Civil Disobedience[1]

THE TACTICS OF GANDHI in securing independence for India and of Martin Luther King Jr. in the American civil rights movement have directed attention in the twentieth century to non-violent resistance as an instrument of political policy. An objection to these tactics has been raised on the grounds that the methods of Gandhi in India or of Martin Luther King in the United States would be ineffective against a Nazi Germany or a Communist China. According to this reasoning the moral power of Gandhi and King was in part due to their dealing with governing authorities which were at least nominally Christian and informed by a Christian conscience. This consideration prompts an examination of the experience of the early Christians with the pagan Roman Empire. Although there are differences between early Christian martyrdom (and the whole tradition of "evangelical pacifism") and modern strategies of non-violent confrontation, the query whether elements of the modern practice or an awareness of them is found among the early martyrs may cast light on the theme of non-violent resistance to persecution and its effectiveness in attaining toleration or other political goals. George Williams discussed "four modalities of violence" in Christian history: dying for the heavenly homeland, holy violence actualized, sublimation of violence in

---

1. 1992 North American Patristics Society Presidential Address. Research for this paper was supported in part by the Research Council of Abilene Christian University through the generosity of the Cullen Foundation.

spiritual warfare, and the conversion of alienation into reconciliation.[2] Early Christian martyrdom falls in the first category: dying for the heavenly homeland.

Early Christian martyrdom has been studied from many standpoints: the meaning of the word,[3] the persecutions by Rome,[4] the concept of martyrdom,[5] its relation to suicide,[6] the theology of martyrdom,[7] as an example of social control,[8] and according to the ethical problems raised.[9] It is proposed here to consider what mutual understanding is gained by examining early Christian martyrdom in relation to modern concerns about civil disobedience. David Daube has defined civil disobedience as involving non-violence and the motivation that the conduct is right and not selfish.[10] He sets a context for our theme but does not himself include the Christian martyrs in his survey.[11] The examination here is limited, with few exceptions, to statements in the early Christian literature of martyrdom—the acts and passions of the martyrs and exhortations to martyrdom.

The importance of martyrdom for the early Christians is demonstrated by the way it was interpreted in terms of major theological motifs. Martyrdom was a baptism of blood, which brought forgiveness of sins to the martyr.[12] It was a eucharist, in which one drank the cup of sufferings of Christ.[13] It was an anticipation of the eschaton, an orthodox version of radically realized eschatology, in which the martyr brought the events of the last days to immediate fruition for himself.[14] It was a defeat of Satan

---

2. Williams, "Four Modalities of Violence," 252–54.
3. Brox, *Zeuge and Märtyrer*; Dehandschutter, "Martyr–Martyrium."
4. Frend, *Martyrdom and Persecution in the Early Church*.
5. Von Campenhausen, *Die Idee des Martyriums in der alten Kirche*.
6. Droge and Tabor, *A Noble Death*.
7. Baumeister, *Die Anfänge der Theologie des Martyriums*.
8. Riddle, *The Martyrs*; Tilley, "Scripture as an Element of Social Control."
9. Wendebourg, "Das Martyrium."
10. Daube, *Civil Disobedience in Antiquity*, 1–4, 43.
11. Cf. Wendebourg, "Das Martyrium," 297–303, on the philosophical idea of a "beautiful death." Tertullian, *Apol.* 50 and Clement of Alexandria, *Str.* 4.8 list pagan examples of endurance of suffering, but Origen claims that although others may have a heroic death, only the "elect race" dies for religion—*mart.* 5.
12. Dassmann, *Sundenvergebung*, 153–71. Cf. M. *Mar.* 11.
13. Kettel, "Martyrium und Eucharistie."
14. Willis, "A Study of Some Eschatological Motifs in the Martyr Literature of the Early Church"; Rordorf, "L'espérance des martyrs chrétiens."

and the demons through identification with the victory of Christ on the cross.[15] The martyr was filled with the Holy Spirit, who gave words to say to the authorities, visions of the other world, and supernatural strength to endure sufferings.[16] Martyrdom was an imitation of Christ, in which one shared in the sufferings of Christ and was brought into direct contact with the Lord,[17] and the glory of Christ himself was manifested in the martyr.[18]

The importance of martyrdom was further emphasized by relating it to divine election and providence. Martyrdom was not for everyone. God chose the worthy for martyrdom. Or, as one author put it, he assigned it to some on account of their worth, and to others he gave it on account of his mercy.[19] According to the mainstream teaching, one was not to volunteer for martyrdom. The church had some unfortunate experiences with those who rushed forward to confess their faith and then did not stand up under the pressure.[20] The doctrine that God chose his martyrs tempered enthusiasm for self-chosen martyrdom; it also highlights the self-consciousness of the church about the significance of martyrdom. The emphasis on the will of God is pertinent to some of the less theological aspects of martyrdom to which this paper addresses itself.

Although more attention seems to be given in the early Christian literature about martyrdom to the theological significance of martyrdom, Christians were not unaware of the practical significance of the act. For instance, the missionary motif was noted. Tertullian's declaration that the blood of the martyrs is seed and by their deeds the martyrs make other disciples[21] has become proverbial. Less well known is the claim of Apollonius, "The more they kill those who believe in God, so much the more will

---

15. Eusebius, *H.E.* 5.1.23 and 27; *M. Apoll.* 47; *M. Fruct.* 7.2; *M. Agap.* 1. 2. 4; Hermas, *sim.* 8.3.6; Origen, *mart.* 42; *Cels.* 8.44.

16. Viller, "Les Martyrs et l'Esprit"; Weinrich, *Spirit and Martyrdom*.

17. Pellegrino, "L'Imitation du Christ dans les Acts des martyrs."

18. Farkasfalvy, "Christological Content."

19. Ps-Cyprian, *laud. mart.* 23. Note also *M. Polyc.* 14; 20; *M. Carp.* 41; 42; *M. Perp.* 21.11; *M. Cyp.* 2.1; *M. Mar.* 2.3; 3.4; *M. Iren.* 5.2; Clement of Alexandria, *str.* 4.12; Hippolytus, *Dan.* III.26; Cyprian, *mort.* 17. "Found worthy of martyrdom"—*didas.* 19 (Connolly, trans., *Didascalia Apostolorum*, 166). Cyprian, *ep.* 81.2 forbids voluntary martyrdom while urging firmness when arrested.

20. *M. Polyc.* 4. The emphasis on martyrdom "according to the will of God" is directed against a Gnostic denial of martyrdom and not Montanist enthusiasm according to B. Dehandschutter, "Le Martyre de Polycarpe." That the early Montanists did not differ from their orthodox opponents on voluntary martyrdom is argued by Tabbernee, "Early Montanism and Voluntary Martyrdom."

21. *Apol.* 50; compare Justin, *dial.* 110; Hippolytus, *Dan.* 2.38.

their numbers grow by God's aid."[22] Justin Martyr, for one, testified to the influence of the martyrs on his own conversion.[23] The martyrs thus truly lived up to their title as "witnesses." Even when they were not able to speak directly to pagan onlookers, as the sources occasionally note occurring,[24] their deed was a public testimony to unbelievers to the gospel.[25] In a world without television spectaculars and Billy Graham campaigns a place on the program at the month's spectacles in the amphitheater was the best advertising available.[26]

Ignatius may have dwelled on the personal aspects of martyrdom, but others were aware of the community dimensions of the deed.[27] A faithful witness confirmed others in the faith and prepared them to resist under similar pressure.[28] Indeed the annual commemoration of the martyr's "birthday to immortality" served expressly to strengthen and train those who would come after.[29] The compiler of the *Martyrdom of Perpetua and Felicitas* in stating the purpose in writing explains that "God always achieves what he promises, as a witness to the non-believer and a blessing to the faithful."[30]

The doctrine that martyrdom was within God's providence highlights further that martyrdom was a witness to the State of its subordination to the God of heaven. The Acts of the Martyrs delighted in contrasts often formulated in sharp antitheses. These Acts feature the demand made of Christians to sacrifice to the pagan gods, so the contest is seen principally in religious terms.[31] This demand lent itself to a contrast between the

---

22. *M. Apoll.* 24. References and quotations are taken from Musurillo, *The Acts of the Christian Martyrs.*

23. Justin, *2 apol.* 12.

24. *M. Carp.* 40; Eusebius, *H.E.* 5.2.4 and 5. The author of the *M. Mar.* makes a direct address to pagans at 6.1.

25. *M. Fruct.* 6.3 for death confirming life and teaching. Reactions by pagan onlookers are noted in *M. Polyc.* 2; 16; *M. Carp.* 45; Eusebius, *H.E.* 5.1.56; *M. Perp.* 17.3.

26. Nock, *Conversion*, 193–202; von Harnack, *The Mission and Expansion of Christianity*, 492–93; von Campenhausen, "Das Martyrium in der Mission."

27. Pellegrino, "Le Sense ecclésial du martyre."

28. *M. Polyc.* 1; 19; Eusebius, *H.E.* 5.1.23, 41–42; *M. Apoll.* 47; *M. Pion.* 22.4; Eusebius, *H.E.* 8.10.11; *M. Mar.* 3.5; 9.2–4; 12.8; Origen, *Cels.* 8.8.

29. *M. Polyc.* 18.

30. *M. Perp.* 1.5. Compare Clement of Alexandria, *Str.* 4.9 for the church confirmed and heathen led to faith by the martyr's confession. Other references for strengthening Christians as the purpose of preserving accounts of martyrdom include *M. Mar.* 1.3 and *M. Pion.* 1.

31. *M. Polyc.* 12; *Mart. Scill.* 3–4; Tertullian, *apol.* 10 says that the chief charge

worship of the one God and the worship of the many gods. When Pionius, presbyter of Smyrna, during the Decian persecution was ordered, "Offer sacrifice," he replied, "My prayers must be offered to God." The proconsul insisted, "We reverence all the gods."[32] But for Christians belief in God was reason not to sacrifice.[33] In contrast to the requirement to sacrifice to the gods, the Christian martyrs could interpret their death as a sacrifice to God.[34] Dasius, martyr under Diocletian, said to the soldiers, "Seeing that you force me to such a despicable act, better is it for me to become a sacrifice to the Lord Christ by my own choice rather than immolate myself to your idol Saturn."[35] Or, the confession of faith itself could be understood as a sacrifice to God.[36]

Quite prominent in the martyr and apologetic literature is the identification of the gods to whom sacrifice was required with demons[37] and the assertion that the demons or the devil were responsible for the persecutions.[38] Hence, to sacrifice to demons was to deny God.[39] It was impossible for Christians "to sacrifice to these demons with their deceptive appearances, for those who sacrifice to them are like them." The gods are dead, and "The living do not offer sacrifice to the dead."[40]

The threat of torture for failure to sacrifice and the promise of rewards for sacrifice set up a quite natural antithesis between temporal and eternal punishments and between present and future rewards. Those who worship God are said to take on his image and become immortal with him, but those who worship the gods take on the image of demons and perish along with them in Gehenna.[41] The *Martyrdom of Polycarp* 2 speaks of those who despised the tortures of this world "buying themselves an

---

against Christians was religious, that is the refusal to sacrifice.

32. *M. Pion.* 19.

33. *M. Agap.* 3.4.

34. Jacob, "Le Martyre, épanouissement du sacerdoce des Chrétiens"; Ferguson, "Spiritual Sacrifice in Early Christianity and its Environment," 1169–70, 1180, 1186.

35. *M. Das.* 5.2; see also *M. Polyc.* 14; *M. Con.* 6.7; *M. Fel.* 30.

36. *M. Iren.* 2.4.

37. *M. Carp.* 6; *M. Crisp.* 1.7; Justin, *1 Apol.* 5; Tertullian, *spect.* 13; Origen, *Cels.* 7.69.

38. *M. Carp.* 17; Eusebius, H.E. 5.1.5 and 25; *M. Mar.*2.2 and 5; Justin, *1 apol.* 57; *2 apol.* 1; Tertullian, *fuga* 2; Origen, *Cels.* 8.43. Ferguson, *Demonology of the Early Christian World*, 121–22.

39. *M. Iren.* 2.2.

40. *M. Carp.* 6 and 12.

41. Ibid., 7.

exemption from the eternal fire." Christians "despise death because of the faith they have in God."[42] On the other hand, eternal punishment was for the persecutors. "You have condemned us, but God will condemn you."[43] Although reference to punishment of persecutors is more frequent, as might be expected, there is also much said about the reward of perseverance.[44] Perhaps in response to criticism of the readiness for martyrdom, it was said that the martyrs were not "rushing toward death but toward life."[45] It was easy for the keen, rhetorical mind of Tertullian to contrast judgment before the proconsul with judgment before God,[46] but the more pedestrian Carpus of Pergamum too looked to the "judgment seat of truth."[47] Eschatological sanctions are a constant feature of the literature about martyrdom. Of the "four modalities of violence" in Christian history identified by George Williams, the martyrs' threats of eschatological punishments are expressions of the category of dying for the heavenly homeland, in which violence is eschatologically postponed.[48]

Although the contest was viewed by Christians as between God and idolatry[49] and not between church and state, there were political implications and these are sometimes explicitly noted. The sacrifices were "for the welfare of the emperors"[50] or were directed to the gods and the image of the emperor,[51] and the decrees to offer sacrifice came from the emperor.[52] The refusal to "obey the gods and submit to the orders of the emperors"[53]

---

42. *M. Iren.* 4.12; compare *M. Con.* 5.

43. *M. Perp.* 18.8.

44. For threats of punishment: *M. Polyc.* 11; Eusebius, *H.E.* 5.1.26; *M. Pion.* 4.24; 7.4; *M. Jul.* 2.4; *M. Agap.* 5.2; *M. Crisp.* 2.2; Ps-Cyprian, *laud. mart.* 19–20. For rewards of perseverance: *M. Just.* (A) 5; *M. Apollon.* 42; *M. Pion.* 7.5; *M. Fruct.* 3.3; 4.3; 7.2; *M. Mont.* 22.2; Ps-Cyprian, *laud. mart.* 7; 9; 11; 21.

45. *M. Pion.* 20.5 and 21.4; for eternal life as the martyr's reward see also *M. Polyc.* 14; *M. Jul.* 3.4; *M. Das.* 4; Hippolytus, *Dan.* 3.24.

46. *Mart.* 2.

47. *M. Carp.* 40.

48. Williams, "Four Modalities of Violence," esp. 15–18.

49. This is clear in Origen, *Mart.* and Cyprian, *Dem.* Tertullian, *Apol.* 28 considers the political charge secondary to the religious charge (see n. 26). Grant, "Sacrifices and Oaths as Required of Early Christians," 12–17 points out that the requirement of sacrifices and oaths was secondary to the charge of being a Christian.

50. *M. Perp.* 6.3; *M. Crisp.* 1.

51. *M. Apoll.* 7; *M. Fruct.* 2.6.

52. *M. Carp.* 4; *M. Agap.* 3.4.

53. *M. Just.* (B) 2.1.

was "to blaspheme the gods and the august emperors."[54] The Christian position, however, was, "A divine decree cannot be quelled by a decree of man."[55] The emperor's command to sacrifice to the gods could not replace God's command to worship him alone.[56] Christians would obey only the edict of Christ.[57] Although the words of Acts 5:29, "We must obey God rather than man," are quoted only once in the Acts of the Martyrs, the description of God in Acts 4:24 as the one "who made heaven and earth and the sea and all that is in them" is frequent and carries the same force in indicating the one who must be obeyed.[58] He is the "Father and king of heaven," to whom the martyr goes at death.[59] God or Christ are often asserted to be king or emperor; in the Acts of the Martyrs this terminology must be in conscious contrast to the earthly ruler.[60] God dispenses kingdoms and sets up kings.[61] Christians claimed for themselves a higher citizenship.[62] After the author of the *Martyrdom of Polycarp* appended to his formula dating the death of Polycarp the phrase, "while Jesus Christ was reigning eternally,"[63] it became a regular feature of this literature to supplement dates with a reference to the reign or kingship of Christ.[64]

This defiance of imperial decrees made Christians guilty of civil disobedience, or even of treason.[65] Nevertheless, the authorities were not desirous of making martyrs, so the accounts of martyrdom are full of the efforts to dissuade Christians from their defiance.[66] In view of modern ethical discussions, note may be taken that the prefect Maximus made the argument to Julius the Veteran that since a higher authority was forcing him to sacrifice he was not responsible for the act, but Julius rejected the

---

54. *M. Carp.* 21.

55. *M. Apoll.* 24.

56. *M. Pion.* 3.2–3; *M. Iul.* 3.3; Origen, *Mart.* 34–35; *Cels.* 8.26, 55.

57. *M. Crisp.* 1.6.

58. Musurillo, *Acts*, 378. The quotation of Acts 5:29 occurs in *M. Fel.* 15–17. For the use of Acts 4:19 in such a context, see Hippolytus, *Dan.* 3.23.

59. Justin, *2 apol.* 2.

60. *M. Polyc.* 9; 17; Eusebius, *H.E.* 5.1.55; *Mart. Scill.* 6; *M. Con.* 3–4.

61. Tertullian, *Apol.* 26; Hippolytus, *Dan.* 3.4; Origen, *Cels.* 8.68.

62. *M. Just.* (C) 1. The sense of contest is heightened in recension C.

63. *M. Polyc.* 21.

64. *M. Pion.* 23; *M. Marcell.* (N) 5.2; *M. Iren.* 6.

65. *M. Agap.* 5.3.

66. For example, *M. Polyc.* 9–12; *M. Carp.* passim; *M. Perp.* 6; *M. Pion.* 4–5; 12; 20; *M. Con.* 3–4; *M. Agap.* 5.2.

argument.⁶⁷ Christians, for their part, insisted that they were taught to respect the authorities.⁶⁸ They honored the emperor⁶⁹ and prayed for him.⁷⁰ As diverse personalities as Tertullian and Origen could argue that the Christians respected the emperor and empire and that Christian prayers were more help than soldiers to the welfare of the empire.⁷¹ By putting the emperor in his proper place, under God and over the gods, Christians commended him to divine favor.⁷² Christian teaching trained good citizens.⁷³

The Christians' obedience to the emperor was limited by their understanding of the divine law. Thus their refusal to obey the decrees concerning sacrifice corresponds to Daube's requirement that civil disobedience be motivated by a higher conviction of what is right. The absence of selfishness, as it pertains to this world, is also evident. The appeal to conscience is sometimes made explicit. The martyr Agape declared, "I refuse to destroy my conscience."⁷⁴ Phileas insisted, "Our conscience with respect to God is prior to all."⁷⁵ Religion, therefore, is not a matter of compulsion. In response to a proconsul's threat to force respect for the gods, Crispina affirmed, "That piety is worthless which forces persons to be crushed against their will."⁷⁶ Thus the Christians claimed "freedom of religion."⁷⁷ The theme of freedom of religion was reiterated by the apologists.⁷⁸

The other feature of civil disobedience noted by Daube is its nonviolence. Martyrdom was certainly a violent act by those who caused it, but the disobedience which provoked it was non-violent. It is true that Christians sometimes were guilty of deliberate provocation.⁷⁹ But the model which was commended as normative Christian conduct showed

---

67. *M. Iul.* 2.5–6.

68. *M. Polyc.* 10; compare Origen, *Cels.* 8.65.

69. *M. Apollon.* 6; 9.

70. *M. Cypr.* 1.2.

71. Tertullian, *apol.* 30–33; Origen, *Cels.* 7.73; compare Cyprian, *Dem.* 20 and Hippolytus, *Dan.* 3.24.

72. Tertullian, *Apol.* 30; 33–34.

73. Origen, *Cels.* 8.74.

74. *M. Agap.* 3.3.

75. *M. Phil.* col. 9, as restored.

76. *M. Crisp.* 2.1.

77. Cyprian, *Dem.* 14.

78. Ferguson, "Voices of Religious Liberty in the Early Church."

79. As in *M. Eupl.* 1. See Kötting, "Martyrium und Provokation."

## Early Christian Martyrdom and Civil Disobedience

a more submissive demeanor in its resistance.[80] Tertullian insisted that Christians had not and would not revolt.[81] A fairly frequent theme in the exhortations to martyrdom and in the apologies is that Christians do not take revenge. This insistence is balanced by the assurance that although Christians do not offer resistance, God will avenge.[82] Christians injure nobody, Tertullian affirms. He countered the charge that Christians hated the human race[83] by saying that they were enemies not of the human race but of human error.[84] In fact, he goes so far as to renounce any form of resistance, even non-violent.[85] This insistence for some authors took the form of complete pacifism—non-participation in military service and avoidance of political office.[86] In the Acts of the military martyrs the refusal of governmental demands takes the form of a choice between the military and the church.[87] The soldier Marinus was confronted by bishop Theotecnus of Caesarea with a choice of the Gospels or the sword, and he chose the Gospels.[88] The recruit Maximilian refused military service because he was a Christian: "I will not serve this world, but only my God."[89] The centurion Marcellus renounced military service seemingly because of the pagan religious practices involved, but then he also refused to fight.[90] The soldier Dasius said, "I do not fight for any earthly king but for the king of heaven,"[91] but it is not clear what kind of fighting he meant. The veteran Julius was a Christian for the twenty-seven years of his military service, but he became a martyr under Diocletian on the grounds that a Christian could not obey the laws to sacrifice.[92] By the time of the persecution under Diocletian there were many Christians in the army and in high positions

---

80. See Clement of Alexandria, *Str.* 4.10 on not provoking martyrdom or persecution.

81. Tertullian, *Apol.* 37.

82. Cyprian, *Dem.* 17; Tertullian, *Apol.* 37; 41; Origen, *Cels.* 3.7–8.

83. Tacitus, *Ann.* 15.44.2–8.

84. Tertullian, *apol.* 39; 41; 37. Bauer, "Das Gebot der Feindesliebe und die alten Christen," deals with how consistently the martyrs practiced love of enemies.

85. Ibid., 37.

86. Michel Spanneut, "La non-violence chez les Pères africains avant Constantin."

87. Texts in translations in Helgeland et al., *Christians and the Military*, 56–66; pacifist interpretation by Hornus, *It Is Not Lawful for Me to Fight*.

88. Eusebius, *H.E.* 7.15.4.

89. *M. Maximil.* 2.1 and 8.

90. *M. Marcell,* (M) 1.1; 4.3.

91. *M. Das.* 7.2.

92. *M. Jul.* 1.3–4; 2.1.

in the government. Some were already there nearly a century earlier when Origen was justifying Christians not taking civil offices because those who were qualified chose to rule the church under the great King and because Christians by their moral influence preserved the order of society.[93] Tertullian had gone further in this direction by affirming that affairs of state were foreign to Christians and they did not aspire to public office.[94] Christians could not be emperors, he indicates, but perhaps because of the idolatrous nature of the office.[95] Such views were a concrete expression of the hatred of the world and separation from the world voiced in the exhortations to martyrdom.[96] Capable of a more positive development was Tertullian's implicit separation of religion and government, anticipating Augustine's City of God.[97]

The Acts of the Martyrs and related literature belong to the history of civil disobedience, and perhaps few exercises of non-violent resistance for the sake of higher law have accomplished as much. Daube states that civil disobedience may be in order to put the government on the right path or to bring it down.[98] In spite of the occasional extreme language against Roman authorities, the implicit purpose of the Christian martyrs seems to have been to set the government on the right path. What is missing from the literature of martyrdom is the conviction that massive civil disobedience would in fact change the laws. The apologists did say that they aimed to achieve this by their arguments. There is not voiced expressly, however, the view that passive resistance was an instrument for political ends. Yet I have no reason to doubt that the steadfastness of the martyrs contributed to the recognition of Christianity and the profound change in political policy effected by Constantine. And the church was clearly not totally innocent of the social and political implications of martyrdom. Polycarp, called upon to curse Christ replied, "For eighty-six years I have been his servant and he has done me no wrong. How can I blaspheme against my king and savior?"[99] He and the host of faithful witnesses before and after him gave a testimony to the supreme claims of God and the limitations of the State. The fruition of the implications of their testimony was long

---

93. Origen, *Cels.* 8.75; 70; 73.
94. Tertullian, *Apol.* 38; 41.
95. Ibid., 21.
96. Tertullian, *mart.* 2; Ps-Cyprian, *laud. mart.* passim.
97. Tertullian, *apol.* 25.
98. Daube, *Civil Disobedience*, 64.
99. M. *Polyc.* 9.

time in coming, but the early Christian witness was an important step in desacralizing the State, elevating the individual conscience, and asserting the value of principles on which religious toleration rests.

# Bibliography

Åkerman, Malte. *Über die Echtheit der letzteren Hälfte von Tertullians Adversus Iudaeos*. Lund: Lindström, 1918.
Aland, Kurt. *Did the Early Church Baptize Infants?* Translated by G. R. Beasley-Murray. 1963. Reprinted, Eugene, OR: Wipf & Stock, 2004.
———. *Die Säulingstaufe im Neuen Testament and in der Alten Kirche*. Theologische Existenz Heute 86. Munich: Kaiser, 1961.
———. *Taufe und Kindertaufe*. Gütersloh: Gütersloher, 1971.
Allard, Guy H. "La nature du De catechizandis rudibus de S. Augustin." PhD diss. Pontificia Universitas Lateranenssi Facultas Theologiae, 1976.
Altaner, Berthold. *Patrology*. 2nd ed. Translated by Hilda C. Graef. New York: Herder & Herder, 1961.
Archer, Gleason L., Jr., trans. *Jerome's Commentary on Daniel*. Grand Rapids: Baker, 1958.
Atchley, E. G. Cuthbert E. *On the Epiclesis of the Eucharistic Liturgy and in the Consecration of the Font*. Alcuin Club Collections 31. Oxford: Oxford University Press, 1935.
Aubineau, M. "Les 318 serviteurs d'Abraham (Gen., XIV, 14) et le nombre des pères au Concile de Nicée (325)." *Revue d'histoire ecclésiastique* 61 (1966) 5–43.
Auf der Maur, Hans Jörg, and Joop Waldram. "*Illuminatio Verbi Divini—Confessio Fidei—Gratia Baptismi*: Wort, Glaube und Sakrament in Katechumenat und Taufliturgie bei Origenes." In *Fides Sacramenti Sacramentum Fidei: Studies in Honour of Pieter Smulders*, edited by Hans Jörg Auf der Maur et al., 41–95. Assen: Van Gorcum, 1981.
Aulén, Gustaf. *Christus Victor: An Historical Study of the Three Main Types of the Idea of Atonement*. Translated by A. G. Hebert. 1961. Reprinted, Eugene, OR: Wipf & Stock, 2003.
Baarda, Tjitze. *Early Transmission of Words of Jesus*. Selected and edited by J. Helderman and S. J. Noorda. Amsterdam: VU Bokhandel, 1983.
Bainton, Roland. "The Origins of Epiphany." In *Early and Medieval Christianity*, 22–38. Boston: Beacon, 1962. Reprinted in *Worship in Early Christianity*, edited by Everett Ferguson, 340–56. SEC 15. New York: Garland, 1993.
Baker, Andy Alexis. "*Ad Quirinum* Book Three and Cyprian's Catechumenate." *JECS* 17 (2009) 357–80.
Bardenhewer, Otto. *Geschichte der altkirchlichen Literatur*. Vol. 1. 2nd ed. Freiburg: Herder, 1913.

*Bibliography*

Bareille, G. "Catéchèse." In *Dictionnaire de Théologie Catholique*, edited by A. Vacant and E. Mangenot, vol. 2, cols. 1877–95. Paris, Letouzey et Ané, 1905.

Barkley, Gary Wayne, trans. *Origen: Homilies on Leviticus 1–16*. FC 83. Washington, DC: Catholic University of America Press, 1990.

Barnard, L. W. Barnard, "The Epistle of Barnabas—A Paschal Homily?" *VC* 15 (1961) 8–22.

———. *Justin Martyr: His Life and Thought*. Cambridge: Cambridge University Press, 1967.

———. "Justin Martyr's Eschatology." *VC* 19 (1965) 86–98.

———. *Studies in the Apostolic Fathers and Their Background*. New York: Schocken, 1960.

Barrett, C. K. "The Eschatology of the Epistle to the Hebrews." In *The Background of the New Testament and Its Eschatology*, edited by W. D. Davies and David Daube, 363–93. Cambridge: Cambridge University Press, 1956.

Barry, Kieren. *The Greek Qabalah: Alphabetic Mysticism and Numerology in the Ancient World*. York Beach, ME: Weiser, 1999.

Barthoulot, Jean, trans. *La Prédication des Apôtres et ses Preuvres: ou la Foi Chrétienne*. Collection Les Pères dans la Foi 3. Paris: Desclée de Brouwer, 1977.

Bauckham, Richard J. "Millennium." In *New Dictionary of Theology*, ed. Sinclair B. Ferguson and David F. Wright, 428–30. Downers Grove, IL: InterVarsity, 1988.

———. "Sabbath and Sunday in the Post-Apostolic Church." In *From Sabbath to Lord's Day: A Biblical, Historical, and Theological Investigation*, edited by D. A. Carson, 252–98. 1982. Reprinted, Eugene, OR: Wipf & Stock, 1999.

Bauer, Walter. "Das Gebot der Feindesliebe und die alten Christen." *Zeitschrift für Theologie und Kirche* (1917) 37–54.

Baumeister, Theofrid. *Die Anfänge der Theologie des Martyriums*. Münsterische Beiträge zur Theologie 45. Münster: Aschendorf, 1980.

Beasley-Murray, G. R. *Baptism in the New Testament*. Grand Rapids: Eerdmans, 1973.

Belche, Jean-Pierre. "Die Bekehrung zum Christentum nach Augustins Buchlein *De catechizandis rudibus*." *Aug* 27 (1977) 26–69, 333–63; 28 (1978) 255–87; 29 (1979) 247–79.

Benoît, André. *Le baptême chrétien au second siècle*. Études d'histoire et de philosophie religieuses 43. Paris: Presses Universitaires de France, 1953.

———. *Saint Irénée: Introduction à l'étude de sa théologie*. Études d'histoire et de philosophie religieuses 52. Paris: Presses universitaires de France, 1960.

Benoît, André, and Charles Munier. *Le Baptême dans 1'Eglise ancienne (Ier–IIIe siècles)*. Traditio Christiana 9. Bern: Lang, 1994.

Bernardi, Jean. *La prédication des Pères Cappadociens: Le prédicateur et son auditoire*. Publications de la Faculté des lettres et sciences humaines de l'Université de Montpellier 30. Paris: Presses universitaires de France, 1968.

Bertrand, Daniel A. *Le Baptême de Jesus: Histoire de l'exégèse aux deux premiers siècles*. Tübingen: Mohr/Siebeck, 1973.

Beskow, Per. *Rex Gloriae: The Kingship of Christ in the Early Church*. Translated by Eric J. Sharpe. Stockholm: Almquist & Wiksell, 1962.

Betz, Hans Dieter, ed. *The Greek Magical Papyri in Translation Including the Demotic Spells*. Chicago: University of Chicago Press, 1986.

Beyenka, Sr. Mary Melchior, trans. *Saint Ambrose: Letters*. FC 26. New York: Fathers of the Church, 1954.

# Bibliography

Bietenhard, Hans. "The Millennial Hope in the Early Church." *SJT* 6 (1953) 12-30.

——. "Das tausendjährige Reich: Eine biblisch-theologische Studie." Theol. diss., Basel, 1945.

Blanc, Cécile. "Le Baptême d'après Origène." *StPatr* 11 (1972) 113-24.

Blum, G. G. "Chiliasmus II: Alte Kirche." In *Theologische Realenzyklopädie*, edited by Horst Robert Balz, 7:729-33. Berlin: de Gruyter, 1981.

Böcher, O. "Chiliasmus I. Judentum and Neues Testament." In *Theologische Realenzyklopädie*, edited by Horst Robert Balz, 7:723-29. Berlin: de Gruyter, 1981.

Bokser, B. Z. "Justin Martyr and the Jews." *Jewish Quarterly Review* 64 (1973-74) 97-122.

Bonner, Campbell. "The Numerical Value of a Magical Formula." *Journal of Egyptian Archaeology* 16 (1930) 6-9.

Bopp, Linus. "Katechese." In *Lexikon für Theologie and Kirche*, edited by Josef Höfer und Karl Rahner, 6:27-28. Freiburg: Herder, 1961.

Botte, Bernard. *Ambroise de Milan: Des Sacrements, Des Mystères, Explication de Symbole*. Sources Chrétiennes 25 bis. Paris: Cerf, 1961.

——. *Les Origines de la Noël et de l'Epiphanie*. Textes et études liturgiques 1. Louvain: Abbaye du Mont César, 1932.

Bouchet, Jean-René. "La vision de l'économie du salut selon S. Grégoire de Nysse." *RSPT* 52 (1968) 613-44.

Braverman, Jay. *Jerome's Commentary on Daniel: A Study of Comparative Jewish and Christian Interpretation of the Hebrew Bible*. Catholic Biblical Quarterly Monograph Series 7. Washington, DC: Catholic University of America Press, 1978.

Bright, Pamela. "Origenian Understanding of Martyrdom and Its Biblical Framework." In *Origen of Alexandria: His World and His Legacy*, edited by Charles Kannengiesser and William L. Petersen, 180-99. Notre Dame: University of Notre Dame Press, 1988.

Brox, Norbert. *Zeuge and Märtyrer: Untersuchungen zur frühchristlichen Zeugnis-Terminologie*. Studien zum Alten und Neuen Testament 5. Munich: Kösel, 1961.

Bruce, Barbara J., trans. *Origen: Homilies on Joshua*. Edited by Cynthia White. FC 105. Washington, DC: Catholic University of America Press, 2002.

Burns, J. P. *Cyprian the Bishop*. Routledge Early Church Monographs. London: Routledge, 2002.

Busch, Benedictus. "De initiatione Christiana secundum sanctum Augustinum." *Ephemerides Liturgicae* 52 (1938) 159-78, 385-483.

Butterworth, G. W., trans. *Origen On First Principles: Being Koetschau's Text of the De principiis Translated into English, Together with an Introduction and Notes*. 1936. Reprinted, New York: Harper & Row, 1966.

Cabrol, Fernand. "Nombres." In *Dictionnaire d'archéologie chrétienne et de liturgie*, edited by Fernand Cabrol and Henri Leclercq, 12:1465-69. Paris: Letouzey et Ané, 1935.

Campbell, James Marshall. *The Influence of the Second Sophistic on the Style of the Sermons of St. Basil the Great*. Catholic University of America Patristic Studies 2. Washington, DC: Catholic University of America, 1922.

Campenhausen, Hans von. "Die Entstehung der Heilsgeschichte: Der Aufbau des christlichen Geschichtsbildes in der Theologie des ersten and zweiten Jahrhunderts." *Saeculum* 21 (1970) 189-212.

# Bibliography

———. *Die Idee des Martyriums in der alten Kirche.* 2nd ed. Göttingen: Vandenhoeck & Ruprecht, 1964.

———. "Das Martyrium in der Mission." In *Kirchengeschichte als Missionsgeschichte*, vol. 1, *Die Alte Kirche*, edited by Heinzgünter Frohnes and Uwe W. Knorr, 71–85. Munich: Kaiser, 1974.

Canning, Raymond. "Augustine on the Identity of the Neighbour and the Meaning of True Love for Him 'As Ourselves'" (Matt 22:39) and "As Christ has Loved Us" (Jn 13:34)." *Aug* 36 (1986) 161–239.

———. "The Augustinian *uti/frui* Distinction in the Relation Between Love for Neighbour and Love for God." *Aug* 33 (1983) 165–231.

———. "The Distinction Between Love for God and Love for Neighbour in St. Augustine." *Aug* 32 (1982) 5–41. Reprinted in *Christian Life: Ethics, Morality, and Discipline in the Early Church*, edited by Everett Ferguson, 703–39. SEC 16. New York: Garland, 1993.

———. "Love of Neighbour in St. Augustine: A Preparation for or the Essential Moment of Love for God?" *Aug* 33 (1983) 5–57.

———. "'Love Your Neighbour as Yourself' (Matt 22:39): St. Augustine on the Lineaments of the Self to Be Loved." *Aug* 34 (1984) 145–97.

———. "The Unity of Love for God and Neighbour." *Aug* 37 (1987) 38–121.

Capelle, D. B. "L'introduction du catéchemenat á Rome." *Recherches de théologie ancienne et médiévale* 5 (1933) 129–54.

Carleton Paget, James N. B. "Barnabas 9:4: A Peculiar Verse on Circumcision." *VC* 45 (1991) 242–51.

———. *The Epistle of Barnabas.* WUNT 2/64. Tübingen: Mohr/Siebeck, 1994.

Cerfaux, Lucien. "Les paraboles du royaume dans l'Évangile de Thomas." *Museon* 70 (1957) 307–27.

Chadwick, Henry. *Augustine.* Past Masters. Oxford: Oxford University Press, 1986.

———, trans. *Dialogue with Heraclides.* In *Alexandrian Christianity.* Library of Christian Classics 2. Philadelphia: Westminster, 1954.

———. "The Evidences of Christianity in the Apologetic of Origen." *StPatr* 2 (1957) 331–39.

———. *Origen: Contra Celsum.* Cambridge: Cambridge University Press, 1953.

Charlesworth, James H., ed. *The Old Testament Pseudepigrapha*, vol. 1, *Apocalyptic Literature and Testaments.* Garden City, NY: Doubleday, 1983.

Chilton, Bruce, ed. *The Kingdom of God.* Issues in Religion and Theology 5. Philadelphia: Fortress, 1984.

Christe, Yves. "The Apocalypse in the Monumental Art of the Eleventh through Thirteenth Centuries." In *The Apocalypse in the Middle Ages*, edited by Richard K. Emmerson and Bernard McGinn, 234–58. Ithaca, NY: Cornell University Press, 1992.

Christopher, Jospeh P. *St. Augustine: The First Catechetical Instruction.* ACW 2. Westminster, MD: Newman, 1952.

Clouse, Robert G. "Millennium, Views of the." In *Evangelical Dictionary of Theology*, edited by Walter A. Elwell, 714–18. Grand Rapids: Baker, 1984.

Cohen, A., trans. *Midrash Rabbah.* Vol. 8, *Ecciesiastes.* London: Soncino, 1939.

Collins, John J. *The Apocalyptic Imagination: An Introduction to the Jewish Matrix of Christianity.* New York: Crossroad, 1984.

———, ed. *Encyclopedia of Apocalypticism.* Vol. 1, *The Origins of Apocalypticism in Judaism and Christianity.* New York: Continuum, 1998.
———, ed. *Semeia* 14: *Apocalypse: The Morphology of a Genre.* Missoula, MT: Scholars, 1979.
Connolly, R. Hugh. *Didascalia Apostolorum: The Syriac Version Translated and Accompanied by the Verona Latin Fragments.* 1929. Reprinted, Ancient Texts and Translations. Eugene, OR: Wipf & Stock, 2010.
———. "The *Explanatio symboli ad initiandos*: A Work of Saint Ambrose." *Texts and Studies* 10 (1952) 28–39.
Countryman, L. William. "Tertullian and the *Regula Fidei.*" *SecCent* 2 (1982) 208–27.
Covolo, E. dal. "'Regno di Dio' nel Dialogo di Giustino con Trifone Giudeo." *Aug* 28 (1988).
Crockett, William R. *Eucharist: Symbol of Transformation.* New York: Pueblo, 1989.
Cross, F. L. *I. Peter: A Paschal Liturgy.* London: Mowbray, 1954.
———, ed. *St. Cyril of Jerusalem's lectures on the Christian sacraments: The Procatechesis and the Five Mystagogical catecheses.* Texts for Students 51. London: SPCK, 1952.
Crouzel, Henri. "Diable et démons dans les homélies d'Origène." *Bulletin littérature ecclésiastique* 94 (1994) 303–31.
———. *Origen.* Translated by A. S. Worrall. San Francisco: Harper & Row, 1989.
———. "Origène et la structure du sacrement." *Bulletin de Littérature Ecclésiastique* 63 (1962) 81–104.
Cyril of Jerusalem. *Catechetical Lectures.* In *NPNF*, trans. E. H. Gifford, series 2, vol. 7. Reprinted, Peabody, MA: Hendrickson, 1994.
Dahl, Nils A. "La terre où coulent le lait et le miel selon Barnabe 6.8–19." In *Aux sources de la tradition chrétienne: Mélanges offers à M. Maurice Goguel*, 62–70. Bibliothèque théologique. Neuchâtel: Delachaux & Niestlé, 1950.
Daley, Brian E. *The Hope of the Early Church: A Handbook of Patristic Eschatology.* Cambridge: Cambridge University Press, 1991.
Daly, Robert, trans. *Origen: Treatise on the Passover and Dialogue with Heraclides.* ACW 54. New York: Paulist, 1992.
Damme, Dirk van. *Pseudo-Cyprian Adversus Iudaeos: Gegen die Judenchristen die älteste lateinische Predigt.* Paradosis 22. Freiburg: Universitätsverlag, 1969.
Daniel, E. Randolph. "Joachim of Fiore: Patterns of History in the Apocalypse." In *The Apocalypse in the Middle Ages*, edited by Richard K. Emmerson and Bernard McGinn, 72–88. Ithaca, NY: Cornell University Press, 1992.
Daniélou, Jean. *The Bible and the Liturgy.* Liturgical Studies 3. Notre Dame, IN: University of Notre Dame Press, 1956.
———. with Regine du Charlat. *La catéchèse aux premiers siècles.* Ecole de la Foi. Paris: Fayard-Mame, 1968.
———. "La Catéchèse dans la Tradition Patristique." *Catéchèse* 1 (1960–61) 21–34. Reprinted in *L'initiation chrétienne*, edited by Adelbert Hamman, 7–20. Paris: Grasset, 1963.
———. "La chronologie des oeuvres de Grégoire de Nysse." *StPatr* 7 (1966) 159–69.
———. "Circoncision et baptême." In *Theologie in Geschichte und Gegenwart: Michael Schmaus zum sechzigsten Geburtstag*, edited by Johann Auer and Hermann Volk, 755–76. Munich: Zink, 1957.
———. *From Shadows to Reality: Studies in the Biblical Typology of the Fathers.* Translated by Wulstan Hibberd. Westminster, MD: Newman, 1960.

## Bibliography

———. "L'histoire du Salut dans la Catéchese." *La Maison-Dieu* 30 (1952) 19–35.
———. "Introduction." In *L'initiation chrétienne*, edited by A. Hamman, 7–20. Lettres chrétiennes 7. Paris: Grasset, 1963.
———. "Le Mystère du cube dans les sermons de Saint Grégoire de Nysse." In *Vom Christlichen Mysterium*, edited by A. Mayr et al., 76–93. Düsseldorf: Patmos, 1951.
———. *Origen*. Translated by Walter Mitchell. New York: Sheed & Ward, 1955.
———. *Origène. Le Génie du christianisme*. Paris: La Table ronde, 1948.
———. *The Origins of Latin Christianity*. Translated by David Smith and John Austin Baker. Edited by John Austin Baker. Philadelphia: Westminster, 1977.
———. *Sacramentum Futuri: Étude sur les origines de la typologie biblique*. Études de théologie historique. Paris: Beauchesne, 1950. (ET = *From Shadows to Reality*.)
———. *The Theology of Jewish Christianity*. Translated and edited by John A. Baker. The Development of Christian Doctrine before the Council of Nicaea 1. Philadelphia: Westminster, 1964.
———. "La typologie millenariste de la semaine dans le christianisme primitif." *VC* 2 (1948) 1–16.
Danker, Frederick W. "Lexicographical Hazards, Pitfalls, and Challenges, with Special Reference to the Contributions of John Edward Gates." In *SBL 1985 Seminar Papers*, 235–41. Atlanta, 1985.
Dassmann, E. *Sundenvergebung durch Taufe, Busse, und Martyrerfürbitte in den Zeugnissen frühchristlichen Frömmigkeit und Kunst*. Münster: Aschendorf, 1973.
Daube, David. *Civil Disobedience in Antiquity*. Edinburgh: Edinburgh University Press, 1972.
Davis, John J. *Biblical Numerology: A Basic Study of the Use of Numbers in the Bible*. Grand Rapids: Baker, 1968.
Dehandschutter, Boudewijn. "Le Martyre de Polycarpe et le développment de la conception du martyre au deuxième siècle." *StPatr* 17.2 (1982) 659–68.
———. "Martyr–Martyrium: Quelques observations à propos d'un christianisme sémantique." In *Eulogia: Mélanges offerts à Antoon A. R. Bastiaensen à l'occasion de son soixante-cinquième anniversaire*, ed. G. J. M. Bartelink et al., 33–39. Instrumenta Patristica 24. Steenbrugis: Abbatia S. Petri, 1991.
De Latte, Robert. "Saint Augustin et le baptême: Etude liturgico-historique du rituel baptismal des adultes chez saint Augustin." *QL* 56 (1975) 177–223.
Demetrakos, D. *Mega Lexikon: Oles tes Hellenikes Glosses* [Greek]. 15 vols. Athens: Dome, 1964.
Didier, J. C. *Le Baptême des enfants dans la tradition de l'église*. Monumenta Christiana Selecta 7. Tournai: Desclée, 1959.
———. "Un cas typique de développement du dogme à propos du baptême des enfants." *Mélanges de science religieuse* 9 (1952) 191–213.
Diehl, Ernst. *Inscriptiones latinae christianae veteres*. 2nd ed. Berlin: Weidmann, 1961.
Dix, Gregory. *The Treatise on the Apostolic Tradition of St. Hippolytus of Rome*. 2nd ed. London: SPCK, 1968.
Dodd, C. H. *The Apostolic Preaching and Its Developments: Three Lectures*. New York: Harper, 1944.
Doignon, Jean. "La scène évangélique du Baptême de Jésus commentée par Lactance (*Divinae institutiones*, 4.15) et Hilaire de Poitiers (*In Matthaeum*, 2, 5–6)." In *Epektasis: Mélanges patristiques offerts au Cardinal Jean Daniélou*, edited by Jacques Fontaine and Charles Kannengiesser, 63–74. Paris: Beauchesne, 1972.

Donfried, Karl Paul. *The Setting of Second Clement in Early Christianity.* NovTSup 38. Leiden: Brill, 1974.
Doval, Alexis. *Cyril of Jerusalem, Mystagogue: The Authorship of the Mystagogical Catecheses.* PMS 17. Washington, DC: Catholic University of America Press, 2001.
———. "The Fourth Century Jerusalem Catechesis and the Development of the Creed." *StPatr* 30 (1997) 296–305.
Drews, P. "Der literarische Charakter der neuentdeckten Schrift des Irenaus 'Zum Erweise der apostolischen Verkündigung.'" *ZNW* 8 (1907) 226–33.
Drijvers, Hans J. W. "Facts and Problems in Early Syriac-Speaking Christianity." *SecCent* 2 (1982) 166–69.
Drobner, H. R. "Augustinus, *Sermo* 227: Eine österliche Eucharistiekatechese für die Neugetauften." *Aug* 41 (1991) 483–95.
Droge, Arthur J., and James D. Tabor. *A Noble Death: Suicide and Martyrdom among Christians and Jews in Antiquity.* San Francisco: Harper, 1991.
Ducatillon, Jeanne. *Basile de Césarée: Sur le Baptême.* SC 357. Paris: Cerf, 1989.
Dugmore, C. W. "Sacrament and Sacrifice in the Early Fathers." *JEH* n.s. 2 (1951) 24–37. Reprinted in *Worship in Early Christianity*, edited by Everett Ferguson, 178–91. SEC 15. New York: Garland, 1993.
Dujarier, Michel. *A History of the Catechumenate: The First Six Centuries.* Translated by Edward J. Hassl. New York: Sadlier, 1979.
Dunbar, David G. "The Delay of the Parousia in Hippolytus." *VC* 37 (1983) 313–27.
Duncan, Edward J. *Baptism in the Demonstrations of Aphraates, the Persian Sage.* SCA 8. Washington, DC: Catholic University of America Press, 1945.
Echle, H. A. "Sacramental Initiation as Christian Mystery—Initiation according to Clement of Alexandria." In *Vom Christlichen Mysterium: Gesammelte Arbeiten zum Gedächtnis von Odo Casel*, edited by Anton Mayer et al., 54–65. Düsseldorf: Patmos, 1951.
Edsman, Carl-Martin. *Le baptême du feu.* Acta Seminarii Neotestamentici Upsaliensis 9. Uppsala: Lundequistka, 1940.
Étaix, Raymond. "Sermon inédit de saint Augustin sur la Circoncision dans un ancien manuscript de Saragosse." *Revue des études augustiniennes* 26 (1980) 62–87.
Evans, Ernest, ed. and trans. *Tertullian's Homily on Baptism.* London: SPCK, 1964.
Farkasfalvy, Denis. "Christological Content and Its Biblical Basis in the Letter of the Martyrs of Gaul." *SecCent* 9 (1992) 7–12.
Faye, Eugène de. *Origen and His Work.* Translated by Fred Rothwell. New York: Columbia University Press, 1929.
———. *Origène, sa vie, son oeuvre, sa pensée.* Bibliothèque de l'Ecole des hautes études. Sciences religieuses 37. Paris: Leroux, 1928.
Fedwick, Paul Jonathan. "The Translations of the Works of Basil before 1400." In *Basil of Casesarea: Christian, Humanist, Ascetic: A Sixteen-Hundredth Anniversary Symposium*, part 2, edited by Paul Jonathan Fedwick, 439–512. Toronto: Pontifical Institute of Mediaeval Studies, 1981.
Ferguson, Everett. *Backgrounds of Early Christianity.* 3rd ed. Grand Rapids: Eerdmans, 2003.
———. "Basil's Protreptic to Baptism." In *Nova et Vetera: Patristic Studies in Honor of Thomas Patrick Halton*, edited by John Petruccione, 70–83. Washington, DC: Catholic University of America Press, 1998. [Reprinted in this vol.]

## Bibliography

———. "The Covenant Idea in the Second Century." In *Texts and Testaments: Critical Studies on the Bible and Early Church Fathers*, edited by W. Eugene March, 135–62. San Antonio: Trinity University Press, 1980. [Reprinted in vol. 1]

———. *Demonology of the Early Christian World*. Symposium Series 12. New York: Mellen, 1984.

———. "The Disgrace and the Glory: A Jewish Motif in Early Christianity." *StPatr* 21 (1989) 86–94. [Reprinted in this vol.]

———. "Divine Pedagogy: Origen's Use of the Imagery of Education." In *Christian Teaching: Studies in Honor of LeMoine G. Lewis*, edited by Everett Ferguson, 343–62. Abilene: Abilene Christian University Bookstore, 1981. [Reprinted in this vol.]

———. *Early Christians Speak*. 3rd ed. Abilene: Abilene Christian University Press, 1999.

———. "Exhortations to Baptism in the Cappadocians." *StPatr* 31 (1997) 112–29. [Reprinted in this vol.]

———. "Inscriptions and the Origin of Infant Baptism." *JTS* n.s. 30 (1979) 37–46. Reprinted in *Conversion, Cathecumenate and Baptism in the Early Church*, edited by Everett Ferguson, 391–400. SEC 11. New York: Garland, 1993. [Reprinted in this vol.]

———. "Irenaeus' *Proof of the Apostolic Preaching* and Early Catechetical Instruction." *StPatr* 18.3 (1989) 119–40. [Reprinted in this vol.]

———. "The Kingdom of God in Early Patristic Literature." In *The Kingdom of God in 20th-Century Interpretation*, edited by Wendell Willis, 191–208. Peabody, MA: Hendrickson, 1987. [Reprinted in this vol.]

———. "The Lord's Supper in Church History: The Early Church through the Medieval Period." In *The Lord's Supper: Believers' Church Perspectives*, edited by Dale R. Stoffer, 21–45. Scottdale, PA: Herald, 1997.

———. "Laying on of Hands: Its Significance in Ordination." *JTS* n.s. 26 (1975) 1–12. Reprinted, *Church, Ministry, and Organization in the Early Church Era*, edited by Everett Ferguson, 147–58. SEC 13. New York: Garland, 1993. [Reprinted in vol. 1]

———. "Love of Enemies and Non-Retaliation in the Second Century." In *The Contentious Triangle: Church, State, and University: A Festschrift in Honor of George Huntston Williams*, Rodney L. Peterson and Calvin Augustine Pater, 81–95. Sixteenth Century Essays & Studies 51. Kirksville, MO: Thomas Jefferson University Press, 1999.

———. "Origen's Demonology." In *Johannine Studies: Essays in Honor of Frank Pack*, edited by James E. Priest, ed., 54–66. Malibu, CA: Pepperdine University Press, 1989.

———. "Preaching at Epiphany: Gregory of Nyssa and John Chrysostom on Baptism and the Church." *CH* 66 (1997) 1–17. [Reprinted in this vol.]

———. "Some Aspects of Gregory of Nyssa's Moral Theology in the Homilies on Ecclesiastes." In *Gregory of Nyssa, Homilies on Ecclesiastes: An English Version with Supporting Studies: Proceedings of the Seventh International Colloquium on Gregory of Nyssa (St. Andrews, 5–10 September 1990)*, edited by Stuart George Hall, 319–36. Berlin: de Gruyter, 1993.

———. "Spiritual Circumcision in Early Christianity." *SJT* 41 (1988) 485–97.

———. "Spiritual Sacrifice in Early Christianity and Its Environment." In *ANRW* II.23.1, 1152–86. Berlin: de Gruyter, 1980.

———, ed. *Personalities of the Early Church*. SEC 1. New York: Garland, 1993.

*Bibliography*

———. "Voices of Religious Liberty in the Early Church." *Restoration Quarterly* 19 (1976) 13–22.

———. "Was Barnabas a Chiliast? An Example of Hellenistic Number Symbolism in Barnabas and Clement of Alexandria." In *Greeks, Romans, and Christians: Essays in Honor of Abraham J. Malherbe*, edited by David L. Balch et al., 157–67. Minneapolis: Fortress, 1990. [Reprinted in this vol.]

Finn, Thomas M. *Early Christian Baptism and the Catechumenate*. 2 vols. Collegeville, MN: Liturgical, 1992.

———. "It Happened One Saturday Night: Ritual and Conversion in Augustine's North Africa." *Journal of the American Academy of Religion* 58 (1990) 589–616.

———. *The Liturgy of Baptism in the Baptismal Instructions of St. John Chrysostom*. SCA 15. Washington, DC: Catholic University of America Press, 1967.

———. "Ritual Processes and the Survival of Early Christianity: A Study of the Apostolic Tradition of Hippolytus." *Journal of Ritual Studies* 3 (1989) 69–90.

Finney, Paul Corby. "Did Gnostics Make Pictures?" *Numen* 14 (1980) 450–54. Reprinted in *Art, Archaeology and Architecture of Early Christianity*, edited by Paul Corby Finney, 84–88. SEC 18. New York: Garland, 1993.

Fitzmyer, Joseph A. *The One Who Is to Come*. Grand Rapids: Eerdmans, 2006.

Folkemer, Lawrence D. "A Study of the Catechumenate." *CH* 15 (1946) 286–307. Reprinted in *Conversion, Cathechumenate, and Baptism in the Early Church*, edited by Everett Ferguson, 244–65. SEC 11. New York: Garland, 1993.

Fortier, P., ed. *Origen: Homélies sur l'Exode*. Sources Chrétiennes 16. Paris, 1947.

Fredouille, Jean-Claude, trans. and ed. *Tertullien: Contre les Valentiniens*, Sources Chrétiennes 280, 281. Paris: Cerf, 1981.

Fredriksen, Paula. "Tyconius and Augustine on the Apocalypse." In *The Apocalypse in the Middle Ages*, edited by Richard K. Emmerson and Bernard McGinn, 20–37. Ithaca, NY: Cornell University Press, 1992.

Frend, W. H. C. *Martyrdom and Persecution in the Early Church: A Study of a Conflict from the Maccabees to Donatus*. Oxford: Blackwell, 1965.

Frick, Robert. *Die Geschichte des Reich-Gottes-Gedankens in der alten Kirche bis zu Origenes und Augustin*. Beihefte zur Zeitschrift für die neutestamentliche Wissenschaft 6. Giessen: Töpelmann, 1928.

Fried, Johannes. "Endzeiterwartung um die Jahrtausendwende." *Deutsches Archiv für Erforschung des Mittelalters* 45 (1989) 381–473.

Friesenhahn, Peter. *Hellenistische Wortzahlenmystik im Neuen Testament*. 1935. Reprinted, Amsterdam: Grüner, 1970.

Froom, Le Roy Edwin. *The Prophetic Faith of Our Fathers*. Vol. 1. Washington, DC: Review & Herald, 1950.

Gardner, Paul D. "'Circumcised in Baptism—Raised through Faith': A Note on Col. 2.11–12." *Westminster Theological Journal* 45 (1983) 172–77.

Germain, Elisabeth. "Baptême et éducation de la foi dans l'église ancienne." *Catéchèse* 22 (1982) 17.

Gingras, George E., trans and ann. *Egeria: Diary of a Pilgrimage*. ACW 38. New York: Newman, 1970.

Gistelinck, Frans. "Lactance et sa théologie baptismale propre à son temps." *QL* 55 (1974) 177–93.

# Bibliography

Grant, Robert M. "Development of the Christian Catechumenate." In *Made Not Born: New Perspectives on Christian Initiation and the Catechumenate from the Murphy Center for Liturgical Research*, 32–49. Liturgical Studies. Notre Dame, 1976.

———. "Irenaeus and Hellenistic Culture." *HTR* 42 (1949) 41–51.

———. *The Letter and the Spirit*. London: SPCK, 1957.

———. "Sacrifices and Oaths as Required of Early Christians." In *Kyriakon: Festschrift Johannes Quasten*, edited by Patrick Granfield and Josef A. Jungmann, 1:12–17. Münster: Aschendorff, 1970.

Gribomont, Jean. "Saint Basile: Le protreptique au Baptême." In *Lex Orandi Lex Credendi: Miscellanea in onore di P. Cipriano Vagaggini*, edited by Gerardo J. Békés and Giustino Farnedi, 71–92. Studia Anselmiana 79. Rome: Editrice Anselmiana, 1980.

Grossi, Vittorino. "Regula veritatis e narratio battesimale in sant' Ireneo." *Aug* 12 (1972) 437–63.

Hall, Stuart. *Melito of Sardis on Pascha and Fragments*. Oxford Early Christian Texts. Oxford: Oxford University Press, 1979.

Hamilton, J. D. B. "The Church and the Language of Mystery: The First Four Centuries." *Ephemerides Theologicae Lovanienses* 53 (1977) 479–94.

Hamman, Adelbert-G. "Introduction." In *La Prédication des Apôtres et ses Preuvres: ou la Foi Chrétienne*. Translated by Jean Barthoulot. Collection Les Pères dans la Foi 3. Paris: Desclée De Brouwer, 1977.

Hamman, André. *Baptism: Ancient Liturgies and Patristic Texts*. Staten Island, NY: Alba House, 1967.

Hanson, R. P. C. *Allegory and Event: A Study of the Sources and Significance of Origen's Interpretation of Scripture*. Richmond: John Knox, 1959.

Harkins, Paul W., trans. and ann. *St. John Chrysostom: Baptismal Instructions*. ACW 31. Westminster, MD: Newman, 1963.

Harmless, William. *Augustine and the Catechomenate*. Collegeville, MN: Liturgical, 1995.

Harnack, Adolf von. *History of Dogma*. Vol. 1. 1900. Reprinted, New York: Dover, 1961.

———. *The Mission and Expansion of Christianity*. Translated by James Moffatt. 2nd ed. 1908. Reprinted, New York: Harper, 1962.

Hart, Columba, and Jane Bishop, trans. *Hildegard of Bingen: Scivias*. Classics of Western Spirituality. New York: Paulist, 1990.

Hedrick, Charles W. "Kingdom Sayings and Parables of Jesus in the *Apocryphon of James*." *NTS* 29 (1983) 1–24.

Hehn, Johannes. *Siebenzahl und Sabbat bei den Babyloniern und im Alten Testament*. Leipziger semitistische Studien 2/5. Leipzig: Hinrichs, 1907.

Heid, Stefan. *Chiliasmus und Antichrist-Mythos: Eine frühchristliche Kontroverse um das Heilige Land*. Hereditas 6. Bonn: Borengässer, 1993.

Heine, Ronald E. *Origen: Homiles on Genesis and Exodus*. FC 71. Washington, DC: Catholic University of America Press, 1982.

———. *Perfection in the Virtuous Life: A Study in the Relationship between Edification and Polemical Theology in Gregory of Nyssa's De vita Moysis*. PMS 2. Cambridge, MA: Philadelphia Patristic Foundation, 1975.

Helgeland, John, Robert J. Daly, and J. Patout Burns. *Christians and the Military: The Early Experience*. Edited by Robert J. Daly. Philadelphia: Fortress, 1985.

Hermans, Albert. "Le Pseudo-Barnabe est-il millenariste?" *Ephemerides theologicae lovanienses* 35 (1969) 849–76.
Herrick, Henry Martyn. *The Kingdom of God in the Writings of the Fathers*. Chicago: University of Chicago Press, 1903.
Hill, Charles E. "Cerinthus and Johannine Christianity." *JECS* 8 (2000) 135–72.
———. "Hades of Hippolytus or Tartarus of Tertullian? The Authorship of the Fragment *De Universo*." *VC* 43 (1989) 105–26.
———. "The Marriage of Montanism and Millennialism." *StPatr* 26 (1993) 142–48.
———. *Regnum Caelorum: Patterns of Future Hope in Early Christianity*. Oxford Early Christian Studies. Oxford: Clarendon, 1992.
Hinson, F. Glenn. *The Evangelization of the Roman Empire: Identity and Adaptability*. Macon, GA: Mercer University Press, 1980.
Hodgson, Robert, Jr. "The Kingdom of God in the School of St. John." In *The Kingdom of God in 20th-Century Interpretation*, edited by Wendell Willis, 163–74. Peabody, MA: Hendrickson, 1987.
Hornus, Jean-Michel. *It Is Not Lawful for Me to Fight: Early Christian Attitudes Toward War, Violence, and the State*. Translated by Alan Kreider and Oliver Coburn. Rev. ed. Christian Peace Shelf Selection. Scottdale, PA: Herald, 1980.
Hotchkiss, Robert V., ed. and trans. *Pseudo-Epiphanius Testimony Book*. Early Christian Literature Series 1. Missoula, MT: Scholars, 1974.
Hübner, Reinhard M. *Die Einheit des Leibes Christi bei Gregor von Nyssa: Untersuchungen zum Ursprung der "physischen" Erlösungslehre*. Philosophia Patrum 2. Leiden: Brill, 1974.
Hvalvik, Reidar. *The Struggle for Scripture and Covenant: The Purpose of the Epistle of Barnabas and Jewish–Christian Competition in the Second Century*. WUNT 2/82. Tübingen: Mohr/Siebeck, 1996.
Jackson, B. Darrell. "Sources of Origen's Doctrine of Freedom." *CH* 35 (1966) 13–23.
Jacob, Réne. "Le Martyre, épanouissement du sacerdoce des Chrétiens, dans la litterature patristique jusqu' an 258." *Mélanges de Science Religieuse* 24 (1967) 57–83, 153–72, 177–209.
Jaeger, Werner. *Early Christianity and Greek Paideia*. Cambridge, MA: Belknap, 1961.
Jeremias, Joachim. *Infant Baptism in the First Four Centuries*. Translated by David Cairns. Library of History and Doctrine. London: SCM, 1960.
———. *Die Kindertaufe in den ersten vier Jahrhunderten*. Göttingen: Vandenhoeck & Ruprecht, 1958.
———. *Nochmals: Die Anfänge der Kindertaufe: Eine Replik auf Kurt Alands Schrift: Die Säuglingstaufe im Neuen Testament und in der alten Kirche*. Theologische Existenz Heute 101. Munich: Kaiser, 1962.
———. *The Origins of Infant Baptism: A Further Study in Reply to Kurt Aland*. Translated by Dorothea M. Barton. Studies in Historical Theology 1. 1963. Reprinted, Eugene, OR: Wipf & Stock, 2004.
Jossa, Giorgio. *Regno di Dio e Chiesa: Ricerche sulla concezione escatologica ed ecclesiologica dell' Adversus haereses di Ireneo di Lione*. Historia Salutis. Serie Storica 2. Naples: D'Auria, 1970.
Jungmann, Josef A. "Katechumenat." In *Lexikon für Theologie and Kirche*, edited by Josef Höfer und Karl Rahner, 6:51–54. Freiburg: Herder, 1961.

# Bibliography

Kavanagh, Denis J., trans. *Saint Augustine: Commentary on the Lord's Sermon on the Mount with Seventeen Related Sermons*. FC 11. New York: Fathers of the Church, 1951.

Kees, Reinhard Jakob. *Die Lehre von der Oikonomia Gottes in der Oratio Catechetica Gregors von Nyssa*. VCSup 30. Leiden: Brill, 1995.

Kelly, J. N. D., trans. and ann. *Rufinus: A Commentary on the Apostles Creed*. ACW 20. Westminster, MD: Newman, 1955.

Kettel, Joachim. "Martyrium und Eucharistie." *Geist und Leben* 30 (1957) 34–46.

Kevane, Eugene. *Catechesis in Augustine*. St. Augustine Lecture Series 1983. Villanova: Villanova University Press, 1983.

Klappert, B. "King, Kingdom." In *NIDNTT*, edited by Colin Brown, 2:372–90. Grand Rapids: Zondervan, 1976.

Klein, Peter K. "Introduction: The Apocalypse in Medieval Art." In *The Apocalypse in the Middle Ages*, edited by Richard K. Emmerson and Bernard McGinn, 159–99. Ithaca, NY: Cornell University Press, 1992.

Kleist, James A. *The Didache, The Epistle of Barnabas, The Epistles and The Martyrdom of St. Polycarp, The Fragments of Papias, The Epistle to Diognetus*. ACW 6. Westminster, MD: Newman, 1948.

Koch, Hal. *Pronoia und Paideusis: Studien über Origenes und sein Verhältnis zurn Platonismus*. Arbeiten zur Kirchengeschichte 22. Berlin: de Gruyter, 1932.

Koch, Hugo. "Tertullianisches." *Theologische Studien and Kritiken* 101 (1929) 462–69.

Kötting, Bernhard. "Martyrium und Provokation." In *Kerygma und Logos: Beiträge zu den geistesgeschichtlichen Beziehungen zwischen Antike und Christentum: Festschrift für Carl Andresen zum 70. Geburtstag*, edited by Adolf Martin Ritter, 329–36. Göttingen: Vandenhoeck & Ruprecht, 1979.

Kraft, Heinz. *Texte zur Geschichte der Taufe, besonders der Kindertaufe in der alten Kirche*. 2nd ed. Kleine Texte für Vorlesungen und Übungen 174. Berlin: de Gruyter, 1960.

Kraft, Robert A. *Barnabas and the Didache*. In *The Apostolic Fathers*, edited by Robert M. Grant. Vol. 3. New York: Nelson, 1965.

———. "Barnabas' Isaiah Text and the 'Testimony Book' Hypothesis." *JBL* 79 (1960) 336–50.

Kretschmar, Georg. "Die Geschichte des Taufgottesdienstes in der alter Kirche." In *Leiturgia: Handbuch des evangelischen Gottesdienst*, vol. 5, *Der Taufgottesdienst*, edited by Karl Ferdinand Müller and Walter Blankenburg, 1–349. Kassel: Stauda, 1964.

Kromminga, D. H. *The Millennium in the Church: Studies in the History of Christian Chiliasm*. Grand Rapids: Eerdmans, 1945.

Lamoreaux, John C. "The Provenance of Ecumenius' Commentary on the Apocalypse." *VC* 52 (1998) 88–108.

Lampe, G. W. H. *A Patristic Greek Lexicon*. Oxford: Clarendon, 1968.

———. *The Seal of the Spirit: A Study in the Doctrine of Baptism and Confirmation in the New Testament and the Fathers*. 2nd ed. London: SPCK, 1967.

Landes, Richard. "Lest the Millennium Be Fulfilled: Apocalyptic Expectations and the Pattern of Western Chronography 100–800 CE." In *The Use and Abuse of Eschatology in the Middle Ages*, edited by Werner Verbeke, Daniel Verhelst, and Andries Welkenhuys, 137–211. Medievalia Lovaniensia, ser. 1, Studia 15. Leuven: Leuven University Press, 1988.

Laporte, Jean. "Models from Philo in Origen's Teaching on Original Sin." In *Living Water, Sealing Spirit: Readings on Christian Initiation*, edited by Maxwell E. Johnson, 101–17. Collegeville, MN: Liturgical, 1995.

Lassiat, P., and H. Lassiat. *Dieu veut-il des hommes libres? La catéchèse de l'Église des Martyrs d'après Irénée de Lyon*. Paris: Mame, 1976.

Lauterbach, Jacob Z., trans. *Mekilta de Rabbi Ishmael*. 3 vols. Philadelphia: Jewish Publication Society, 1933–35. Reprinted, 1949.

Lawson, John. *The Biblical Theology of Saint Irenaeus*. London: Epworth, 1948.

Lawson, R. P. *Origen: The Song of Songs Commentary and Homilies*. ACW 26. New York: Newman, 1957.

Leclercq, Henri. "Catéchèse. Catéchisme. Catéchumène." In *Dictionnaire d'archéologie chrétienne et de liturgie*, edited by Fernand Cabrol and Henri Leclercq, II.2:2530–79. Paris: Letouzey & Ané, 1925.

Leclercq, Jean. "L'idée de la royauté du Christ dans l'œuvre de Saint Justin." *L'Année Théologique* 7 (1946) 83–95.

Lerner, Robert E. "The Medieval Return to the Thousand-Year Sabbath." In *The Apocalypse in the Middle Ages*, edited by Richard K. Emmerson and Bernard McGinn, 51–71. Ithaca, NY: Cornell University Press, 1992.

———. "Refreshment of the Saints: The Time after Antichrist as a Station for Earthly Progress in Medieval Thought." *Traditio* 32 (1976) 97–144.

Lewis, Warren. "Peter John Olivi: Prophet of the Year 2000." 2 vols. PhD diss., University of Tübingen, 1972.

Lienhard, Joseph T., trans. *Origen: Homilies on Luke, Fragments on Luke*. FC 94. Washington, DC: Catholic University of America Press, 1996.

Leipoldt, Johannes. *Die urchristliche Taufe im Lichte der Religionsgeschichte*. Leipzig: Dörffling & Franke, 1928.

Liddell, H. G., and R. Scott. *Greek–English Lexicon with Revised Supplement*. Edited by H. S. Jones and R. McKenzie. 9th ed. Oxford: Clarendon, 1996.

Lightfoot, J. B. *The Apostolic Fathers*. Part I, vol. 2. London: Macmillan, 1890.

———. *Saint Paul's Epistles to the Colossians and to Philemon*. London: MacMillan, 1879.

Lindemann, Andreas, and Henning Paulsen. *Die Apostolischen Väter: Greichisch-deutsche Parallelausgabe*. Tübingen: Mohr/Siebeck, 1992.

Löfstedt, B., ed. *Zenonis Veronensis Tractatus*. Corpus Christianorum. Series Latina 22. Turnhout: Brepols, 1971.

Lombardo, Gregory J., trans. *St. Augustine on Faith and Works*. ACW 48. New York: Newman, 1988.

Lowry, S. "The Confutation of Judaism in the Epistle of Barnabas." *Journal of Jewish Studies* 11 (1960) 1–33. Reprinted in *Early Christianity and Judaism*, edited by Everett Ferguson, 303–35. SEC 6. New York: Garland, 1993.

Lukken, G. M. *Original Sin in the Roman Liturgy: Research into the Theology of Original Sin in the Roman Sacramentaria and the Early Baptismal Liturgy*. Leiden: Brill, 1973.

Lundberg, Per. *La typologie baptismale dans l'ancienne église*. ASNU 10. Uppsala: Lundequistka, 1942.

Luneau, Auguste. *L'Histoire du salut chez les Pères de l'Église: La Doctrine des ages du monde*. Théologie historique 2. Paris: Beauchesne, 1964.

## Bibliography

Lupi, J. "Catechetical Instruction in the Church of the First Two Centuries." *Melita Theologica* 9 (1956) 64.

Maertens, Th. *Histoire et pastorale du rituel du catéchumenat et du baptême.* Paroisse et Liturgie: Collection de Pastorale Liturgique 56. Bruges: Biblica, 1962.

Malingrey, Anne-Marie. *Philosophia: Étude d'un groupe de mots dans la littérature grecque, des Presocratiques au IVe siècle après J.-C.* Études et commentaires 40. Paris: Klincksieck, 1961.

Markus, R. A. *End of Ancient Christianity.* Cambridge: Cambridge University Press, 1990.

Marrou, Henri I. *A History of Education in Antiquity.* Translated by George Lamb. 1956. Reprinted, New York: Mentor, 1964.

———. *St. Augustine and His Influence through the Ages.* Translated by Patrick Hepburne-Scott. Texts of St. Augustine translated by Edmund Hill. New York: Harper & Brothers, 1957.

Marsh, H. G. "The Use of ΜΥΣΤΗΡΙΟΝ in the Writings of Clement of Alexandria with Special Reference to his Sacramental Doctrine." *JTS* 37 (1936) 64–80.

Martimort, Aimé-Georges. "L'inconographie des catacombs et la catéchèse antique." *Rivista di archeologia cristiana* 25 (1949) 105–14.

Matter, E. Ann. "The Apocalypse in Early Medieval Exegesis." In *The Apocalypse in the Middle Ages*, edited by Richard K. Emmerson and Bernard McGinn, 38–50. Ithaca, NY: Cornell University Press, 1992.

McArthur, A. Allan. *The Evolution of the Christian Year.* Greenwich, CT: Seabury, 1953.

McDonnell, Killian. "Jesus' Baptism in the Jordan." *TS* 56 (1995) 209–36.

McEleney, Neil J. "Conversion, Circumcision, and the Law." *NTS* 20 (1974) 319–41.

———. "153 Great Fishes (John 21, 11)—Gematriacal Atbash." *Biblica* 58 (1977) 411–17.

McGinn, Bernard. "Angel Pope and Papal Antichrist." *CH* 47 (1978) 155–73.

———, trans. *Apocalyptic Spirituality: Treatises and Letters of Lactantius, Adso of Montier-en-Der, Joachim of Fiore, the Franciscan Spirituals, Savonarola.* Classics of Western Spirituality. New York: Paulist, 1979.

———. *The Calabrian Abbot: Joachim of Fiore in the History of Western Thought.* New York: Macmillan, 1985.

———. "The End of the World and the Beginning of Christendom." In *Apocalypse Theory and the Ends of the World*, edited by Malcolm Bull, 59–89. Oxford: Blackwell, 1995.

———. *Visions of the End: Apocalyptic Traditions in the Middle Ages.* New ed. Records of Civilization 96. New York: Columbia University Press, 1998.

McHugh, Michael P., trans. *Saint Ambrose: Seven Exegetical Works.* FC 65. Washington, DC: Catholic University of America Press, 1972.

McLynn, Neil B. *Ambrose of Milan: Church and Court in a Christian Capital.* Transformation of the Classical Heritage 22. Berkeley: University of California Press, 1994.

Meeks, Wayne A., and Robert L. Wilken. *Jews and Christians in Antioch in the First Four Centuries of the Common Era.* Sources for Biblical Study 13. Missoula, MT: Scholars, 1978.

Metcalfe, W., trans. *Gregory Thaumaturgos Address to Origen.* Translations of Christian Literature, ser. 1: Greek Texts 13. London: SPCK, 1920.

Metzger, Marcel. "Enquêtes autour de la prétendue 'Tradition apostolique.'" *Ecclesia Orans* 9 (1992) 7-36
———. "Nouvelies perspectives pour la prétendue tradition apostolique." *Ecclesia Orans* 5 (1988) 241-59.
Meyer, Marvin, and Richard Smith, eds. *Ancient Christian Magic: Coptic Texts of Ritual Power*. 1994. Reprinted, Princeton: Princeton University Press, 1999.
Michiels, Guibert. "L'initiation chrétienne selon saint Ambroise." *Les Questions Liturgiques et Paroissiales* 34 (1953) 109-14, 164-69.
Miller, Betsey Fordyce. "Study of the Theme of 'Kingdom'; The Gospel according to Thomas: Logion 18." *NovT* 9 (1967) 52-60.
Minns, Denis. *Irenaeus*. Washington, DC: Georgetown University Press, 1994.
Mohrmann, Christine. "Encore une fois: *paganus*." *VC* 6 (1952) 109-21.
Moreschini, C., and P. Gallay, trans. *Grégoire de Nazianze: Discourse 38-41*. SC 358. Paris: Cerf, 1990.
Mossay, Justin. *Les fêtes de Noël et de l'Epiphanie: D'après les sources littéraires cappadociens au IVe siècle*. Textes et études liturgiques 3. Louvain: Abbaye du Mont César, 1965.
Mueller, Dieter. "Kingdom of Heaven or Kingdom of God?" *VC* 27 (1973) 266-76.
Mühlenberg, Ekkehard. *Gregorii Nysseni Oratio Catechetica, Opera Dogmatica Minora, Pars IV* in *Gregorii Nysseni Opera*, III, Pars IV. Leiden: Brill, 1996.
Muldowney, Mary Sarah, trans. *Saint Augustine: Sermons on the Liturgical Seasons*. FC 38. New York: Fathers of the Church, 1959.
Musurillo, Herbert. *The Acts of the Christian Martyrs*. Oxford: Clarendon, 1971.
———. "History and Symbol: A Study of Form in Early Christian Literature." *TS* 18 (1957) 357-86.
Mutzenbecher, Almut, ed. *Maximi Episcopi Taurinensis: Collectionem Sermones antiquam nonnullis sermonibus extravagantibus adiectis*. Corpus Christianorum Series Latina 23. Turnhout: Brepols, 1962.
Nautin, Pierre, and P. Husson, trans. and eds. *Origène: Homélies sur Jérémie*. SC 238. Paris: Cerf, 1977.
Neri, Umberto, trans. and comm. *Basilio di Cesarea, Il Battesimo: Testo, traduzione, introduzione e commento*. Testi e ricerche di scienze religiose 12. Brescia: Paideia, 1976.
Neusner, Jacob. *Aphrahat and Judaism: The Christian-Jewish Argument in Fourth-Century Iran*. Studia post-Biblica 19. Leiden: Brill, 1971.
———. "The Jewish-Christian Argument in Fourth Century Iran: Aphrahat on Circumcision, the Sabbath, and the Dietary Laws." *Journal of Ecumenical Studies* 7 (1970) 282-90.
Nigg, Walter. *Das Ewige Reich: Geschichte einer sehnsucht und einer Enttäuschung*. Berlin: Weiss, 1953.
Nock, Arthur Darby. *Conversion*. Oxford: Clarendon, 1933.
Olbricht, Thomas H. "The Education of a Fourth Century Rhetorician." *Western Speech* 29 (1965) 29-36.
Osborn, Eric Francis. *Justin Martyr*. Beiträge zur historischen Theologie 47. Tübingen: Mohr/Siebeck, 1973.
Otranto, Georgia. "La tipologia di Giosué nel 'Dialogo con Trifone ebreo' di Giustino." *Aug* 15 (1975) 29-48.

# Bibliography

Oulton, John Ernest Leonard. *Alexandrian Christianity: Selected Translations of Clement and Origen.* Library of Christian Classics 2. Philadelphia: Westminster, 1954.

Outler, Albert C. "Origen and the *Regulae fidei.*" *CH* 8 (1939) 212–21.

Patrick, John, trans. "Origen's Commentary on the Gospel of Matthew." In *Ante-Nicene Fathers,* vol. 10, edited by Allan Menzies, 409–512. 1885. Reprinted, Grand Rapids: Eerdmans, 1951.

Paulin, Antoine. *Saint Cyrille de Jerusalem: Catéchète.* Lex orandi 29. Paris: Cerf, 1959.

Paverd, Frans van de. "Anaphora, Intercessions, Epiclesis and Communion-rites in John Chrysostom." *Orientalia christiana periodica* 49 (1983) 303–39.

———. *Zur Geschichte der Messliturgie in Antiocheia and Konstantinopel gegen Ende des vierten Jahrhunderts: Analyse der Quellen bei Johannes Chrysostomos.* Orientalia Christiana Analecta 187. Rome: Pontificio Instituto Orientale, 1970.

———. *St. John Chrysostom, the Homilies on the Statues: An Introduction.* Orientalia Christiana Analecta 239. Rome: Pontificio Instituto Orientale, 1991.

Peebles, Bernard M., trans. *Saint Augustine.* FC 2. New York: Fathers of the Church, 1947.

Pelikan, Jaroslav. *Development of Christian Doctrine: Some Historical Prolegomena.* New Haven: Yale University Press, 1969.

Pellegrino, M. "L'Imitation du Christ dans les Acts des martyrs." *La Vie Spirituelle* 98 (1958) 38–54.

———. "Le Sense ecclésial du martyre." *Revue de sciences religieuses* 35 (1961) 152–75.

Peretto, Elio, ed. *Ireneo di Lione: Epideixis, Antico catechismo degli adulti.* Cultura cristiana antica. Rome: Borla, 1981.

Perkins, Pheme. "Irenaeus and the Gnostics: Rhetoric and Composition in *Adversus Haereses* book one." *VC* 30 (1976) 193–200.

Perler, Othmar. "Typologie der Leiden des Herrn in Melitons *Peri Pascha.*" In *Kyriakon: Festschrift Johannes Quasten,* edited by Patrick Granfield and Josef A. Jungmann, 1:256–65. Münster: Aschendorff, 1970.

Phillips, L. Edward. "Hippolytus and the So-Called 'Apostolic Tradition': Evidence for Authorship Reconsidered." A paper presented to the North American Patristic Society, Chicago, 30 May 1996.

Plumpe, Joseph C. *Mater Ecclesia: An Inquiry into the Concept of the Church as Mother in Early Christianity.* SCA 5. Washington, DC: Catholic University of America, 1943.

Poirier, John C. "Montanist Pepuza-Jerusalem and the Dwelling Place of Wisdom." *JECS* 7 (1999) 491–507.

Porter, Stanley E., ed. *The Messiah in the Old and New Testaments.* Grand Rapids: Eerdmans, 2007.

Prigent, Pierre. *Justin et l'Ancien Testament: L'argumentation scripturaire du traité de Justin contre toutes les hérésies comme source principale du Dialogue avec Tryphon et de la première Apologie.* Études bibliques. Paris: Lecoffre, 1964.

———. "Le Millénium dans l'Apocalypse johannique." In *L'Apocalyptique,* edited by F. Raphaël et al., 139–56. Études d'histoire des religions 3. Paris: Geuthner, 1977.

———. *Les Testimonia dans le Christianisme primitif: L'Épître de Barnabé I—XVI et ses sources.* Études bibliques. Paris: Gabalda, 1961.

Prigent, Pierre, and Robert A. Kraft. *Épître de Barnabé.* SC 172. Paris: Cerf, 1971.

Prostmeier, Ferdinand R. *Der Barnabasbrief.* Kommentar zu den apostolischen Vätern 8. Göttingen: Vandenhoeck & Rüprecht, 1999.

# Bibliography

Puniet, Pierre de. "Catechumenate." In *DACL*, edited by Fernand Cabrol and Henri Leclercq, II.2:2579–621. Paris: Letouzey & Ané, 1925.
Pusey, Karen, and John Hunt. "Jewish Proselyte Baptism." *Expository Times* 95 (1984) 141–45.
Quacquarelli, Antonio. "Note retoriche sui *Testimonia* di Cipriano." *Vetera Christianorum* 8 (1971) 181–209.
Quasten, Johannes. *Patrology*. Vol. 1. Utrecht: Spectrum, 1950.
———. *Patrology*. Vol. 2. Westminster, MD: Newman, 1953.
———. *Patrology*. Vol. 3. Utrecht: Spectrum, 1960.
Quasten, Johannes, and A. Di Berardino. *Patrology*. Vol. 4. Westminster Christian Classics. Westminster, MD: Newman, 1986.
Rahner, Hugo. "Taufe und geistliches Leben bei Origenes." *Zeitschrift für Askese und Mystik* 7 (1932) 205–23.
Rambo, Lewis. *Understanding Religious Conversion*. New Haven: Yale University Press, 1993.
Reeves, Marjorie. *Joachim of Fiore and the Prophetic Future*. London: SPCK, 1976.
Reeves, Marjorie, and Beatrice Hirsch-Reich. *The Figurae of Joachim of Fiore*. Oxford–Warburg Studies. Oxford: Clarendon, 1972
Reicke, Bo. *The Disobedient Spirits and Christian Baptism: A Study of 1 Pet. III. 19 and Its Context*. Acta Seminarii Neotestamentici Upsaliensis 13. Copenhagen: Munksgaard, 1946.
Renoir, E. "Chiffre de la bête." In *Dictionnaire d'archéologie chrétienne et de liturgie*, edited by Fernand Cabrol, 3:1341–53. Paris: Letouzey et Ané, 1913.
Richardson, Peter, and Martin B. Shukster. "Barnabas, Nerva, and the Yavnean Rabbis." *JTS* n.s. 34 (1983) 31–55.
Riddle, Donald W. *The Martyrs: A Study in Social Control*. Chicago: University of Chicago, 1931.
Riesenfeld, Harald. "Sabbat et Jour du Seigneur." In *New Testament Essays: Studies in Memory of T. W. Manson*, edited by A. J. B. Higgins, 210–17. Manchester: Manchester University Press, 1959.
Riggi, C. "La catéchèse adaptée aux temps chez Epiphane." *StPatr* 17 (1982) 160–68.
Riley, Hugh M. *Christian Initiation: A Comparative Study of the Interpretation of the Baptismal Liturgy in the Mystagogical Writings of Cyril of Jerusalem, John Chrysostom, Theodore of Mopsuestia, and Ambrose of Milan*. SCA 17. Washington, DC: Catholic University of America Press, 1974.
Roberts, Alexander, and James Donaldson, eds. *Ante-Nicene Fathers*. 9 vols. 1887–96. Reprinted, Grand Rapids: Eerdmans, 1951.
Robinson, William. "Historical Survey of the Church's Treatment of New Converts with Reference to Pre- and Post-Baptismal Instruction." *JTS* 42 (1941) 42–53.
Rordorf, Willy. "L'espérance des martyrs chrétiens." In *Forma Futuri: Studi in onore del Cardinale Michele Pellegrino*, 445–61. Turin: Bottega d'Erasmo, 1975.
———. *Sunday: The History of the Day of Rest and Worship in the Earliest Centuries of the Christian Church*. Translated by A. A. K. Graham. Philadelphia: Westminster, 1968.
Russell, D. A., and N. G. Wilson. *Menander Rhetor*. Oxford: Clarendon, 1981.
Russell, D. S. *Divine Disclosure: An Introduction to Jewish Apocalyptic*. Minneapolis: Fortress, 1992.
Saber, Georges. "Le Baptême dans l'Épitre de Barnabé." *Melto* 4 (1968) 194–214.

## Bibliography

Säflund, Gösta. *De Pallio and die stilistische Entwicklung Tertalliana*. Skrifter utgivna av Svenska institutet i Rom 80. 8. Lund: Gleerup, 1955.

Sage, Michael M. *Cyprian*. PMS 1. Cambridge, MA: Philadelphia Patristic Foundation, 1975.

Saumagne, Charles. *Saint Cyprien, évêque de Carthage et "pape" d'Afrique, 248-258: Contribution à l'étude des "persécutions" de Dèce et de Valérien*. Etudes d'Antiquités africaines. Paris: Éditions du Centre national de la recherche scientifique, 1975.

Savon, Hervé. "Le prêtre Eutrope et la 'vraie circoncision.'" *Revue de l'histoire des religions* 199 (1982) 273–302; 381–404.

———. *Saint Ambroise devant l'exégèse de Philon le Juif*. Paris: Études Augustiniennes, 1977.

Saxer, Victor, and Gabriella Maestri. *Cirillo e Giovanni di Gerusalemme: Catechesi prebattesimali e mistagogiche*. Milan: Paoline, 1994.

Scheck, Thomas P., trans. *Origen: Commentary on the Epistle to the Romans Books 1–5*. FC 103. Washington, DC: Catholic University of America Press, 2001.

Schiller, Gertrud. *Ikonographie der christlichen Kunst*. Vol. 3, *Die Auferstehung and Erhöhung Christi*. 2nd ed. Gütersloh: Gütersloher/Mohn, 1986.

Schiller, Gottfried. "Zur urchristlichen Tauflehre: Stilistische am Barnabasbrief." *ZNW* 49 (1958) 31–52.

Schlosser, H. "Moses." In *Lexikon der christlichen Ikonographie*, edited by Englebert Kirschbaum, 3:286–88 (fig. 2 and 5). Rome: Herder, 1971.

———. "Quellwunder." In *Lexikon der christlichen Ikonographie*, edited by Englebert Kirschbaum, 3:487–88. Rome: Herder, 1971.

Schmidt, Karl Ludwig. "βασιλεύς." In *Theological Dictionary of the New Testament*, edited by Gerhard Kittel, 1:549–93. Translated by Geoffrey Bromiley. Grand Rapids: Eerdmans, 1964.

Schoedel, William R. "Philosophy and Rhetoric in the *Adversus Haereses* of Irenaeus." *VC* 13 (1959) 22–32.

Schürer, Emil. *The History of the Jewish People in the Age of Jesus Christ (175 B.C.—A.D. 135)*. Vol. 2. Revised and edited by Geza Vermes, Fergus Millar, and Matthew Black. Edinburgh: T. & T. Clark, 1979.

Schweizer, Eduard. *Erniedrigung und Erhöhung bei Jesus und seinen Nachfolgern*. Abhandlungen zur Theologie des Alten und Neuen Testaments 28. Zürich: Zwingli, 1962.

———. *Lordship and Discipleship*. Studies in Biblical Theology 1/28. Naperville, IL: Allenson, 1960.

Searle, Mark. "Infant Baptism Reconsidered." In *Living Water, Sealing Spirit: Readings on Christian Initiation*, edited by Maxwell E. Johnson, 365–409. Collegeville, MN: Liturgical, 1995.

Seeberg, Alfred. *Der Katechismus der Urchristenheit*. 1903. Reprinted, Theologische Bücherei 26. Munich: Kaiser, 1966.

Segal, Alan F. "Jewish Christianity." In *Eusebius, Christianity, and Judaism*, edited by Harold W. Attridge and Gohei Hata, 326–51. Studia post-Biblica 42. Leiden: Brill, 1992.

Sethe, Kurt. *Von Zahlen und Zahlworten bei den alten Ägyptern und was für andere Völker und Sprachen daraus zu lernen ist*. Schriften der Wissenschaftlichen Gesellschaft Strassburg 25. Strassburg: Trübner, 1916.

Shea, William H. "The Sabbath in the Epistle of Barnabas." *Andrews University Seminary Studies* 4 (1966) 149-75.
Shippee, Arthur B. "Antioch's Separate Catechetical Classes and Curricula." Paper read at the annual meeting of the North American Patristic Society, Chicago, 31 May 1996.
Shukster, Martin B., and Peter Richardson. "Temple and *Bet Ha-midrash* in the Epistle of Barnabas." In *Anti-Judaism in Early Christianity*, edited by Stephen G. Wilson 17-31. 2 vols. Studies in Christianity and Judaism 2, 3. Toronto: Wilfred Laurier University Press, 1986.
Simon, Marcel. *Verus Israel: étude sur les relations entre chrétiens et juifs dans l'empire romain (135-425)*. Bibliothèque des écoles françaises d'Athènes et de Rome 166. Paris: Boccard, 1964.

―――. *Verus Israel: A Study of the Relations between Christians and Jews in the Roman Empire (135-425)*. Translated by H. McKeating. Littman Library of Jewish Civilization. New York: Oxford University Press, 1986.

Skarsaune, Oskar. "Baptismal Typology in Barnabas 8 and the Jewish Background." *St Patr* 18 (1989) 221-28.

―――. *The Proof from Prophecy: A Study in Justin Martyr's Proof-Text Tradition*. NovTSup 56. Leiden: Brill, 1987.

Slusser, Michael. *St. Gregory Thaumaturges: Life and Works*. FC 98. Washington, DC: Catholic University of America Press, 1998.
Smith, Christopher R. "Chiliasm and Recapitulation in the Theology of Irenaeus." *VC* 48 (1994) 312-31.
Smith, Joseph P., trans. and ed. *St. Irenaeus Proof of the Apostolic Preaching*. ACW 16. Westminster, MD: Newman, 1952.
Smith, M. A. "Did Justin Know the *Didache*?" *StPatr* 7 (1966) 287-90.
Smulders, Pierre. "The *Sitz im Leben* of the Old Roman Creed." *StPatr* 13 (1975) 409-21.
Solano, Jesus, ed. *Textos eucaristicos primitivos*. Madrid: Editorial Catolica, 1952.
Sophocles, E. A. *Greek Lexicon of the Roman and Byzantine Periods*. New York: Ungar, 1870.
Spanneut, Michel. "La non-violence chez les Pères africains avant Constantin." In *Kyriakon: Festschrift Johannes Quasten*, edited by Patrick Granfield and Josef A. Jungmann, 1:36-39. Münster: Aschendorff, 1970.
Strack, Hermann L., and Paul Billerbeck. *Kommentar zum Neuen Testament aus Talmud and Midrasch*. Vol. 3. Munich: Beck, 1961.
Strecker, Georg. *Das Judenchristentum in den Pseudoklementinen*. TU 70. Berlin: Akademie, 1958.
Stroup, George W. *The Promise of Narrative Theology: Recovering the Gospel in the Church*. Atlanta: John Knox, 1981.
Surkau, Hans Werner. "Katechetik." In *Die Religion in Geschichte und Gegenwart*, 3rd ed., edited by Kurt Galling, 3:1179-86. Tübingen: Mohr/Siebeck, 1959.
Tabbernee, William. "Early Montanism and Voluntary Martyrdom." *Colloquium* 17 (1985) 33-43.
Taylor, T. M. "The Beginning of Jewish Proselyte Baptism." *NTS* 2 (1955-56) 193-98.
Ter-Mekerttschian, Karapet, and Erwand Ter-Minassiantz. *Des Heiligen Irenäus Schrift zum Erweise der Apostolischen Verkündigung in Armenischer Version Entdeckt*. TU 31.1. Leipzig: Hinrichs, 1907.

## Bibliography

Thompson, T. *St. Ambrose, "On the Mysteries" and the Treatise "On the Sacraments" by an Unknown Author.* Edited with Introduction and notes by J. H. Srawley. London: SPCK, 1919.

Tilley, Maureen A. "Scripture as an Element of Social Control: Two Martyr Stories of Christian North Africa." *HTR* 83 (1990) 383-97.

Tollinton, R. B., trans. *Selections from the Commentaries and Homilies of Origen.* London: SPCK, 1929.

Touton, J. "La méthode catéchètique de St. Cyrille de Jérusalem comparée à celles de St. Augustin et de Théodore de Mopsueste." *Proche-Orient chrétien* 1 (1951) 265-85.

Trakatellis, Demetrius C. *The Pre-Existence of Christ in Justin Martyr.* Harvard Dissertations in Religion 6. Missoula, MT: Scholars, 1976.

Tränkle, Hermann, ed. *Q.S.F. Tertulliani Adversus Iudaeos.* Wiesbaden: Steiner, 1964.

Trigg, Joseph W. "A Fresh Look at Origen's Understanding of Baptism." *StPatr* 17.2 (1982) 959-65.

Turck, André. "Aux origines du catéchuménat." *RSPT* 48 (1964) 20-31.

———. "*Catéchein* et *Catéchèsis* chez les premiers Pères." *RSPT* 47 (1963) 361-72.

———. *Évangélisation et catéchèse aux deux premiers siècles.* Parole et mission 3. Paris: Cerf, 1962.

Turner, C. H. "Prolegomena to the *Testimonia* and *Ad Fortunatum* of St. Cyprian." *JTS* 31 (1930) 225-46.

Turner, H. E. W. *The Patristic Doctrine of Redemption: A Study of the Development of Doctrine during the First Five Centuries.* London: Mowbray, 1952.

Usener, Hermann, and Ludwig Radermacher. *Dionysii Halicarnasei quae exstant,* vol. 6. Bibliotheca scriptorum Graecorum et Romanorum Teubneriana. 1929. Reprinted, Stuttgart: Teubner, 1965.

Van der Lof, L. J. "The Date of the *De catechizandis rudibus*." *VC* 16 (1962) 198-204.

Van der Meer, F. *Augustine the Bishop: Church and Society at the Dawn of the Middle Ages.* London: Sheed & Ward, 1961.

Van Voorst, Robert E. *The Ascents of James: History and Theology of a Jewish-Christian Community.* Society of Biblical Literature Dissertation Series 112. Atlanta: Scholars, 1989.

Vermes, Geza. "Baptism and Jewish Exegesis: A New Light from Ancient Sources." *NTS* 4 (1957-58) 308-19.

Vesco, Jean-Luc. "La lecture du Psautier selon l'Épître de Barnabé." *Revue biblique* 93 (1986) 5-37.

Viciano, Alberto. "Principios de hermenéutica biblica en el tratato 'Adversus Iudaeos' de Tertuliano." *Biblia y Hermenéutica* (Pamplona, 1986) 637-44.

Vigne, Daniel. *Christ au jourdain—Le Baptême de Jésus dans la tradition judeo-chrétienne.* Etudes bibliques 16. Paris: Gabalda, 1992.

———. "Enquête sur Basilide." In *Recherches et Tradition: Mélanges patristiques offerts à Henri Crouzel, SJ.*, edited by André Dupleix, 285-313. Théologie historique 88. Paris: Beauchesne, 1992.

Viller, M. "Les Martyrs et l'Esprit." *Recherches de science religieuse* 14 (1924) 544-51.

Völker, Walther. *Das Vollkommenheitsideal des Origenes: Eine Untersuchung zur Geschichte der Frömmigkeit und zu den Anfängen christlicher Mystik.* Beiträge zur historischen Theologie 7. Tübingen: Mohr/Siebeck, 1931.

Wagner, Sr. M. Monica, trans. *Saint Basil: Ascetical Works.* FC 9. Washington, DC: Catholic University Press, 1950.

Way-Rider, R. "Justin Martyr's Use of Some Pagan and Jewish Material." Paper read at the Seventh International Conference on Patristic Studies, Oxford, 10 September 1975.

Weinrich, William C. *Spirit and Martyrdom: A Study of the Work of the Holy Spirit in Contexts of Persecution and Martyrdom in the New Testament and Early Christian Literature*. Washington, DC: University Press of America, 1981.

Wendebourg, Dorothea. "Das Martyrium in der Alten Kirche als ethische Problem." *Zeitschrift für Kirchengeschichte* 98 (1987) 295–320.

Wengst, Klaus. *Tradition und Theologie des Barnabasbriefes*. Arbeiten zur Kirchengeschichte 42. Berlin: de Gruyter, 1971.

Werner, Martin. *The Formation of Christian Dogma: An Historical Study of Its Problem*. New York: Harper, 1957.

Wilken, Robert L. "The Interpretation of the Baptism of Jesus in the Later Fathers." *StPatr* 11.2 (1972) 268–77.

———. *John Chrysostom and the Jews: Rhetoric and Reality in the Late 4th Century*. Transformation of the Classical Heritage 4. Berkeley: University of California Press, 1983.

———. *Judaism and the Early Christian Mind*. Yale Publications in Religion 15. New Haven: Yale Univesity Press, 1971.

Williams, George Hunston. "Four Modalities of Violence, With Special Reference to the Writings of George Sorel, Part One." *Journal of Church and State* 16 (1974) 11–30.

———. "Four Modalities of Violence, With Special Reference to the Writings of George Sorel, Parts Two and Three." *Journal of Church and State* 16 (1974) 237–61.

Williams, John. "Purpose and Imagery in the Apocalypse Commentary of Beatus of Liebana." In *The Apocalypse in the Middle Ages*, edited by Richard K. Emmerson and Bernard McGinn, 217–33. Ithaca, NY: Cornell University Press, 1992.

Williams, Norman Powell. *The Ideas of the Fall and of Original Sin: A Historical and Critical Study*. Bampton Lectures 1924. London: Longmans, Green, 1927.

Williamson, Paul. *Gothic Sculpture 1140–1300*. Pelikan History of Art. New Haven: Yale University Press, 1995.

Willis, Robert Wayne. "A Study of Some Eschatological Motifs in the Martyr Literature of the Early Church." Thesis, Abilene Christian University, 1966.

Windisch, Hans. *Der Barnabasbrief*. Handbuch zum Neuen Testament. Ergänzungsband. Die Apostolischen Väter 3. Tübingen: Mohr/Siebeck, 1920.

Winslow, Donald F. "Orthodox Baptism—A Problem for Gregory of Nazianzus." *StPatr* 14 (1976) 371–74.

———. "The Polemical Christology of Melito of Sardis." *StPatr* 7.2 (1982) 765–76.

Worley, Robert C. *Preaching and Teaching in the Earliest Church*. Philadelphia: Westminster, 1967.

Wright, David F. "How Controversial Was the Development of Infant Baptism in the Early Church?" In *Church, Word, and Spirit: Historical and Theological Essays in Honor of Geoffrey W. Bromiley*, edited by James E. Bradley and Richard A. Muller, 45–63. Grand Rapids: Eerdmans, 1987.

———. "The Origins of Infant Baptism—Child Believers' Baptism?" *SJT* 40 (1987) 1–23.

Yarnold, *The Awe-inspiring Rites of Initiation: Baptismal Homilies of the Fourth Century*. 2nd ed. Edinburgh: T. & T. Clark, 1994.

*Bibliography*

Ysebaert, J. *Greek Baptismal Terminology: Its Origin and Early Development.* Græcitas Christianorum primæva 1. Nijmegen: Dekker & Van de Vegt, 1962.

# Ancient Sources Index

**OLD TESTAMENT**

## Genesis

| | |
|---|---|
| 1 | 216 |
| 1:1 | 10 |
| 1:2 | 75 |
| 1:28 | 55 |
| 2:2–3 | 204, 209 |
| 2:7 | 55, 63n51 |
| 2:15 | 82, 82n59 |
| 2:17 | 220 |
| 3:19 | 63n51 |
| 3:22 | 54, 63 |
| 5:5 | 220n30 |
| 6–9 | 72 |
| 6:14 | 72 |
| 7:13 | 252 |
| 14:14 | 250 |
| 17:11 | 144 |
| 17:23 | 250 |
| 21:15–19 | 129 |
| 22:9–10 | 129 |
| 24:15–20 | 129 |
| 26:18–22 | 129 |
| 49:8–12 | 168 |

## Exodus

| | |
|---|---|
| 2:2–4 | 130 |
| 3:1–6 | 128 |
| 4:1–5 | 128 |
| 6:30 | 145 |
| 17:1–7 | 59 |
| 17:8–13 | 169 |
| 17:11 | 171 |
| 19:5 | 144n1 |
| 19:10–11 | 78 |
| 23:13 | 206n32 |
| 31:13–17 | 204 |
| 33:1 | 54 |
| 33:3 | 54, 55 |

## Leviticus

| | |
|---|---|
| 1:9 | 72 |
| 11:24 | 136 |
| 12:2–7 | 83 |
| 12:3 | 146, 252 |
| 12:8 | 83, 157n11 |
| 16 | 169 |
| 20:24 | 54 |
| 26:11 | 144 |
| 26:40 | 145 |

## Numbers

| | |
|---|---|
| 19 | 56 |
| 20:2–13 | 59 |
| 27:1 | 3n9 |
| 31:21–24 | 72n18 |

## Deuteronomy

| | |
|---|---|
| 1:25 | 54 |
| 10:16 | 145, 146n5 |
| 30:6 | 145 |

## Ancient Sources Index

### Joshua

| | |
|---|---|
| 3 | 70 |
| 4:9 | 130 |
| 5:3 | 148 |
| 5:9 | 72, 148 |

### 2 Samuel

| | |
|---|---|
| 7:12–16 | 178 |

### 1 Kings

| | |
|---|---|
| 18:30–40 | 130 |
| 18:33–35 | 115 |

### 2 Kings

| | |
|---|---|
| 2:6–14 | 128 |
| 2:8 | 71 |
| 2:9 | 72 |
| 2:12 | 72 |
| 2:14 | 71 |
| 5 | 71 |
| 5:1–14 | 130 |
| 5:9 | 72 |
| 5:10 | 71 |

### Job

| | |
|---|---|
| 14:4 | 72n18, 83, 157n11 |
| 14:4–5 | 79n46, 82, 83, 84n63 |

### Psalms

| | |
|---|---|
| 1 | 61, 61n40 |
| 1:1 | 54 |
| 1:3 | 54, 61, 63 |
| 1:3–6 | 54, 61n41 |
| 1:4–6 | 61 |
| 8:5–6 | 173 |
| 8:5 | 173 |
| 12 | 61 |
| 14–15 | 61n40 |
| 21:23 | 55, 65n67 |
| 22 | 170 |
| 22:6 | 173 |
| 24:4 | 204 |
| 24:5 | 130n22 |
| 26–27 | 61n40 |
| 33:6 | 114, 122 |
| 34:5 | 130 |
| 34:11 | 134 |
| 38:17 | 173 |
| 41:3 | 55 |
| 42:2 | 130n22 |
| 45 | 178 |
| 46:10 | 134 |
| 51:5 | 79n46, 83, 157n11 |
| 67:18 | 60n36 |
| 72 | 174 |
| 72:6 | 175 |
| 78:15–17 | 59 |
| 78:25 | 115 |
| 90:4 | 200, 205, 216, 220, 230 |
| 104:24 | 128n15 |
| 106:16 | 60 |
| 107:4 | 55 |
| 110 | 168 |
| 110:7 | 170n21 |
| 118:22 | 171 |
| 132:12 | 178 |
| 143:6 | 130n22 |
| 150:4 | 226 |

### Ecclesiastes

| | |
|---|---|
| 3 | 121 |
| 3:1–2 | 113 |

### Isaiah

| | |
|---|---|
| 1:13 | 206 |
| 1:16 | 114, 122, 130n22 |
| 8:14 | 173 |
| 11:4 | 171 |
| 16:1–2 | 53, 60n37 |
| 16:1 | 59, 60, 60n35 |
| 28:16 | 64n59 |
| 33:16–18 | 53, 60 |
| 33:18 | 61 |
| 35:1–2 | 130n22 |
| 42:10 | 70 |
| 44:3 | 204 |
| 45:2–3 | 53, 60 |
| 49:5 | 55 |
| 49:20 | 126 |
| 50:5–7 | 170 |
| 52:2–4 | 170 |
| 53 | 168, 170, 173, 174 |

| | |
|---|---|
| 53:3 | 171 |
| 53:7 | 171 |
| 53:9 | 137 |
| 58:1–9 | 28 |
| 60:8 | 126 |
| 61:10 | 132n31 |
| 65:17–25 | 220 |
| 65:22 | 220 |

## Jeremiah

| | |
|---|---|
| 2:12–13 | 53 |
| 2:13 | 57, 57n20, 59, 60n35 |
| 4:3–4 | 153 |
| 4:4 | 84n63, 145, 146n5 |
| 5:3 | 265 |
| 5:13 | 3n9 |
| 6:10 | 145 |
| 9:26 | 145, 146n5 |
| 17:22 | 204 |
| 20:7 | 261 |
| 31:31–34 | 67n77 |
| 31:33 | 46n118 |

## Ezekiel

| | |
|---|---|
| 11:19–20 | 265 |
| 11:19 | 55 |
| 20:6 | 54 |
| 20:15 | 54 |
| 36:25–27 | 130n22 |
| 36:26 | 55 |
| 44:7 | 145 |
| 44:9 | 145 |
| 47:1–12 | 54, 63 |
| 47:9 | 54 |

## Daniel

| | |
|---|---|
| 2 | 178 |
| 2:34ff. | 173 |
| 7 | 168, 178, 192 |
| 7:13–14 | 173 |
| 7:13 | 171 |
| 7:27 | 178 |
| 9:24–27 | 55 |

## Joel

| | |
|---|---|
| 2:13 | 153 |

## Micah

| | |
|---|---|
| 4 | 169 |

## Zephaniah

| | |
|---|---|
| 3:19 | 54 |

## Haggai

| | |
|---|---|
| 1:9 | 134 |

## Zechariah

| | |
|---|---|
| 3 | 170 |
| 3:1–5 | 173 |
| 3:3 | 130, 130n22 |
| 9:9 | 171 |
| 12 | 168 |
| 12:10–14 | 168 |
| 12:10 | 173 |
| 12:12 | 173 |

## Malachi

| | |
|---|---|
| 1:11 | 188 |
| 1:14 | 188 |
| 4:4 | 171 |

## NEW TESTAMENT

## Matthew

| | |
|---|---|
| 1:18 | 137 |
| 1:20 | 137 |
| 2 | 194 |
| 3:8 | 137 |
| 3:11 | 73, 76n31, 87, 137 |
| 3:14 | 137 |
| 3:15 | 73, 138, 138n47 |
| 5–7 | 24n28 |
| 5:10 | 190 |
| 5:44–45 | 131 |
| 6:33 | 178 |
| 8:11–12 | 178, 179 |
| 9:9 | 131 |
| 11:12 | 178 |
| 11:28 | 114 |
| 11:29 | 134 |
| 12:29 | 218 |

## Ancient Sources Index

### Matthew (continued)

| | |
|---|---|
| 18:2–4 | 84 |
| 18:3 | 139 |
| 18:23–35 | 121 |
| 19:13–15 | 85 |
| 19:14 | 85 |
| 19:28 | 76n31, 249 |
| 22:39 | 44n105 |
| 25 | 33 |
| 25:14–30 | 108 |
| 25:25 | 122, 123 |
| 25:31–46 | 28 |
| 25:34 | 178 |
| 28:19 | 79, 119, 129 |

### Mark

| | |
|---|---|
| 1:4 | 137 |
| 10:38 | 56n15, 85, 86 |

### Luke

| | |
|---|---|
| 1:6 | 138 |
| 1:36 | 138 |
| 2:21 | 252 |
| 2:22 | 82, 83 |
| 3:3 | 77, 137, 137n45 |
| 3:7–8 | 87 |
| 3:15–16 | 74n25, 76 |
| 3:22 | 77 |
| 4:1 | 78 |
| 5:6 | 249 |
| 6 | 24n28 |
| 6:13 | 249 |
| 6:20 | 190 |
| 7:30 | 139 |
| 12:50 | 56n15, 75n29, 85, 86 |
| 16:16 | 178 |
| 17:21 | 185 |
| 19:1–9 | 131 |
| 24:26 | 166 |

### John

| | |
|---|---|
| 1:26 | 87, 135 |
| 1:31 | 138 |
| 1:33 | 73, 136, 138, 139 |
| 2:21 | 65n67 |
| 3:3–7 | 98, 99 |
| 3:3 | 78, 79, 107 |
| 3:5 | 50, 70, 75, 78, 79, 85, 85n66, 107, 119, 127, 127n10, 164 |
| 4:13–14 | 130n22 |
| 6:35 | 64n61 |
| 6:45–48 | 64n61 |
| 7:37 | 130n22 |
| 8:46 | 137 |
| 9 | 128 |
| 13:8 | 73 |
| 13:10 | 73 |
| 19:34 | 61n41 |
| 20:1 | 252 |
| 20:19 | 252 |
| 20:22–23 | 77 |
| 20:26 | 252 |
| 21:11 | 249 |

### Acts

| | |
|---|---|
| 1:11 | 167 |
| 2 | 251 |
| 2:3 | 137 |
| 2:38 | 22n21, 57n19, 65n69, 66n74, 114 |
| 3:16 | 65n69 |
| 4:24 | 275 |
| 5:29 | 275 |
| 7 | 14 |
| 7:8 | 144 |
| 8 | 108 |
| 8:12–16 | 75 |
| 8:13–19 | 78 |
| 8:27–39 | 122 |
| 8:38–39 | 66n72 |
| 9:1–22 | 131 |
| 10:44 | 78 |
| 13:16ff. | 14 |
| 15:9 | 65n69 |
| 18:8 | 22n21 |
| 19:1–7 | 137 |
| 19:2–5 | 74 |
| 19:3–5 | 73 |
| 19:4 | 138 |
| 22:16 | 57n19 |

### Romans

| | |
|---|---|
| 2:25 | 147 |

|  |  |  |  |
|---|---|---|---|
| 2:29 | 145, 147, 150 | 3:24–25 | 264 |
| 4:11 | 144, 150 | 3:24 | 266 |
| 6 | 107 | 3:27 | 107 |
| 6:1–11 | 98, 119 | 4:1–4 | 264 |
| 6:2 | 116n28 | 5:17–21 | 190 |
| 6:3–4 | 75, 79, 80 | 5:21 | 178 |
| 6:3 | 78, 132 | 5:22 | 34n63 |
| 6:4 | 76n31, 79n46 | 5:23 | 34n63 |
| 6:5–6 | 83 | | |
| 6:5 | 116n28 | | |
| 6:8–10 | 87 | | |

## Ephesians

|  |  |
|---|---|
| 1:13 | 150 |
| 2:15 | 70 |
| 2:18–22 | 65n69 |
| 4:8 | 77 |
| 4:22 | 80 |
| 4:24 | 70, 80 |
| 4:30 | 150 |
| 5:5 | 178, 189 |

|  |  |
|---|---|
| 6:13 | 116n28 |
| 8:14 | 78 |
| 8:29 | 99n55 |
| 10:8 | 65n70 |
| 10:14–17 | 65n70 |

## 1 Corinthians

|  |  |
|---|---|
| 2:9 | 180n13 |
| 3:16 | 65n67 |
| 6:9 | 178 |
| 6:9–10 | 189 |
| 6:19 | 65n67 |
| 7:1 | 53n10 |
| 7:25 | 53n10 |
| 8:1 | 53n10 |
| 8:4 | 53n10 |
| 10:1–4 | 69, 70 |
| 10:2 | 71, 116, 130n20 |
| 10:4 | 115 |
| 12:1 | 53n10 |
| 13:9–10 | 264 |
| 15 | 187 |
| 15:24 | 185 |
| 15:28 | 199 |
| 15:50 | 177 |
| 16:1 | 53n10 |

## Philippians

|  |  |
|---|---|
| 2 | 170 |
| 3:3 | 150 |
| 3:21 | 76n31 |

## Colossians

|  |  |
|---|---|
| 1:15 | 99n55 |
| 1:18 | 99n55 |
| 2:9–12 | 81 |
| 2:10–13 | 147n8 |
| 2:11–12 | 149, 149n16, 150 |
| 2:11 | 117, 120, 149, 150, 152 |
| 2:12 | 149n14 |
| 3:9–10 | 80 |

## 2 Thessalonians

|  |  |
|---|---|
| 2 | 187 |

## 2 Corinthians

|  |  |
|---|---|
| 1:22 | 150 |
| 3:3 | 65n67 |
| 5:17 | 65n67 |
| 5:19 | 65n69 |
| 6:15–16 | 65n69 |

## 1 Timothy

|  |  |
|---|---|
| 4:6 | 65n70 |

## 2 Timothy

|  |  |
|---|---|
| 2:18 | 187 |

## Galatians

|  |  |
|---|---|
| 2:20 | 132 |

## Titus

|  |  |
|---|---|
| 2:11–13 | 135 |

## Titus *(continued)*

| | |
|---|---|
| 3:5 | 72, 75, 76n31, 79n46, 98, 98n50, 107, 127n10 |

## Hebrews

| | |
|---|---|
| 2:10 | 92 |
| 2:12 | 65n67 |
| 3:8 | 65n67 |
| 3:10 | 65n67 |
| 4:1–11 | 211 |
| 4:9 | 205 |
| 4:12 | 154 |
| 6:1–2 | 3 |
| 9:28 | 167 |
| 10:22 | 72 |

## James

| | |
|---|---|
| 1:21 | 65n69 |
| 2:5 | 178 |

## 1 Peter

| | |
|---|---|
| 1:3 | 98 |
| 1:11 | 166 |
| 1:23 | 65n67, 98 |
| 2:2 | 65n67 |
| 2:22 | 77, 137 |
| 3:15 | 134 |
| 3:20–21 | 72, 252 |
| 3:21 | 72 |
| 4:13 | 166–167n3 |
| 5:1 | 166–167n3 |
| 5:10 | 166–167n3 |

## 2 Peter

| | |
|---|---|
| 1:11 | 178 |
| 3:8 | 200, 201n2, 205, 216 |

## 1 John

| | |
|---|---|
| 5:6 | 61n41 |
| 5:8 | 75n29 |

## Revelation

| | |
|---|---|
| 1:6 | 218 |
| 1:9 | 218 |
| 1:11 | 252 |
| 5:10 | 218 |
| 6:9–11 | 218, 222 |
| 7:2 | 241 |
| 12:6 | 250 |
| 12:9–12 | 218 |
| 12:10–12 | 218 |
| 12:10 | 218 |
| 13:18 | 249 |
| 15:2–4 | 218 |
| 18:20 | 218 |
| 20 | 218, 218n22, 227, 232, 238, 240, 250 |
| 20:1–7 | 233 |
| 20:1–6 | 231 |
| 20:2–4 | 249 |
| 20:4–6 | 220, 229, 232 |
| 20:4 | 218 |
| 20:6 | 249 |
| 21 | 231 |

# APOCRYPHA AND PSEUDEPIGRAPHA

## 2 Baruch

| | |
|---|---|
| 26–30 | 216 |
| 29:5 | 219 |

## 1 Enoch

| | |
|---|---|
| 10:19 | 219 |
| 76–77 | 245 |
| 91:12–17 | 245 |
| 93:2–10 | 245 |

## 2 Enoch

| | |
|---|---|
| 33:1 | 206n31 |
| 33:1–2 | 245 |

## 4 Ezra

| | |
|---|---|
| 2.10–13 | 193 |
| 7.28 | 216 |
| 7.30 | 208n45 |

# Ancient Sources Index

*5 Ezra*

| 2.38 | 183 |

*Jubilees*

| 4:29–30 | 220n30 |
| 15:26 | 144 |
| 23:27 | 220n30 |

*Sirach*

| 24 | 223n43 |

*Testament of Benjamin*

| 9.3 | 167n4 |

*Testament of Isaac*

| 8.6 | 216n15 |

## DEAD SEA SCROLLS AND RELATED TEXTS

*Community Rule*

| 3–4 | 118n34 |
| 5.4–5 | 145 |

*Habakkuk Pesher*

| 11.13 | 145 |

## PHILO

*De Opificio Mundi*

| 89–128 | 245 |

*Questions on Genesis*

| 3.48 | 145 |

*Special Laws*

| 1.1–11 | 145 |
| 1.8–20 | 245 |

## MISHNAH, TALMUD, AND RELATED LITERATURE

### MISHNAH

*Mikwaoth*

| 3.3 | 57 |

*Nedarim*

| 3.11 | 144 |

*Parah*

| 12.11 | 57n21 |

*Pesachim*

| 8.8 | 57 |
| 10.4 | 166n1 |

*Tamid*

| 7.4 | 206n32 |

### BABYLONIAN TALMUD

*Hullin*

| 10.4 | 58 |

*Nedarim*

| 32a | 144 |

*Sanhedrin*

| 99a | 216n13 |

*Shabbat*

| 132b | 144 |
| 135a | 144 |
| 137b | 144 |

*Shebiith*

| 109 | 58 |

*Sukka*

| 21b | 62n45 |

309

*Ancient Sources Index*

## *Yebamoth*

| | |
|---|---|
| 22a | 58 |
| 23a | 58 |
| 46a–b | 58n26 |
| 46a | 58 |
| 47b | 58 |
| 48b | 58 |
| 62a | 58 |
| 112 | 58 |

## *Yoma*

| | |
|---|---|
| 3.9 | 169n17 |
| 6.1 | 169n17 |

## OTHER RABBINIC WORKS

### *Midrash Rabbah*

Genesis

| | |
|---|---|
| 4.3.2 | 250 |

Ecclesiastes

| | |
|---|---|
| 1.8.4 | 58 |
| 28–29 | 58n24 |

### *Midrash on Psalms*

| | |
|---|---|
| 90.17 | 216n15 |

### *Mekhilta on Exodus*

| | |
|---|---|
| 19.5 | 144–145n1 |
| 23.13 | 206n32 |

### *Pesiqta Rabbati*

| | |
|---|---|
| 1.7 | 216n13, 216n14, 216n15 |
| 8:8 | 57 |

### *Tanhuma*

| | |
|---|---|
| 7b | 216n15 |

## APOSTOLIC FATHERS

### *1 Clement*

| | |
|---|---|
| 23.4 | 61n42 |
| 42.3 | 188 |
| 50.3 | 188 |
| 61.1 | 188 |

### *2 Clement*

| | |
|---|---|
| 5.5 | 189 |
| 6.9 | 149n17, 189 |
| 7.6 | 149n17 |
| 8.6 | 149n17 |
| 9.6 | 189 |
| 11.3–4 | 61n42 |
| 11.7 | 189 |
| 12 | 180, 180n12, 189 |
| 12–17 | 180n13 |
| 14.3–5 | 149n17 |
| 17.5 | 189 |

### *Didache*

| | |
|---|---|
| 1–6 | 24 |
| 2.1 | 26n40 |
| 7.2–3 | 66n73 |
| 8.2 | 188 |
| 9.4 | 188 |
| 10.5–6 | 188 |
| 14.3 | 188 |

## Shepherd of Hermas

Mandates

| | |
|---|---|
| 4.3.1 | 57n19 |
| 6.2 | 118n34 |

Similitudes

| | |
|---|---|
| 8.3.6 | 271n15 |
| 9.12.3 | 190 |
| 9.12.4 | 190 |
| 9.12.5 | 190 |
| 9.12.8 | 190 |
| 9.15.2 | 190 |
| 9.15.3 | 190 |
| 9.16.2 | 66n72 |
| 9.16.2–4 | 191 |

| | |
|---|---|
| 9.16.3 | 164n21 |
| 9.16.3–4 | 149n17 |
| 9.16.4 | 66n72 |
| 9.16.6 | 66n72 |
| 9.17.4 | 149n17 |
| 9.20.2 | 191 |
| 9.20.3 | 191 |
| 9.29.1–3 | 97n45 |
| 9.29.2 | 191 |
| 9.31.2 | 191 |
| 13.1 | 190 |
| 13.2 | 190 |

# NEW TESTAMENT APOCRYPHA AND PSEUDOEPIGRAPHA

## Acts of John

| | |
|---|---|
| 8 | 198 |
| 22 | 198 |
| 106 | 198 |

## Apocalypse of Paul

| | |
|---|---|
| 21–22 | 230n73 |

## Gospel of Peter

| | |
|---|---|
| 13.56 | 207n35 |

## Gospel of Thomas

| | |
|---|---|
| 3 | 180n11, 198n35 |
| 17 | 180n13 |
| 20 | 198n35 |
| 22 | 180, 180n12, 198 |
| 27 | 185, 198n35 |
| 46 | 198n35 |
| 49 | 198n35 |
| 53 | 145 |
| 54 | 198n35 |
| 57 | 198n35 |
| 76 | 198n35 |
| 82 | 198n35 |
| 96–99 | 198n35 |
| 107 | 198n35 |
| 109 | 198n35 |
| 113 | 180n11, 198n35 |
| 114 | 198n35 |

# GREEK, LATIN, AND SYRIAC WORKS

## Acts of Carpus, Papylus, and Agathonice

| | |
|---|---|
| 4 | 274n52 |
| 6 | 273n37, 273n40 |
| 7 | 273n41 |
| 12 | 273n40 |
| 17 | 273n38 |
| 21 | 275n54 |
| 40 | 272n24, 274n47 |
| 45 | 272n25 |

## Acts of Cyprian

| | |
|---|---|
| 1.2 | 276n70 |

## Acts of Euplus

| | |
|---|---|
| 1 | 276n79 |

## Acts of Justin

| | |
|---|---|
| 1 | 275n62 |
| 2.1 | 274n53 |
| 3.3 | 22n19 |
| 5 | 274n44 |

## Acts of Marcellus

| | |
|---|---|
| 1.1 | 277n90 |
| 1.3 | 272n30 |
| 2.2 | 273n38 |
| 2.3 | 271n19 |
| 2.5 | 273n38 |
| 3.4 | 271n19 |
| 3.5 | 272n28 |
| 4.3 | 277n90 |
| 5.2 | 275n64 |
| 6.1 | 272n24 |
| 9.2–4 | 272n28 |
| 12.8 | 272n28 |

# Ancient Sources Index

## Acts of Maximilian

| | |
|---|---|
| 2.1 | 277n89 |
| 2.8 | 277n89 |

## Acts of Phileas

| | |
|---|---|
| 9 | 276n75 |

## Acts of the Scillitan Martyrs

| | |
|---|---|
| 3–4 | 272n31 |
| 6 | 275n60 |

## Ambrose

### On Abraham

| | |
|---|---|
| 1.4.2.5 | 36n72 |
| 1.7.59 | 36n72 |
| 1.9.89 | 36n72 |

### De bono mortis

| | |
|---|---|
| 1–29 | 37 |
| 30–57 | 37 |

### Commentary on Luke

| | |
|---|---|
| 7.7 | 231n76 |

### Epistles

| | |
|---|---|
| 20.4 | 38n81 |
| 72 | 146 |
| 72.9 | 146, 151n25 |

### Explanatio symboli ad initiandos

| | |
|---|---|
| 9 | 39 |
| 11 | 39 |
| 12 | 38 |

### Expositio Evangelii secundum Lucam

| | |
|---|---|
| 6.104–109 | 38n82 |
| 6.104 | 38n82 |
| 6.107 | 38n82 |

### De Fide

| | |
|---|---|
| 1 | 250 |

### De fuga saeculi

| | |
|---|---|
| 3.15 | 37n76 |
| 4.17 | 38 |

### On Isaac

| | |
|---|---|
| 8.74 | 37 |

### On Jacob

| | |
|---|---|
| 1.6.20 | 37 |
| 1.6.22 | 37 |
| 1.8.35 | 37 |
| 1.9.41ff | 37 |

### On Joseph

| | |
|---|---|
| 1.2 | 37 |
| 2.8 | 37 |

### On the Mysteries

| | |
|---|---|
| 1:1 | 3n9 |
| 1.1 | 36 |
| 1.2 | 35 |
| 1.3 | 39 |
| 1.3–4 | 40 |
| 3.9–18 | 39 |
| 4.21 | 39 |
| 4.25 | 39 |
| 5.28 | 39, 40n89 |
| 6.31–33 | 41 |
| 8.43–49 | 39 |
| 9.50–52 | 39–40 |
| 9.58 | 39 |
| 9.59 | 39 |
| 34 | 132n29 |

### De officiis ministrorum

| | |
|---|---|
| 1.50.260 | 146n4 |

### On Psalms

| | |
|---|---|
| 1.47–48 | 231n77 |
| 118 | 147n7 |

### On the Sacraments

| | |
|---|---|
| 1.1.1 | 40 |
| 1.1.2 | 40 |

# Ancient Sources Index

| | |
|---|---|
| 1.2.5 | 40 |
| 1.2.6 | 40 |
| 1.2.8 | 40 |
| 1.3.9–10 | 40n86 |
| 1.5.13–1.6.43 | 39n85 |
| 1.5.15 | 40, 40n86 |
| 1.5.16 | 40 |
| 2.1.2 | 40 |
| 2.2.3–2.3.9 | 39n85 |
| 2.2.6 | 40 |
| 2.2.7 | 40 |
| 2.3.9 | 40 |
| 2.4.10–13 | 40 |
| 2.5.14 | 40 |
| 2.6.19 | 40 |
| 2.7.20 | 39n83, 40n89 |
| 2.7.20–22 | 40 |
| 2.7.23 | 40 |
| 3.1.2 | 40 |
| 3.1.4–7 | 40–41 |
| 3.1.7 | 40 |
| 3.2.8–10 | 40 |
| 3.4.11–13 | 40 |
| 4.4.14 | 41 |
| 4.4.17–20 | 40n86 |
| 4.4.19 | 41 |
| 5 | 41 |
| 5.1 | 115n26 |
| 5.3.17 | 41 |
| 5.4.18–30 | 41 |
| 6.3.11–6.4.19 | 41 |
| 6.5.22–25 | 41 |

## Aphrahat

*Demonstrations*

| | |
|---|---|
| 11 | 153 |
| 11.11 | 153–154 |
| 11.12 | 154 |

## Apostolic Constitutions

| | |
|---|---|
| 6.14.5 | 153n31 |
| 6.15 | 153n31 |
| 7.22 | 114–115n24 |
| 7.39 | 43n101 |
| 7.41–44 | 114–115n24 |
| 8.6.2 | 13n48 |
| VII.39 | 4n17, 6 |

## Aristides

*Apology*

| | |
|---|---|
| 16 | 192 |

## Asterius

*Homilies*

| | |
|---|---|
| 6 | 153n29 |

## Athanasius

*Festal Letters*

| | |
|---|---|
| 39 | 24n29 |

## Athenagoras

*Plea*

| | |
|---|---|
| 1.3 | 193 |
| 6.3 | 193 |
| 18 | 193 |
| 37.1 | 193 |

## Augustine

*On Catechizing Beginners*

| | |
|---|---|
| 2.4.45 | 44 |
| 2.5.47 | 44 |
| 4.8 | 44, 50n131 |
| 5.9 | 49 |
| 6.10 | 43, 44 |
| 7.11 | 43, 44 |
| 14.21 | 44 |
| 15 | 43 |
| 16–25 | 43 |
| 16.24–25 | 44 |
| 17.27–28 | 44 |
| 17.28 | 43, 174n46 |
| 19.31 | 43 |
| 22.39 | 43 |
| 23.41 | 44 |
| 24.44–45 | 43 |
| 25.46 | 44 |
| 25.47–48 | 44 |
| 25.48 | 44, 45n113 |
| 26.51–27.55 | 43 |
| 27.55 | 44 |

## Ancient Sources Index

### On Christian Combat

| | |
|---|---|
| 13.14 | 50n131 |
| 13.14–33.35 | 46 |

### City of God

| | |
|---|---|
| 20 | 232 |
| 20.6 | 232n85 |
| 20.6–9 | 250 |
| 20.7 | 201n10, 232n84, 232n86 |
| 20.8 | 232n87 |
| 20.9 | 232n88 |
| 22.29 | 232n89 |
| 22.30 | 43n103, 201n10, 232n86 |
| 22.30.5 | 203 |

### Enchiridion

| | |
|---|---|
| 3.8 | 50n131 |
| 9–113 | 46 |
| 114–116 | 46 |
| 117–121 | 46 |

### Epistles

| | |
|---|---|
| 187.11.34 | 148 |

### Exposition on Psalms

| | |
|---|---|
| 40.10 | 45n114 |
| 81 | 42 |
| 81.2 | 45n113 |
| 81.8 | 45n111 |
| 81.10 | 45 |
| 81.18 | 45 |
| 93 | 43n103 |
| 122 | 45 |
| 125 | 45 |
| 126 | 45 |

### On Faith and Works

| | |
|---|---|
| 1.1 | 47 |
| 6.9 | 47, 50 |
| 7.11 | 47 |
| 8.12 | 47 |
| 9.14 | 21n14 |
| 13.19 | 21n14 |
| 14.21 | 47 |
| 18.33 | 21n14 |
| 19.35 | 21n14, 47 |
| 20.36 | 47 |
| 27.49 | 47 |

### De gratia Christi et de peccato originali

| | |
|---|---|
| 2.2–4 | 156n9 |

### Against Julian

| | |
|---|---|
| 3.5 | 156n9 |
| 3.11 | 156n9 |
| 6.7.18 | 147 |

### De peccatorum meritis

| | |
|---|---|
| 1.23 | 156n9 |
| 1.28 | 156n9 |
| 1.39 | 156n9 |
| 3.2 | 156n9 |
| 3.39 | 156n9 |

### Retractiones

| | |
|---|---|
| 2.38 | 47 |

### Sermons

| | |
|---|---|
| 56–59 | 43 |
| 56.2 | 47 |
| 57.1 | 47 |
| 97A.3 | 45n111 |
| 132 | 42 |
| 148 | 45n114 |
| 199–204 | 45n110 |
| 211–214 | 46 |
| 212–218 | 43 |
| 212.2 | 46, 46n118 |
| 213 | 46 |
| 213.9 | 46 |
| 214 | 46 |
| 215 | 46 |
| 224–229 | 43 |
| 224 | 48 |
| 224.1 | 48 |
| 224.4 | 48 |
| 225.4 | 48 |
| 227 | 48 |
| 228.1 | 48 |
| 228.2 | 48 |

| | | | |
|---|---|---|---|
| 229 | 48 | | 111, 112, 113, 114, 115–116, 117, 120, 120n38, 122 |
| 229A | 48 | | |
| 250 | 45n114 | | |
| 259 | 232n84 | 2 | 107–108n64, 107n51, 107n54, 107n61, 108n65, 113, 115, 116, 117, 119, 120, 120n38, 122 |
| 259.2 | 43n103 | | |
| 260 | 43, 49 | | |
| 272 | 43, 48 | | |
| 301A.8 | 45n113 | 3 | 107n63, 111, 113, 115, 116, 118, 121–122, 130n21 |
| 339.8 | 45n111 | | |
| | | 4 | 107n51, 107n62, 108n70, 112, 113, 115, 116, 117, 118, 122, 123 |

*Tractates on the Gospel of John*

| | | | |
|---|---|---|---|
| 1–12 | 44n106 | | |
| 4 | 42 | 5 | 101n6, 101n7, 101n9, 102n16, 103n24, 104n29, 104n32, 108n69, 108n71, 111, 112, 113, 114, 115, 116, 117–118, 119, 120, 120n39, 121, 122, 123 |
| 4.12–14 | 45n112 | | |
| 4.13 | 44n106, 45n112 | | |
| 9.6 | 43n103 | | |
| 10 | 42 | | |
| 10.10 | 44n106 | | |
| 11 | 42 | 6 | 105n34, 105n40, 107n50, 108n66, 108n68, 111, 114, 115, 116, 117, 118, 121, 122 |
| 11.1 | 44n106 | | |
| 11.2 | 44n106 | | |
| 11.3 | 46 | 7f | 111 |
| 11.4 | 44n106, 45n111, 46, 50 | 7 | 101n5, 103n25, 107n59, 109n74, 111–112, 113, 114, 115, 118, 119, 121, 122, 123 |
| 11.6 | 50 | | |
| 12.3 | 50 | | |
| 15.9 | 43n103 | 8 | 102n13, 116, 118 |
| 44.2 | 50 | | |
| 122.6 | 250 | | |
| 122.8 | 250 | | |

*On the Holy Spirit*

| | |
|---|---|
| 12.28—15.35 | 117n32 |
| 14.31—15.36 | 120n38 |
| 14.31–33 | 116n30 |
| 15.35 | 115n25 |

## Bardesanes

*On Fate*

201n9

*Homilies*

| | |
|---|---|
| 13 | 100n1 |
| 13.2 | 148 |

## Basil of Caesarea

*On Baptism*

| | |
|---|---|
| 1.2 | 40n88, 119, 119–120n37, 120, 120n38, 120n39, 136n43 |
| 1.3 | 119–120n37 |
| 2.1 | 119, 119–120n37, 120 |

## Clement of Alexandria

*Eclogae Propheticae*

| | |
|---|---|
| 31 | 145 |

*Exhortation to Holy Baptism*

| | |
|---|---|
| 1–2 | 40n88 |
| 1 | 101n3, 101n4, 101n6, 106n48, 107n53, 107n61, |

*Exhortation*

| | |
|---|---|
| 9 | 196 |
| 10 | 196 |
| 11 | 196 |

## Ancient Sources Index

### Instructor

| | |
|---|---|
| 1.6.28.3 | 226 |
| 1.9.78.2 | 60n35 |
| 2.1 | 196 |
| 2.3 | 196 |
| 2.4.41.4 | 226 |
| 2.8 | 145 |
| 3.7 | 196 |
| 3.11 | 196–197 |

### Miscellanies

| | |
|---|---|
| 2.4 | 197 |
| 2.6 | 210n54 |
| 2.7 | 210n54 |
| 2.15 | 210n54 |
| 2.18 | 210n54 |
| 2.19 | 197 |
| 2.20 | 210n54 |
| 3.12.86 | 63n53 |
| 3.13.92 | 180n12 |
| 4.2 | 178n9 |
| 4.7.45.1 | 226 |
| 4.8 | 270n11 |
| 4.9 | 272n30 |
| 4.10 | 277n80 |
| 4.12 | 271n19 |
| 4.25 | 64n65, 164n21, 211n57 |
| 4.25.160.1–2 | 97n45 |
| 5.2 | 178n9 |
| 5.8 | 210n54 |
| 5.10 | 210n54 |
| 6.8 | 210n54 |
| 6.11 | 251 |
| 6.16 | 210, 210n54, 211, 212n60, 251 |
| 6.45 | 180n12 |
| 9.36 | 180n12 |

### Who Is the Rich Man That Is Saved?

| | |
|---|---|
| 19 | 197 |
| 21 | 178n9, 197 |
| 21.6 | 226 |
| 31 | 178n9 |
| 32 | 197 |
| 42.15 | 226 |

## Commodian

### Instructions

| | |
|---|---|
| 43 | 201n7 |
| 44 | 201n7 |
| 80 | 201n7 |

## Cyprian

### Epistles

| | |
|---|---|
| 18.2 | 27 |
| 23 | 13n49 |
| 58.4 | 146–147 |
| 62.8 | 131n24 |
| 63.8 | 59n31, 59n34 |
| 73.22 | 27 |
| 81.2 | 271n19 |

### To Fortunatus on Martrydom

| | |
|---|---|
| 12 | 229n67 |
| 13 | 229n67 |

### On the Lord's Prayer

| | |
|---|---|
| 13 | 229 |

### On Mortality

| | |
|---|---|
| 26 | 229n67 |

### Patience

| | |
|---|---|
| 23–24 | 170n23 |

### In Praise of Martyrdom

| | |
|---|---|
| 7 | 274n44 |
| 9 | 274n44 |
| 11 | 274n44 |
| 17 | 271n19 |
| 19–20 | 274n44 |
| 21 | 274n44 |
| 23 | 271n19 |

### Testimonia ad Quirinium

| | |
|---|---|
| 1 | 27, 28 |
| 1.1–4 | 28 |
| 1.5–18 | 28 |
| 1.8 | 153n32 |

| | | | |
|---|---|---|---|
| 1.8–18 | 15 | 3.5 | 116–117n31 |
| 1.12 | 153n32 | 3.8 | 32 |
| 1.19–24 | 15, 28 | 3.10 | 32 |
| 1.20 | 252 | 3.12 | 66n72 |
| 2 | 27, 28 | 3.15 | 30n56, 32 |
| 2.1–6 | 14 | 3.16 | 32 |
| 2.1–7 | 15 | 4 | 32, 33 |
| 2.7–9 | 14 | 4.2 | 30n56, 32 |
| 2.7–12 | 15 | 4.16 | 33 |
| 2.10 | 14 | 4.18 | 30n56 |
| 2.11 | 14 | 4.21 | 30n56 |
| 2.12 | 14 | 4.23 | 30n56 |
| 2.13 | 15, 170n23 | 4.24 | 30n56 |
| 2.13–23 | 14, 15 | 4.37 | 32 |
| 2.24 | 14 | 5 | 31n59, 32 |
| 2.25–27 | 14, 15 | 5.6 | 152 |
| 2.28–30 | 14 | 5.10–11 | 32 |
| 2.30 | 28 | 5.12 | 32 |
| 3 | 27, 28 | 6 | 32, 33 |
| 3.1 | 28 | 6–9 | 32 |
| 3.3 | 28 | 7 | 32 |
| 3.8 | 28 | 7.1 | 32 |
| 3.11 | 28 | 7.14 | 32 |
| 3.12–13 | 28 | 7.15–16 | 32 |
| 3.16 | 27 | 8 | 32 |
| 3.21 | 28 | 9 | 32 |
| 3.22 | 28 | 10 | 32 |
| 3.25–27 | 28–29 | 10–15 | 32 |
| 3.98 | 29 | 10.2 | 33 |
| 3.114 | 29 | 10.8 | 33 |
| 3.116 | 29 | 10.16 | 33 |
| 3.119 | 29 | 10.20 | 32–33 |
| | | 11 | 32 |

## Cyril of Alexandria

*Homilies on the Pascha*

| | |
|---|---|
| 6 | 151n23 |

## Cyril of Jerusalem

*Catechetical Lectures*

| | | | |
|---|---|---|---|
| 1 | 31, 31n59 | 11.13–17 | 33 |
| 2 | 31, 31n59 | 11.21 | 33 |
| 2.6 | 30n56 | 12 | 32 |
| 2.9 | 30n56 | 12.2 | 33 |
| 2.20 | 31 | 12.5ff | 33 |
| 3 | 31n59, 32 | 12.6 | 30n56 |
| 3.2 | 32 | 12.13 | 33 |
| | | 12.26 | 30n56 |
| | | 12.28 | 33 |
| | | 12.33–34 | 30n56 |
| | | 13 | 32 |
| | | 13.7 | 33 |
| | | 13.9ff | 33 |
| | | 13.13 | 32 |
| | | 14 | 32 |

## Ancient Sources Index

*Catechetical Lectures (continued)*

| | |
|---|---|
| 14.1 | 33 |
| 14.3–20 | 33n61 |
| 14.3ff | 33 |
| 14.15 | 33 |
| 14.21 | 33 |
| 14.22–23 | 33n61 |
| 14.24 | 33n61 |
| 14.26 | 33 |
| 14.27–28 | 33n61 |
| 14.29 | 33n61 |
| 14.30 | 33 |
| 15 | 32, 33 |
| 15.1 | 135n39 |
| 15.1–2 | 175n47 |
| 15.9 | 33 |
| 15.23 | 33 |
| 15.26 | 33 |
| 15.33 | 33 |
| 16 | 33 |
| 16.3 | 34n62 |
| 16.3–4 | 33 |
| 16.4 | 34 |
| 16.6–10 | 34 |
| 16.12 | 34n62 |
| 16.16 | 34n62 |
| 16.17 | 34, 34n62 |
| 16.18 | 34n62 |
| 16.22 | 34, 34n62 |
| 16.25–31 | 33 |
| 17 | 33 |
| 17.5 | 33 |
| 17.6–12 | 33 |
| 17.13–31 | 33 |
| 17.14 | 115n25 |
| 17.32–38 | 33 |
| 17.34 | 33–34 |
| 17.35–36 | 34 |
| 17.38 | 34n63 |
| 18 | 31 |
| 18.1 | 30n56, 34 |
| 18.2–21 | 34 |
| 18.20 | 30n56, 34 |
| 18.22–27 | 34 |
| 18.25 | 34 |
| 18.27–31 | 34 |
| IV.2 | 3n9 |
| XII | 5n19 |

*Mystagogical Catechesis*

| | |
|---|---|
| 1–3 | 114–115n24 |
| 1.2–3 | 130n20 |
| 1.2–8 | 132n30 |
| 2.4 | 114, 114–115n24, 115n25, 132n30 |

*Procatechesis*

| | |
|---|---|
| 4 | 30 |
| 5 | 30 |
| 6 | 30 |
| 8 | 30 |
| 8–16 | 114–115n24 |
| 16 | 30–31 |

*Didascalia Apostolorum*

| | |
|---|---|
| 6.18 | 201n11 |
| 24 | 153 |

*Egeria*

*Journal*

| | |
|---|---|
| 46 | 5n18, 43n101 |

*Ephraim the Syrian*

*Hymns for Epiphany*

| | |
|---|---|
| 3.1 | 153n33 |
| 3.4 | 153n33 |
| 3.13 | 153n33 |

*Epiphanius*

*Adversus Haereses*

| | |
|---|---|
| 8.6 | 148 |
| 30.33 | 147 |
| 33.5 | 145 |
| 48.14 | 223 |

*Epistle of Barnabas*

| | |
|---|---|
| 1.3 | 62, 66n73 |
| 1.4 | 62n46 |
| 1.4.6 | 62 |
| 2 | 56, 206n28 |
| 2.6 | 58n28 |
| 3 | 56, 206n28 |

## Ancient Sources Index

| | | | |
|---|---|---|---|
| 3.1 | 59 | 9.7 | 146 |
| 3.3 | 57n21, 59 | 10 | 53, 204 |
| 3.6 | 56 | 10.10 | 61 |
| 4 | 208 | 10.11 | 64n60 |
| 4.8 | 57n21, 62, 67 | 10.12 | 67, 146 |
| 4.10 | 206n28 | 11–12 | 56 |
| 4.11 | 67 | 11 | 53–54, 64, 65, 67n78, 151, 204 |
| 4.13 | 188 | | |
| 5.1 | 56, 67 | 11.1 | 53, 64, 65, 66, 67, 151n24 |
| 5.9 | 65n70, 66 | 11.1b | 56 |
| 5.13 | 61 | 11.2–11 | 59 |
| 6 | 64, 65, 65n67, 210n54 | 11.2–3 | 59 |
| 6.3 | 62, 64n59 | 11.2 | 58n29, 59, 66n73, 67 |
| 6.7 | 64, 67 | 11.3 | 60n37 |
| 6.7–19 | 64 | 11.4–5 | 59, 67 |
| 6.8 | 64 | 11.4 | 60, 66 |
| 6.8–19 | 54–55, 62, 64n62 | 11.5–6 | 61n41 |
| 6.9 | 62, 62–63n50, 64 | 11.5 | 59, 60, 61, 66n73 |
| 6.9–10 | 62–63n50 | 11.6–8 | 56, 59, 61 |
| 6.10–16 | 62–63n50 | 11.6 | 62n45, 64, 66n73, 67 |
| 6.11 | 57, 64, 66, 97n45 | 11.7 | 59, 61 |
| 6.11–16 | 62–63n50 | 11.8 | 61, 62, 62n45, 64, 65n70, 66, 67 |
| 6.13 | 64, 66 | | |
| 6.14 | 64, 65, 66 | 11.8a | 56n13 |
| 6.15 | 65, 66 | 11.8c | 56n13 |
| 6.16–17 | 66 | 11.9–11 | 59, 63 |
| 6.16 | 65, 67 | 11.9–10 | 64 |
| 6.17–19 | 62–63n50 | 11.9 | 62, 63, 63n53 |
| 6.17–18 | 62–63n50 | 11.9b | 56n13 |
| 6.19 | 206n28 | 11.10–11 | 67 |
| 6.21 | 206n28 | 11.10 | 59, 63, 63n54, 66n73 |
| 6.31 | 62 | 11.11 | 62, 63, 64, 65, 65n70, 66, 67 |
| 7 | 169n17 | 11.11a | 56n13, 59 |
| 7–8 | 53, 204 | 11.11c | 56n13 |
| 7.2 | 57 | 12 | 56 |
| 7.3 | 57, 63 | 12.1–11 | 67 |
| 7.5 | 57 | 12.1 | 53, 56, 61 |
| 7.11 | 188 | 12.2 | 62 |
| 8.3 | 65n70, 66 | 12.3 | 62 |
| 8.5–6 | 188 | 12.7 | 61, 62 |
| 8.5f | 181 | 13–14 | 53, 59, 204 |
| 8.5 | 61, 62, 64n59 | 13.2 | 53 |
| 8.17 | 61 | 14.3 | 58n28 |
| 9 | 53, 204, 206n28 | 14.5 | 57 |
| 9.1–9 | 67 | 15 | 53, 56, 202, 203, 204, 208, 225 |
| 9.3 | 146 | | |
| 9.4 | 151n24 | 15.1–9 | 251 |
| 9.7–9 | 250 | 15.1–5 | 203 |

319

## Ancient Sources Index

### Epistle of Barnabas (continued)

| | |
|---|---|
| 15.1–3 | 204 |
| 15.1 | 53, 205 |
| 15.4 | 204, 205 |
| 15.5–7 | 209 |
| 15.5 | 203, 205, 206, 208 |
| 15.6–9 | 203 |
| 15.6–7 | 205 |
| 15.8 | 203, 206, 207, 209 |
| 15.9 | 206, 207 |
| 16 | 53, 65, 204, 206n28 |
| 16.1 | 53, 62, 65 |
| 16.2 | 62 |
| 16.6 | 65 |
| 16.7–10 | 54–56, 65, 66 |
| 16.7–9 | 65 |
| 16.7–8 | 65, 66 |
| 16.7 | 66n75 |
| 16.8–9 | 66 |
| 16.8 | 57, 62, 65, 66, 66n74 |
| 16.9 | 62, 65 |
| 17.1 | 62 |
| 18 | 118n34 |
| 19.7 | 62 |
| 21.1 | 188 |
| 21.8 | 63n52 |
| 61.7 | 62n48 |
| 81–83 | 56 |
| 156 | 210n54 |

### Eusebius

#### Church History

| | |
|---|---|
| 3.20.4 | 193, 225n46 |
| 3.28.2 | 191 |
| 3.39.11–13 | 219n26, 230n70 |
| 3.39.12 | 191 |
| 4.26.7 | 193 |
| 4.26.8 | 193 |
| 5.1.3 | 256n5 |
| 5.1.5 | 273n38 |
| 5.1.23 | 271n15, 272n28 |
| 5.1.25 | 273n38 |
| 5.1.26 | 274n44 |
| 5.1.27 | 271n15 |
| 5.1.41–42 | 272n28 |
| 5.1.55 | 275n60 |
| 5.1.56 | 272n25 |
| 5.2.4 | 272n24 |
| 5.2.5 | 272n24 |
| 5.18.2 | 223 |
| 6.2.15 | 256n4 |
| 6.7 | 235n100 |
| 6.15 | 256n6 |
| 6.18–19 | 256n8 |
| 7.15.4 | 277n88 |
| 7.24–25 | 227n58 |
| 7.24.1–2 | 230n70 |
| 7.25.7 | 228n59 |
| 8.10.11 | 272n28 |

#### Commentary on Psalms

| | |
|---|---|
| 90.4 | 230n71 |
| 91.2–3 | 230n71 |

#### Demonstratio evangelica

| | |
|---|---|
| 4.16 | 174n45 |
| 9.17 | 174n45 |
| 14 | 276n77 |
| 17 | 277n82 |
| 20 | 276n71 |

#### Life of Constantine

| | |
|---|---|
| 1.3 | 230n69 |

#### Praise of Constantine

| | |
|---|---|
| 3.5 | 230n69 |

#### Preparation for the Gospel

| | |
|---|---|
| 13.12.9–11 | 210n56 |

### Gregory of Elvira

#### Tractatus

| | |
|---|---|
| 4 | 147n9 |
| 4.20 | 145n2 |
| 4.28 | 152n28 |

## Ancient Sources Index

## Gregory of Nazianzus

*Carmina*

| 1.1.9 | 164n22 |
|---|---|

*On Holy Baptism*

| 1 | 106n44, 106n45, 108n71 |
|---|---|
| 2 | 106n47, 107n57 |
| 3 | 106n42, 106n45, 106n46, 107n60, 107n62, 107n63 |
| 4 | 106n43, 106n45, 106n47, 107n49, 107n57, 107n58, 107n62 |
| 6 | 106n45 |
| 7 | 106n47, 107n49, 107n59, 107n62 |
| 8 | 107n57 |
| 9 | 107n61 |
| 10 | 106n45, 107n49, 107n58, 108n67 |
| 11 | 104n31, 104n33, 106n46, 106n47 |
| 11–12 | 104n27 |
| 12 | 106n46, 106n47, 107–108n64, 108n69, 108n71 |
| 13–14 | 101n3 |
| 13 | 102n11, 107n63 |
| 14 | 101n4, 101n6, 101n7, 102–103n20, 103n24, 108n66 |
| 15 | 107n49, 108n70 |
| 16 | 102n18, 106n46, 108n66 |
| 17 | 105n37, 107n49, 107n58 |
| 18 | 106n46, 107n49 |
| 19 | 102n19 |
| 20–21 | 103n21 |
| 20 | 103n24, 106n47 |
| 21 | 106n46 |
| 22–23 | 103n22 |
| 22 | 106n45, 106n46 |
| 23 | 106n46, 107n49 |
| 24 | 101n3, 101n6, 102n15, 106n45, 106n47, 107n61 |
| 25 | 106n47 |
| 26–27 | 108n68 |
| 26 | 105n36, 106n47, 107–108n64, 107n49 |
| 27 | 106n46, 106n47, 107n57 |
| 28 | 105n38, 105n39, 106n47, 107n49 |
| 29–30 | 103n23 |
| 31 | 106n46 |
| 32 | 106n46, 107n58, 107n62 |
| 34 | 106n45, 106n46, 106n47, 107–108n64, 107n62 |
| 35 | 107n62, 108n65 |
| 36–37 | 106n45 |
| 36.359–428 | 100n1 |
| 38–41 | 109n75 |
| 38 | 106n45 |
| 44 | 106n46, 106n47 |
| 45 | 104n28, 107n49 |
| 46 | 106n45, 109n76 |

*Oration*

| 10 | 122 |
|---|---|
| 11f | 122 |
| 14 | 121 |
| 15 | 122 |
| 16 | 121 |
| 17 | 121, 122 |
| 20 | 121 |
| 26 | 121 |
| 31 | 121 |
| 40 | 100n1, 111n9, 120, 121n42, 122n44 |
| 40.28 | 164n22 |

## Gregory of Nyssa

*Adversus eos qui baptismum differunt*

| 46.416–32 | 100n1 |
|---|---|
| 46.416C | 101n3, 106n41, 106n48, 107n62 |
| 46.417A | 107–108n64, 107n63 |
| 46.417B | 101n5, 107–108n64, 108n70, 108n71 |
| 46.417C | 108n65 |
| 46.417D | 101n6, 101n10 |
| 46.420A | 101n8, 106n48 |
| 46.420B | 101n10, 106n48 |
| 46.420C | 103n24, 106n48 |
| 46.421A | 103n24, 108n66 |
| 46.421A–B | 109n73 |
| 46.421C | 104n28, 108n68 |
| 46.421D | 101n6, 105n35 |

321

## Ancient Sources Index

*Adversus eos qui baptismum differunt (continued)*

| | |
|---|---|
| 46.424A | 106n48, 107n55 |
| 46.424B | 106n45, 106n48, 107n52, 107n62, 107n63 |
| 46.424D | 106n48 |
| 46.425A | 103n26, 104n30, 106n48 |
| 46.425B | 106n48, 107n56 |
| 46.425B–D | 102n17 |
| 46.428A | 102n14, 106n48 |
| 46.428B | 107n56 |
| 46.429A–B | 108n69 |
| 46.429B | 106n48, 109n73 |
| 46.429C | 106n48, 107n56, 107n62 |
| 46.429D | 106n48, 107n62, 109n73 |
| 46.432A | 106n45, 106n48, 109n73 |

*On the Baptism of Christ*

| | |
|---|---|
| 9.225.10–9.227.4 | 40n86 |
| 9.228.9–22 | 40n90 |
| 221.6–9 | 126 |
| 221.12 | 126 |
| 221.18 | 126 |
| 222.3–4 | 126 |
| 222.13–223.11 | 142 |
| 222.16 | 126 |
| 222.20–21 | 126 |
| 222.23–223.1 | 126 |
| 223.2 | 126 |
| 223.14–16 | 126 |
| 223.20–21 | 127 |
| 223.20–24 | 142 |
| 223.22–25 | 127 |
| 223.25 | 142 |
| 224.4–5 | 126–127 |
| 224.27–225.1 | 127 |
| 225.1–226.8 | 142 |
| 225.10–11 | 127 |
| 225.18–20 | 127 |
| 225.21–24 | 127 |
| 225.26–226.8 | 128 |
| 226.8–227.4 | 128 |
| 226.23 | 128 |
| 227.5–7 | 128 |
| 228.6–7 | 128 |
| 228.24 | 129 |
| 229.6–230.5 | 142 |
| 230.11 | 129 |
| 230.15–16 | 129 |
| 230.17 | 129 |
| 230.19–237.22 | 129, 142 |
| 231.3 | 129 |
| 231.7–8 | 129 |
| 231.18–19 | 129 |
| 232.14–22 | 129 |
| 232.19–22 | 142 |
| 233.2–3 | 130 |
| 233.6–7 | 130 |
| 233.9–10 | 130 |
| 233.9–14 | 142 |
| 233.24 | 130 |
| 235.13 | 130 |
| 235.15 | 130 |
| 235.18–19 | 130 |
| 236.6–7 | 130 |
| 237.23–240.20 | 142 |
| 237.25–27 | 131 |
| 238.6 | 131 |
| 238.12–16 | 131 |
| 239.4 | 131 |
| 239.5 | 131 |
| 239.7–8 | 131 |
| 239.20–240.4 | 142 |
| 239.24 | 132 |
| 239.24–25 | 132 |
| 240.4–5 | 132 |
| 240.12 | 132 |
| 240.21–242.3 | 142 |
| 240.23–241.1 | 132 |
| 241.19 | 132 |
| 241.19–21 | 140n50 |
| 241.21 | 132 |
| 242.2–3 | 132 |

*Catechetical Oration*

| | |
|---|---|
| 1–4 | 89n3 |
| 2.67.64–2.70.18 | 99n55 |
| 2.344.20–2.346.5 | 99n55 |
| 3.1.105.19–3.1.106.11 | 97n46 |
| 3.1.227.4–9 | 92–93n25 |
| 5–8 | 89n3 |
| 5.1 | 89n1 |
| 7.1.34–8.14 | 96n38 |
| 8.1.203 | 97n43 |
| 8.204.8 | 97n43 |

## Ancient Sources Index

| | | | | | |
|---|---|---|---|---|---|
| 9–32.10 | 89n3 | 88.23–89.14 | 99n56 |
| 9.223.2 | 98n49 | 89.5–17 | 94n30 |
| 9.224–25.225.24 | 97n46 | 89.6–92.25 | 90n7 |
| 9.224.4–5 | 99n57 | 89.10–12 | 99n61 |
| 9.227–7–26 | 91n13 | 89.20–21 | 93n27 |
| 9.227.4–7 | 97n44 | 89.20–24 | 94n31 |
| 9.228–13–26 | 93n26 | 89.21 | 93n28 |
| 9.228.22–9.229.18 | 96n41 | 90.1–16 | 94n32 |
| 9.237–23–9.238–11 | 97n43 | 90.16–91.5 | 94n33 |
| 9.238.11–17 | 97–98n47 | 91.4–5 | 98n50, 98n54 |
| 9.239.5–8 | 98n48 | 91.4–9 | 98n49 |
| 15.16–20.25 | 91n16 | 91.10–92.8 | 95n35 |
| 22–26 | 127n11 | 91.14–18 | 99n56 |
| 32.11–40 | 89n3 | 91.19–23 | 90n5 |
| 33 | 128n15 | 92.6–10 | 99n56 |
| 35 | 40n90, 128–129n17 | 92.8–20 | 95n34 |
| 37 | 127–128n13 | 92.11–25 | 90n8, 95n36 |
| 40.6–41.8 | 91n16 | 92.13–25 | 90n5 |
| 82.1–5 | 90n4 | 92.18–19 | 99n56 |
| 82.1–14 | 98n54 | 93.1–98.6 | 90n9 |
| 82.2 | 98n49 | 93.4 | 99n60 |
| 82.5–86.5 | 90n6 | 93.5–6 | 99n58 |
| 82.6 | 99n58 | 98.7–102.3 | 90n10 |
| 82.10 | 99n58 | 98.8–11 | 96n37 |
| 82.16 | 99n60 | 98.16–99.5 | 96n38 |
| 82.16–17 | 90n5 | 98.18–19 | 98n53 |
| 82.17 | 98n50 | 99.13–16 | 96n40 |
| 82.20–21 | 90n12 | 99.14 | 99n60 |
| 82.21 | 99n58 | 99.14–18 | 98n51 |
| 82.23–84.5 | 91n13 | 99.17–18 | 98n50 |
| 83.15–16 | 91n14 | 100.1–4 | 98n54 |
| 83.21 | 99n58 | 100.2–7 | 96n41 |
| 84.18 | 99n60 | 100.7–8 | 96n39 |
| 84.85.3 | 91n17 | 100.9 | 99n58 |
| 85.3–86.5 | 92n20 | 100.17–22 | 99n60 |
| 85.5–86.1 | 91n13 | 100.18–19 | 98n53 |
| 85.10–11 | 98n52 | 100.19 | 99n58 |
| 85.13–86.3 | 99n60 | 101.4–6 | 96n42 |
| 85.23 | 98n50 | 101.4 | 99n60 |
| 86.6 | 91n19, 93n28 | 101.19–102.2 | 98n51 |
| 86.6–7 | 92n24 | 101.23–102.2 | 96n42 |
| 87.12–14 | 98n54 | 102.3 | 98n51 |
| 87.17–18 | 92–93n25 | 102.4–11 | 97n43 |
| 88.2–5 | 93n26 | 102.4–106.18 | 90n11 |
| 88.3 | 99n58 | 102.6 | 89n1 |
| 88.10–11 | 93n27 | 102.9 | 98n50, 99n58 |
| 88.12–18 | 98n54 | 102.12–24 | 97n44 |
| 88.16–18 | 98n54 | 102.21–22 | 98n54 |

## Ancient Sources Index

*Catechetical Oration (continued)*

| | |
|---|---|
| 102.21 | 98n51 |
| 102.24–103.10 | 97n46 |
| 102.24 | 98n50 |
| 103.2 | 98n49 |
| 103.5 | 98n49 |
| 103.9–10 | 91n15 |
| 103.10–104.10 | 97–98n47 |
| 103.20 | 98n49 |
| 104.10–12 | 98n51 |
| 104.11 | 98n50 |
| 104.12–16 | 98n48 |

*Testimonies against the Jews*

| | |
|---|---|
| 17 | 168n12 |

*Against Those Who Delay Baptism*

| | |
|---|---|
| | 111n9, 122, 123 |

# Hippolytus

*Antichrist*

| | |
|---|---|
| 44 | 75n48 |
| 45 | 229n64 |
| 59 | 229n65 |
| 61 | 228n63 |
| 65 | 228n62 |

*Apostolic Tradition*

| | |
|---|---|
| 16 | 13n49, 19n5, 49 |
| 17 | 13n47, 19n9, 49 |
| 18 | 13n49 |
| 18.1 | 19n10 |
| 19 | 13n49, 19n6 |
| 19.2 | 27n46 |
| 20 | 13n47, 21n15 |
| 20.2 | 19n9 |
| 20.3 | 66n75 |
| 20.3–4 | 19n7 |
| 20.8 | 19n7, 19n8 |
| 21 | 13n47, 21n15, 132n30 |
| 21.9 | 19n10, 66n75 |
| 21.10 | 66n75 |
| 21.12–18 | 19n10 |
| 22–23 | 13n47 |
| 23 | 21n15 |
| 23.2 | 64n63 |
| 23.13 | 21n15 |
| 27 | 13n47 |
| 32 | 21n15 |
| 33 | 13n47, 21n15 |
| 35 | 13n47 |
| 37–38 | 13n47 |
| 41 | 13n47 |
| 42 | 13n47 |

*Commentary on Daniel*

| | |
|---|---|
| 1.21.4–5 | 229n65 |
| 2.37.3–4 | 229n65 |
| 2.38 | 271n21 |
| 3–4 | 275n61 |
| 3.23 | 275n58 |
| 3.24 | 274n45, 276n71 |
| 3.31.3 | 229n65 |
| 4.10.1–2 | 228n62 |
| 4.11.4 | 228n63 |
| 4.23 | 228 |
| 4.23–24 | 201n4 |
| 4.58 | 228 |
| III.26 | 271n19 |

*Refutation of all Heresies*

| | |
|---|---|
| 5.2 | 198 |
| 5.3 | 198 |
| 5.4 | 198 |
| 6.45 | 248 |
| 9.7 | 139n49 |
| 10.30 | 228 |

# Ignatius

*Ephesians*

| | |
|---|---|
| 16.1 | 189 |
| 19.3 | 189 |

*Philadelphians*

| | |
|---|---|
| 3.3 | 189 |

*Romans*

| | |
|---|---|
| 6.13 | 189 |

## Irenaeus

### Against Heresies

| | |
|---|---|
| 1.1 | 248 |
| 1.1.3 | 248 |
| 1.3 | 8n32 |
| 1.3.1 | 248 |
| 1.3.2 | 248 |
| 1.10.1 | 170n21 |
| 1.14–16 | 248 |
| 1.14.4 | 250 |
| 1.14.5 | 212n61 |
| 1.14.6 | 212n60 |
| 1.15.2 | 248 |
| 1.24.3 | 248 |
| 1.24.7 | 248 |
| 1.30.13 | 177n4 |
| 2.20–21 | 248 |
| 2.20–25 | 248 |
| 2.22.1 | 248 |
| 2.22.4–5 | 248 |
| 2.24.1 | 248 |
| 2.28.3 | 194 |
| 3.7.1f | 164n21 |
| 3.11.8 | 194, 251 |
| 3.12.13 | 194 |
| 3.16.4 | 194 |
| 3.17.1–2 | 64n65 |
| 3.18.7 | 194 |
| 3.21.9 | 194 |
| 4.6.2 | 170n25 |
| 4.8.1 | 194 |
| 4.16.1 | 195 |
| 4.18.6 | 178n5 |
| 4.20.5 | 195 |
| 4.21.1 | 195 |
| 4.22.2 | 195 |
| 4.24.2 | 195 |
| 4.25.3 | 195 |
| 4.27.1 | 195 |
| 4.27.2 | 195 |
| 4.33.1 | 171n27 |
| 4.33.11 | 195 |
| 4.34.3 | 195 |
| 4.38.1 | 263n39 |
| 5.9–14 | 177n4 |
| 5.23.2 | 201n2, 201n11 |
| 5.27.1 | 178n5 |
| 5.28.1 | 195 |
| 5.28.3 | 201n2, 201n11 |
| 5.29.2–30.4 | 249 |
| 5.30.4 | 195, 252 |
| 5.31–36 | 220, 250 |
| 5.31.1 | 224 |
| 5.32.1 | 195, 221n34, 224 |
| 5.33.2 | 195, 201n2, 201n11 |
| 5.33.3 | 195 |
| 5.33.3–4 | 219n27 |
| 5.34.3 | 196 |
| 5.35.1 | 196 |
| 5.35.2 | 221n34 |
| 5.35.3 | 196 |
| 5.36.2 | 196 |
| 5.36.3 | 196 |
| 14.16.1–2 | 150 |
| 28.2 | 178n5 |
| 40.2 | 178n5 |

### Proof of the Apostolic Preaching

| | |
|---|---|
| 1 | 7, 10, 13, 25, 193 |
| 1–2 | 8, 9 |
| 1–6 | 25 |
| 2 | 13, 25 |
| 3 | 13, 25, 26, 64n65, 97n45, 149n17 |
| 3–7 | 8, 9 |
| 6 | 10, 11n44, 12, 25, 26 |
| 7 | 26 |
| 8–29 | 9 |
| 8–42a | 8, 10 |
| 12 | 16n59 |
| 20 | 25n35 |
| 25 | 16n59 |
| 26 | 16n59 |
| 28 | 25, 194 |
| 30 | 9, 26 |
| 30–88 | 9 |
| 31 | 14 |
| 32 | 11, 16n59 |
| 32–36 | 9 |
| 33 | 16n59 |
| 36 | 194 |
| 37 | 14 |
| 41 | 10, 13, 25, 194 |
| 41–42 | 10 |

## Ancient Sources Index

*Proof of the Apostolic Preaching (continued)*

| | |
|---|---|
| 42 | 9 |
| 42–43 | 10 |
| 42–85 | 10 |
| 42b–97 | 8, 11 |
| 43 | 11, 14 |
| 43–51 | 15 |
| 44–46 | 9 |
| 46 | 194 |
| 47 | 194 |
| 48 | 170n21 |
| 49 | 26 |
| 50–51 | 14 |
| 51–64 | 15 |
| 52 | 194 |
| 53–58 | 14 |
| 53–85 | 9 |
| 56 | 194 |
| 57 | 194 |
| 58 | 194 |
| 59 | 14 |
| 61 | 194 |
| 62 | 14 |
| 63 | 14 |
| 64 | 14, 194 |
| 68–77 | 14 |
| 68–82 | 15 |
| 74 | 194 |
| 78 | 14 |
| 79–81 | 14 |
| 83–84 | 14 |
| 83–85 | 15 |
| 84 | 194 |
| 85 | 14 |
| 86 | 10 |
| 86–97 | 10 |
| 87 | 13, 25, 26 |
| 87–96 | 15 |
| 87–98 | 25 |
| 89–96 | 15 |
| 89–97 | 9 |
| 91–95 | 43n102 |
| 95 | 13, 25, 26, 194 |
| 96 | 26 |
| 98–100 | 8, 9 |
| 98 | 10, 12, 25 |
| 99–100 | 12 |
| 100 | 26 |

## Isidore of Pelusium

*Epistles*

| | |
|---|---|
| 1.125 | 148 |

## Jerome

*Commentary on Amos*

| | |
|---|---|
| 1.3.9–10 | 247 |
| 2.5.3 | 252 |

*Commentary on Daniel*

| | |
|---|---|
| 7.17 | 231n80 |

*Commentary on Ezekiel*

| | |
|---|---|
| 11.36 | 231n81 |

*Commentary on Isaiah*

| | |
|---|---|
| 6.14.1 | 231n78 |
| 18 | 231n80 |

*Commentary on Jeremiah*

| | |
|---|---|
| 19.10–11 | 231n80 |
| 31.38ff | 231n80 |

*Commentary on Zephaniah*

| | |
|---|---|
| 1.14 | 231n78 |

*Epistles*

| | |
|---|---|
| 121 | 75n47 |

## John of Chrysostom

*Baptismal Instructions*

| | |
|---|---|
| 1.10–26 | 132n30 |
| 2.20–21 | 132n30 |
| 3.5–7 | 136n44 |
| 3.6 | 164n22 |
| 4.17–33 | 131n26 |
| 9.12–15 | 136n44 |
| 9.13–20 | 136n41 |
| 12.6 | 136n44 |
| 12.15–20 | 131n26 |

## Ancient Sources Index

*On the Baptism of Christ*

| | |
|---|---|
| 1 | 45n113, 126n9, 131n27 |
| 1.363–364 | 133, 142 |
| 1.363 | 133 |
| 1.364 | 133–134 |
| 1.365 | 134, 142 |
| 2–3 | 40n88 |
| 2 | 175n47 |
| 2.365–369 | 142 |
| 2.365–366 | 135 |
| 2.365 | 135 |
| 2.366 | 136 |
| 3.365–369 | 142 |
| 3.366 | 136 |
| 3.367 | 137 |
| 3.368 | 138 |
| 3.369 | 138 |
| 4.369–370 | 140, 142 |
| 4.369 | 138–139, 142 |
| 4.370 | 140, 142 |
| 4.371 | 141 |
| 4.371–372 | 141 |
| 4.372 | 141 |

*De Lazaro*

| | |
|---|---|
| 6.7 | 139n49 |

*Homilies*

| | |
|---|---|
| 28.1 | 135n39 |

*Homilies on 2 Corinthians*

| | |
|---|---|
| 3.7 | 151 |

*Homilies on Acts*

| | |
|---|---|
| 1.2 | 134n38 |

*Homilies on Colossians*

| | |
|---|---|
| 6.2 | 152 |

*Homilies on Ephesians*

| | |
|---|---|
| 2.2 | 151 |

*Homilies on John*

| | |
|---|---|
| 3.17 | 135n39 |
| 14.1 | 153 |
| 28.1 | 75n47 |
| 33.2 | 147 |

*Homilies on Matthew*

| | |
|---|---|
| 10.1 | 138n47 |
| 10.2 | 137n45 |
| 12.1–4 | 138n47 |
| 12.1 | 138n47 |
| 12.3 | 138n47 |
| 12.4 | 137n45 |

*Homilies on Romans*

| | |
|---|---|
| 6.2 | 147 |

## John of Damascus

*An Exact Exposition of the Orthodox Faith*

| | |
|---|---|
| 4.25 | 148 |

## Justin Martyr

*1 Apology*

| | |
|---|---|
| 1.39 | 9n40 |
| 1.45 | 9n40 |
| 3.2 | 23 |
| 3.4 | 23 |
| 5 | 273n37 |
| 6 | 23n23, 26n39 |
| 11 | 192 |
| 13 | 23, 26n39 |
| 13.3 | 24n31 |
| 14 | 23 |
| 15–17 | 23 |
| 18 | 24 |
| 19 | 24, 91n13 |
| 21 | 23 |
| 21.15 | 174n41 |
| 22 | 23 |
| 23.2 | 24n31 |
| 31 | 23, 26n39 |
| 32–35 | 23 |
| 39 | 43n102 |
| 40 | 23 |
| 41 | 23 |
| 41.4 | 188n34 |

# Ancient Sources Index

## 1 Apology (continued)

| | |
|---|---|
| 42 | 170n20 |
| 45 | 23, 43n102 |
| 47–53 | 23 |
| 50 | 271n21 |
| 52 | 167n7 |
| 57 | 273n38 |
| 61 | 23, 64n65, 164n21 |
| 61.2 | 22n20 |
| 61.10 | 57n19 |
| 65 | 23n23 |
| 65.1 | 22 |
| 66.1 | 22, 57n19 |
| 67 | 23n23 |

## 2 Apology

| | |
|---|---|
| 1 | 273n38 |
| 2 | 275n59 |
| 2.19 | 179 |
| 12 | 272n23 |

## Dialogue with Trypho

| | |
|---|---|
| 1 | 237n109 |
| 2.8 | 167n5 |
| 7.4 | 191 |
| 9.1 | 192 |
| 10.2 | 192 |
| 10.3 | 151 |
| 11–30 | 15 |
| 14 | 57 |
| 14.1 | 57n20, 60n35 |
| 14.8 | 168n10 |
| 16 | 151 |
| 18.2 | 152 |
| 19 | 151, 152 |
| 19.2 | 57n20, 60n35, 67n78 |
| 24.2 | 151 |
| 28.4 | 151 |
| 29.1 | 57n20, 67n78, 152 |
| 30.3 | 23n25 |
| 31 | 178n6 |
| 31–62 | 15 |
| 32 | 192 |
| 32.2 | 168n11 |
| 33 | 170n21 |
| 33.2 | 168n11 |
| 34 | 192 |
| 34.2 | 168n11 |
| 39 | 192 |
| 40–42 | 16n59 |
| 41 | 207n34 |
| 41.4 | 151 |
| 43.2 | 152 |
| 46 | 192 |
| 47.1 | 151 |
| 49.2 | 168n12 |
| 51 | 192 |
| 52.1 | 168n14 |
| 52.4 | 169n16 |
| 56 | 178n7 |
| 63 | 178n7 |
| 63–78 | 15 |
| 63.1 | 23n25 |
| 65 | 178n6 |
| 68.52 | 178n6 |
| 73.1 | 188n34 |
| 76.4 | 178n8 |
| 76.12 | 178n6 |
| 79.2 | 178n6 |
| 80 | 182n19, 186 |
| 80–81 | 219 |
| 80.2 | 224 |
| 80.4 | 224 |
| 80.5 | 220, 224, 250 |
| 81 | 201n1 |
| 81.1–3 | 220n30 |
| 81.4 | 220 |
| 86 | 178n7 |
| 86–105 | 15 |
| 86.1 | 61n41 |
| 86.4 | 61n41 |
| 92 | 151 |
| 93 | 26n40 |
| 106–108 | 15 |
| 109–110 | 9n40 |
| 109–111 | 43n102 |
| 109–end | 15 |
| 110 | 271n21 |
| 110.2 | 169n15 |
| 111 | 169 |
| 113 | 16n59 |
| 113.6f | 151 |
| 114.4 | 151 |
| 114.5 | 60n35 |
| 116 | 192 |

## Ancient Sources Index

| | |
|---|---|
| 117 | 192 |
| 118.2 | 178n6 |
| 120 | 192 |
| 120.5–6 | 178n8 |
| 121 | 193 |
| 131 | 193 |
| 132 | 16n59 |
| 132.1 | 23n25 |
| 134 | 16n59 |
| 137.1 | 151 |
| 138 | 16n59, 61n41 |
| 140 | 193 |
| 140.2 | 178n8 |

### Lactantius

*Divine Institutes*

| | |
|---|---|
| 4.12 | 174n45 |
| 4.15 | 40n87, 148n12 |
| 4.17 | 148 |
| 7 | 222 |
| 7.14 | 222 |
| 7.22 | 201n5 |
| 7.22–23 | 222 |
| 7.24 | 201n5 |
| 7.25.5 | 222 |
| 7.26 | 201n5 |

*Epitome*

| | |
|---|---|
| 72 | 201n5 |

### Martyrdom of Agape

| | |
|---|---|
| 1.2.4 | 271n15 |
| 3–4 | 273n33 |
| 3.3 | 276n74 |
| 3.4 | 274n52 |
| 5.2 | 274n44, 275n66 |
| 5.3 | 275n65 |

### Martyrdom of Apollonius

| | |
|---|---|
| 6 | 276n69 |
| 7 | 274n51 |
| 9 | 276n69 |
| 24 | 272n22, 275n55 |
| 42 | 274n44 |
| 47 | 271n15, 272n28 |

### Martyrdom of Conon

| | |
|---|---|
| 3–4 | 275n60, 275n66 |
| 5 | 274n42 |
| 6.7 | 273n35 |

### Martyrdom of Crispina

| | |
|---|---|
| 1 | 274n50 |
| 1.6 | 275n57 |
| 1.7 | 273n37 |
| 2.1 | 276n76 |
| 2.2 | 274n44 |

### Martyrdom of Dasius

| | |
|---|---|
| 4 | 274n45 |
| 5.2 | 273n35 |
| 7.2 | 277n91 |

### Martyrdom of Felix the Bishop

| | |
|---|---|
| 15–17 | 275n58 |
| 30 | 273n35 |

### Martyrdom of Fructuosus and Companions

| | |
|---|---|
| 2.6 | 274n51 |
| 3.3 | 274n44 |
| 4.3 | 274n44 |
| 6.3 | 272n25 |
| 7.2 | 271n15, 274n44 |

### Martyrdom of Irenaeus, Bishop of Sirmium

| | |
|---|---|
| 2.2 | 273n39 |
| 2.4 | 273n36 |
| 4.12 | 274n42 |
| 5.2 | 271n19 |
| 6 | 275n64 |

### Martyrdom of Julius the Veteran

| | |
|---|---|
| 1.3–4 | 277n92 |
| 2.1 | 277n92 |
| 2.4 | 274n44 |
| 2.5–6 | 276n67 |

329

## Ancient Sources Index

### Martyrdom of Julius the Veteran (continued)

| | |
|---|---|
| 3–4 | 274n45 |
| 3.3 | 275n56 |

### Martyrdom of Montanus and Lucius

| | |
|---|---|
| 22.2 | 274n44 |

### Martyrdom of Perpetua and Felicitas

| | |
|---|---|
| 1.5 | 272n30 |
| 6.3 | 274n50, 275n66 |
| 17.3 | 272n25 |
| 18.8 | 274n43 |
| 21.11 | 271n19 |

### Martyrdom of Peter with Simon

| | |
|---|---|
| 9 | 180n12 |
| 94 | 180n12 |

### Martyrdom of Pionius

| | |
|---|---|
| 1 | 272n30 |
| 3.2–3 | 275n56 |
| 4–5 | 275n66 |
| 4.24 | 274n44 |
| 7.4 | 274n44 |
| 7.5 | 274n44 |
| 12 | 275n66 |
| 19 | 273n32 |
| 20 | 275n66 |
| 20.5 | 274n45 |
| 21.4 | 274n45 |
| 22.4 | 272n28 |
| 23 | 275n64 |

### Martyrdom of Polycarp

| | |
|---|---|
| 1 | 272n28 |
| 2 | 272n25, 273 |
| 2.1 | 271n19 |
| 4 | 271n20 |
| 9 | 275n60, 278n99 |
| 9–12 | 275n66 |
| 9.3 | 190 |
| 10 | 276n68 |
| 11 | 274n44 |
| 12 | 272n31 |
| 14 | 273n35, 274n45 |
| 14.1–2 | 225n49 |
| 16 | 272n25 |
| 17 | 275n60 |
| 17.1 | 225n49 |
| 17.3 | 190 |
| 18 | 272n29 |
| 19 | 272n28 |
| 19.2 | 225n49 |
| 20.2 | 190, 225n49 |
| 21 | 275n63 |
| 21.2 | 190 |
| 22.1 | 190 |
| 22.3 | 190 |
| 41 | 271n19 |
| 42 | 271n19 |

### Melito of Sardis

*On Pascha*

| | |
|---|---|
| 1–45 | 16 |
| 47–48 | 16 |
| 49–56 | 16 |
| 57–65 | 16 |
| 66–71 | 16 |
| 72–99 | 16 |
| 83–89 | 16 |
| 100–105 | 16 |

### Methodius

*Banquet*

| | |
|---|---|
| 7.6 | 147 |
| 8.2 | 222n40 |
| 9 | 222n39 |
| 9.1 | 201n6, 222 |
| 9.3 | 222 |
| 9.5 | 222 |

*On the Resurrection*

| | |
|---|---|
| 1.14 | 91n13 |
| 3.2.5 | 222n40 |

## Novatian

*De Trinitate*

| | |
|---|---|
| 29 | 34n63 |

## Odes of Solomon

| | |
|---|---|
| 4.10 | 64n63 |
| 11.2–3 | 150 |
| 11.5 | 61n39 |
| 11.8 | 63n55 |
| 11.12–23 | 63 |
| 11.18 | 63n55 |
| 12.2 | 62n45 |
| 17.6–16 | 60 |
| 17.10 | 60 |
| 22.12 | 191 |
| 23.12 | 191 |
| 24 | 60n38 |
| 38.16–22 | 61n41 |
| 38.17 | 61n41 |

## Origen

*Against Celsus*

| | |
|---|---|
| 1.7 | 86–87n71 |
| 1.56 | 174n44 |
| 2.6 | 264n44 |
| 3.7–8 | 277n82 |
| 3.15 | 86–87n71 |
| 3.34 | 258n17 |
| 3.49 | 257n15 |
| 3.61 | 260n30 |
| 3.62 | 261n31 |
| 4.13 | 75n28 |
| 4.16 | 263n40 |
| 4.19 | 262n36 |
| 4.99 | 259 |
| 5.15 | 75n28 |
| 5.31 | 259n26 |
| 6.22 | 246 |
| 6.56 | 260n29 |
| 7.28–30 | 227n53 |
| 7.50 | 259n23 |
| 7.60 | 263n38 |
| 7.69 | 273n37 |
| 7.733 | 276n71 |
| 8.8 | 272n28 |
| 8.11 | 199 |
| 8.26 | 275n56 |
| 8.43 | 273n38 |
| 8.44 | 271n15 |
| 8.55 | 275n56 |
| 8.65 | 276n68 |
| 8.68 | 275n61 |
| 8.70 | 278n93 |
| 8.73 | 278n93 |
| 8.74 | 276n73 |
| 8.75 | 278n93 |
| 111.51 | 13n48 |

*Commentary on 1 Corinthians*

| | |
|---|---|
| 1.17 | 75 |

*Commentary on Ephesians*

| | |
|---|---|
| 4.5 | 69n5 |

*Commentary on Genesis*

| | |
|---|---|
| 3 | 82n59 |

*Commentary on John*

| | |
|---|---|
| 1.182 | 80n48 |
| 6.23.125 | 73 |
| 6.23.166 | 78n36 |
| 6.32.162 | 74 |
| 6.32.187–193 | 86–87n71 |
| 6.33.165 | 87 |
| 6.33.166 | 87 |
| 6.33.166–167 | 74 |
| 6.33.168 | 74 |
| 6.33.169 | 74–75, 79n45 |
| 6.42.220 | 71n13 |
| 6.43.223 | 75 |
| 6.43.224 | 75n29 |
| 6.43.226–6.48.249 | 69 |
| 6.43.227 | 69 |
| 6.44.228 | 71 |
| 6.44.229 | 71n12 |
| 6.44.229–230 | 70n7 |
| 6.44.232 | 82 |
| 6.46.238 | 71 |
| 6.47.242–245 | 71 |
| 6.48.250 | 72 |
| 6.56.290–291 | 85 |

## Ancient Sources Index

### Commentary on John (continued)

| | |
|---|---|
| 10.43.298 | 87n73 |

### Commentary on Matthew

| | |
|---|---|
| 10.9 | 264n42 |
| 10.10 | 264n41 |
| 10.14 | 264n46 |
| 12.16 | 258n19 |
| 12.20 | 87n75 |
| 13.16 | 84 |
| 13.27 | 79n46 |
| 15.6–9 | 85 |
| 15.11 | 261n34 |
| 15.23 | 75n28, 76n31, 79n46, 80n48 |
| 16.6 | 85–86 |
| 49 | 73 |

### Commentary on Romans

| | |
|---|---|
| 2.1.2 | 85n68 |
| 2.12.4 | 81 |
| 2.13 | 146 |
| 2.13.2 | 81 |
| 3.1.11 | 72n17 |
| 3.1.12 | 78n37, 80n50 |
| 5.2.11 | 79n42 |
| 5.8.2 | 80n48 |
| 5.8.3 | 75n27 |
| 5.8.6 | 73n21 |
| 5.8.7 | 87n75 |
| 5.8.10 | 80n48, 87n72 |
| 5.8.12 | 80n48 |
| 5.8.13 | 80n48 |
| 5.9 | 157n11 |
| 5.9.2 | 80n49 |
| 5.9.11 | 83 |
| 5.10.2 | 87n74 |
| 5.10.4 | 87n72, 87n76 |
| 8.5.3 | 79n43 |

### Commentary on the Song of Songs

| | |
|---|---|
| 2.8 | 70n7 |
| 2.10 | 78n36 |

### Exhortation to Martyrdom

| | |
|---|---|
| 2 | 274n46 |

| | |
|---|---|
| 30 | 86 |
| 34–35 | 275n56 |
| 39 | 86 |
| 42 | 271n15 |

### On First Principles

| | |
|---|---|
| 1.3.2 | 78n37, 87n75 |
| 1.4.8 | 86–87n71 |
| 2.10.4 | 75n28 |
| 2.10.6 | 260n30 |
| 2.11.1 | 255n2 |
| 2.11.2–3 | 226 |
| 2.11.4 | 256n3 |
| 2.11.6 | 227n54 |
| 2.11.6–7 | 227n55, 250 |
| 2.11.7 | 267n52, 267n53 |
| 2.11.16 | 266n51 |
| 3.1.13 | 260n30 |
| 3.1.15 | 265n48 |
| 3.2.3f | 118n34 |
| 3.3.3 | 258n21 |
| 3.3.4 | 118n34 |
| 3.5.4 | 259n22 |
| 3.5.8 | 259n24 |
| 3.6.8f | 266n50 |
| 4.1.22 | 227n53, 250 |
| 4.26 | 268n54 |
| 5 | 227 |

### Homilies on Exodus

| | |
|---|---|
| 5.1 | 70 |
| 5.2 | 80n49 |
| 5.4 | 80n51 |
| 5.5 | 70, 80n51 |
| 6.2.5 | 78n38 |
| 8.4 | 78n37 |
| 8.4–5 | 87n72 |
| 8.5 | 78n37 |
| 10.4 | 78n37, 79n44 |
| 11.7 | 78n36 |

### Homilies on Ezekiel

| | |
|---|---|
| 1.2 | 261n33 |
| 2.5 | 80n50 |

## Ancient Sources Index

### Homilies on Genesis

| | |
|---|---|
| 1.7 | 263n39 |
| 3.4–7 | 145 |
| 3.6 | 151n22 |
| 10.5 | 81n53 |
| 104–110 | 72n16 |

### Homilies on Jeremiah

| | |
|---|---|
| 1.16.2 | 80n49 |
| 2.3.1–2 | 75–76 |
| 5:13 | 3n9 |
| 5.13 | 86–87n71 |
| 5.14 | 84n63 |
| 6.2 | 266n49 |
| 10.11.3 | 259n27 |
| 16.5.2 | 79n47 |
| 18.6 | 263n37 |
| 18.15 | 262n35 |
| 20.1 | 261n34 |

### Homilies on Joshua

| | |
|---|---|
| 1.7 | 81 |
| 4.1 | 71 |
| 4.2 | 79n47, 80n49 |
| 5.1 | 71 |
| 5.2 | 71 |
| 5.5 | 148n11 |
| 5.5–6 | 81n57 |
| 5.9 | 70n10 |
| 6.1 | 81 |
| 9.4 | 79n44 |
| 10.3 | 79n47 |
| 15.7 | 77n35 |
| 26.2 | 87n76 |

### Homilies on Judges

| | |
|---|---|
| 7.2 | 80n48, 80n51, 86 |
| 8.5 | 80n52 |

### Homilies on Leviticus

| | |
|---|---|
| 1.4.6 | 72 |
| 2.4.4–5 | 85 |
| 2.4.6 | 78n37 |
| 6.2.5 | 87n77 |
| 6.5.2 | 86n70 |
| 8.3 | 157n11 |
| 8.3.5 | 82–83 |
| 8.4 | 252 |
| 9.4.4 | 78n36 |
| 14.3 | 83 |
| 14.4 | 84 |
| 15.3 | 75n28 |

### Homilies on Luke

| | |
|---|---|
| 7.1 | 73n24 |
| 14.1 | 81–82 |
| 14.5 | 82, 157n11 |
| 14.6 | 76 |
| 21.3–4 | 77n34 |
| 21.4 | 77 |
| 22.5 | 88n78 |
| 22.6 | 88n78 |
| 22.8 | 88n78 |
| 24.2 | 76 |
| 26.3 | 76 |
| 27.5 | 77 |
| 28.4 | 79n41 |
| 29.2 | 78n39 |
| 33.5 | 71–72 |

### Homilies on Numbers

| | |
|---|---|
| 3.1 | 78n40 |
| 6.4 | 145n2 |
| 12.4 | 87n76 |
| 15.4 | 80n48 |
| 25.6 | 71n18 |
| 26.4 | 71n13, 227 |
| 27.1 | 3n9, 263n39 |

### On the Pasch

| | |
|---|---|
| 4.29–36 | 79n46 |

### On Prayer

| | |
|---|---|
| 5 | 185n30 |
| 17.9 | 263n39 |
| 25 | 198–199 |
| 29.13 | 258n20 |

### Selections on the Psalms

| | |
|---|---|
| 118 | 148n11 |

## Ancient Sources Index

### Paulinus

*Vita Ambrosii*

| | |
|---|---|
| 8.36 | 42n96 |

### Polycarp

*Philippians*

| | |
|---|---|
| 2.3 | 190 |
| 5.3 | 190 |
| 9.2 | 225 |
| 12.2 | 225 |

### Pseudo-Clement

*Epistle to James*

| | |
|---|---|
| 14 | 198 |

*Homilies*

| | |
|---|---|
| 1.6 | 192 |
| 11.26 | 197 |
| 13.21 | 197 |
| 20.2 | 197 |

*Recognitions*

| | |
|---|---|
| 1.6 | 192 |
| 1.24 | 197 |
| 1.33–71 | 172 |
| 1.42.1 | 184 |
| 1.48 | 59 |
| 1.49 | 197 |
| 1.49–50 | 172n34 |
| 1.50 | 174n43 |
| 1.55.4 | 184 |
| 1.69 | 170n20, 172n32, 197 |
| 2.20 | 198 |
| 2.21 | 178n10 |
| 3.20 | 178n10 |
| 5.9 | 197 |
| 6.9 | 197 |
| 8.10–12 | 197 |
| 37 | 178n10 |
| 41 | 178n10 |
| 46 | 178n10 |

### Pseudo-Tertullian

*Adversus omnes haereses*

| | |
|---|---|
| 1 | 248 |

### Rhetorica ad Herennium

| | |
|---|---|
| 1.3.4 | 8n34 |
| 3.9.16–18 | 8n37 |

### Sentences of Sextus

| | |
|---|---|
| 311 | 197 |

### Sibylline Oracles

| | |
|---|---|
| 2.347 | 193 |
| 4.165–169 | 58 |
| 8.245–250 | 61n41 |

### Tatian

*Oration*

| | |
|---|---|
| 9 | 193 |
| 39 | 193 |

### Tertullian

*Adversus Praxean*

| | |
|---|---|
| 1.10.1 | 11n44 |
| 3.4.2 | 11n44 |

*De anima*

| | |
|---|---|
| 37.4 | 252 |
| 55 | 224 |

*Apology*

| | |
|---|---|
| 10 | 272n31 |
| 21 | 278n95 |
| 25 | 278n97 |
| 26 | 275n61 |
| 28 | 274n49 |
| 30 | 276n72 |
| 30–33 | 276n71 |
| 33–34 | 276n72 |
| 37 | 277n81, 277n82, 277n84, 277n85 |
| 38 | 278n94 |

## Ancient Sources Index

| | |
|---|---|
| 39 | 277n84 |
| 41 | 277n82, 277n84, 278n94 |
| 50 | 270n11 |

*On Baptism*

| | |
|---|---|
| 3 | 131n24 |
| 12 | 164n21 |
| 13 | 64n65 |
| 18.4 | 165 |
| 19 | 16n56 |

*De corona*

| | |
|---|---|
| 2 | 13n48 |
| 3 | 64n63 |

*De Fuga in Persecutione*

| | |
|---|---|
| 2 | 273n38 |

*Against the Jews*

| | |
|---|---|
| 3 | 146n5 |
| 8 | 173n40 |
| 9 | 173n40 |
| 10.79–82 | 153 |
| 13 | 207n35 |
| 13.13–15 | 60n35 |
| 14 | 172 |
| 14.10 | 173n39 |

*Against Marcion*

| | |
|---|---|
| 3 | 11n45 |
| 3.6.2ff | 171n29 |
| 3.7 | 172, 173 |
| 3.7.1 | 171n28 |
| 3.8.1 | 171n29 |
| 3.15 | 154n34 |
| 3.24 | 201n3, 221, 222 |
| 4.33 | 179 |
| 5.13.7 | 145n2 |

*Ad Martyras*

| | |
|---|---|
| 2 | 278n96 |

*De praescriptione*

| | |
|---|---|
| 13 | 11n44 |

*On Repentance*

| | |
|---|---|
| 6 | 13n48 |

*De resurrectione*

| | |
|---|---|
| 25.11–13 | 62n49 |

*On the Soul*

| | |
|---|---|
| 37 | 201n3 |
| 37.11 | 221n36 |
| 55 | 221n36 |
| 58.1 | 221n36 |
| 58.8 | 221n36 |

*De spectaculis*

| | |
|---|---|
| 13 | 273n37 |

*Ad uxorem*

| | |
|---|---|
| 1.2.3 | 145n2 |

*De virginibus velandis*

| | |
|---|---|
| 1 | 11n44 |

## Theodore of Mopsuestia

*Sermons*

| | |
|---|---|
| 4 | 132n29 |

## Theodoret of Cyrus

*Quaestiones*

| | |
|---|---|
| 27 | 115n26 |

## Theophilus

*To Autolycus*

| | |
|---|---|
| 2.14 | 133n35 |
| 2.15 | 251 |
| 2.16 | 57n19, 64n65, 97n45, 164n21 |

## Victorinus of Pettau

*Commentary on Revelation*

| | |
|---|---|
| 1.7 | 75n48 |

## Ancient Sources Index

*On the Creation of the World*

|  |  |
|---|---|
|  | 201n8 |

## Zeno

*Invitation to the Baptismal Font*

| 1.12 | 110n1 |
|---|---|
| 1.23 | 110n1 |
| 1.32 | 110n1 |
| 1.49 | 110n1 |
| 1.55 | 110n1 |
| 2.14 | 110n1 |
| 2.23 | 110n1 |
| 2.28 | 110n1 |

# CLASSICAL AUTHORS

## Aristotle

*Metaphysics*

| 1.5.1–2 | 245 |
|---|---|
| 14.6.3–5 | 246 |
| 985b–986a | 245 |
| 1093a–b | 246 |

*Rhetoric*

| 3.8.4 | 8n33 |
|---|---|
| I.iii.4 | 8n34 |
| III.xiii.4 | 8n33 |

## Cicero

*De Inventione*

| 1.19 | 8n34 |
|---|---|
| 1.27 | 9n39 |
| 1.33 | 9n38 |

*De Oratore*

| 4 | 8n33 |
|---|---|
| 11.79 | 8n36 |
| 27 | 8n33 |
| 122 | 8n33 |

*De Re Publica*

| 6.12 | 246 |
|---|---|
| 6.17 | 246 |
| 6.18 | 246 |

*Topica*

| 97–99 | 8n33 |
|---|---|

## Dionysius of Halicarnasus

*Ars rhetorica*

| 3.243–244 | 113n20 |
|---|---|
| 6.265f | 113n19 |

## Quintilian

*Institutio oratoria*

| 3.9.1–3 | 8n35 |
|---|---|

## Tacitus

*Annals*

| 15.44.2–8 | 277n83 |
|---|---|

## Theon

*Progymnasmata*

| 12 | 8n37 |
|---|---|

# Subject Index

Abraham, 9, 129, 144, 146, 250
Abrasax, 247–48
accommodative language, educational imagery and, 262–63
*Acts of John*, 184, 198
*Acts of Justin*, 22
*Acts of the Martyrs*, 275, 278–79
Adam, 9, 33, 63, 84, 157, 238–39
*Ad Fortunatum de exhortatione martyrii* (Cyprian), 27
*Ad Quirinium* (Cyprian), 14–15, 27
*Adversus Iudaeos* (Tertullian), 172–73
*Adversus Marcionem* (Tertullian), 172–73
*Against Celsus* (Origen), 185, 199, 257, 259–60
*Against Heresies* (Irenaeus), 8, 11, 194–96, 220–21
*Against Marcion* (Tertullian), 221–22
*Against the Jews* (Cyprian), 57n20, 153
*Against Those Who Delay Baptism* (Gregory of Nyssa), 121–22
agape, 276
Aland, Kurt, 155–56, 158
Alexander Minorita, 238
Alexander the Great, 234
allegory, educational imagery and, 264
Alpha and Omega, 253
Ambrose of Milan
  on catechesis, 18, 34–41, 51
  on circumcision, 146
amillennialism
  number symbolism and, 250
  prior to Constantine, 224–29
*Anagennesis*, 127n10

Andrew of Caesarea, 233–34
Anselm of Havelberg, 237
Antichrist
  eschatology and, 220, 233–43
  number symbolism and, 249
anti-Judaism
  of Cyprian, 28, 33
  in *Epistle of Barnabas*, 59
  in two comings of Christ theme, 171–72
Apharat, 153–54
*Apocalypse of Paul*, 230
*Apokatastasis*, 95
Apollonius, 271–72
Apologists, interpretations of kingdom of God, 182
*Apology* (Melito of Sardis), 193
Apostles' Creed, 2, 38, 46
*Apostolic Constitutions*, 4–6, 6–7n24, 153n31
Apostolic Fathers
  eschatology and, 225
  kingdom of God, interpretations of, 181–82
*Apostolic Tradition* (Hippolytus), 2, 21, 21nn15–16, 49
Aqiba (Rabbi), 216
Aquinas, Thomas, 238–39
Arians, 33
Aristides, 192
art, eschatology in, 234, 238
*Ascents of James II*, 174
Asterius, 152–53
Athenagoras, 193
Auf der Maur, Hans Jörg, 86

337

## Subject Index

Augustine of Hippo
  on catechesis, 18, 42–51
  on circumcision, 147–48
  on Decalogue, 44
  eschatology and, 231–33, 236–39
  on infant baptism, 156–58
  number symbolism and, 201, 203, 250
  *Proof of the Apostolic Preaching*, parallels with, 3–7
  on sin, 84

Babylonia, number symbolism in, 245–46
baptism
  Basil of Caesarea on (*See* Basil of Caesarea)
  blessings of, 105–7, 126–29
  catechesis on, 32, 35–36, 38–41, 44–48
  circumcision, relationship to, 67n78, 81–82, 144, 148–54 (*See also* circumcision)
  cleansing and, 57, 59–61, 65–66, 97–99, 107–8
  clinical baptism, 103–5
  clothing and, 132n29
  of Constantine, 30, 111, 165
  cross and, 56–57, 61–62
  death, relationship to, 80, 92–95, 98–99, 116, 128–29
  in *Dialogue with Trypho*, 57, 61
  emergency baptism, 159, 163–65
  in *Epistle of Barnabas*, 52–67
  eucharist, relationship to, 139–41
  faith and, 95–97
  fasting and, 114
  fire and, 75–76, 95
  forgiveness and, 107–8
  fruit and, 63–64
  grace and, 78, 90–92, 131
  Gregory of Nazianzus on (*See* Gregory of Nazianzus)
  Gregory of Nyssa on (*See* Gregory of Nyssa)
  Holy Spirit and, 63, 65, 67, 70, 74–78, 116–17, 139
  infant baptism (*See* infant baptism)
  of Jesus, 69, 73–75, 77–79, 120n38, 126, 135–39
  Jewish baptism contrasted, 136–37
  Jewish washing contrasted, 57, 59–61, 65–66
  Jews and, 125
  of John the Baptist, 73–75, 87–88, 120n38, 136–37
  Jordan River, crossing of, 70–72
  Justin Martyr on, 57, 61
  Lactantius on, 148
  land and, 64–65
  life expected of baptized persons, 108–9, 131–32
  martyrdom, relationship to, 85–86, 270
  Moses and, 58, 61, 113, 120, 128, 130
  Old Testament foreshadowings of, 69–73, 129–31
  in *Oratio Catechetica*, 89–99
  Origen on, 68–88, 155–56
  pagans and, 125
  Pasch and, 111, 113, 124
  Paul and, 69–70, 81–82, 131, 137
  prayer and, 90–92, 114
  procrastination, warnings against, 101–3, 111, 121–22
  proselyte baptism, 57–58
  Pseudo-Clementines on, 184
  rebirth and, 97–99, 107
  Red Sea, crossing of, 69–71, 129n19, 130, 130n20
  in Reformed tradition, 148
  as regeneration, 79, 127, 130–31
  repentance and, 86–88
  resurrection, relationship to, 80, 92–95, 98–99, 116, 128–29
  righteousness and, 138–39
  ritual baptism, 58–59
  Satan and, 130
  as seal, 67, 117, 123
  sickbed baptism, 103–5, 115, 122
  sin and, 66–67, 83–84, 117–19, 123, 137
  temple and, 65
  temptation and, 132
  Tertullian on, 85

338

## Subject Index

washing of feet by Jesus, 72–73
water and, 56–57, 61–64, 90–93, 127–29
*Baptismal Instructions* (Chrysostom), 136n41, 136n44
Bardesanes, 201
Barnabas. See *Epistle of Barnabas*
Barnard, L.W. Barnard, 53
Barrett, C. K., 207–8
Basilides, 212, 248
Basil of Caesarea
  blessings of baptism, 105–7
  cleansing and, 107–8
  clinical baptism, 103–5
  Cyril of Jerusalem and, 113–14
  exhortation to baptism by, 100–109
  *Exhortation to Holy Baptism*, 110–23
  forgiveness and, 107–8
  on John the Baptist, 113, 120
  life expected of baptized persons, 108–9
  procrastination, warnings against, 101–3
  rebirth and, 107
  sickbed baptism, 103–5
Basil the Great, 148
Beatus, 236
Bede (The Venerable), 235–36
Benedict, 239–40
Benedictines, 240
Beskow, Per, 172
blessings of baptism, 105–7, 126–29
Bonaventura, 241
Boniface VIII, 242
Bosker, B. Z., 172
Byzantine Empire, eschatology in, 233–39

Caiaphas, 172
Cain, 113
Campbell, J. M., 112–13
Cappadocian Fathers. *See* Basil of Caesarea; Gregory of Nazianzus; Gregory of Nyssa
Carpus of Pergamum, 274
catechesis, 18–51
  Ambrose on, 18, 34–41, 51

  Augustine on, 18, 42–51
  on baptism, 32, 35–36, 38–41, 44–48
  Chrysostom on, 38, 42, 48
  Cicero on, 8–9
  in *City of God*, 43–44
  Cyprian on, 18, 26–29
  Cyril of Jerusalem on, 3, 5, 18, 29–34, 38–41, 46, 51
  in *Didache*, 3, 24
  "distinctive community" and, 22–24
  doctrinal component of, 3
  Easter, during, 29–31, 34–35, 38–39, 48–49
  in *Epistle of Barnabas*, 28
  on eucharist, 39–41, 48
  on faith, 32, 47–48
  fasting and, 28
  on Father, 23, 39, 46
  Greco-Roman concepts and, 35–36
  Gregory of Nyssa on, 41
  "heavenly city" and, 42–49
  Hippolytus on, 2, 21
  historical background of, 1–6
  "history of salvation" approach to, 4–6, 10–11, 16, 25–26
  on Holy Spirit, 33–34
  Irenaeus on, 24–26, 28
  on Jesus, 32–33
  Justin Martyr on, 22–24, 28
  Lent, during, 29–30, 36–37, 42–43, 46
  Lord's Prayer and, 46–47, 50
  martyrdom and, 26–29
  moral component of, 3, 36–38
  on Moses, 37, 39
  mystagogical catecheses, 35–36, 41
  "orthodox church" and, 29–34
  overview, 18–21, 49–51
  in *Proof of the Apostolic Preaching*, 28
  Red Sea, crossing of, 39, 44–45
  on resurrection, 34
  on sin, 30–31
  on Son of God, 23–24, 46
  "state church" and, 34–41
  terminology of, 20–21
  Tertullian on, 28

## Subject Index

Catechetical Lectures (Cyril of Jerusalem), 3, 5, 30–31
Celsus, 257
Cerinthus, 183, 186, 223
Charlemagne, 235
children, baptism of. See infant baptism
chiliasm
  defined, 214, 214n3
  of Irenaeus, 221
  number symbolism and, 250
Chi-Rho, 253
Christ. See Jesus
Chronicle (Eusebius of Caesarea), 235
Chrysostom, John
  on catechesis, 38, 42, 48
  on circumcision, 147, 151–53
  Epiphany sermons on baptism, 124–25, 132–43
  on infant baptism, 164
Church History (Eusebius), 178, 191, 193
Cicero
  on catechesis, 8–9
  on number symbolism, 246
circumcision, 144–54
  Ambrose on, 146
  Apharat on, 153–54
  Asterius on, 152–53
  Augustine on, 147–48
  baptism, relationship to, 67n78, 81–82, 144, 148–54
  Basil the Great on, 148
  Chrysostom on, 147, 151–53
  Cyril of Alexandria on, 151
  Cyril of Jerusalem on, 152
  death and, 146–47
  in Dialogue with Trypho, 151–52
  Epiphanius on, 147–48
  in Epistle of Barnabas, 151, 153
  Eutropius on, 147–48
  figurative meanings of, 145–48
  Holy Spirit and, 150–54
  Isidore of Pelusium on, 148
  Jesus on, 145
  Jews and, 153
  John of Damascus on, 148
  Justin Martyr on, 151–152

  Lactantius on, 148
  metaphorical meanings of, 145–48
  Methodius on, 147
  in New Testament, 149–51
  in Old Testament, 145
  Origen on, 145–46, 148, 150–51
  Paul on, 144, 150
  Ptolemy on, 145
  in Rabbinic tradition, 144
  in Reformed tradition, 148
  as removal of sin of flesh, 148–49
  resurrection and baptism and, 146–47
  as seal, 144, 149–50, 152
City of God (Augustine)
  catechesis in, 43–44
  eschatology in, 232
  number symbolism in, 203
civil disobedience, martyrdom and, 269, 275–79
cleansing, baptism
  Cappadocian Fathers and, 107–8
  Jewish washing contrasted, 57, 59–61, 65–66
  in Oratio Catechetica, 97–99
Clement of Alexandria
  generally, 256
  eschatology and, 226, 235
  on kingdom of God, 178, 184–85, 196–98
  on martyrdom, 272n30
  number symbolism and, 210–12, 251
Clement of Rome
  eschatology and, 225
  on kingdom of God, 182
clinical baptism, 103–5
clothing, baptism and, 132n29
Commentary on 1 Corinthians (Origen), 75
Commentary on Daniel (Augustine), 231
Commentary on Daniel (Hippolytus), 228, 235
Commentary on John (Origen), 69–71, 75, 82, 85
Commentary on Matthew (Origen), 76n31, 84–86

*Subject Index*

*Commentary* on Revelation (Bede), 236
*Commentary* on Romans (Origen), 73, 81, 83–84
*Commentary* on the Apostles' Creed (Rufinus), 30
*Commentary* on the Song of Songs (Origen), 257n14
Commodian, 201
consistent eschatology, 176–77
Constantine
  baptism of, 30, 111, 165
  conversion of, 236
Conventual Franciscans, 241–42
Coptic Christians, number symbolism among, 246
Council of Constantinople, 30
Council of Nicaea, 30
Crispina, 276
cross, baptism and, 56–57, 61–62
Crouzel, Henri, 68
Cyprian of Carthage
  anti-Judaism of, 28, 33
  on catechesis, 18, 26–29
  on circumcision, 146–47
  eschatology and, 218, 229, 231
  on infant baptism, 155–57
  number symbolism and, 252
  *Proof of the Apostolic Preaching* and, 14–15
  on two comings of Christ, 170
Cyril of Alexandria, 151
Cyril of Jerusalem
  Basil of Caesarea and, 113–14
  on catechesis, 3, 5, 18, 29–34, 38–41, 46, 51
  on circumcision, 152
  on Gnosticism, 33–34
  on Marcionites, 34
  on two comings of Christ, 174–75

Daniélou, Jean
  on baptism, 68, 81
  on catechesis, 3, 7, 14, 16, 27, 41, 51
  on educational imagery, 257, 268
  on number symbolism, 202
  on two comings of Christ theme, 172

Dante, 243
Dasius, 273, 277
Daube, David, 270, 276, 278
David, 9, 14, 249
*De Abraham* (Ambrose), 36
death
  baptism, relationship to, 80, 92–95, 98–99, 116, 128–29
  circumcision and, 146–47
  martyrdom (*See* martyrdom)
*De bono mortis* (Ambrose), 37
Decalogue
  Augustine on, 44
  number symbolism in, 204
*De catechizandis rudibus* (Augustine), 3–4, 6–7
Decian persecution, 26–27, 29
de Faye, Eugène, 256–57
*De fuga saeculi* (Ambrose), 38
*De Ioseph* (Ambrose), 37
*De Isaac* (Ambrose), 38
*De Jacob et vita beata* (Ambrose), 37
Demetrius of Alexandria, 256
*Demonstration of the Apostolic Preaching* (Irenaeus). See *Proof of the Apostolic Preaching* (Irenaeus)
*Demonstrations* (Apharat), 153–54
*De Mysteriis* (Ambrose), 35–36, 39
DePuniet, 2
*De Sacramentis* (Ambrose), 35–36, 39–41
*De Trinitate* (Novatian), 34n63
*Dialogue with Trypho* (Justin Martyr)
  baptism in, 57, 61
  circumcision in, 151–52
  eschatology in, 219–20
  kingdom of God in, 182, 192–93
  *Proof of the Apostolic Preaching* and, 15
  two comings of Christ in, 168–70
*Didache*
  catechesis in, 3, 24
  kingdom of God in, 181–82, 188
*Didascalia Apostolorum*, 153
Diehl, Ernst, 158–63
Diocletian persecution, 29, 273, 277
Dionysius of Alexandria, 218, 227–228

341

## Subject Index

disgrace and glory theme. *See* two comings of Christ theme
*Divine Institutes* (Lactantius), 222
Dix, Gregory, 149–50
Docetism, refutation in *Proof of the Apostolic Preaching*, 12
doctrinal component of catechesis, 3
Domitian, 225
Donatists, 47
Drews, P., 13
Dujarier, Michael, 7

earth, baptism and, 94–95
Easter, catechesis during, 29–31, 34–35, 38–39, 48–49
educational imagery, 254–268
   accommodative language, 262–63
   allegory and, 264
   free will and, 264–65
   God as love, 261
   grace and, 264–65
   Old Testament and New Testament, relationship of, 263–64, 266
   physicians contrasted, 260–61
   prophecy and, 258
   punishment and, 259–62
   redemption and, 256–57
   "School of Christ," 258
   souls, training of, 258–59, 266–67
   virtue and, 257
   wrath of God, 261
Egeria, 5
Egypt, number symbolism in, 244, 246
*Egyptian Church Order*, 2
election, martyrdom and, 271
Eliezer ben Hyrcanus (Rabbi), 216
Elijah, 71, 113, 115–17, 128, 130, 168
Elisha, 39, 71, 128, 130
emergency baptism, 159, 163–65
*Enchiridion* (Augustine), 46, 50
Epiphanius
   on circumcision, 147–48
   eschatology and, 223
Epiphany, 124, 124–25n4
Epiphany sermons on baptism
   Chrysostom, 124–25, 132–43
   Gregory of Nyssa, 124–32, 142–43
   overview, 124–25, 142–43

*Epistle of Barnabas*
   background, 52–53
   baptism in, 52–67
   catechesis in, 28
   circumcision in, 151, 153
   eschatology in, 207–9, 225
   Gnosticism and, 212
   kingdom of God in, 181, 188
   number symbolism in, 200–212, 250–51
   purpose of, 53
*Epistle of the Apostles*, 183
*Epistle to Diognetus*, 182, 191–92
*Epistle to James* (Clement of Alexandria), 184, 198
Erythraean Sibyl, 237
eschatology, 213–43
   amillennialism, 224–29, 250
   Antichrist and, 220, 233–43
   Apostolic Fathers and, 225
   in art, 234, 238
   Augustine and, 231–33, 236–39
   Augustine on, 231–33
   in Byzantine Empire, 233–39
   in *City of God*, 232
   Clement of Alexandria and, 226, 235
   Clement of Rome and, 225
   consistent eschatology, 176–77
   Cyprian and, 218, 229, 231
   in *Dialogue with Trypho*, 219–20
   Dionysius of Alexandria and, 227–28
   Epiphanius and, 223
   in *Epistle of Barnabas*, 207–9, 225
   Eusebius and, 218, 227, 230, 235
   Hegesippus and, 225
   Hermas and, 225
   Hippolytus and, 218, 228, 232, 235
   Holy Spirit and, 240–42
   Ignatius and, 225
   inaugurated eschatology, 177
   individuals, place of, 230
   intermediate state of dead and, 217–18
   Irenaeus and, 217, 219–21, 224–25
   Jewish apocalypticism, 215–217
   Joachim of Fiore and, 239–43

## Subject Index

Justin Martyr and, 218–20, 224
kingdom of God, focus on, 229–30
Lactantius and, 222
martyrdom, relationship to, 270
in medieval West, 233–39
Methodius and, 222–23
in Middle Ages, 233–39
millennialism, 214, 214n3, 221, 250
Mongol invasions, impact of, 236
Montanists and, 223
Muslim invasions, impact of, 234–36
Origen and, 218, 226–27, 230–34
overview, 213–15
Papias and, 218–19
Polycarp and, 225
postmillennialism, 214
premillennialism, 217–23
present political kingdom, focus on, 230
realized eschatology, 176
Sabbath and, 204–11
Tertullian and, 218, 221–22, 224
Theophilus of Antioch and, 235
Victorinus of Pettau and, 222
eucharist
 baptism, relationship to, 139–141
 catechesis on, 39–41, 48
 martyrdom, relationship to, 270
Eusebius of Caesarea
 eschatology and, 218, 227, 230, 235
 kingdom of God and, 191, 193
Eutropius, 147–48
Eve, 113
*Exhortation* (Clement of Alexandria), 196
*Exhortation to Holy Baptism* (Basil of Caesarea), 110–23
 *On Baptism* compared, 119–20
 doctrinal points, 115–17
 Gregory of Nazianzus compared, 120–23
 Gregory of Nyssa compared, 120–23
 liturgical matters, 114–15
 metaphors and illustrations in, 112–13
 moral concerns, 117–19
 as protrepic, 112

rhetorical features, 111–13
Scripture, use of, 113–14
sin and, 117–19
*Exhortation to Martyrdom* (Origen), 86
*Explanatio symboli ad initiandos* (Ambrose), 38
*Expositio Evangelii secundum Lucam* (Ambrose), 38n82
*Exposition of the Orthodox Faith* (John of Damascus), 234

faith
 baptism and, 95–97
 catechesis on, 32, 47–48
 Paul on, 47
*Faith, Hope, and Love* (Augustine), 46
fasting
 baptism and, 114
 catechesis and, 28
Father. *See also* Trinity
 age of, 239
 catechesis on, 23, 39, 46
 in *Proof of the Apostolic Preaching*, 10–12
*Fifth Ezra*, 183
*Figurae* (Joachim of Fiore), 240n118
fire, baptism and, 75–76, 95
*First Apology* (Justin Martyr), 23–24
 kingdom of God in, 192
 two comings of Christ theme in, 171, 173
*First Clement*, 188
forgiveness, baptism and, 107–8
*Fourth Ezra*, 193, 216
Fourth Lateran Council, 241
Franciscans, 241–42
Francis of Assisi, 241
Frederick II, 236
free will, educational imagery and, 264–65
fruit, baptism and, 63–64

Gandhi, Mohandas, 269
Gaudentius of Brescia, 232
Gerhoh of Reichersburg, 237
Gnosticism
 Cyril of Jerusalem on, 33–34

343

## Subject Index

*Epistle of Barnabas* and, 212
Irenaeus on, 24
kingdom of God and, 179-80, 186-87
number symbolism among, 248
refutation in *Proof of the Apostolic Preaching*, 11-13, 177
*Gospel of Thomas*, 180, 185, 198
grace
  baptism and, 78, 90-92, 131
  educational imagery of, 264-65
  infant baptism and, 159-61
Graham, Billy, 272
Greece, number symbolism in, 245-47
Gregory of Nazianzus
  generally, 111
  Basil of Caesarea compared, 120-23
  blessings of baptism, 105-7
  cleansing and, 107-8
  clinical baptism, 103-5
  exhortation to baptism by, 100-109
  forgiveness and, 107-8
  life expected of baptized persons, 108-9
  procrastination, warnings against, 101-3
  rebirth and, 107
  sickbed baptism, 103-5
Gregory of Nyssa
  generally, 111, 256
  on catechesis, 41
  Epiphany sermons on baptism, 124-32, 142-43
  exhortation to baptism by, 89-99, 100-109, 120-23
Gregory Thaumaturgus, 254
Gribomont, Jean, 110, 112
Groh, John E., 178

Hadrian, 52
Hagar, 129
Hall, Stuart, 16
Harmless, William, 42
Harnack, Adolf von, 6
Hegesippus
  eschatology and, 225
  on kingdom of God, 179, 193
Henry IV, 237-38

Heraclas, 256
Hermans, Albert, 208, 210
Hermas of Rome
  eschatology and, 225
  on kingdom of God, 181, 190-91
Hilarianus, 232
Hilary of Poitiers, 231
Hildegard of Bingen, 238
Hill, Charles, 217-18
Hippolytus of Rome
  on catechesis, 2, 21
  eschatology and, 218, 228, 232, 235
  on kingdom of God, 180, 198
  number symbolism and, 201, 209
historical background of catechesis, 1-6
"history of salvation" approach to catechesis
  overview, 4-6
  in *Proof of the Apostolic Preaching*, 10-11, 16, 25-26
Holy Spirit. *See also* Trinity
  age of, 239
  baptism and, 63, 65, 67, 70, 74-78, 116-17, 139
  catechesis on, 33-34
  circumcision and, 150-54
  eschatology and, 240-42
  martyrdom and, 271
  number symbolism and, 250
  in *Proof of the Apostolic Preaching*, 9-10
*Homilies* (Clement of Alexandria), 192, 197
*Homilies on Exodus* (Origen), 70
*Homilies on Jeremiah* (Origen), 75
*Homilies on Joshua* (Origen), 71, 81
*Homilies on Judges* (Origen), 86
*Homilies on Leviticus* (Origen), 82-83, 85
*Homilies on Luke* (Origen), 71-72, 76-77, 81-83
*Homily on the Pascha* (Melito of Sardis), 15-16
*Hypostasis of the Archons*, 248

idolatry, martyrdom and, 274-75
Ignatius of Antioch

## Subject Index

eschatology and, 225
  on kingdom of God, 181, 189
  on martyrdom, 272
inaugurated eschatology, 177
infant baptism, 155–65
  Augustine on, 156–58
  Chrysostom on, 164
  Cyprian on, 155–57
  emergency baptism and, 163–65
  grace and, 159–61
  infant sinfulness and, 156
  innocence and, 158–59
  inscriptions and, 158–64
  neophytes, 161–63
  Origen on, 82–85, 155–56, 164
  original sin and, 155–58, 164
  peace and, 158–59
  Tertullian on, 158, 165
innocence, infant baptism and, 158–59
inscriptions, infant baptism and, 158–64
*Instructor* (Clement of Alexandria), 196–97
invocation of heavenly grace, baptism and, 90–92
Irenaeus
  on catechesis, 24–26, 28
  chiliasm of, 221
  eschatology and, 217, 219–21, 224–25
  on Gnosticism, 24
  on kingdom of God, 178–79, 183, 186, 193–96
  on Marcionites, 24
  millennialism of, 221
  number symbolism and, 201, 208–9, 248–52
  *Proof of the Apostolic Preaching* (See *Proof of the Apostolic Preaching* (Irenaeus)
Isaac, 129
Ishmael, 129
Isidore of Pelusium, 148
isopsephy, 247–48

Jacob, 129–30, 168
Jaeger, Werner, 257
James, 172

Jeremias, Joachim, 155–56, 163
Jerome, 235, 247
Jesus
  baptism of, 69, 73–75, 77–79, 120n38, 126, 135–39
  catechesis on, 32–33
  on circumcision, 145
  martyrdom and, 85–86
  as Messiah, 168, 171, 174–75
  number symbolism and, 201, 248–49
  Origen on, 258
  two comings of, 166–75
  washing of feet by, 72–73
Jewish apocalypticism, 215–17
Jewish baptism, 136–37
Jewish washing, baptism contrasted, 57, 59–61, 65–66
Jews
  in *Ad Quirinium,* 14–15
  circumcision and, 153
  number symbolism among, 245–46
Joachim of Fiore, eschatology and, 239–43
John of Damascus, 148, 234
John of Parma, 241
John the Baptist
  baptism of, 73–75, 87–88, 120n38, 136–37
  Basil of Caesarea on, 113, 120
Jordan River, crossing of, 70–72
Joshua, 130, 169, 173
Judas, 141
Julius Africanus, 235
Julius the Veteran, 275–77
Justin Martyr
  on baptism, 57, 61
  on catechesis, 22–24, 28
  on circumcision, 151–52
  eschatology and, 218–20, 224
  Irenaeus and, 15
  on kingdom of God, 178–79, 182, 186, 192–93
  on martyrdom, 272
  number symbolism and, 201, 209, 250
  on two comings of Christ, 167–74

## Subject Index

King, Martin Luther, Jr., 269
kingdom of God, 176–99
  Apologists, interpretations by, 182
  Apostolic Fathers, interpretations by, 181–82
  Clement of Alexandria on, 178, 184–85, 196–98
  Clement of Rome on, 182
  in *Dialogue with Trypho*, 182, 192–93
  in *Didache*, 181–82, 188
  in *Epistle of Barnabas*, 181, 188
  eschatology, focus in, 229–30
  Eusebius and, 191, 193
  in *First Apology*, 192
  as future, 176–77
  Gnosticism, controversy with, 179–80, 186–87
  Hegesippus on, 179, 193
  Hermas on, 181, 190–91
  Hippolytus on, 180, 198
  Ignatius on, 181, 189
  Irenaeus on, 178–79, 183, 186, 193–96
  Jews, debate with, 179, 187
  Justin Martyr on, 178–79, 182, 186, 192–93
  language regarding, 188–99
  in miscellaneous writings, 183–84
  Origen on, 185–86, 198–99
  overview, 186–87
  Papias on, 182, 186
  Paul and, 177
  political situation, impact of, 179
  as present, 176
  as present and future, 177
  Pseudo-Clementines on, 178, 184
  Stoicism and, 184
  as symbolic, 177
  temporal outline, 176–77
  Tertullian on, 179
Kleist, James A., 202–3, 207
Koch, Hal, 256–58, 268
Kraft, Robert, 203–4
Kromminga, D. H., 208

Laban, 129–30
Lactantius
  on baptism, 148
  on circumcision, 148
  eschatology and, 222
  number symbolism and, 201, 208
  on two comings of Christ, 174
Lampe, G. W. H., 149–50, 178, 186
land, baptism and, 64–65
Landes, Richard, 235
Last Supper, 2
Leclercq, H., 22
Lent, catechesis during, 29–30, 36–37, 42–43, 46
leprosy, 71–72
Lerner, Robert, 238
Lewis, LeMoine G., 254–56
life expected of baptized persons, 108–9, 131–32
Logos, 260–61, 263
Lombard, Peter, 241
Lord's Prayer, 2, 46–47, 50
love, God as, 261
Lupi, J., 3

Maertens, T., 3, 7, 49
Malherbe, Abraham J., 200
Manicheans, 33–34
Marcianus, 8, 13
Marcion, 170–71, 223
Marcionites
  Cyril of Jerusalem on, 34
  Irenaeus on, 24
  refutation in *Proof of the Apostolic Preaching*, 11–13
  two comings of Christ theme and, 170–71, 175
Marcus the Valentinian, 212, 248
Marinus, 277
martyrdom, 269–79
  baptism, relationship to, 85–86, 270
  catechesis and, 26–29
  civil disobedience and, 269, 275–79
  Clement of Alexandria on, 272n30
  election and, 271
  eschatology, relationship to, 270
  eucharist, relationship to, 270
  Holy Spirit and, 271
  idolatry and, 274–75
  Ignatius on, 272

## Subject Index

Jesus and, 85–86
Justin Martyr on, 272
non-violence and, 269–70, 276–79
obedience to emperor and, 275–76
of Polycarp of Smyrna, 278
providence of God and, 272–73
sacrifice, relationship to, 273–76
Satan and, 270–71
Tertullian on, 271, 274
theological significance of, 271–72
*Martyrdom of Perpetua* and *Felicitas*, 272
*Martyrdom of Polycarp*, 179, 190, 225, 273, 275
Matthew, 131
Maximilian, 277
Maximus, 275
Melito of Sardis, 15–16, 193
Messiah, Jesus as, 168, 171, 174–75
Methodius
  on circumcision, 147
  eschatology and, 222–23
  number symbolism and, 201, 208, 249–50
Middle Ages, eschatology in, 233–39
millennialism
  defined, 214, 214n3
  of Irenaeus, 221
  number symbolism and, 250
*Mimesis*, 92
*Miscellanies* (Clement of Alexandria), 197
Mithraism, 246
Mithras, 247
Mongol invasions, impact on eschatology, 236
Montanists, 33–34, 186, 223
moral component of catechesis, 3, 36–38
Moses
  baptism and, 58, 61, 113, 120, 128, 130
  catechesis on, 37, 39
  number symbolism and, 245
  two comings of Christ theme and, 169
*Muratorian Fragment*, 170, 252
Murray, Robert, 178

Muslim invasions, impact on eschatology, 234–36
mystagogical catecheses, 35–36, 41
*Mystagogical Catecheses* (Cyril of Jerusalem), 5, 30, 40

Naaman, 71, 130
Naassenes, 180
neophytes, 161–63
Nepos, 227
Nerva, 52
New Testament
  circumcision in, 149–51
  educational imagery, relationship to Old Testament, 263–64, 266
  number symbolism in, 248–49
  premillennialism in, 218
Nicene Creed, 38, 250
Noah, 72, 139
non-violence, martyrdom and, 269–70, 276–79
Novatian, 34n63
number symbolism, 244–53
  Alpha and Omega, 253
  amillennialism and, 250
  among Coptic Christians, 246
  among Gnostics, 248
  among Jews, 245–46
  Antichrist and, 249
  Augustine and, 201, 203, 250
  in Babylonia, 245–46
  chiliasm and, 250
  Chi-Rho, 253
  Cicero on, 246
  in *City of God*, 203
  Clement of Alexandria and, 210–12, 251
  Cyprian and, 252
  in Decalogue, 204
  in Egypt, 244, 246
  eight, 210–12, 246, 248, 252–53
  in *Epistle of Barnabas*, 200–212, 250–51
  forty, 245
  four, 244, 251
  gemátria, 247
  in Greece, 245–47
  Hippolytus and, 201, 209

## Subject Index

Holy Spirit and, 250
Irenaeus and, 201, 208-9, 248-52
isopsephy, 247-48
Jesus and, 201, 248-49
Justin Martyr and, 201, 209, 250
Lactantius and, 201, 208
Methodius and, 201, 208, 249-50
millennialism and, 250
Moses and, 245
in New Testament, 248-49
nine, 246
9,999, 248
in Old Testament, 245-46
100, 253
153, 249-50
Paul and, 252
pleroma, 248
Sabbath and, 204-11, 251-52
Satan and, 249-50
seven, 210-12, 244-46, 252
seventy, 245
six, 210-12, 250-51
666, 249
ten, 245-46, 251
in Ten Commandments, 204
Tertullian and, 201, 249, 252
Theophilus of Antioch and, 251
thirty, 248
three, 246
318, 250
365, 247
Trinity and, 251
twelve, 245-46, 249
Victorinus of Pettau and, 201, 208

obedience to emperor, martyrdom and, 275-76
*Odes of Solomon*, 183-84, 191
Oecumenius, 233-34
Old Testament
    baptism, foreshadowings of, 69-73, 129-31
    circumcision in, 145
    educational imagery, relationship to New Testament, 263-64, 266
    number symbolism in, 245-46
    *Proof of the Apostolic Preaching*, basis of, 13-15

two comings of Christ theme and, 170
Olivi, Peter John, 242
*On Baptism* (Basil of Caesarea), 110, 119-20
*On Catechizing Beginners* (Augustine), 43-44
*On Christ and the Antichrist* (Hippolytus), 228
*On Christian Combat* (Augustine), 46, 50n131
*On Faith and Works* (Augustine), 21n14, 47, 49-50
*On Prayer* (Origen), 198-99
*On Promises* (Dionysius of Alexandria), 227
*On the Baptism of Christ* (Chrysostom), 132
*On the Baptism of Christ* (Gregory of Nyssa), 126, 131
*On the Cause of the Universe* (Hippolytus), 228
*On True Circumcision* (Eutropius), 147-148
*Oratio Catechetica* (Gregory of Nyssa), baptism in, 89-99
    *apokatastasis* in, 95
    apologetic purpose of, 89
    cleansing and, 97-99
    death and resurrection and, 92-95, 98-99
    earth and, 94-95
    faith and, 95-97
    fire and, 95
    invocation of heavenly grace and, 90-92
    *mimesis* in, 92
    physical birth analogy and, 90-91
    prayer and, 90-92
    rebirth and, 97-99
    Trinity in, 96
    water and, 90-93
*Oration* (Tatian), 193
Origen
    on angels and demons, 118
    on baptism, 68-88, 155-56
    on circumcision, 145-46, 148, 150-51

## Subject Index

educational imagery (*See* Educational imagery)
eschatology and, 218, 226–27, 230–34
as intellectual, 254–56
on Jesus, 258
on kingdom of God, 185–86, 198–99
on obedience to emperor, 276
as teacher, 256
on two comings of Christ, 174
original sin, infant baptism and, 155–58, 164

*Palingennesia*, 127n10
*Panegyric to Origen* (Gregory Thaumaturgus), 254
Pantaenus, 256
Papias of Hierapolis
  eschatology and, 218–19
  kingdom of God and, 182, 186
Parousia, 218, 228
Pasch, baptism and, 111, 113, 124
Passover, 16, 166
Paul
  baptism and, 69–70, 81–82, 131, 137
  on circumcision, 144, 150
  on faith, 47
  kingdom of God and, 177
  number symbolism and, 252
peace, infant baptism and, 158–59
pedagogical imagery. *See* Educational imagery
Pelagians, 47, 156
Peter, 72, 172
Phileas, 276
*Philippians* (Polycarp), 190, 225
Philo, 145, 245
physical birth analogy, baptism and, 90–91
Pionius, 273
*Plea* (Athenagoras), 193
Pleroma, 248
Polycarp of Smyrna
  eschatology and, 225
  kingdom of God and, 190
  martyrdom of, 278

postmillennialism, 214
prayer, baptism and, 90–92, 114
premillennialism
  intermediate state of dead and, 217–218
  in New Testament, 218
  prior to Constantine, 218–223
Prigent, P., 170–171, 203
*Procatechesis* (Cyril of Jerusalem), 30–31
procrastination of baptism, warnings against, 101–3, 111, 121–22
*Proof of the Apostolic Preaching* (Irenaeus), 1–17
  apologetic purpose of, 7
  Augustine, parallels with, 6–7
  catechesis in, 28
  catechetical purpose of, 6–7, 11–13
  Cicero on, 8–9
  *Dialogue with Trypho* and, 15
  Docetism, refutation of, 12
  doctrinal outline of, 9–10
  false teachers and, 12, 16–17
  Father in, 10
  Gnosticism, refutation of, 11–13, 177
  "history of salvation" approach to catechesis in, 10–11, 16, 25–26
  Holy Spirit in, 9–10
  Justin Martyr and, 15
  kingdom of God in, 193–194
  Marcionites, refutation of, 11–13
  Mileto of Sardis and, 15–16
  Old Testament basis of, 13–15
  prophecy and, 13–15
  purpose of, 8
  rhetorical outline of, 8
  Son of God in, 9–11, 13–14
  Trinity in, 9–11
prophecy, educational imagery and, 258
proselyte baptism, 57–58
providence of God, martyrdom and, 272–73
psalmody, 114
Pseudo-Clementines
  on baptism, 184
  on kingdom of God, 178, 184

## Subject Index

two comings of Christ theme and, 171, 174
*Pseudo-Epiphanius Testimony Book*, 170
Pseudo-Methodius, 234–35
Ptolemy, 145
punishment, educational imagery and, 259–62
Pythagoras, 245–46
Pythagoreans, 211, 246

Quasten, Johannes, 27, 202
Quintillian, 8
Quirinus, 27–28

Rabbinic tradition, circumcision in, 144
Rachel, 129
Rambo, Lewis, 19–20
realized eschatology, 176
Rebekah, 129
rebirth, baptism and
  Cappadocian Fathers on, 107
  in *Oratio Catechetica*, 97–99
*Recognitions* (Clement of Alexandria), 172, 178, 184, 192, 197–98
redemption, educational imagery and, 256–57
Red Sea, crossing of
  as baptism, 69–71, 129n19, 130, 130n20
  in catechesis, 39, 44–45
Reformed tradition
  baptism in, 148
  circumcision in, 148
*Refutation of All Heresies* (Hippolytus), 198, 228
regeneration, baptism as, 79, 127, 130–31
*Regnum Dei* (Robertson), 178
*Regula fidei*, 86
repentance, baptism and, 86–88
resurrection
  baptism, relationship to, 80, 92–95, 98–99, 116, 128–29
  catechesis on, 34
  circumcision and, 146–47
*Revelations* (Pseudo-Methodius), 234
*Rhetorica ad Herennium* (Aristotle), 8

righteousness, baptism and, 138–39
ritual baptism, 58–59
Robertson, A., 178
Rordorf, W., 203
Rufinus, 30, 71, 82–83

Sabbath
  eschatology and, 204–11
  number symbolism and, 204–11, 251–52
Sabellians, 33–34
sacrifice, relationship to martyrdom, 273–76
Säflund, Gösta, 173
Satan
  baptism and, 130
  martyrdom and, 270–71
  number symbolism and, 249–50
Savon, Hervé, 145–148, 150
scapegoats, 169n17
Schiller, Gottfried, 53
"School of Christ," 258
Schweitzer, Albert, 176–77
Schweizer, Eduard, 166
seal
  baptism as, 67, 117, 123
  circumcision as, 144, 149–50, 152
*Second Baruch*, 216, 219
*Second Clement*, 180, 189
Seeberg, Alfred, 2
*Sentences of Sextus*, 184, 197
Septimius Severus, 235
Sermon on the Mount, 24n28, 26
Shea, William H., 208–9
sickbed baptism, 103–5, 115, 122
Simon, Marcel, 172
Simon Magus, 183
sin
  Augustine on, 84
  baptism and, 66–67, 83–84, 117–19, 123, 137
  catechesis on, 30–31
  circumcision as removal of, 148–49
  original sin, infant baptism and, 155–58, 164
Sinaiticus, 60
Skarsaune, Oskar, 168–69, 171–72
Smith, Joseph P., 7
Son of God. *See also* Trinity

## Subject Index

age of, 239
catechesis on, 23–24, 46
in *Proof of the Apostolic Preaching*, 9–11, 13–14
Spiritual Franciscans, 241–43
Stephen, 14
Stoicism, kingdom of God and, 184
Strecker, Georg, 172
*Stromata* (Clement of Alexandria), 210, 210n54

Tatian, 193
temple, baptism and, 65
temptation, baptism and, 132
Ten Commandments
  Augustine on, 44
  number symbolism in, 204
Tertullian
  on baptism, 85
  on catechesis, 28
  eschatology and, 218, 221–22, 224
  on infant baptism, 158, 165
  on kingdom of God, 179
  on Marcion, 171
  on martyrdom, 271, 274
  on non-violence, 277
  number symbolism and, 201, 249, 252
  on obedience to emperor, 276
  on two comings of Christ, 172–74
*Testaments of the Twelve Patriarchs*, 167
*Testimonia* (Cyprian), 18
Theodore of Mopsuestia, 42, 46, 48
theological significance of martyrdom, 271–72
Theophilus of Antioch
  eschatology and, 235
  number symbolism and, 251
Theotecnus of Caesarea, 277
Thornton, L. S., 149
Tränkle, Hermann, 173
Trigg, Joseph, 69
Trinity
  history and, 239
  number symbolism and, 251
  in *Oratio Catechetica*, 96
  in *Proof of the Apostolic Preaching*, 9–11

troup, George W., 1
Turck, André, 2–3, 7
two comings of Christ theme, 166–75
  as anti-Jewish polemic, 171–72
  as anti-Marcionite argument, 170–71
  as creedal summary of Christ, 169–70
  Cyprian on, 170
  Cyril of Jerusalem on, 174–75
  in *Dialogue with Trypho*, 168–70
  in *First Apology*, 171, 173
  Justin Martyr on, 167–74
  Lactantius on, 174
  Marcionites and, 170–71, 175
  Moses and, 169
  in Old Testament testimonia to Christ, 170
  Origen on, 174
  Pseudo-Clementines and, 171, 174
  scapegoats and, 169n17
  Tertullian on, 172–74
Tyconius, 231, 236

Ubertino of Casale, 242
Uzziah, 239–40

Valentinus, 212
Vespasian, 52
Victorinus of Pettau
  eschatology and, 222
  number symbolism and, 201, 208
violence, Christianity and, 269–70
virtue, educational imagery and, 257

Waldram, Joop, 86
washing of feet by Jesus, 72–73
water, baptism and, 56–57, 61–64, 90–93, 127–29
Way-Rider, R., 15
Wengst, Klaus, 203
*Who Is the Rich Man That Is Saved?* (Clement of Alexandria), 197
Williams, George, 269, 274
wrath of God, 261
Wright, David F., 68, 84

Zacchaeus, 131